WITHDRAWN

Illinois Central College
Learning Resources Center

FUTURE TENSE

THE CINEMA OF
SCIENCE FICTION

FUTURE TENSE

THE CINEMA OF SCIENCE FICTION

John Brosnan

St. Martin's Press,
New York

Foreword

It has been a pleasure to read this volume: the right book published at the right time. John Brosnan, an experienced and thoughtful critic of the cinema, has equally professional knowledge of the specialized world of science fiction. Now, at a time when the sf film appears to be bursting into popularity, he has written the definitive history of the birth and growth of these films. I have much enjoyed this book and now feel replete with the details of sf cinematic history. But, being a science fiction author myself, I am greatly interested in where the sf film is going as well as where it has been. So I paid special attention in this book to the opinions of film producers, special effects men, screen writers and sf writers about what the sf film is and what sort of future it is likely to have.

One thing was instantly obvious: all these opinions are wrong. (If you have heard that science fiction writers are a contentious lot, you are right.) I say this not to belittle the observations of my fellow writers, most of whom are serious and thoughtful artists, but to point out what appears to be a self-evident fact that they have all missed. This is that, *when film-makers talk about 'science fiction films', they are really talking about the same old films they have always made—only tarted up with some of the mechanical trappings of sf.*

This is a serious statement and should not be dismissed as a casual insult. It is simply an observation of the truth. When, in the past, real science fiction writers have been involved in the making of an sf film, like H. G. Wells in *Things to Come* or Arthur C. Clarke in *2001*, the result was a real sf film without the need of quote-marks round the sf. The rest of the time we have had the machinery but not the soul. Do you doubt this? If you do, then glance at what the giants of the film industry have learned from the recent success of the sf film. Look at the last page of the last chapter of this book and see what *real* sf they are planning for our future. They seriously think that things like *Starship Invasions, The Terrible Jaw Man, Star Crash*, etcetera, can be something more than the desperate rubbish described by their titles.

Why will they be bad? Because they will have cobbled-together, derivative plots ground out by bored screenwriting hacks. These overly familiar stories will be magically transformed into 'sf' by the addition of sf furniture. This does not mean they will be science fiction at all. Dressing an actor in a dentist's smock does not make him a scientist; nor does putting him into a tin suit make him a robot. If the author of the screenplay does not know what a scientist really is or what a robot could possibly be, then the film, no matter how much it *looks* like science fiction, will not *be* science fiction.

The film-makers have still to get this message. Science fiction is something different. Its creation requires a strange and rare kind of writer. It is a quirk, a talent, an attitude, an indescribable difference that is nevertheless always present. The first film producer to recognize this fact will be a rich man – witness how successful 'almost sf' films have been recently. Science fiction's popularity has been growing for years and has never been bigger than it is now. For the very first time, science fiction books are on the bestseller lists. In January 1978 the *New York Times* Book Section announced: 'Publishers expect the public's appetite for the genre to continue unabated . . . and many are doubling – in some cases tripling – the number of titles they'll publish.' So the audience is there, and something should be done to bring them into the cinemas.

If a failed-sf film like *Close Encounters of the Third Kind* can make millions, think of the profits that a real sf movie could generate.

Star Wars is a real science fiction film; therefore it deserves every greenback it has earned. It is not sophisticated sf, but then it never pretended to be: it is juvenile, the best of Buck Rogers and *Planet Stories* woven together to please the young and the young at heart. We who like to read the stuff have experienced it all before. But it was fun to see all the mechanics spelled out in living colour. *Star Wars* is all action, and in between the shooting and crashing there are none of the ridiculous 'drama' scenes of actors in strange clothes trying to take the stupid plot seriously. Instead there is humour – and what a change that makes!

Close Encounters, on the other hand, is not sf, but rather mysticism of the smarmiest kind. I always feel contempt for those who pander to weaknesses – people who sell narcotics to children or practise crooked schemes to pry life savings from old-age pensioners. *Close Encounters* cynically uses the trappings of science to deliver the strongly anti-science message of pie-in-the-sky. It tells us not to use our brains and energy to improve mankind's state by means of science. It reveals that science is only flashing lights and strange sounds – which a lot of people have always suspected – good only for luring from the skies Superior Beings who will care for us. Is this attitude any different from that of the South Sea Cargo Cults, which involve the building of crude bamboo replicas of aeroplanes to entice cargo planes bearing their manna from heaven? The effects in this film were incredible and spectacular – the sf trappings. The message they carried, though, is anti-sf, anti-science and pro-mysticism of the most debilitating sort.

It is exasperating that no one to date seems able to separate the look of sf from its ideas. Trumbull himself, the master of the special effects in *Close Encounters*, doesn't understand this point. In the pages of this book he is quoted as saying that he is so proud of his work on this film that he will never do special effects again for anybody apart from himself. Instead he intends to make another film of his own. Really? What will his film be *about* – and which sf author will write it? When will he – and everyone else – learn that setting a film in a spaceship does not make it science fiction? Just as the film-makers ignore science, so they also ignore science fiction while pretending that they are producing it. Until they change their ways we are only going to get the trappings on the cinema screen without the substance. It is not the science that is important but the attitude towards science. And until this changes we will continue only to get more of the same.

If this sounds too gloomy I hold out one small hope for the future. A single producer recognizes this fact. His name is Lester Goldsmith and perhaps some day he will be honoured for his observation of the seemingly obvious – that science fiction films should be written by science fiction authors. He plans to have the authors themselves write screenplays of their already successful sf novels. Obvious? It may be after the fact – but no one else in a position of authority appears to have noticed it. When Mr Goldsmith's plans come to fruition they might very well usher in the final and successful era of science fiction films.

We can only wait, hope – and see.

Harry Harrison

Introduction

Any discussion of science fiction films must begin with an examination of science fiction. Though no two people will agree as to the precise meaning of the term, it may help if its chief components are identified. In the first place, it is perhaps worth stating that science fiction must involve science in some way. It is not fiction necessarily *about* science but fiction that invariably uses science as a basis for extrapolation; the scientific element, though it may be very small, still remains the *raison d'être* for a science fiction story. But what is meant by 'science'? In most people's minds science fiction is still exclusively associated with technology – usually in the form of spaceships, robots and other futuristic devices, all of which involve the 'hard' sciences. But 'science' is a blanket term that covers a wide variety of subjects, including the 'soft' sciences of biology, sociology, psychology and so on, and any definition of science fiction must take into account the multiplicity of science.

The origins of science fiction are disputed. Recently describing how he evolved the plot of *Star Wars*, the film's writer and director George Lucas said: 'Originally I wanted to make a "Flash Gordon" movie, with all the trimmings, but I couldn't obtain the rights to the character. So I began researching and went back and found where Alex Raymond [who had done the original Flash Gordon comic strips in the newspapers] had got his idea from. I discovered that he'd got his inspiration from the works of Edgar Rice Burroughs, and especially from his "John Carter of Mars" series of books. I read through that series, then found what had sparked Burroughs off was a science fantasy called *Gulliver on Mars* written by Edwin Arnold in 1905. That was the first story in this genre that I have been able to trace. Jules Verne had got pretty close, I suppose, but he never had a hero battling against space creatures or having adventures on another planet.'[1] Lucas, fine film-maker though he is, leaves a lot to be desired as a researcher; one obvious story he failed to mention was *The First Men in the Moon* by H. G. Wells, published in 1901. While Wells's protagonists didn't behave in the approved Burroughs fashion by donning leather jock-straps and leaping about the landscape skewering the natives with fancy sword-play, they certainly did have some adventures 'up there', despatching a few of the ultra-frail Selenites in a manner that John Carter would have appreciated.

As a literary genre, science fiction is a side-product of modern science, though some of its devices had been employed by earlier writers of satire or fantasy. Its origins properly lie in the 18th century, in the Age of Reason and the beginning of the Industrial Revolution, when technology first allowed Man to cut loose from Nature and, more importantly, to bring about *changes* – in the landscape, in a whole way of life, in Nature itself. But with this apparent triumph of Man over his external world came also doubt and guilt. Was technology basically a good thing? Did Man have the right to flout the laws of Nature? By flouting those laws, was he also flouting God? These questions have echoed down through science fiction, and science fiction films, ever since.

In his book *The Billion Year Spree* Brian Aldiss makes a good case for Mary Shelley's *Frankenstein* (1818) being regarded as one of the first real sf novels. The methods that Frankenstein uses to create his artificial man, though only vaguely described, are undoubtedly scientific and reflect this new approach to the manipulation of the external world: that is, by technological means as opposed to alchemy or other forms of magic. In the book Shelley has Frankenstein visit a university professor who warns him against the old ways of the alchemists and persuades him to follow the path of modern science. 'Symbolically,' writes Aldiss, 'Frankenstein turns away from alchemy and the past towards science and the future – and is rewarded with his horrible success.' As a result many science fiction films were to fall into the horror category, and vice versa.

Many writers during the 19th century used existing technology as a basis for extrapolation. Edgar Allen Poe, for instance, along with Mary Shelley, helped to fuse science fiction with the Gothic, a development from which the genre has never really escaped.

But the first generally recognized science fiction writer was the Frenchman Jules Verne, who, after writing a number of plays, began producing novels in the 1860s and kept up a prodigious output until his death in 1905. Much of his work dealt with marvellous machines or inventions that provide the means for exotic journeys of exploration, but whilst he was something of a visionary Verne lacked that radical spark – the subversive way of looking at life and the universe – which marks the modern science fiction writer. Verne was basically a conservative, and while a few of his characters, like Nemo and Robur, posed as outcasts of society he himself was a pillar of the establishment and a good Catholic (so far he is the only sf writer to have been blessed by the Pope for his work). His attitude towards technology was ambiguous – he relished machines, as is evidenced by his long and loving descriptions of their workings, but as he grew older he doubted Man's ability to control them. Significantly, in one of his last books, published in 1904, Robur is destroyed by a bolt of lightning, presumably of divine origin, when, in his flying machine, he declares himself 'Master of the world'.

The first *modern* science fiction writer was H. G. Wells, a genuine radical in his attitude towards the nature of mankind, society, politics and human relationships (sex never figured much in Verne's work). George Orwell wrote of Wells:'Back in the 1900s it was a wonderful thing to discover H. G. Wells. There you were, in a world of pedants, clergymen, and golfers, with your future employers exhorting you to "get on or get out", your parents systematically warping your sex life, and your dull-witted schoolmasters sniggering over their Latin tags; and here was this wonderful man who could tell you all about the inhabitants of the planets and the bottom of the sea, and who *knew* that the future was not going to be what respectable people imagined.'[2] But, like Verne, Wells was ambiguous in his attitude towards technology – he believed that science used rightly could enable common man to throw off most of the shackles that created 'lives of quiet desperation', but he was also profoundly pessimistic about humanity as a whole and its ability to cope with the new scientific discoveries. After successfully prophesying both the First and Second World Wars he died in 1946 forecasting the destruction of the world in an atomic war.

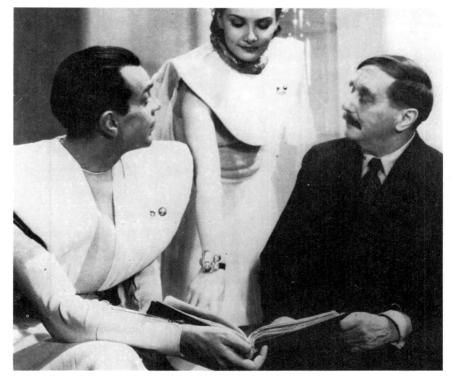

Raymond Massey, Margaretta Scott and the father of modern science fiction himself, H. G. Wells, on the set of Things to Come.

While Verne and Wells can both be described as sf writers, the scientific content in their work was completely different, and this difference was later to have a fundamental effect on the structure of the sf genre. Verne was basically machine-orientated – he dealt with the 'hard' sciences, and engineering in particular, whereas Wells was involved with the 'soft' sciences of biology and sociology. Wells did use machines in his work but they were often no more than convenient devices to get his story underway, as in the case of his time machine or the anti-gravity sphere that takes his protagonists to the moon. Wells never went into great details about his wondrous inventions and, amusingly, this annoyed Verne, who once complained that Wells had more or less cheated with *The First Men in the Moon*. Verne claimed that while he himself had gone to a great deal of trouble designing and explaining the giant cannon he used to get his characters to the moon (or at least around it) in *From the Earth to the Moon*, Wells had merely created 'Cavorite', an impossible substance, and hey presto! man was on the moon. Yet, ironically, Wells had a much better grasp and overall understanding of science than Verne ever had, despite the latter's ostentatious display of 'scientific' detail in his books. Verne's technical descriptions were often inaccurate and he rarely bothered to keep up with contemporary scientific progress (for instance, if he had taken advantage of the information on submersible craft available at the time he wrote *20,000 Leagues Under the Sea* in 1870 he could have designed a much more efficient Nautilus submarine), while Wells's inventions, no matter how fanciful, were usually rooted in prevailing scientific theory. Wells, of course, had had the benefit of a scientific training – he had studied biology under Thomas Huxley – and was for a time a teacher, whereas Verne had first studied to be a lawyer, then became a stockbroker before turning playwright and finally successful novelist: his involvement in science was always that of an amateur. The main difference in their respective approaches to science was that Verne dealt primarily with specifics, while Wells dealt with science's effect as a whole upon society. Thus the scope of Wells's work was always much broader than Verne's, and yet for many years it was Verne who had the greater influence on the science fiction genre.

As a separate genre fiction really began in the 1920s and was the creation of a man called Hugo Gernsback. Born in Luxembourg, he emigrated to the USA in 1904, determined to become a successful inventor having been trained as an electrical engineer. A few years later he was publishing the world's first radio magazine called *Modern Electrics* and in 1911 he serialized within it a story of his own called *Ralph 124C 41 + : A Romance of the Year 2660*. The story was full of futuristic inventions and appallingly written, and set the pattern for much of the magazine science fiction that followed. Like Verne, Gernsback was in love with machinery, and this blinkered view of science dominated both his own work and that of writers who later sold material to him. In 1926 he started publishing *Amazing Stories*, the first magazine devoted to stories of 'scientifiction' (later modified to science fiction) and thus, at a stroke, created the science fiction ghetto, cutting the genre off from the mainstream of literature.

The dominance of the machine and related 'hard' sciences in magazine science fiction – which for many years was the only form of sf there was – continued right through the 1930s and 1940s, even though the field had become increasingly sophisticated, due mainly to the influence of John W. Campbell. Campbell had written a number of popular sf stories and serials in the early 1930s, such as *The Black Star Passes* and *The Mightiest Machine*, but it was as the editor of *Astounding* magazine that he had most influence in the field. For one thing he stressed the need for magazine sf writers to learn how to write, which was a definite breakthrough, but his prime interest wasn't in good literature but in engineering, and how the principles of engineering could be applied to most aspects of life, including politics.

It wasn't until the 1950s, when the first big science fiction boom was underway and the general public was beginning to assimilate the idea that space travel was a real possibility, that science fiction writers began to discard their spaceships and futuristic hardware in favour of mining the softer sciences for their story ideas. In the 1960s science fiction metamorphosed into forms that bore no resemblance at all to the earlier magazine sf. This was the period when writers like Michael Moorcock, J. G. Ballard, Brian Aldiss, Harlan Ellison and others started experimenting with the genre – playing with its traditions and devices and turning it inside out, much to the disgust of Campbell's engineers who immediately reached for their blasters (the shooting still hasn't quite stopped). It wasn't so much the new styles that the older sf adherents resented as the loss of the basic optimism that had permeated most of science fiction up until then. Sf was growing up, and the days when a man could increase his brain power to the 'nth' magnitude by doing a few mental exercises and then whittle the universe down to size were past. Today science fiction is a vast hydra consisting of many totally different genres and ranging in quality from sublime to atrocious.

It has long been evident that there is a fundamental difference between the science fiction cinema and written science fiction. John Baxter, in his book *Science Fiction in the Cinema*, noted: 'Sf film's sources lie remote from science fiction and its visual style is likewise drawn from other areas, primarily the semi-visual world of the comic strip. Sf film offers simple plots and one-dimensional characters in settings so familiar as to have the quality of ritual. It relies on a set of visual conventions and a symbolic language, bypassing intellect to make a direct appeal to the senses.

Written sf is usually radical in politics and philosophy; sf cinema, like the comic strip, endorses the political and moral climate of its day.' Baxter also correctly perceives the different attitudes towards science in written sf and the sf cinema. 'It is not difficult,' he writes, 'to see a direct relationship between the fear of science and the film-maker's habit of contrasting humanistic protagonists with forces that attempt unsuccessfully to over-whelm the human mind, but the fear and distrust of science reaches its most obvious form in films devoted to the threat of knowledge. Probably there is no more common line if sf cinema than: "There are some things Man is not meant to know." It expresses the universal fear all men have of the unknown and the inexplicable, a fear written sf rejects but which has firmly entrenched itself in the sf cinema.'[3]

This diverging attitude towards science between writers and film-makers exists basically because scriptwriters have never understood even the basic principles of science or the workings of technology. The sf writers, on the other hand, were always writing for a specialised audience that was much more knowledgeable about science than the general public was (particularly from the 1920s through to the 1950s), and even the least competent pulp magazine hack had to acquire some knowledge of basic scientific theories if he wanted to keep making money in the field. But the film scriptwriters never had to make a similar effort. Why should they have? They were writing for the mass cinema audiences, and what did *they* know about science? About as much as the scriptwriters – which is why so many of the early movies that are labelled 'science fiction' aren't really sf at all. They may be full of mad scientists and weird inventions, but they are really fantasies about evil warlocks and magicians who are called scientists because to the early film-makers science and magic were interchangeable – being difficult to understand, mysterious and not to be trusted. Of course there is an abundance of reasons why science shouldn't be trusted, but no one can really make an anti-science picture unless he has some understanding of what exactly he is attacking.

Even during the sf film boom of the 1950s Hollywood scriptwriters got over the science parts by sleight-of-hand and other magic tricks. One wand they often waved was 'atomic radiation', which is not to be confused with the real thing. During the 1950s Hollywood's version of atomic radiation was responsible for all manner of strange things; it turned men into steel, made men shrink and made them grow, turned them into animated slime, awoke prehistoric monsters from their age-long sleep, caused ants to grow into colossi, provoked sea monsters into committing gigantic anti-social acts. It did all of these things and more, but never did it actually make anyone radioactive. Even when the original material came from a *bona fide* science fiction writer the scriptwriter could be depended upon to impose his own customary stamp on the story, usually throwing out the real sf elements in the process. The same applied when technical experts were hired by film producers to add a tinge of authenticity in the early days of the sf boom; the technical information was poorly incorporated by the scriptwriters, who didn't want their screenplays cluttered up with 'boring' scientific logic. In the same way, when it actually came to the making of his historical epics, Cecil B. DeMille would throw out all the historical facts his own teams of researchers had painstakingly unearthed.

Of course this hybrid product of science fiction and the cinema has included a lot of marvellous entertainment and some classic films over the years, and it would be churlish to disregard these simply because they don't fulfil one's personal criteria of what makes good science fiction. John Baxter maintains, both in his own book and in Chapter 10 of this one, that as sf literature and sf cinema are two totally different media they will never successfully merge. I disagree. Many young film-makers (like George Lucas, Steven Spielberg, Michael Crichton and Brian De Palma) have grown up with science fiction, in all its various guises, and are familiar with its traditions and rules. There are signs that the sf cinema is now catching up with written sf. *Star Wars*, for instance, has put 1930s and 1940s pulp magazine space opera on the screen at last, combining the flashy, cardboard universe of E. E. Smith with the scope of Asimov's *Foundation* series, plus a touch of Van Vogt's mysticism. Maybe we'll be watching vintage Bester, Aldiss, Moorcock, Harrison, Delaney, Disch and Ballard in the 1980s.

Two of the real stars of Star Wars.

1 Yesterday's Tomorrow (1900–30)

The Lumière brothers gave the first public demonstration of their 'cinematography machine' in Paris in 1895; seven years later Georges Méliès made his film *Le Voyage Dans La Lune* (*A Trip to the Moon*), probably the first film actually based, however loosely, on the work of an sf writer, though elements of sf can be detected in the trick photography of the earliest films.

Méliès was the son of wealthy parents who indulged him in his desire to be a magician by buying him a theatre, the Théâtre Robert-Houdin, where he produced a series of very popular conjuring shows. In 1895 he witnessed the Lumière brothers' demonstration of moving pictures and was immediately impressed. He tried first, unsuccessfully, to buy their equipment; then in 1896 he managed to obtain a projector from the English film pioneer Robert Paul, who had developed, independently, his own motion picture equipment at the same time as the Lumière brothers. Méliès converted the projector into a camera and was soon making his own films, but being a magician by inclination he concentrated on the medium's potential for trickery and from 1897 onwards made a number of increasingly elaborate movies that utilized both photographic effects and the stage effects that he had built into his theatre. Most of his films, with the exception of his 'reconstructed actualities', which were reconstructions of contemporary and historical events, were made purely as entertainments, with the emphasis on humour, and this also applied to *Le Voyage Dans La Lune*. Though incorporating elements of Verne's *From Earth to the Moon* and Wells's *First Men in the Moon* the film was played strictly for laughs. The moon projectile is loaded into a space gun by a line of grinning chorus girls; the Man in the Moon is shown with the projectile stuck in his eye; the moon travellers encounter a group of cardboard lunar inhabitants (vaguely resembling Wells's Selenites) who tend to explode when tapped with an umbrella, and all are returned safely home, due to the 'pull of the Earth's gravity', in time to see a statue being erected in their honour. Similarly absurd was *Le Voyage À Travers L'Impossible* (*An Impossible Voyage*), in which a high-speed train takes off from the summit of a mountain, travels through space and falls into the sea before returning to dry land, all achieved with Méliès' repertoire of primitive but ingenious special effects, including stop-motion photography, split-screen multiple exposures, giant moving cut-outs and live action combined with full-scale mechanical backgrounds. In 1907 he applied the same treatment to Verne's *Twenty Thousand Leagues Under the Sea* though it's doubtful whether the illustrious French writer would have approved of the half-naked sea nymphs whom Méliès' underwater explorer encounters.

In England science fiction was treated more seriously in Charles Urban's *The Airship Destroyer*, made in 1909. Urban was an American who had originally come to England as a representative of the Thomas Edison Company but later set up his own film company. Inspired, no doubt, by the work of H. G. Wells, *The Airship Destroyer* is about a mystery attack on London by a fleet of airships. Through the use of model work we see buildings being blown up, prototype tanks destroyed and railroads wrecked, but the film's young hero, an inventor, saves the day by launching a number of radio-controlled flying torpedoes at the airships. The film proved a popular success and prompted sequels like *The Aerial Anarchists* and *The Pirates of 1920*, both made in 1911.

Meanwhile in America the Edison company had made the first version of *Frankenstein* (a print of which was recently rediscovered) in 1910. Directed by J. Searle Dawley and starring Charles Ogle as the Monster, it lasts for only about fifteen minutes but in spirit is much closer to Mary Shelley's original than the later Universal version made in 1931, and Ogle's make-up was obviously fashioned on Shelley's description of Frankenstein's creation.

But after this first flurry science fiction cinema fell quiet for the next few years, though there appeared the occasional sf-related film such as the American *A Bolt from the Sky* (1913), a short one-reeler about a scientist who is killed by a meteorite, and one of the few films in which a scientist is victim rather than instigator of catastrophic events. The scientist in Abel Gance's experimental film of 1914 *La Folie du Dr Tube* (*The Madness of Dr Tube*) was more conventional – he goes insane while experimenting with light waves – as was the one in the 1915 two-reel production *The Secret Room* (directed by Tom Moore, who also starred in it), who brings about a mind exchange between a normal man and an idiot – a theme that was to become popular in sf films.

In 1915 came one of the first important German contributions to the genre – *Homunculus* (also known as *Homunculus Der Führer*), a six-part serial directed by Otto Rippert and starring Olaf Fonss, Friedrich Kuhne, Mechtild Their and Maria Carmi. Based on a novel by Robert Reinert, it concerns the attempt of a scientist to create an artificial man whose mind consists of pure reason uncluttered by emotion. Lacking a 'soul', however, the creature automatically becomes evil. After establishing himself dictator of a large but unnamed country he plans to conquer the world but, like Verne's character in *Master of the World*, he is struck dead by a bolt of lightning. The idea that free will is an illusion and that one's personal morality is shaped and controlled by external events was also the theme of the German film *Alraune*, made in 1918 (the first of many versions). It was based on the novel by Hanns Heinz Ewers which stirred up controversy in the German-speaking world in the early 1900s. Its story was built around the idea of artificial insemination. It concerns a scientist who impregnates a prostitute with the semen of a convicted murderer. He adopts the resulting baby, a girl, and raises her himself as part of an experiment to test his theories on the relationship between character and environment. But the girl is irredeemably tainted both by the nature of her true 'parents' and the soulless way in which she was conceived, growing up into an evil woman who takes pleasure in driving men to suicide.

A much less murky theme provided the stimulus for the big American sf film of 1916 – none other than *Twenty Thousand Leagues Under the Sea* by the clean-limbed Jules Verne. Directed by Stuart Paton, it was produced by Carl Laemmle's Universal company, the studio that was to become best known for its series of horror and sf-related film in the 1930s such as *Frankenstein, The Invisible Man, Dracula* and so on. But the most interesting aspect of the 1916 *Twenty Thousand Leagues* was the involvement in its making of a man called J. Ernest Williamson, who, with his brother George, had developed the first efficient technique for filming underwater. They built an underwater chamber, which they called the 'photosphere', which was spherical and made of thick steel, containing one large porthole. The 'photosphere' was attached to a barge floating overhead by a long tube made of removable metal sections which were wide enough to permit a man to climb through them. Air was pumped down the tube into the sphere from the barge above, and the whole structure was strong enough to be lowered to a depth of about eighty feet. The Williamsons first tested it in the clear waters off Nassau in the Bahamas and made a short film which included shots of native boys diving for coins and a man attacking a shark with a knife. Their underwater films soon attracted attention and when Universal decided to film Verne's novel Ernest and his brother were hired to handle the sea footage. The director Stuart Paton concocted some absurd additions to the Verne story which included the discovery of a scantily-clad girl on an isolated island. But Ernest Williamson, according to his autobiography published many years later, was determined to remain as faithful as possible to the original as far as his part in the production was concerned.

'To vindicate Verne the dreamer was my problem – to make Jules Verne's dream come through,' he wrote, 'but where were the unique and extraordinary props? No doubt there were plenty of obsolete submarines

The Nautilus submarine, circa 1916, as it appeared in Stuart Paton's version of 20,000 Leagues Under the Sea.

The Nautilus 38 years later (but more reflective of the Victorian era than the 1916 Nautilus) in a scene from the Walt Disney version of 20,000 Leagues, *directed by Richard Fleischer.*

knocking about that would serve as the Nautilus, but my confidence was soon punctured. I found it impossible to get hold of a submarine.' But this didn't stop Williamson for long – he had his own metal submarine specially built. He claims it was a hundred feet long and could be operated by one man. But on the first trial run, watched by the Governor of the Bahamas, things went wrong. 'I knew it could be submerged but I was not so confident that it could be raised to the surface with entire success at the first attempt. Ordinarily I planned to handle the Nautilus myself but on this occasion I trusted her to an assistant who was clad in a diving suit as a precaution. All was going well . . . up rose the railed platform, up came the rounded cigar-shaped hull. And then! Cries of dismay from the spectators. Wildly the craft rolled. It heeled from side to side in imminent danger of turning turtle and drowning the man within. And then slowly, smoothly, the Nautilus rolled back and came to rest at an even keel. I saw the Governor slap the Chief of Police on the back and heard him exclaim: "By Jove, these motion pictures fellows – you can't baffle them, you know."

'Accordingly, preparations were made to film the first episode in Jules Verne's tale, the ramming of the *Abraham Lincoln*. It was not such smooth sailing as I thought it would be. My Nautilus did not possess the great "iron spur" that Captain Nemo had provided on his submarine. He might ram a frigate with ease, "passing through it like a needle through sackcloth", but for me to drive my submarine into the hull of the old brig might result in the destruction of the undersea craft with perhaps no great damage to the tough, old-fashioned warship we were supposed to destroy.'[4]

One might ask at this point why Williamson didn't make use of models, as the 1954 Disney version of the film was later to do (see Chapter 4). This was simply because model work would have been regarded as 'cheating' by audiences of the day. The techniques for filming models relatively realistically weren't developed until the 1920s; before then, model shots were always very obvious and film-makers avoided such trickery as much as possible. So Williamson was obliged to create the effect of the Nautilus ramming another vessel with full-scale props. Somehow he had to suggest that the frigate had received a sudden, violent shock, and one of his assistants came up with the bizarre idea of placing water-filled barrels on the deck and at a given signal rolling them in unison from one side of the ship to the other, thus causing her to list heavily. A local rum importer was willing to loan the film company the necessary barrels and all through the night fifty men sweated to fill them with sea water and then place them on greased runways. The next day, just as they were preparing to go back to sea, the owner of the barrels appeared and demanded their immediate return, so for Williamson it was back to the drawing board.

Again I read and reread my copy of *Twenty Thousand Leagues* trying to find a way out. At last I had it! In the story the frigate fired a shot at the Nautilus from a distance, the first shot missing the submarine, the second striking it but glancing off. Here was my chance, my way out of the dilemma. I would have the frigate fire at the oncoming Nautilus at close range, and in the cloud of powder smoke and the tense excitement of the scene no one would notice whether or not the *Abraham Lincoln* registered a "terrible shock".

'Jockeying the vessels into position as they surged through the open sea I ran the Nautilus diagonally under the frigate's bows. Cameras clicked. The uniformed crew of the warship rushed excitedly forward and peered with amazed faces over the bulwarks. Then the impersonator of Verne's great character, Ned Land, raised his weapon and heaved with all his strength. But he had forgotten a most important detail. He had failed to have the line which he was holding coiled, free to run with the harpoon. As the harpoon sped through the air the rope whipped into a loop, wrapped about the actor's neck and came within an ace of flinging him from his perch into the sea.'

There were other problems: first, the cannon exploded prematurely, leaving two of the crew with burns to the face and suffering from temporary blindness, and then the sharks came. 'The triangular fins were cutting the water around the frigate. Scraps of food thrown overboard had attracted them. The actors who were to take the parts of Ned Land, Professor Arronax and Conseil flatly refused to throw themselves overboard as the story demanded. And nor could I blame them. Doubles had to be provided to act their parts in this phase of the scene.'[5] (One wonders how the doubles were led to jump into the shark-infested sea.)

Despite all the problems Williamson finally achieved what he wanted on film and, together with footage shot by Stuart Paton, the picture was released in 1916 in time to coincide with the news that a German U-boat had slipped through the blockades and sunk a dozen British ships outside New York. With the sudden new interest in submarines the film was assured of success, but audiences particularly marvelled at the underwater sequences which included many shots of the denizens of the deep in their natural habitat for the first time. Probably the most spectacular of the underwater scenes involved a fight between a couple of divers and a giant octopus. With their customary dislike of admitting to the use of fakery both the film-makers and the studio created the impression in their publicity that the octopus was real. It was nearly twenty years later that Williamson admitted, somewhat shamefacedly, that the octopus had not been real after all. Instead it had been constructed out of rubber and operated from within by a hard-hat diver (who wore a metal helmet with an air hose leading to the surface). The tentacles contained springs that kept them coiled, but when compressed air was forced into them the tentacles straightened out, and when the air was released they again coiled. The diver, inside the octopus head, manipulated a series of levers that fed the air into the tentacles, and the result was relatively effective if a little primitive by today's standards.

After the success of *20,000 Leagues* Williamson hoped to make a film version of *Mysterious Island*, but it wasn't until the mid-1920s that the project got underway. It was an ill-fated picture, as we shall see later in this chapter. Meanwhile in other parts of the world sf-related films continued to be made sporadically. In 1917 Denmark produced *Himmelskibet* (*Heaven Ship*), directed by Forest Holger-Madsen, about a group of Earthmen who travel to Mars in a prop-driven aircraft. The Mars they discover is a veritable utopia whose inhabitants live lives of peace and happiness in a world apparently designed by a landscape gardener. They decide to take back a Martian emissary, a beautiful girl, who they hope will spread the message of sweetness and light on corrupt old Earth. There is some initial opposition, however, from a villainous politician who attempts to discredit the Martian, but all ends happily when he is struck by lightning – an occupational hazard for villains in those days.

Scientists, mad or otherwise, continued to be a staple ingredient of the genre. In *The Greatest Power*, made by Metro in 1917 and directed by Edwin Carewe, an American scientist not only discovers a cure for cancer but also a super-explosive substance called 'exonite'. At first he plans to give it to all the nations of the world so that it will act as a deterrent against war, but by the end of the picture he comes to his senses and gives the exonite exclusively to the USA: an interestingly prophetic film if 'atomic bomb' is substituted for 'exonite'. Another prophetic idea, that of germ warfare, was used in *The Green Terror*, a British film made in 1919. An evil scientist and a financier plot to buy up a vast stock of wheat grain and release an artificially-created germ that will destroy the bulk of the world's wheat harvest, thus making themselves a fortune. But the idea is really used as little more than a device on which to hang a conventional thriller story involving a kidnapped heiress, private detectives, mistaken identities, disguises and so on. Directed by Will P. Kelling, it was adapted from an Edgar Wallace story and contains all his usual narrative gimmicks.

H. G. Wells' benign scientist Professor Cavor is portrayed fairly accurately in the 1919 British Gaumont production of *The First Men in the Moon*, directed by J. V. Leigh and starring Bruce Gordon, Lionel D'Arragan, Hector Abbas, Cecil Morton York and Heather Thatcher (who also starred in *The Green Terror* mentioned above), but the Wells story has been changed somewhat by the film-makers. The core of the novel, like so much of Wells's early work, concerned the theme of both natural evolution and artificial evolution – the deliberate manipulation of mankind into specialized forms. This theme dominates such books as *The Island of Dr Moreau*, *The Time Machine* and even *War of the Worlds*, but probably reaches its peak in *First Men in the Moon* in which Wells toys with a concept that would later be known as 'genetic engineering' (*Moreau* was a cruder experiment along the same lines). What really interested Wells was not the journey to the moon but the description of Selenite society with its total control over the individual and the shaping of each member of that society to fit a specific role or task (*Brave New World* is an updated rewrite of *First Men*, and Orwell also admitted a debt to Wells). But this aspect was more or less ignored in the first film version (as it was in the second, made in 1964), and was replaced by a triangular love affair and a scheming villain.

Critical reaction to the film was generally favourable. One reviewer wrote: 'Primarily perhaps the film is a notable feat of studio-craft. The scenes on the moon, which naturally constitute the outstanding feature of the production, have been staged with genuine skill and imagination, which do great credit to Mr J. V. Leigh and his technical staff. The landing of the two explorers amidst the wild and desolate lunar mountains, which tower mysteriously in the chill and eerie twilight, is a situation of altogether novel power and suggestiveness. In the picture of the Grand Lunar's glittering palace Mr Leigh strikes an almost poetic note. In their grotesque beauty and originality some of these settings are worthy of the fantastic art of the Russian ballet. Wisely, we think, the lunar episodes are studio scenes throughout. It would have been possible to stage many of the mountain pictures against natural backgrounds but the element of unreality introduced by the use of artificial settings and lighting is by no means a disadvantage in a picture which aims at creating an extramundane atmosphere.'[6]

Also in 1919 came *The Ghost of Slumber Mountain* made by stop-motion photography innovator Willis H. O'Brien, who later went on to make *The Lost World* and *King Kong*. His first commercially-released film was *The Dinosaur and the Missing Link*, bought by the Thomas Edison Company in 1915. Though it only ran for about five minutes of screen time it had taken two months to make. Between 1916 and 1918 O'Brien made a number of similar animated films for the Edison Company but by 1919 had decided to take the stop-motion process one step further by including live actors with his animated creatures. The result was *The Ghost of Slumber Mountain*, released in 1919, which ran for about fifteen minutes and opened with a man telling some youngsters about a camping trip into remote mountains. In a flashback we see him discover the deserted cabin of Mad Dick, a hermit who is now supposed to haunt the place. That night he visits the cabin and encounters Mad Dick's ghost, which hands him a telescope and tells him to look down into the valley. To his amazement the man sees a number of dinosaurs down there, including a Brontosaurus, a flying reptile and two Triceratopses engaged in combat. The victor is then attacked by an Allosaurus which, after killing the three-horned Triceratops, looks up and sees the man. The ghost immediately disappears as the large flesh-eater charges up the mountain. Just as it is about to reach him the man wakes up. It had, he tells the youngsters to their obvious disappointment, all been a dream.

But unlike his previous films this one was played fairly straight and the scenes with the dinosaurs were obviously designed to shock audiences rather than amuse them. The dinosaurs themselves, for the first time, were realistically portrayed, O'Brien having consulted a distinguished palaeontologist at the American Museum of Natural History. Seemingly obsessed by prehistoric monsters, O'Brien returned to the theme again and again during his career in the film industry and established the 'giant-monster-versus-mankind' formula which was to prove the mainstay of so many sf films, particularly during the 1950s.

In 1920 came the German sf-fantasy *Algol*, directed by Hans Werkmeister and starring Emil Jannings. No prints of the film seem to have survived, but the story concerns a female spirit on the star Algol who journeys to Earth and becomes romantically involved with an Earthman, offering to make him master of the world through the power of a machine she creates. The expressionistic settings, designed by poet-architect Paul Scheerbart, attracted favourable comment at the time of the film's release.

A version of *Dr Jekyll and Mr Hyde* was also made in America in 1920 (there had already been at least six previous versions, the first being made in 1908) starring John Barrymore in the title role and directed by John S. Robertson. The short novel on which it was based, *The Strange Case of Dr Jekyll and Mr Hyde* by Robert Louis Stevenson, published in 1886, can be described as a prototype sf story, not only because it features a mad scientist and a wonder drug, but because of its attitude towards the nature of modern man and his so-called higher morality. Stevenson's suggestion that civilization may only be skin-deep prefigures the theme that was to dominate the work of H. G. Wells, who later admitted to Stevenson's influence. Subsequent film versions of *Dr Jekyll and Mr Hyde* picked up the implication that Jekyll wasn't merely being taken over by the 'evil' side of his personality but rather was *regressing* back to a primitive state. This was especially obvious in the 1931 version in which Fredric March's make-up was based on the appearance of Neanderthal man. However, in the 1920 production, Barrymore, with plenty of absurd leers and exaggerated gestures, plays him simply as a caricature of evil. And on top of that the whole experience turns out to be nothing but a dream – a popular device in fantasy-related films of that period.

Also dealing with the theme of primitive man, though on a less ambitious level, was *Go and Get It* made in 1920 and directed by Marshall Neilan and Henry R. Symonds from a scenario by Marion Fairfax. The story owes a sizeable debt to Poe's *Murders in the Rue Morgue*. Set in a newspaper office, it involves a male and a female reporter who are in a race with a rival newspaper to solve a series of mysterious murders. It turns out that a celebrated surgeon has transplanted the brain of a condemned criminal into the body of a gorilla, which had promptly killed the surgeon and set out to wreak vengeance on those responsible for the criminal's execution. A few years later H. G. Wells provided the uncredited inspiration for a film called *A Blind Bargain*, a 1922 Lon Chaney vehicle produced by Sam Goldwyn and directed by Wallace Worsley. Though based on a book called *The Octave of Claudius* by Barry Pain it obviously owed much to Wells's *Island of Dr Moreau* with its story of a scientist experimenting with a combination of man and beast. Lon Chaney plays Dr Lamb, yet another brilliant surgeon who is attempting to create a new race of men by grafting monkey glands onto humans. In one of his previous experiments Dr Lamb has permanently crippled a man who is both dumb and half-animal (also played by Lon Chaney). A young man in desperate need of money for an expensive operation to save his mother's life attempts to rob him but Dr Lamb overcomes him and then offers to save

Wallace Worsley, director of A Blind Bargain, *is flanked by two of the beast men who feature in the film (Lon Chaney is on the right).*

his mother if he will submit to one of the doctor's surgical experiments. The young man agrees, but later the beast-man and the doctor's wife urge him to flee, and when he hesitates they show him the cages containing the results of the doctor's previous experiments – half-human creatures of great strength. Once again the young man is taken by surprise and overcome by the villainous Dr Lamb, but during the struggle the crippled mute releases one of the creatures from its cage, which then breaks the doctor's back. Amusingly, the following advice was given in a trade magazine to potential exhibitors of the movie: 'Talk a story of unusual strength with a topical flavour. The newspapers lately have been giving prominence to gland grafting.'[7] It is easy to see how this film provided the template for so many of the horror-sf films that followed – mad scientist creates monster, and is eventually destroyed by monster.

Time travel, a popular sf subject, wasn't exploited much in the early movies. It was touched on in *Ghost of Slumber Mountain*, mentioned above, and also in the 1921 *The Connecticut Yankee at King Arthur's Court* (the first of three versions; others followed in 1931 and 1948), based on Mark Twain's satirical fantasy. One might argue that Twain's character, who is hit on the head and wakes up to find himself in England at the time of King Arthur's reign, doesn't really go back in time but is merely dreaming, but that is to quibble. Time travel itself is a fantasy, even when used in the context of the hardest of 'hard' science fiction stories, and in any case Twain's story fulfils the traditions of the typical sf time travel story – that of a time traveller who journeys into either the past or the future and brings about changes in the society he finds there. In Twain's book the entertainment is created by the anachronisms that his character introduces to Arthur's kingdom, such as modern plumbing, telephones and jousting on bicycles instead of horseback. The 1921 film version, directed by Emmet J. Flynn and starring Harry C. Myers and Pauline Stark, kept to the spirit of the original.

Time travel was treated more 'scientifically' in *The Sky Splitter*, a short one-reel film made by John R. Bray in 1922 – a comedy in which a scientist, testing a new spaceship, exceeds the speed of light and finds himself reliving his own life. Time, or rather the manipulation of it, provided the basis for the French sf comedy *Paris Qui Dort* (*Paris Asleep*, also known as *The Crazy Ray*). Made in 1923 by René Clair, it concerned a scientist who accidentally freezes all of Paris into a split-second of time with an experimental ray. Not all the city's inhabitants are frozen, however: a small number are mysteriously unaffected by the ray and most of them take advantage of their position by breaking out of their social rôles and having a good time. But the film's young protagonist, a night-watchman on the Eiffel Tower, retains his sense of social responsibility and persuades the revellers to seek out the source of the phenomenon.

They do so and Paris returns to normal, while the night-watchman goes back to the Eiffel Tower accompanied by the scientist's beautiful young daughter. Made with style and charm by Clair the film still retains much of its humour when seen today. It is said to have been inspired by a 1913 French comedy film called *Onesime Horloger*, made by Jean Durand and featuring the famous clown Ernest Bourbon (known as 'Onesime') as a lovesick suitor who tampers with time in order to speed up the arrival of his wedding-day, with the result that his son outgrows him almost before the honeymoon is concluded.

Meanwhile, in Russia, science fiction was being used for a much more serious purpose – to spread the message of Marx to Mars. *Aelita*, made in 1924 and based on a novel by Alexei Tolstoy, concerned a

A startling crowd scene, consisting of Martian slaves, from the 1924 Russian film Aelita.

Moscow engineer who is dissatisfied with life on Earth and plans to build a machine which will take him to Mars. Suspecting his wife of having an affair with his next-door neighbour he shoots her during a jealous quarrel and then flees his house, intending to leave for Mars immediately. He eventually makes the journey accompanied by two men – a cheerful Red Army soldier who wants to take the revolution to Mars, and a detective who is after him for murdering his wife. On Mars he becomes romantically involved with the Martian queen Aelita, but her Prime Minister has him and his companions imprisoned in the caves where the Martian slaves are kept. With the help of Aelita's servant girl the Red Army soldier escapes and instigates an uprising of the slaves. But just when success seems assured they are betrayed, to the engineer's horrified amazement, by Queen Aelita, which goes to prove that a good Russian should never trust an aristocrat, no matter how beautiful she may be. So great is his shock that he wakes up to find himself in a Moscow railway station. It had, of course, all been a dream. Returning home he finds that his wife is unhurt and that she hadn't been carrying on with his neighbour after all. Once again content to be a part of the Soviet paradise on Earth, he burns the plans for his invention and returns to his normal life.

Aelita was directed by Yakov Protazanov, a leading Russian director before the revolution who had emigrated to Paris in 1917, where he stayed for a few years, making several films. He decided to return to Russia in the early 1920s, and *Aelita* was one of his first projects after his return. The film was coolly received by the Russian critics who didn't consider it 'artistic' enough, but it was popular with the Russian public and many babies born that year were named Aelita despite the aristocratic connotations. The film is best remembered for the cubist designs of its sets and costumes.

Aelita's engineer protagonist is at first resistant to the Party message but eventually learns the error of his ways.

Another Russian sf-related film was *The Death Ray*, directed in 1924 by Lev Kuleshov from a scenario by the famous Russian director and film theorist Vsevolod Pudovkin. The film was more an exercise in style than a serious work in its own right and was deliberately fashioned to resemble the popular foreign serials of the time, with all the usual sensational ingredients. The plot revolves breathlessly around a new deadly weapon developed in an unnamed country and the efforts to keep it out of the hands of a powerful fascist group whose methods and style alarmingly foreshadow Hitler's stormtroopers. Pudovkin himself played the chief villain – a Jesuit priest no less – but regretted it later when a stunt fall from a four-storey window resulted in a two-week hospital stay. In addition the film was very poorly received.

The Hands of Orlac was a 1925 Austrian production directed by Robert Weine and starring Conrad Veidt as a pianist whose hands, severely injured in an accident, are replaced by those of an executed murderer. The pianist then discovers that he has inherited the murderer's homicidal tendencies along with his hands and fights a losing battle to prevent himself being dominated by the dead man. Though it can be described as a marginal sf film its theme has more in common with the supernatural than with science, as did most of the so-called sf films of the period. And, as the German film *Alraune* had also done, it puts forward the then-popular theory that evil is an external force over which the individual has no control, thus separating morality from free will. Other film historians have claimed that the particular popularity of that idea in Germany reflects a specific German national characteristic of the time, namely that Germans regarded themselves as empty vessels waiting to be dominated by whatever ruling power prevailed – which, of course, would explain the ease of Hitler's take-over and the later pleas of 'We were not responsible'. But, with hindsight, such intellectual games are easy to play and are much too pat to be convincing. The idea certainly wasn't exclusive to Germany, and it's worth remembering that *The Hands of Orlac* was based on a novel by a Frenchman. The fear of possession is an old and universal one and is still in evidence today (witness the success of *The Exorcist*); the theme has been used often in sf cinema, usually involving aliens from outer space who take over the minds of human beings or duplicate their bodies.

The year 1925 saw the making of Fritz Lang's *Metropolis*, which has been described as the first major science fiction film but is really a Gothic epic. The absurdity of the story doesn't detract from the visual power of the film – it can be described, with justification, as a classic piece of cinema rather than sf cinema. The action is set in a vast city of the future neatly divided into the downtrodden masses and a ruling élite. A member of the latter is a young man called Freder, who is the son of the city's ruler, John Frederson. Freder, who spends most of his time running about in outsize

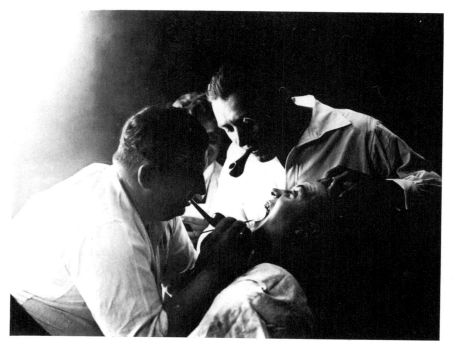

Cameraman Karl Freund (left) and director Fritz Lang (right) supervise the make-up on an unfortunate member of the Metropolis *cast.*

Fritz Lang and Brigitte Helm (with saxophone) relax for the photographer during the making of Metropolis.

white knickerbockers having fun with his friends, doesn't know of the workers' existence until he encounters a beautiful girl called Maria who comes from 'down below'. He tries to follow her when she returns below and finds himself in a nightmarish world where men work unceasingly to tend vast machines and themselves are reduced to mere human cogs within the city's mechanical bowels. Freder is horrified by what he sees but persuades a worker to change clothes with him so he can continue his search for Maria. Eventually he finds her in a church beneath the city where she is preaching on the subject of good worker-employer relationships. The basis of her message seems to be that the two parties should at least meet and discuss the situation now and again – hardly revolutionary, but upsetting enough to John Frederson who is spying on the meeting. Frederson then instructs an evil scientist called Rotwang to construct a robot double of Maria, and they test out her effectiveness in a night-club where, dressed in a scanty costume, she performs an erotic dance. The test is successful – not a bolt shows through her human disguise and the male patrons are quickly driven into a frenzy of lust. Then, in the clothes of the saintly Maria, she leads the workers in a violent revolt which results in the wrecking of the city's machinery. Meanwhile the real Maria, who has been imprisoned by Rotwang, manages to escape just in time to rescue the children of the workers from a flood caused by the wrecked machinery. The workers, believing that their children have been drowned, turn on the robot Maria and burn her at the stake. While the robot is burning someone in the crowd notices that on the top of a nearby building another Maria is being pursued by the sinister Rotwang. Freder immediately dashes off to rescue her and the crowd, including John Frederson, watch in horror as the drama high above them unfolds. But all ends happily for everyone except Rotwang who falls to his death; Freder brings Maria safely down to the ground while Frederson is persuaded to be nicer to the workers. The film closes with a shot of him shaking hands, without much obvious enthusiasm, with their spokesman while the workers look on approvingly, no doubt forgetting that they will probably have to work twenty-four hours a day for the next ten years to repair all the damage.

The main absurdity in the story is the absence of any reason why Frederson should want to cause a revolution that would destroy the city he rules. The plot and action of *Metropolis* are really on the level of a serial melodrama, which makes the contrast with its powerful imagery all the greater. Though supposedly set in the future there is little that is futuristic about the city; the New York of the time would have seemed more modern. Metropolis is a purely Gothic city, for all its skyscrapers and the occasional shot of aeroplanes (which execute tight curves in the air without tilting their wings). As noted already, most scientists in the early cinema were merely magicians in modern disguise, but in *Metropolis* there is no attempt to disguise Rotwang's magical nature – he lives in a bizarre house with a pentagram inscribed over the door. Rotwang is definitely a sorcerer of the old school, and though he builds a robot he uses magic to transform the stiff, metallic figure into the smooth and supple doppelganger of Maria (a marvellous performance by Brigitte Helm).

The main creative force behind *Metropolis* was Fritz Lang's. Though he originally trained as an architect he soon became a graphic artist and for a time supported himself by selling cartoons and caricatures. As a result of wounds sustained in the First World War he turned to writing and began selling melodramatic thrillers. Then he entered the film industry and started to make films on similar subjects. One of his first was *The Spiders* (*Die Spinnen*) made in 1919 about a group of men who attempt to take over the world using Inca gold, and later he made the first of the famous *Dr Mabuse* films about an evil genius who also plans world conquest. Many of his films during this period, including *Metropolis*, contained sf elements. When the Nazis came to power Lang was offered the headship of the National-Socialist film industry by Goebbels, who told him that Hitler had been enormously impressed by *Metropolis*. However Lang, like many other film-makers in Germany, left the country and after a spell in France emigrated to America where he continued to make films. Edgar G. Ulmer, another German director who later worked in America and who had been Lang's assistant on many of his German films including *Metropolis, Die Niebelungen* (1924), *Spione* (1927) and *M* (1932), described how such films were made: 'At that time, up to the coming of sound, there were *two* directors in each picture: a director for the dramatic action and for the actors, and then the director for the picture itself who established the camera angles, camera movements etc. There had to be teamwork. Our sets were built in perspective with rising or sloping floors. Everything was constructed through the viewfinder. So what happened was you could only take one shot in that set if you had a room. If there were ten shots of it, you built ten sets of that one room. Because the one eye was the point of the perspective, the furniture was built in perspective. That's where the great visual flair of the pictures came from. It gave you, of course, a completely controlled style. When you look at the old UFA [Germany's famous pre-war film studio that produced *Metropolis* etc.] pictures today, you're startled at how precise every shot is. Because a set was built for each one. Fritz Lang was a designer too. He designed advertising posters when he came to Berlin. Lang had an unbelievable energy and stick-to-itiveness; you could never stop him. He saw what he wanted in the picture. Nothing could distract him, he would do it fifty times.' Ulmer, however, did not get on well with Lang. 'Not at all. Because on the set he

Lloyd Hughes (below) confronts an unfriendly inhabitant of The Lost World *(played by Bull Montana).*

was the incarnation of the Austrian who became the Prussian general. A sadist of the worst order you can imagine. He was a great picture-maker who fortunately married the best scenario writer in Germany, Thea von Harbou.'[8] (Thea von Harbou, who wrote the novel on which *Metropolis* was based, collaborated with Lang on the scenarios and scripts of a number of his films, including *Woman in the Moon* and *M*.)

While *Metropolis* was being filmed a more prosaic foray into fantasy was being made in America – a film version of Conan Doyle's novel *The Lost World* about the discovery of prehistoric animals on the top of a remote plateau in South America. In charge of the special effects was Willis H. O'Brien, and the film involved the most ambitious use of model animation up to that time. Not only would fifty different dinosaur models be used but for the first time live actors would appear in the same shots as the models; previously shots of the actors had been intercut with footage of the monsters. He achieved this special effect by matting out a portion of the dinosaur scenes on the negative and then printing into these areas shots of the actors photographed against matching backgrounds.

The climax of the story involved the transportation of a Brontosaurus from the Amazon basin to London. As it is being unloaded from the ship it breaks out of its cage and rampages through the city leaving a trail of destruction and sending terrified Londoners running in all directions. It then attempts to walk across Tower Bridge but the structure crumbles under its weight and the dinosaur is last seen swimming out to sea.

These sequences were the most ambitious in the film and involved some major innovations in O'Brien's animation techniques as well as the construction of a huge set representing two London streets, peopled with two thousand extras together with two hundred cars and six London buses. O'Brien used an early automatic matting process to put his model Brontosaurus into the midst of the action. The model was animated against a stark white background and the resulting footage was printed in two ways: as a negative with the animal appearing against a black background, and as a high-contrast positive with the animal in silhouette against clear film. The latter was used as a matte in the printing of street footage, producing a copy in which the area of the dinosaur was left unexposed on each frame of film. Into this area the original negative of the model was then printed, and the result was a Brontosaurus in a London street.

The story was relatively faithful to the Conan Doyle original for about the first two-thirds of the way, then goes off on its own. In the book Challenger's party encounter a whole tribe of primitive men, not just one, and there is no volcanic eruption (ever since this film, primitive lost worlds have been blowing up with monotonous regularity – recent examples of the genre, *The Land That Time Forgot* and *The People That*

Time Forgot, both end with an obligatory bang). In the book the expedition takes back to London not a Brontosaurus but an egg which later hatches a pterodactyl. The idea of loosing a prehistoric monster in the streets of a modern city has appealed to film-makers ever since. It provided the basis for *King Kong* and later *The Beast from 20,000 Fathoms, Gorgo, Godzilla* and all their countless relations.

Despite the success of *The Lost World* O'Brien had difficulty in interesting film companies in other animation projects until RKO bought an idea of his entitled *Creation*. The story, which seems to owe much to Edgar Rice Burroughs' 1924 novel *The Land That Time Forgot*, concerned a group of people on a yachting expedition to South America who are taken on board a Chilean submarine when a typhoon approaches their vessel. In the turmoil that follows the arrival of the typhoon an undersea earthquake causes the submarine to be sucked down a long tunnel, and it finally emerges in a lake surrounded by jungle and the walls of a volcanic crater. The occupants of the submarine then have a series of fatal encounters with the prehistoric wildlife, which includes a giant rhinoceros, and the survivors are forced to revert to a Stone Age way of life. They manage to keep alive long enough to be rescued by the Chilean air force just as a volcanic eruption occurs (as in the film of *The Lost World*). A great deal of work was done on the project; models were constructed, sets built, and a few sequences were even filmed, but RKO decided to abandon it. So *Creation* itself never reached the screen, though much of the preparatory work, and some of the models, were incorporated into the making of *King Kong* several years later – the film that marked the peak of O'Brien's career.

In 1928 Fritz Lang, still in Germany, made what was probably the nearest thing to straight science fiction among all his films – *Die Frau Im Mond* (*Woman in the Moon*). The story itself, by Thea von Harbou, is weak but the film is technically interesting, even prophetic in some respects, and it was the first film to attempt to portray realistically the mechanics of space travel. The plot revolves around a young engineer called Helius who is jilted by his girlfriend Friede. To take his mind off his broken romance he becomes involved in the plans of a scientist friend of his, Professor Manfeldt, to build a rocketship capable of reaching the moon. It is the Professor's theory that the moon's surface contains gold in pure form, and this attracts the attention of a group of villainous financiers who attempt to sabotage the project. After various incidents the two groups join forces; the rocket is constructed and then launched towards the moon. These sequences are the most impressive from a scientific point of view – technical advisers on the film were German rocket experts Hermann Oberth and Willy Ley (Oberth later worked on rocket designs for the Nazis) and their spaceship design was remarkably prophetic (too much so for Hitler who later had all the prints of the film seized). Not only was the

Straps hanging *(illogically) from the ceiling and leather loops nailed to the floor enabled the astronauts in the 1928* Die Frau im Mond *to cope with the lack of gravity.*

rocket multi-staged but the scene where it is moved on tracks out of its vast hangar towards the launching pad is similar to later real-life scenes at Cape Canaveral. The film even included the first use of the now traditional countdown in connection with the launching of a rocket. But once the rocket lands safely on the moon scientific authenticity comes to an end. Not only is there air on the moon but the lunar surface is covered with snow and the whole setting resembles the Swiss Alps. After gold is found in a cave filled with bubbling pools of mud the story becomes increasingly melodramatic, and it ends with the young couple Helius and Friede deciding to stay on the moon, where presumably they live happily ever after, or at least until their food runs out.

Another German film of 1928 was a remake of *Alraune*, directed and written by Henrik Galeen and starring Brigitte Helm (the star of *Metropolis*) as the girl produced by artificial insemination. Paul Wegener, most famous for his portrayal of the Golem in the film of the same name (which he also directed) played the scientist who makes use of a condemned murderer and a prostitute to create the beautiful and totally evil Alraune (who nevertheless undergoes a change of heart at the end of the film). British audiences were naturally confused when the film was first released (under the title of *Daughter of Destiny*) since all references to artificial insemination had been removed by the censor. What remained was a strange story about a girl who acts very badly towards her loving foster father for no apparent reason.

*Brigitte Helm and
Paul Wegener in
the 1928 version
of* Alraune.

Alraune was remade two years later by UFA, again starring Brigitte Helm but without Wegener, this time directed by Richard Oswald, and yet again in 1952. The last version, also known as *Unnatural*, starred Hildegard Knef and Erich von Stroheim, and, directed by Fritz Rotter, it completely reversed the story by making the scientist the evil character who exploits the innocent Alraune. He finally shoots her dead and the film ends with him on his way to a fog-shrouded gallows.

Earlier in this chapter mention was made of a film version of *Mysterious Island*, another project of J. Ernest Williamson who had made the successful 1916 version of *20,000 Leagues*. Williamson finally interested MGM in his scenario for the film, but he soon came face to face with a problem, which he described in his autobiography: 'I was to learn that Jules Verne hadn't written a story big enough for this Hollywood crowd. The powers had definitely decided they would not film his romantic adventure story which my version followed closely. It must be something more than that, something larger, something "Big"! And the Abraham Lincoln atmosphere with its Civil War characters was definitely *out*. For technical reasons the story was now to be laid in Russia. Captain Nemo was to be Russian, the whole cast were to be Russian. These ethnological changes were satisfactory to me providing the story was right and the undersea possibilities were still open.'[9]

Williamson finally got the go-ahead to start shooting the location material in 1926, but no sooner had he and his crew arrived in the Bahamas than most of their boats and equipment were wrecked by a hurricane. Despite this major setback Williamson was soon at work, but he then encountered other obstacles – all of which originated in Hollywood. It seemed that the studio couldn't make up its mind about the film's basic content and kept changing things around. Directors came and went, as did

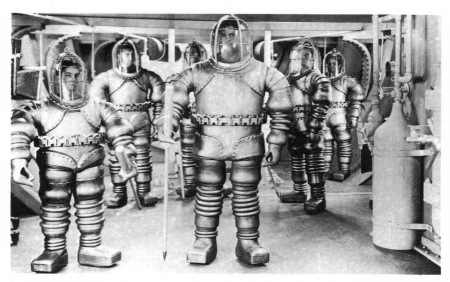

'This is no laughing matter' seems to be the silent message in this scene from the 1928 Mysterious Island.

leading members of the cast, which meant that material had to be re-shot endlessly. Altogether it took nearly four years and a million dollars to complete the film, and the result was spectacular but hardly something that Jules Verne would have recognized. Captain Nemo's name had been changed to Count Dakkar, and he was played by Lionel Barrymore. Dakkar, like Nemo, has an island base on which he and his workmen live and work, perfecting a mysterious ship. On the day that the first experimental model of the submarine sets out on a trial run the Russians invade the island, kill many of the workmen and capture Dakkar. Eventually he and his surviving assistants escape in a second experimental submarine in which they sink to the bottom of the sea. Donning heavy metal diving suits they start to explore the sea bed and encounter a giant octopus and an undersea dragon (a photographically enlarged lizard), also a horde of little creatures who look like relatives of Donald Duck. These underwater sequences, a combination of Williamson's actual underwater shots and footage shot 'dry' in the studio (the little duck-like creatures were actually midgets in costumes who 'swam' with the aid of piano wire), are quite impressive, and the final version of the film would probably have been a big success if the project hadn't been rammed by a technological innovation as deadly to silent films as Nemo's Nautilus had been to conventional shipping. By the time the film was finally ready for release, sound had arrived.

Sound effects were hastily added to the film (which, in the final version, was directed by Lucien Hubbard) but *Mysterious Island*, despite favourable critical reaction, sank almost without trace. It was the end of one era and the beginning of another.

2　Things That Came (1930–40)

The discovery by the film companies that audiences actually wanted sound – that they *preferred* talkies to silent films – panicked the studios, and almost overnight the style of movies changed. The fluid visuals of the typical silent film were replaced by static scenes in which the actors, no longer able to venture outdoors, huddled together in rooms and talked into plants or articles of furniture containing the all-important microphone – and talked and talked and talked. The problem lay in finding them something to talk about (in silent films many actors and actresses simply used to mouth the words 'so and so and so' endlessly into the camera). All of a sudden film-scenario writers were required to fill countless pages with dialogue, and as many of them weren't even capable of writing their own names this caused problems. Frantic film producers started looking elsewhere for suitable talkie material; they very quickly discovered the theatre. It was an ideal solution because in plays, they learned, there was always lots of talk and, more importantly, it took place indoors. This meant that, for a time, films relying on visual spectacle, like the science fiction ones (though the term was not then in general use) went out of fashion. Willis H. O'Brien, for instance, was unable to generate any interest in his animation projects for several years. In retrospect it might look as if the time was ripe for the sf film to evolve into something more sophisticated – to become a platform for ideas rather than merely a showcase for special effects (H. G. Wells was certainly interested in using films in this way) but this development didn't take place. Film-makers soon realized that it was possible to combine sound and spectacle, so the cinema once again reverted to its normal, low-minded self, with the emphasis once again on action rather than ideas.

In the intervening period, however, came an sf-related talkie that took itself very seriously indeed. Called *High Treason* it was made in Britain in 1929 and was based on a play by Pemberton Billing which reflected the strong pacifist movement in Europe between the two world wars. The time is 1940 – a 1940 when the two most powerful political alliances in the world are called the United Atlantic States and the Federated States of Europe. They are in danger of declaring war on each other, so 25 million people of all nationalities have formed a Peace League to try and prevent

A 1929 view of the London of the 'future' in High Treason.

such a thing happening. When an argument between two soldiers over a card game at the frontier threatens to spark off the feared holocaust after the Peace League building has been bombed, the President of the Peace League assassinates the President of the European States to prevent him from declaring war. He then makes a broadcast to the world which conciliates the Atlantic States and successfully averts bloodshed. The film ends with him bravely facing execution for the murder of the European leader. Directed by Maurice Elvey, who had started directing in 1912 and later went on to make the English remake of *The Tunnel*, it attracted favourable critical comment, particularly in Britain, where one reviewer wrote: 'It confirms the impression that the talking picture is the medium in which Britain is qualified to lead the world. Comparisons with the great German film *Metropolis* will naturally arise but as popular entertainment such comparisons must be in favour of the British film . . . The forecast of London and New York in the future shows imagination of design within the bounds of possibility, and steers clear of the exaggerated phantasy of *Metropolis*. Neither has Mr Elvey relied overmuch on tricks of the camera. The lighting is effective and the sensational scenes of the flooding of the Channel Tunnel and the destruction by bombs of the Peace League building are most realistic and impressive.'[10] All of which reads like embarrassing chauvinism today, especially since *High Treason* with its dated sermonizing has been all but forgotten while the timeless *Metropolis* still proves its popularity with audiences. Nor can the basic contradiction in the film's pacifist message be easily overlooked: the leader of the peace group has to become a murderer to achieve his pacifist aims. That sort of behaviour gives pacifism a bad name.

New York of 1980 as imagined by the makers of the 1930 musical Just Imagine. *It was obviously inspired by* Metropolis, *but Fritz Lang had originally been inspired to make* Metropolis *by his first view of the New York skyline.*

With sound came the musical, which rapidly developed into one of the most popular film genres. The first major science fiction film of the 1930s produced by Hollywood was, indeed, a musical. Called *Just Imagine* it was directed in 1930 by David Butler, whose first film was *Fox Movietone Follies of 1929* and who later went on to direct Shirley Temple films. Lavish and very expensive, it concerned a man struck by lightning while playing golf in 1930 who wakes to find himself in New York in 1980. He is befriended by two young men, known by numbers instead of names, who show him the city and its marvels. The huge model set of New York is really the film's most interesting aspect. Obviously inspired by *Metropolis* but much more elaborate than the city in the German film, it cost a quarter of a million dollars to build and contained miniature skyscrapers supposedly 250 storeys high as well as a canal network for ocean liners. The futuristic New York's wonders included pills for nourishment, TV phones, automatic doors, heated hand-driers, personal aircraft and a slot-machine that produced test-tube babies at the drop of a coin. However the film's main concern isn't the future but the romantic problems of one of the young men, J21. He has fallen in love with a girl called LN 18 but, due to a New York decree of the future, if two men wish to marry the same girl she must choose the one with the most accomplishments. So, to prove himself, J21, with two companions, volunteers to fly to Mars in an experimental space craft. They encounter some Martian flappers and J21 further complicates his love-life by falling in love with one of them. All this is interspersed with several forgettable musical numbers, including such classics as 'The Romance of Elmer Stremingway', 'Old Fashioned Girl' and 'Never Swat a Fly' (the latter being about the love-life of blow flies). Another liability is the performance of comedian El Brendel as the man from 1930: his customary dumb yokel routine hasn't improved with age. The film contains many in-jokes that have become very dated over the years; for instance all the cars have Jewish names, a joke on Henry Ford's then well-known anti-Semitism.

To Fox's surprise *Just Imagine* failed badly at the box-office, and it seems likely that the Fox executives didn't blame the weak story or the unmemorable songs so much as the science fiction elements. It had long been a Hollywood belief that the quickest way to lose money was to make a fantasy picture and no doubt this latest failure provided added confirmation. Perhaps if *Just Imagine* had been a huge success it might have produced a wider variety of sf movie themes instead of which the use of sf elements became almost exclusively confined to horror movies. For the year after *Just Imagine* saw Universal's version of *Frankenstein* which *was* a success and once again firmly linked science fiction with the Gothic. For the next two decades the science fiction cinema, with a few notable exceptions, was dominated by mad scientists and their unholy creations.

Frankenstein was directed by the young Englishman James Whale, who had originally been brought to Hollywood to direct the film version of R. C. Sherriff's famous play *Journey's End* about a group of First World War

El Brendel (centre) is introduced to the fashions of '1980'.

soldiers. Whale had originally trained as a commercial artist and later worked as a theatrical scenery designer, and he brought a definite visual flair to his filming of *Frankenstein*. With his atmospheric lighting, smooth tracking shots and numerous low-angle shots that made effective use of the high-ceiling sets he succeeded in making a film that is still visually interesting today (unlike Tod Browning's static *Dracula*, which has dated badly). Whale, as a former theatre director, was also able to draw good performances from his cast, especially Boris Karloff as the monster. The film's major deficiency lies with the script, which was written by Garrett Fort, Edward Faragoh and Robert Florey. Mary Shelley's basic theme revolved around a question of metaphysics; her creature was intelligent and articulate, and able to voice his existentialist anguish at the way in which he had been brought to life. He *knew* he had been made a monster with no place in the world of men and was thus able to face Frankenstein directly with his guilt, yet the problems of the film monster seem to arise almost solely because of a mix-up of brains, a criminal one being used by mistake. This device was one of Florey's contributions to the script (originally Florey, a Frenchman, was to have directed *Frankenstein* with Bela Lugosi as the monster, but the two test reels he shot were rejected by Universal) and effectively clouds and confuses Shelley's theme. It also shows that film writers of the time had curious ideas about the nature of the human brain; no attempt is made to keep the brain alive and the problem of cell degeneration is completely ignored. No effort is made to communicate with the personality within the brain that must have remembered a former life; instead, the creature is treated as a totally *new* being. Even the brain's criminal 'taint' is forgotten along the way since most of the monster's subsequent actions seem to arise from its fear and confusion rather than from any deliberately evil intent.

Nevertheless it is arguable that Karloff's mute, shambling interpretation of the monster is far more cinematically impressive than Shelley's intelligent, articulate creation would have been, and when the monster learns to speak in the sequel *Bride of Frankenstein* it loses some of its magic. For all its faults, particularly the weak script with its leaden dialogue, *Frankenstein* is a great movie which possesses its own unique power – a power which owes more to the medium of the cinema than it does either to Mary Shelley or to science fiction.

After Dr Frankenstein, mad scientists came fast and furious out of Hollywood and onto the screens of the world. Nineteen thirty-two – a vintage year for mad scientists – saw *Dr Jekyll and Mr Hyde*, *Doctor X*, *Island of Lost Souls* and *The Mask of Fu Manchu*. The 1932 version of *Dr Jekyll* is probably the best of all; it certainly has more vitality than the slicker 1941 remake. Directed by Rouben Mamoulian, it starred Fredric March as the noble humanitarian Dr Jekyll who only wants to do good but comes unstuck when he attempts to isolate evil from the human character and instead turns himself into a monster. As noted earlier, this version of the Robert Louis Stevenson story, adapted by Samuel Hoffenstein and Percy Heath, suggests that evil is somehow connected with man's animal heritage, a point of view which is quite different from the orthodox religious view of the nature of evil which had usually held sway in supernatural movies up until then. When Jekyll first takes his drink of potion he is transformed into an ape-man, with an ape-man's increased appetite for sensual experience, whether it be food, drink or sex. The latter drive dominates Hyde but with it comes an increased appreciation of the joys of cruelty, and Hyde's dealings with his female victim, a pathetic prostitute, well played by Miriam Hopkins, become progressively more sadistic as Hyde grows more and more ape-like. In other words, the script-writers equate sadism with the primitive – not a concept likely to find much favour nowadays. But whatever the legitimacy of its theme, the 1932 *Dr Jekyll* is an above-average film, thanks to a good script and a masterful central performance by March, who swings from the saintly Dr Jekyll to the energetic excesses of Hyde with great gusto.

A similar theme of dark and primitive forces being unleashed from within the mind was used in *Doctor X*, directed by Michael Curtiz and adapted by Robert Tasker and Earl Baldwin from a play by Howard M. Comstock and Allen C. Miller. It's a marvellously absurd horror movie that pulls out all the stops. The police are investigating a series of gruesome murders in which the victims have all been partially eaten. Suspicion falls on the Academy of Surgical Research run by Doctor Xavier (played by Lionel Atwill, who was to specialize in mad scientists) as several of the professors at the institute have connections with cannibalism. Two of the suspects were once shipwrecked in a lifeboat with a third scientist who had mysteriously vanished by the time they were picked up by a passing ship – the two survivors looking suspiciously well-fed. Another scientist, called Wells, is an expert on the subject of cannibalism, and we are introduced to him from behind a jar containing a pulsating human heart. 'If this experiment is successful we will be nearer the secret of life,' he tells the detectives. Like the evil Rotwang in *Metropolis* he wears a black glove, but his hand is completely artificial and he is able to detach it from his arm. 'An empty sleeve is revolting to most people,' he remarks while waving a pencil up it. Of course it is Wells who turns out to be the killer – he has developed a synthetic flesh which he uses to fashion not only a new hand of incredible strength but also a living disguise that transforms him into a monster. The living material also causes Wells's inner monster to break out and take over: 'There *isn't* any Wells!' screams Wells (played by Preston Foster) in the final showdown with the forces of law and order.

With their film of *The Island of Lost Souls* Paramount managed to combine mad scientists, man-made monsters and the theme of beasts-into-men all in one. It was, of course, based on H. G. Wells's novel *The Island of Dr Moreau* and marked the first time that one of his works had received the Hollywood treatment. In 1925 Cecil B. DeMille had purchased the rights to *War of the Worlds* for Paramount but the obvious problems in transferring the story to the screen caused DeMille to abandon the project. In 1930 Paramount actually offered it to the Russian film-maker Eisenstein, but though it reached the script stage he also withdrew from the project. Paramount again tried unsuccessfully to make the film in 1932 but it would be another twenty years before a version (by George Pal) would finally reach the screen. The script of *The Island of Lost Souls* was written by Waldemar Young and Philip Wylie, the latter being a science fiction writer himself (ironically, his novel *When Worlds Collide*, which he wrote with Edwin Balmer, was bought by Paramount in 1934 as a possible project for DeMille, but once again it was George Pal who finally brought it to the screen in 1951). Young and Wylie diluted much of the impact of Wells's book and inserted a typical Hollywood love interest, but for all their alterations the film remains relatively faithful to Wells's theme. As the evil vivisectionist Dr Moreau, who is attempting to transform animals into men using crude and barbaric methods, Charles Laughton gives a hypnotic performance. A leering, whip-cracking monster, he is much more terrifying than his hapless creations, but he isn't mad: he *knows* what he's doing – which makes him even more disturbing. Of course he has nothing to do with Wells's character whose cruelty springs from a scientific zeal that makes him oblivious to the feelings of his subjects. Laughton's Moreau is just plain evil and he obviously relishes every moment of it. His performance, along with the atmospheric island settings (the exteriors were actually filmed outdoors instead of in a studio, which is unusual for an early talkie) and a better-than-average script, help to make *Lost Souls*, which was directed by Erle C. Kenton, a memorable film. It is certainly far superior to the 1977 version.

Boris Karloff, who so often suffered at the hands of mad scientists during his career, had the opportunity to deal out the pain himself when he played the oriental super-villain Dr Fu Manchu in MGM's *The Mask of Fu Manchu*, based on the novel by Sax Rohmer. Produced by Irving Thalberg and directed by Charles Brabin and Charles Vidor it is a typically lavish MGM picture of the period with marvellously stylized sets designed by Cedric Gibbons. As Fu Manchu, Karloff lisps his way enjoyably through the role, torturing and murdering in the most esoteric ways possible, with the assistance of his equally evil daughter, played by Myrna Loy. The plot involves Fu's search for Ghengis Khan's death mask and sword, which he intends to use as symbols to arouse the oriental races in a war against the white nations. There is a very spectacular climax in which Fu's electrical death-ray machine goes out of control and destroys both him and his followers. The electrical effects were created by Ken Strickfaden, who also provided the machinery used in Frankenstein's laboratory.

Meanwhile in Germany the science fiction film hadn't fallen victim to the mad scientist syndrome, and 1932 saw the release of two totally different sf-related productions. One was *L'Atlantide*, directed by G. W. Pabst and based on the popular 1919 novel by Pierre Benoit about Antinea, the mysterious Queen of Atlantis – now an underground city beneath a North African desert – who lures a succession of men to their doom and then keeps their preserved bodies on display in a bizarre trophy room. The similarities between this and H. Rider Haggard's *She* are obvious, and like the latter book *L'Atlantide* has been filmed several times, the first version being a French one made in 1921, directed by Jacques Feyder. Of the various versions the Pabst one is generally regarded as the best, a judgement based not only on the visual élan of his direction but also on Brigitte Helm's striking performance as the Queen. French- and English-language versions of the 1932 production were made simultaneously with different casts, with the exception of Brigitte Helm who appeared in all three.

F.P.1 Antwortet Nicht (*F.P.1. Does Not Answer*), directed by Karl Hartl, was Germany's other contribution to the genre that year. Based on a novel by Kurt Siodmak, who also wrote the screenplay with Walter Reisch, it has been described as in the tradition of *Metropolis* and *Die Frau Im Mond*, but Hartl was no Fritz Lang. *F.P.1.* is a very slow-moving and weakly-plotted film ostensibly about the construction of a giant floating runway to be moored in the middle of the Atlantic, but it is actually more concerned with a tedious love triangle. The central character is an egotistical aviator (played by Hans Alber acting as if he's wandered in from an opera) who helps his best friend, a designer, convince a shipyard to build the F.P.1. (Floating Platform 1). The sister of the three shipyard owners falls in love with the aviator but he leaves her to fly non-stop around the world from Berlin to Berlin. However he doesn't return for two and half years – it transpires he had crash-landed in Australia and was too embarrassed to emerge from the Bush. By the time he returns F.P.1.is completed and in position in the Atlantic and the girl has switched her affections to the aviator's friend who is now in command of the platform. A saboteur attempts to sink the F.P.1. but all ends happily. The designer gets the girl and the aviator joins an expedition to capture a giant South American condor. Rather on the level of a mediocre pulp novel, it has nothing of the slickness, vitality or humour of similar Hollywood products of the period. Even the model work, which is somewhat sparse,

Paul Hartmann and Sybille Schmitz look anxious on 'Floating Platform Number One', and for good reason.

Artist's rendition of the floating platform that featured in the disappointing F.P.I. Antwortet Nicht.

isn't very convincing. The only real source of entertainment is the overacting of Hans Alber and the languid posing of the statuesque Sybille Schmitz. A young Peter Lorre also appears in the film, but he doesn't have much to do except stand around looking mournful, and for good reason.

1933 was also a vintage year for sf films, and the one that towers above them all is undoubtedly *King Kong*. Much has been written about this film, and its epic story has been interpreted in many ways – sexually, politically and racially. It is full of so much striking imagery that it is easy to see symbolic undertones in almost every frame. A popular film will often reflect contemporary attitudes and fears without its makers realizing it; one of the most popular interpretations is that King Kong represents the American black, a creature who is taken forcibly from his homeland to America where he is exploited in chains but then breaks free and conquers New York, snarling his defiance at the world. Certainly many young American blacks identified with Kong and conversely the film reflected white America's fear of the black man. Gorillas, as menacing creatures, had been featuring in American films since the early silent days, often in serials and in such films as *The Unholy Three* (1925 and 1930), *The Murders in the Rue Morgue* (1914 and 1932) and even *Sign of the Cross* (1932); usually, at some point in the story, they threaten a beautiful white girl with 'a fate worse than death'. *King Kong* takes the metaphor of sexual threat to its ultimate limit: the Skull Island natives offer to buy Ann Darrow (Fay Wray, whose hair had been dyed blonde for the part) from Carl Denham (Robert Armstrong); 'Tell them she's not for sale!' snarls her would-be lover John Driscoll (Bruce Cabot); but then the natives steal her in the middle of the night and offer her, after an erotic ceremony, to their god. The white man, Driscoll (who is actually more neanderthal than Kong thanks to Cabot's acting style), eventually wins her back but later loses her again when Kong's huge arm penetrates the sanctuary of Ann's own bedroom and snatches her up. The film is a treasure-trove of Freudian symbols: a fifty-foot-tall ape who becomes sexually infatuated with a girl; who kills his pursuers by dislodging them from a massive tree trunk; who then slowly undresses her (in the famous sequence missing from most prints), sniffing his fingers as he does so, after first wrestling with a giant snake-like creature; and who finally, with the girl, climbs to the top of New York's tallest phallus. If Freud hadn't existed it would have been necessary to invent him after *King Kong*.

King Kong was mainly the creation of three men: Merian C. Cooper, Ernest B. Schoedsack and Willis H. O'Brien. The first two, who produced and directed the picture, were not conventional Hollywood film-makers but had made their names by producing a series of true-life adventure films shot in a number of exotic locations and under the most difficult conditions: films such as *Grass*, shot in Turkey and Iran and released in

1925, *Chang*, a jungle spectacular filmed in Thailand and released in 1927, and *Rango*, set in the Dutch East Indies and released in 1930. In 1930 Schoedsack said of their films: 'The point is that I have my own ideas about making motion pictures. Everyone seems to think that stories, to be vital, must have a love interest. A picture can't be good unless it's built around a throbbing scene between a male and a female. That's a mistake, as Cooper and I tried to show with *Grass* and *Change*. We focus our lenses, not on silly close-ups of love-sick females, but on the elemental clashes between nations and their fundamental problems, between man and nature.'[11] An ironic statement from a man who was to collaborate on one of the most incredible love stories in motion picture history! *King Kong* came about when David O. Selznick was put in charge of the ailing RKO studio to see what could be salvaged from the company's various abandoned projects. To assist him he brought in Merian C. Cooper, who at that time was planning to make a film about a giant ape on the rampage in a big city (he claimed that his first idea was of the giant ape on top of a building battling a fleet of planes) and originally he intended to use a real ape, photographically enlarged, in the film but changed his mind when he became familiar with O'Brien's techniques. Examining the footage of *Creation* that had been shot before the money ran out Cooper was impressed with the realism of the animated creatures and saw that his giant ape might be achieved by stop-motion photography.

There's still controversy over exactly who contributed what to the story of *King Kong*. Various people receive an actual credit on the picture; Ruth Rose (Schoedsack's wife) and James A. Creelman (who also wrote the screenplay for Cooper and Schoedsack's *The Most Dangerous Game*) are both credited with the screenplay, while Cooper himself and Edgar Wallace are credited with conceiving the idea, though it's doubtful whether the latter had anything to do with the original idea or the script since the famous English novelist and playwright died shortly after arriving in Hollywood. Also credited was Horace McCoy (best known for his novel *They Shoot Horses, Don't They?*), who worked as Creelman's assistant on the picture, but one person who *didn't* receive any credit for any of the story elements was Willis H. O'Brien himself; yet so many of the action sequences must first have been conceived by him purely in terms of animation. Much of the structure of the film, and many of the set-pieces, came from O'Brien's storyboard. Many things in *King Kong* can be traced to earlier O'Brien projects such as *The Lost World* and the unfinished *Creation*; for instance the idea of a giant prehistoric monster running amuck in a modern city comes from O'Brien's version of *The Lost World*, as does the log spanning a vast chasm which is then dislodged by a monster (an image used in both *The Lost World* and *Creation*), and the sequence where Kong reels in Ann Darrow and Driscoll as they attempt to climb down the vine leading from his lair is an elaboration of a similar sequence in *The Lost World*. Without doubt O'Brien contributed more to the overall structure of *King Kong* than he has been given credit for.

But everyone has always agreed that the film represents O'Brien's finest achievement in the area of model animation. His models merge perfectly with a story of almost epic proportions, with the result that the special effects, while vitally important, don't take over the film to the extent where the story becomes a mere appendage (as often happens with films built around model animation). In *King Kong* the story itself is always the dominant element.

Definitely not a classic is the sequel that was hurriedly made in 1933 – *Son of Kong*. Once again it stars Robert Armstrong as Carl Denham, film producer and showman, who returns to Skull Island looking for buried treasure – Kong's activities in New York having left him with a few debts and lawsuits. On the island he encounters the son of Kong, a young white ape a mere twelve feet tall. Denham earns Little Kong's gratitude by saving him from a bed of quicksand and is in turn saved by the ape when he is later menaced by a giant bear. There are other battles with prehistoric monsters and the film ends with Skull Island sinking into the sea, Little Kong's last act being to save Denham from drowning. After the success of *King Kong* the production team had immediately been given the go-ahead by the studio to make an even more spectacular sequel, but the allotted budget was a mere $250,000 (*Kong* had officially cost $650,000 but the actual cost was nearer $500,000). So, since they couldn't make the sequel bigger, they decided to make it funnier, with the result that Little Kong, with his constant mugging, ended up being too funny for words. Despite

Robert Armstrong, watched by Helen Mack, applies first-aid to an appendage belonging to King Kong's son in Son of Kong.

the script the special effects in *Son of Kong* are of a high standard and compare well with those in *King Kong*, but O'Brien himself was embarrassed by the picture and didn't like to discuss it in later years.

Whether or not *King Kong* can be described as a true work of science fiction is open to debate: as scientific extrapolation none of it seems very plausible, but, as noted in the Introduction, scientific knowledge was never one of the requirements needed for a successful Hollywood scriptwriter. At least sf writers are usually aware of scientific flaws and try to disguise them with pseudo-science; for instance, they've long got around Einstein's law regarding the impossibility of travel faster than the speed of light by taking a short-cut through 'hyper space'. No doubt H. G. Wells was aware of the fact that a totally transparent man would also be totally blind, since the light would pass straight through the retinas of the eyes without exciting the optic nerves, but instead he diverted attention to all the other problems of being invisible (such as half-digested meals still being visible within the body for several hours) in his marvellous book *The Invisible Man*.

Many of the more interesting elements in Wells's novel were discarded when it came to be adapted for the screen but the film *The Invisible Man* (1931) still remains a very impressive and entertaining piece of work, though Wells himself didn't share that opinion. He was, however, fortunate in having a very talented team of people involved in the production of the film; the director was James Whale, who had directed *Frankenstein*, the script was written by the playwright R. C. Sherriff, Claude Rains played the invisible man, and top effects man John P. Fulton handled the special effects. Whale and Sherriff may have diluted some of the horror in their adaptation, but they did concentrate on the strong streak of black humour that runs through the book and the result was a very amusing picture in which the comedy was more than a shade sick. There is also a great deal of gleeful anarchy in it, and one feels that Whale and Sherriff had more sympathy with the invisible man, who has been turned into a raving megalomaniac due to a side effect of the invisibility drug, than with his victims; they certainly seemed to derive pleasure from making the British policemen in the film look ridiculous.

As the mad scientist Griffin, Claude Rains gives a memorable performance despite being heard but not seen for most of the film: in the early scenes his face is covered in bandages and it is not until he dies in hospital that the audience receives a glimpse of him. For the rest of the film he is entirely invisible or represented by various articles of apparently empty clothing – shirt, trousers, dressing gown and so on. John P. Fulton, in charge of the effects department at Universal for many years, made use of an improved travelling matte system based on one originally devised by effects innovator Frank Williams, whose assistant he had once been.

The Invisible Man's efforts to find a cure for his unique medical problem are all in vain.

Meanwhile German film-makers were still trying to devise effective ways of travelling to America. After establishing a floating platform in the Atlantic as a way station for aircraft in *FP.1. Antwortet Nicht*, they devised a tunnel linking Europe with America in *Der Tunnel* made in 1933. This obsession with reaching America was probably an unconscious reflection of the fact that many German film-makers knew they would really be making the journey sooner or later, either lured by Hollywood promises or to escape the Nazi menace. The rather curious official reason for the building of the tunnel in the film was 'the promotion of world peace'. Directed by Kurt Bernhardt and scripted by Kurt Siodmak (based on a novel by Bernard Kellerman), *Der Tunnel* was of a very high standard technically, though once again the actual story left much to be desired. The various natural disasters that occur during the excavation of the tunnel – cave-ins, floods and volcanic eruptions – are realistically staged (the film's associate producer was killed during the shooting of one such sequence) and far superior to the British version of the film made the following year. Called *The Tunnel* (though also known as *The TransAtlantic Tunnel*) it was directed by Maurice Elvey, who had made *High Treason*, and scripted by Clemence Dane and L. du Garde Peach from Siodmak's own adaptation of his German screenplay. Though it lacked much of the spectacle of the German version it followed roughly the same story, the one big difference being that the European end of the tunnel was now sited in England, which makes the new reason for building the tunnel – 'to establish a permanent peace between the English-speaking nations' – even more difficult to understand.

Set vaguely in a future world that has TV phones but whose people still wear clothes from the early 1930s it concerns a young engineer, McAllan, whose one burning ambition is to see a trans-Atlantic tunnel built. Mr Lloyd, England's richest man, helps him to realize his vision. Work on the tunnel occupies McAllan's mind so much that he begins to neglect his wife and their young son. Called to America to create public interest in the project, he is photographed for the papers with Mr Lloyd's beautiful daughter (secretly in love with McAllan). When McAllan's wife sees the photographs she is upset but bravely attempts to take her mind off her grief by volunteering to work as a nurse in the tunnel. But, and here things really start going downhill, she contracts 'tunnel fever' and goes blind (not to be confused with 'tunnel vision'). She therefore retires to a country hideaway but McAllan thinks that she has deserted him, and throws himself even more totally into his work. The years pass. McAllan's own son, grown up and also working in the tunnel, is killed after a volcanic explosion. Finally the last few feet of rock are blasted away and the English tunnellers link up with the Americans.

Critics at the time of the film's release, while appreciating the special

Two views of future transport as seen by British film-makers of the past: (above) *a car from the 1929* High Treason; (below) *a rail vehicle from the 1934* The Tunnel *(both directed by Maurice Elvey).*

effects created by J. Whitehead, B. Guidobaldi and A. Stroppa, were not taken with the script. They also noted that though the events spanned two decades clothing fashions did not change.

Another 1934 British sf film, which has more or less been forgotten now, was *The Secret of the Loch* directed by Milton Rosmer (best known as an actor, though he directed a number of films as well) and scripted by Billie Bristow and Charles Bennett. Bennett scripted several of Hitchcock's early British thrillers and later worked in Hollywood where he became involved with science fiction film producer/director Irwin Allen, with whom he co-scripted such films as *Voyage to the Bottom of the Sea* (1961), *Five Weeks in a Balloon* (1962) and the 1960 version of *The Lost World*. *The Secret of the Loch* owes a lot to the latter Conan Doyle story, involving an eccentric scientist, a journalist in love with his daughter and – of course – the Loch Ness monster.

Films concerning worldwide catastrophes, whether natural, man- or alien-made, became very popular during the 1950s but were rather scarce in the 1930s. There was the 1930 French film *La Fin Du Monde* (*The End of the World*) made by Abel Gance about a comet striking the Earth and also the planned DeMille production of *When Worlds Collide*, which was later abandoned. One such film that did reach the screen was RKO's *Deluge*, directed by Felix E. Feist and adapted by John Goodrich and Warren B. Duff from a novel by S. Fowler Wright. However the makers of *Deluge* made a vital mistake that a master showman like DeMille would have avoided at all costs: they start the film with what should have been the climax – the destruction of most of the world – and then fill up the remainder of the running time with a very conventional love story. The film begins with the meteorological offices in New York being puzzled by strange weather conditions, which are then followed by an eclipse of the sun in true biblical fashion. Disaster strikes in the form of worldwide earthquakes and floods, and the special effects in these sequences are truly remarkable, especially in those scenes showing New York's forest of

(Above) *New York City is destroyed in* Deluge; *while* (below) *Sydney Blackmer seems surprised to have survived the meteorological traumas.*

skyscrapers first collapsing and then being swamped by a huge tidal wave. (Ned Mann and William B. Williams are officially credited for the effects but apparently Willis H. O'Brien also worked on these sequences.) But all this spectacle comes to an end with the first reel; from then on the film is concerned with the story of the survivors. One of them, Martin, believes his wife and children have died, so he becomes romantically involved with a girl called Claire. At the end of the film however, he discovers that his wife and family are still alive but Claire solves everything by calmly swimming off in the general direction of oblivion, making the sort of gesture film heroines rarely make these days.

The musical comedy *It's Great to Be Alive* was directed in 1933 by Alfred Werker for Fox. It was actually a remake of a 1924 film called *The Last Man on Earth* and based on a story by John D. Swain in which an epidemic kills all males over fourteen except one. He naturally becomes a much-prized specimen to the women who have taken over the governments of the world and there are clashes over who should own him.

As the 1930s progressed the mad scientists continued their own take-over of the sf film genre, and even the Germans succumbed to their influence in the 1934 production of *Gold*, just as they were succumbing to a different type of madman in reality. Directed by Karl Hartl (who had directed *F. P. 1.*) it concerned a villainous Englishman who builds a vast machine capable of turning lead into gold – the old alchemist's dream. Hans Alber, the posturing hero from *F.P.1.*, plays a German engineer who is hired by the villain to work on the machine, which is situated in Scotland. Basically a mediocre adventure film, though rather more entertaining than *F.P.1.*, its climactic sequences showing the machine getting out of control amidst huge electrical explosions are very spectacular. Some people have suggested that the English villain, who is rat-faced and has a tendency to rant wildly, was Hartl's sly dig at Hitler, but if this was so it must have been too subtle for the Führer to grasp as Hartl was one German film-maker who didn't depart hastily for America.

Back in America Dr Frankenstein was again meddling with things Man Was Not Meant to Know in *The Bride of Frankenstein* (1935), this time aided by the very camp Dr Praetorius, who has also succeeded in creating a form of human life by using very different methods. Showing Frankenstein a number of tiny human figures that he keeps in bell-jars he says: 'While you were playing with dead flesh I went to the original seed! Forsake the charnel house!' Frankenstein regards Praetorius' creations with alarm. 'But this isn't science,' he cries. 'It's more like magic!' Science indeed has little place in this picture but it remains James Whale's most interesting work and his most daring in terms of pushing his idiosyncratic tastes in black humour to the limits. The most outrageous element in the film is the character of Dr Praetorius, played by Ernest Thesiger, a friend of Whale's from the London theatre, and one memorable scene shows him happily eating his supper in a shadowy burial vault while chatting to part of a skeleton that he has mounted on top of the tomb. The film as a whole is quite bizarre and ends with a classic sequence when the artificial woman created by Frankenstein and Praetorius as a mate for the original monster (again played by Karloff) takes one look at the monster and screams. The embittered monster then throws a lever that sends up the hill-top laboratory almost as far as Whale was sending up the horror genre itself.

The following year Karloff turned up as a mad scientist in *The Invisible Ray* directed by Lambert Hillyer. Karloff plays a physicist called Janos Rukh who lives with his blind mother in an observatory high in the Carpathian mountains. He has a theory that centuries ago a meteor containing a special radioactive element landed in Africa, but his efforts to persuade other people to help him locate the substance are in vain. Eventually he makes it to the site of the meteorite on his own but is infected by the radiation. Now able to kill with just a touch of his hand, leaving a glowing hand-print on his victims, and also able to project deadly beams from his eyes, he hunts down the people who had earlier refused to help him, but is finally destroyed when his mother deprives him of the drugs that keep him alive.

Revenge also provided the motive for *The Devil Doll* made the same year (1936) by Tod Browning from a screenplay by Garrett Fort, Guy Endore, Erich von Stroheim and Browning himself. Loosely based on the novel *Burn, Witch, Burn!* by Abraham Merritt, it starred Lionel Barrymore as a man wrongly convicted of fraud and sent to Devil's Island. He escapes with an old man who turns out to be a scientist who has discovered a means of shrinking living things – purely for the good of mankind, of course, as he thinks that it will be cheaper to transport livestock from country to country if cows and pigs are reduced to the size of puppies. But Barrymore steals the device and returns to the city where he disguises himself as an old lady toymaker. He then sends his enemies what appear to be dolls but are actually tiny humans in a trance-like state. In the middle of the night they come to life and carry out his murderous instructions which they receive telepathically. The story is absurd, but the special effects are above-average for the time and the illusion of miniaturization is perfectly created by the use of giant sets and skilfully executed travelling mattes, the work of MGM's effects department.

Standing apart from all the science fiction and fantasy films of the 1930s was *Things to Come*. It was unique for many reasons – for its scope, its ambition, its sheer portentousness – but mainly because it was written by H. G. Wells himself. He had become involved in the film industry through the efforts of the Hungarian film-maker Alexander Korda, who was based in England during the 1930s and who in 1934 persuaded the world-

famous author to adapt his own book *The Shape of Things to Come* for the screen. Wells had always been interested in the cinema and was dissatisfied with Hollywood's versions of his work, so the opportunity to adapt his own material must have been especially attractive. But more importantly, it would provide him with yet another medium – and a medium of mass popularity – to spread his message to the world. Unfortunately, by that time, messages were about the only things he *was* producing. Nearing seventy years of age, the writer who had once presented his ideas in stories that were innovatory, exciting, daring and, most of all, entertaining, had been replaced by an elder statesman who had discarded fiction, considering his early output to be nothing but frivolous fantasies, and who was now giving his ideas *direct* to the world. The message, in other words, had overcome the medium. And not only was he engaged in pointing out the many dangers that faced mankind but he was now also supplying the answers – a dangerous course for any artist, since answers have an embarrassing habit of looking silly in a very short time while the original questions retain their relevance. Not surprisingly, it is his earlier work that is still immensely popular while his later polemical output is largely ignored.

Most of Wells's answers to the problems of the world seemed, in the 1930s, to reside in a touching faith in technology – a technology in the hands of the 'right people', of course, a group of enlightened, beneficent technocrats who would enable mankind, through the use of rationality, to overcome the grubby, emotional and aggressive beast that dwells within. This is the message that he promoted in his screenplay for Korda, a screenplay that was to undergo many transformations before it reached the screen.

Korda must have known he was asking for trouble in letting Wells, who had no previous experience in writing for the cinema, write the screenplay, but it was obviously the price he was prepared to pay to induce the famous author to lend the project his valuable name. When Wells finally delivered the first draft Korda found it more or less unusable and asked Wells to try again. It says something for Korda's legendary charm that Wells did. To assist Wells Korda brought in a writer called Lajos Biro, a fellow Hungarian who had worked in Hollywood and on previous Korda productions. In his notes accompanying the published script of *Things to Come* Wells wrote: 'This was my first film treatment written by the Author for actual production and he found much more difficulty in making it than he did any of its successors . . . What is before the reader here is the last of several drafts. An earlier treatment was made, discussed, worked upon for a little and discarded. It was a 'prentice effort and the Author owes much to the friendly generosity of Alexander Korda, Lajos Biro and Cameron Menzies, who put all their experience at his

Part of the vast 'Everytown' of the future in Things to Come *– a plastic Utopia with all the appeal of a modern shopping complex.*

disposal during the revision.

'They were greatly excited by the general conception, but they found the draft quite impracticable for production. A second treatment was then written. This, with various modifications, was made into a scenario of the old type. This scenario again was set aside for a second version, and this again was revised and put back into the form of the present treatment. Korda and the Author had agreed upon an innovation in film technique, to discard the elaborate detailed technical scenario altogether and to produce directly from the descriptive treatment here given. We have found this worked very well in practice – given a competent director. But this time, however, the Author, now almost through the toils of his apprenticeship, was in a state of fatigue towards the altered, revised and reconstructed text, and, though he had done his best to get it into tolerable film prose, he has an uneasy sense that many oddities and awkwardnesses of expression that crept in during the scenario have become now so familiar to him that he has become blind to them and unable to get rid of them.'[12]

The film begins in a city square which looks suspiciously like Oxford Circus but is labelled 'Everytown' (actually it was all a vast studio-contained set complete with cars, buses and other traffic). It is 1940 and war is imminent as we enter the home of the film's central figure John Cabal, played by Raymond Massey, who is warning his unheeding friends that 'If we don't end war, war will end us.' Soon afterwards the threat becomes a reality as enemy bombers are reported to be approaching the city. The crowds flee from the city square as anti-aircraft guns are brought in and aimed at the sky. Then the bombs fall, the buildings explode and by the time the raid is over the centre of Everytown is a ruin. The following scenes consist of a long montage showing the progress of a war that lasts for decades. In the mid-1960s the film slows down again and we are back in Everytown, now little more than a pile of rubble with only a few buildings still standing and ruled over by a feudal warlord called the Chief (Ralph Richardson, giving the liveliest performance in the whole picture), who is Wells's symbol of all that is wrong with mankind. Despite the almost-total destruction around him the Chief is still pursuing a war of his own – with the nearby Hill People – and is oblivious to the suffering around him. Most of Europe is in the grip of a plague called the 'Wandering Sickness' which causes its victims to wander aimlessly around like zombies. Then a strange black aircraft arrives and lands in the town. It is piloted by John Cabal wearing a helmet at least four feet high and two feet wide that might have looked fine on the designer's drawing board but looks somewhat odd on the actor. He tells the Chief that he is a representative of a society of scientists who call themselves the Airmen and who are going to reform the world. The Airmen are really Wells's *deus ex machina* – his cavalry who arrive in the nick of time and save the world.

Raymond Massey, as the leader of the 'Airmen', surveys the fallen 'Boss' (Ralph Richardson) in Things to Come.

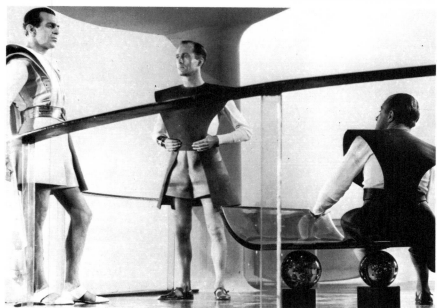

Raymond Massey (left) as Oswald Cabal, scientific supervisor of 'Everytown'.

He doesn't give us any information about them: how they came into being, how they developed into an efficient, stable society in the midst of worldwide chaos, or along what lines their society is run. Cabal merely states that he represents 'Law and sanity', but whose law, and whose sanity?

The Chief is not impressed by Cabal or his message and has him thrown into prison while he prepares his latest attack on the Hill People, but Cabal succeeds in getting a message through to his colleagues and the sky is soon filled with giant, unwieldy-looking aircraft. They spray the area with a knock-out gas and then land without resistance, bringing the rule of the Chief to an end. The Chief, incidentally, has mysteriously died from the effects of the harmless gas, the suggestion being that the whiff of 'sanity' was too much of a shock for his corrupt soul.

The next reel is concerned with the rebuilding of Everytown as the Airmen make good their promise to transform the world. We see vast machines at work cutting deep into the rock and huge buildings being constructed. Then, in the year 2036, we see the completed new version of Everytown – a white and gleaming underground complex that has all the plastic appeal of a modern shopping centre. Apparently in charge of it all is Oswald Cabal (again played by Massey), the grandson of John Cabal, but he is opposed by a sculptor called Theotocopulous (Cedric Hardwicke) who represents the city's artists and maintains that all this scientific progress is getting out of hand and that there should be a return to the time when life was 'short and hot and merry', whenever that was. Theo and his followers are particularly against a planned expedition to the moon which will be achieved by firing a manned projectile from a huge cannon. Despite all the opposition from the artists Cabal goes ahead with the project. The space craft is loaded into the gun and even though a horde of Theo's followers invade the area and begin to clamber up the sides of the vast mechanism, not heeding a warning about the shock wave, Cabal orders the gun to be fired. The film ends with Cabal and his friend Passworthy watching the projectile's journey towards the moon on a large 'space mirror'.

Seen today *Things to Come* has dated badly. Wells's dialogue is both ponderous and pompous and most of the characters are lifeless symbols rather than believable people. But the flaws in the screenplay aside, the film is also disappointing in the technical sense, despite Korda's hiring of a number of Hollywood's top experts. One of the main problems lay in Korda's choice of William Cameron Menzies as director. Menzies was a former production designer, who had designed the sets for Fairbanks's 1923 version of *The Thief of Bagdad*, later worked on two D. W. Griffith films, and in 1928 won the first Academy Award to be given for art direction (or 'interior decoration' as it was then called). He had never directed a whole feature film by himself before, though he had co-directed *Chandu the Magician* with Ray Taylor in 1932. This lack of experience shows up not only in the uninteresting treatment of the actors but also in the lack of continuity between various camera set-ups, thus making an already episodic film seem yet more disjointed. Even the much-lauded special effects in *Things to Come* are disappointing in spite of all the effort and expertise that went into them.

In charge of the effects was Ned Mann, a Hollywood colleague of Menzies who had also worked on *Thief of Bagdad* and who had created impressive effects for such films as DeMille's *Madam Satan* (1930) in a sequence involving a giant airship that breaks loose from its mooring above New York during a storm, and *Deluge* (1934). Mann brought several of the top American effects men with him, including Harry Zech, an expert on rear projection, Jack Thomas, who specialized in optical effects, Ross Jacklin, a model builder, Paul Morell, who was a travelling matte expert, Eddie Cohen, who was an effects cameraman, and Lawrence Butler, who handled full-sized mechanical effects. Yet much of the model work is unconvincing, particularly in the montage sequences involving futuristic tank battles and in the climactic scenes showing the vast crowd which swarms towards the space gun and obviously consists of hundreds of model figures being pulled jerkily along little tracks. Perhaps the budget, which was only £350,000 – not a vast amount for such an ambitious picture, even in those days – placed too many limitations upon the effects men.

When, in *Things to Come*, Cabal asks Passworthy the question : 'All the Universe or nothingness. Which shall it be, Passworthy?' it is clear what Wells thinks the answer should be and it's an answer that a whole generation of sf writers agreed with. The idea that mankind's existence can somehow be fulfilled by spreading out into space and populating the universe is one that is still firmly held by many of the older sf writers. To them it is automatically A Good Thing – a self-evident truth that doesn't even need to be argued about. Yet no one has yet provided a good, rational explanation as to why this should be, though it has been suggested that part of man's primal drive is to spread out, explore and populate new worlds, and this may be so. It is a difficult thing to prove one way or the other. If the human race does indeed now possess such a desire it may not be the result of genetic imprinting but instead something created by science fiction writers themselves.

Things to Come, being both pro-science and pro-space travel, was a rarity among sf films of the 1930s in that it reflected ideas, themes and attitudes being propounded in the sf magazines. People who thought of space travel as a possibility were definitely in a minority then, even in scientific circles, and most of the enthusiasts for the idea were to be found within the sf magazine readership. Those were the days when any attempt to discuss the subject seriously with non-sf readers (or 'mundanes' as they came to be known) could result in ridicule and scorn, thus reinforcing the image sf fans had of themselves as a persecuted but intellectually superior group whose beliefs would one day be vindicated in the eyes of the world. One can perhaps draw amusing parallels between them and the early Christians in Rome who were waiting for the Second Coming to achieve a similar result for *their* religion. Some 1930s sf fans even believed that they would become a powerful force in the world, and there was talk of forming their own Utopia – made up of élite technocrats. But this idea thankfully never caught on with the sf movement as a whole.

However space travel *was* taken for granted in one area of the cinema, in the feature films' poor relations – the serials. While in the full-length films mad scientists were still proving that there were Things Man Shouldn't Fool Around With, the heroes of the serials, such as Flash Gordon and Buck Rogers, were blithely zooming from planet to planet in cardboard rockets supported by almost non-existent budgets. The origins of the serials were different from those of the mainstream sf cinema. *Flash Gordon* and *Buck Rogers* were both based on comic strips which in turn drew their sources of inspiration from the pulp magazines (Buck Rogers was originally a character in a novel by Phillip Nowlan serialized in *Amazing* magazine): thus they reflected a different attitude to science and technology. These weren't regarded as evils in themselves, they were simply tools to be used by the hero or the villain to gain the upper hand. Flash Gordon's loyal helper Dr Zarkov, who could always be depended upon to produce a fantastic invention at the drop of a hat, certainly wasn't evil or mad, though he did look a little bemused at times. The serials were really the nearest thing to space opera – an sf sub-genre that flourished in the 1930s and 1940s and is still immensely popular with sf readers – to reach the screen for many years.

The serials were aimed primarily at children so they were usually of low quality both in script and in production values. *Flash Gordon*, the most famous of the sf serials, was better than most as far as sets and special effects were concerned, but like the others its blatant absurdities provide most of the entertainment when seen today. The first Flash Gordon serial was made in 1936 and starred Buster Crabbe as Flash, Jean Rogers as his girlfriend Dale Arden, Frank Shannon as Dr Zarkov and Charles Middleton as the villain Ming the Merciless. Directed by Frederick Stephani, who also wrote the script along with George Plympton, Basil Dickey and Ella O'Neill, the plot consisted of the usual serial-type collection of almost unrelated incidents, each one ending with a well-contrived cliff-hanger. The framing story involved Flash, Dale and Zarkov making a journey to the planet Mongo in Zarkov's experimental, back-yard spaceship to try

Buster Crabbe (second from right) as the legendary Flash Gordon.

and find the cause of a sudden outbreak of volcanic activity on Earth. They discover that Mongo's ruler, Ming, is behind it all and that he plans to invade the Earth. Flash and friends then spend the next twelve episodes trying to survive all the various hazards that Ming confronts them with, including prehistoric monsters, shark-men, bird-men, clay-men and mind-destroying rays, before they destroy him in the final reel. But Ming returned in the next serial, *Flash Gordon's Trip to Mars*, made in 1938, and also in the third and final one, *Flash Gordon Conquers the Universe*, in 1939. Sf serials continued to be made during the 1940s on ever-decreasing budgets but devotees of the genre usually agree that the period between 1935 and 1940 represents their Golden Age.

H. G. Wells's technology-based utopia in *Things to Come* was apparently not what the audiences of 1936 wanted. Despite attracting many favourable critical responses the film did very badly at the box-office. Yet another picture set in a utopia was a tremendous success that same year. This was *Lost Horizon*, directed by Frank Capra from the novel by James Hilton, and it concerned a group of travellers who, having just escaped from war-torn China, crash-land in the Himalayas and are then taken to the city of Shangri-La, a white, middle-class fantasy land which looks as if its architect had served his apprenticeship designing the foyers of 1930s cinema palaces.

Why audiences should have responded so whole-heartedly to Hilton and Capra's bland utopia while by-passing Wells's and Korda's is an interesting question. Apart from Capra being a more capable film-maker than Menzies *Lost Horizon* probably provided the 1930s cinema-goers with *instant* wish-fulfilment. To reach Hilton's utopia all you had to do was climb a mountain, whereas with Wells you had to endure decades of horrific war before there was a chink of light in the clouds; there was no easy way of reaching *his* utopia. Obviously Wells's grim and prophetic vision of a World War starting in 1940 was the last thing that the audiences of 1936 wanted to contemplate.

Things to Come didn't mark the end of Wells's association with Korda. Shortly afterwards Wells wrote a screenplay based on his story 'The Man Who Could Work Miracles' and the result, directed by Lothar Mendes (another Hungarian colleague of Korda's), was much more satisfying than the former film. Basically a satirical fantasy, it contained all Wells's usual comments on the stupidity of mankind but they were now presented in a very amusing and entertaining way. The story concerned a humble shop assistant in a drapery store (drawing upon Wells's own experiences in just such a job) who is casually granted omnipotent powers by three passing gods. At first he uses his power to perform simple and unimaginative tricks but gradually becomes more ambitious – willing a girl to fall in love with him, making himself ruler of the world, building himself a suitable palace out of thin air, and finally even bringing the Earth itself to a deadstop, with drastic results. Ned Mann's special effects are much more convincing in this film than in *Things to Come*.

But the failure of *Things to Come*, like the failure of *Just Imagine* six years earlier, served to deter other film producers from taking a chance with more ambitious science fiction films. So with very few exceptions it was back to the mad scientists and the laboratory-created monsters. Dr X returned in the guise of Humphrey Bogart in *The Return of Dr X* directed by Vincent Sherman in 1939; Dr Frankenstein returned in *The Son of Frankenstein* directed by Rowland V. Lee the same year; and even Boris Karloff was back in the familiar role of resuscitated corpse in *The Man They Could Not Hang* made the same year.

One of the exceptions was *Non-Stop New York*, an English film made in 1937 and directed by Robert Stevenson (who later went to Hollywood and became one of the regular directors for the Disney studio, making *Mary Poppins* among many others) from a script by Kurt Siodmak, who later changed his name to Curt and also went to Hollywood. Set in the near future it was mainly a thriller and murder mystery that takes place almost entirely on board a large transatlantic airliner.

Elsewhere it was all mad scientists, the trend continuing well into the 1940s – a decade that was to prove the poorest of all in terms of sf cinema.

3   Interval (1940–50)

One of the minor side-effects of the Second World War was to help cause, some years after it ended, a boom in science fiction, but during the actual war years the science fiction cinema reached its lowest ebb and remained there until the end of the decade. While real-life scientists, mad or otherwise, were working in various countries on weapons far beyond the imagination of Hollywood scriptwriters (though not beyond that of sf writers), the cinema's collection of mad scientists were still busy with such innocuous goals as trying to turn men into apes or vice versa, making people invisible or simply shrinking them in size. If only the situation could have been reversed the world might have remained a much less disturbing place.

The evil Doctor Thorkel in *Doctor Cyclops* lures a group of scientists to his remote laboratory in Peru to assist him with his research, and when they prove troublesome reduces them all to an average height of twelve inches. They manage to escape from him (he's very short-sighted) and hide in the surrounding jungle despite threats from various animals, but, knowing that they will soon automatically regain their full size, he tracks them down, shoots one and then attempts to burn the others to death.

The shrunken victims of the evil Dr Thorkel attempt to kill their tormentor in Dr Cyclops.

Believing he has killed them all Thorkel returns to his cabin to sleep, but the three minute survivors creep in, destroy his spectacles and lure him to an open mine shaft where he falls to his death. Though really just a straightforward melodrama the film does contain two significant if unintentional hints of the approaching apocalypse. One is that Thorkel draws the power for his device from a 'radium mine' beside his laboratory; and the other is that, with his shaven head and thick glasses, he resembles what was to become the caricature of the 'beastly Jap' by the end of the war. It was obviously just a strange coincidence since, when the film was made in 1939, there was no real anti-Japanese feeling in the US and therefore no reason for the makers to have their villain appear Japanese.

Directed by one of the makers of *King Kong*, Ernest B. Schoedsack, it's a fast-paced, inventive film, though the dialogue is awful and the acting undistinguished with the exception of Albert Dekker's portrayal of the cold-blooded and ruthless Doctor Thorkel. As with Laughton's version of Dr Moreau his evil isn't a by-product of scientific zeal but a deliberate choice of action. The special effects in *Doctor Cyclops* are ingeniously contrived and very convincing, the illusion of miniaturization being achieved by the combined use of giant props and rear projection, the latter process handled by Farciot Edouart, one of Hollywood's most important innovators in this area of trick photography.

A more benign type of mad scientist was portrayed by Boris Karloff in *The Ape*, directed in 1940 by William Nigh and written by Curt Siodmak and Richard Carroll and based on a play by Adam Hull Shirk. It concerns a Dr Adrian who, after the death of his wife and daughter from polio, decides that paralysis may be cured by means of a serum containing fluid extracted from spines of human beings. After killing an ape which has escaped from a circus, Adrian dons its skin and starts killing off the town's most objectionable citizens in order to obtain the necessary fluid to experiment upon Frances, a young female victim of polio whom he has befriended. While wearing his gorilla suit he is mistaken for the escaped ape and shot by the sheriff's men, but as he lies dying Frances arrives, cured of her paralysis, and he realizes that he has succeeded in his work.

In 1943 Karloff's rival Bela Lugosi also went on the rampage after spinal fluid, in a film called *The Ape Man* (also known as *Lock Your Doors*) directed by William Beaudine and based on a story called 'They Creep in the Dark' by Karl Brown. Having injected himself with the spinal fluid of a gorilla, Lugosi is obliged to hide himself away in a cellar after an excessive growth of body-hair and other ape-like characteristics have manifested themselves. He spends the rest of the film trying to obtain human bodies from which he can extract enough spinal fluid to reverse the process. He doesn't succeed, of course, and meets his inevitable fate. But Lugosi

Two mad scientists from the 1940s: (right) *Boris Karloff as Dr Adrian in* The Ape; (below) *Erich von Stroheim as Professor Mueller in* The Lady and the Monster (*first film version of* Donovan's Brain).

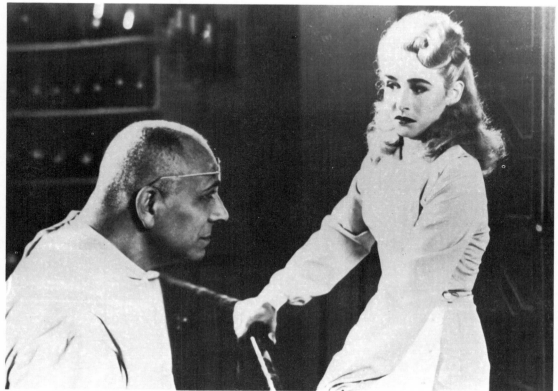

returns, clean-shaven and alive, in *Return of the Ape Man* (1944, directed by Philip Rosen from a script by Robert Charles), as Professor Dexter who, along with John Carradine's Professor Gilmore, discovers a method of reviving the dead. Naturally they first test out their discovery on a prehistoric ape found preserved in ice. When complications arise Dexter murders Gilmore and transfers his brain to the ape's body. Understandably annoyed, the ape-thing then becomes violent, escapes, and murders a few people before finally turning on Dexter and killing him too. Then, like most laboratory-produced monsters in these films, it is destroyed in a fiery holocaust. *Return of the Ape Man*, like the previous two ape films, was produced by Monogram Studios, a company famous for the cheap quality of its films (it was the subsidiary of the Allied Artists Corporation).

Little better were the horror films made at Columbia during the early 1940s, most of which featured Boris Karloff as resident mad scientist. Even Lon Chaney had a chance of playing a mad scientist in 1945 – in a film called *Strange Confession* directed by John Hoffman.

Curt Siodmak was at his busiest in Hollywood during the 1940s but his screenplays tended to have a foot in both the pseudo-science and the horror camps. Strangely enough he had nothing to do with the screenplay of the first film adaptation of his most famous novel, *Donovan's Brain*. Under the title of *The Lady and the Monster* it was directed by George Sherman and scripted by Dane Lussier and Frederick Kohner. Incredibly neither Boris Karloff nor Bela Lugosi appears in it; instead the cast includes Vera Ralston, Richard Arlen and Erich von Stroheim. The first of three film versions of the novel, the story is basically the same in all of them: financial wizard W. H. Donovan is killed when his plane crashes in the desert but a scientist, whose laboratory is near the scene of the crash, removes Donovan's undamaged brain from his body and keeps it alive in a glass tank. Donovan's personality, however, is so dominant that the brain gradually takes over the minds of those people around it, forcing them to carry out Donovan's evil plans, and all, of course, ends in disaster. However, instead of investigating the reactions of the disassociated brain to its total sensory deprivation, Siodmak turns his story into yet another description of innocence being overcome by an evil supernatural force. What the original idea called for was a *science fiction* writer rather than one who was really, despite his customary trappings of pseudo-science, an exponent of Gothic horror, or rather Gothic soap opera.

Siodmak was on safer ground with his story for *The Invisible Woman* which he wrote in collaboration with Joe May. It was his second excursion into invisibility – he and May had written the story for *The Invisible Man Returns*, starring Vincent Price, in 1939 which May had directed. (May, like Siodmak, was a self-exiled German and had been prominent in the German film industry from its earliest days directing serials and thrillers; his real name was Joseph Mandel.) *The Invisible Woman*, directed by A. Edward Sutherland, is a light and moderately amusing film whose only real claim to fame was that it featured one of the first full-frontal female nudes in the commercial cinema. True, it was an invisible nude, but in 1940 it was the thought that counted to the adolescent males in the audience.

In 1942 it was the turn of female audiences to be titillated by the sight of the invisible Jon Hall who appeared, as it were, in *The Invisible Agent*. Curt Siodmak's screenplay had the son of the original invisible man, now calling himself Frank Raymond, volunteering to the US authorities, shortly after Pearl Harbor, to use what little remained of the invisibility serum on a secret mission in Germany. He is then parachuted, invisible, from a plane over Berlin and once on the ground he makes successful contact with a female agent (Ilona Massey) who, understandably, takes a little time to adjust to his unique 'appearance'. Soon afterwards she receives a visit from the head of the 'Secret Nazi Police' who discloses that Hitler plans an immediate attack on the USA. With the girl's help the invisible man secures a list belonging to a Japanese spy called Ikito (Peter Lorre doing a sort of villainous Mr Moto routine) which contains the names of all the Nazi and Japanese spies in America. Ikito almost succeeds in trapping him with a silk net lined with sharp hooks, but, though injured, he escapes. Then he and the girl commandeer a German bomber and fly back to England, a stunt performed with casual regularity in Hollywood films during the war. Though pure escapism, *The Invisible Agent* is completely different in tone from the frivolous *The Invisible Woman*, a sign of how quickly even comic book characters were harnessed to the propaganda machine. It's a typical Hollywood irony that in this case it should have been a German writer providing the propaganda.

The war was ignored in the next instalment of the Invisible Man saga, but the downbeat mood was continued in *The Invisible Man's Revenge*, a 1944 production directed by Ford Beebe and written by Bertram Millhauser. Jon Hall once again played the lead character but for the first time since the 1933 version he was an unsympathetic one, and his end was suitably macabre – killed by an invisible Great Dane. And with that the invisible man saga came to an end on the cinema screen, though the character did re-emerge on TV, first in a British-made series in 1957 and then in an American one in 1975.

From 1945 to 1950 there seems to have been a total absence of Hollywood-made sf films, even of the mad scientist variety. In Britain it was much the same, with one or two minor exceptions. One of these was *Counterblast*, made in 1948 and directed by the Austrian film-maker Paul

L. Stein. It was written by Jack Whittingham, a veteran British screenwriter who later co-wrote *Thunderball*, and based on a story by Guy Morgan. In it Mervyn Johns plays Dr Karl Bruckner, a fanatical Nazi scientist who escapes from a POW camp and travels to London where he assumes the identity of an Australian scientist due to take up a post as a bacteriologist at a medical research centre near Oxford. His mission is to continue to try and devise a means of inoculating the German people against a virulent plague germ that a group of surviving Nazis have created and are planning to unleash upon the world. Bruckner murders the real Australian scientist and all goes well for him at first, but then various people become suspicious and he is ordered by his Nazi superiors to kill his female assistant (Nova Pilbeam). He refuses and kills one of his Nazi colleagues instead, which leads to his real identity being discovered. Forced to flee the country, he attempts to escape by hiding in a ship on its way to Rotterdam but is killed when a deadly gas is pumped into the ship's hold to fumigate it. The symbolism of his death is obvious. The film is an oddity not only because it deals somewhat ahead of its time with the terrible prospect of germ warfare but also because, among the mad scientist films of the 1940s, its villain, though he becomes an almost sympathetic character by the end, is a *real* monster – a genuine reflection of the Nazi-induced catastrophe that had so recently traumatized the whole world.

Totally unconnected with reality was the mad scientist in the 1949 British film *The Perfect Woman*, directed by Bernard Knowles from a script by George Black and Knowles himself, and based on a play by Wallace Geoffrey and Basil Mitchell. Played by Stanley Holloway the scientist in this sf comedy builds a robot (played by Pamela Devis) in the image of his niece (Patricia Roc) and then hires a young playboy (Nigel Patrick) and his valet (Miles Malleson) to test it out by taking it to a luxury hotel for the night. The playboy is simply to pretend that 'it' is his wife and to see whether the staff at the hotel accept it as real. But the real niece, who is intrigued by the playboy, takes the robot's place and has a good deal of fun pretending to be a robot while the two men are busy pretending that she's anything but. Her fun ends, however, when she is undressed by them (or rather, *partly* undressed – this *is* 1949) and put to bed, so she puts through an urgent call to her housekeeper (Irene Handl) and asks her to bring the real robot to the hotel. In the meantime the playboy's rich aunt arrives and when he attempts to prove his innocence by sticking a pin in the 'robot' he is rewarded by a very feminine shriek. His aunt is not amused but later the robot is produced and she is persuaded to see the pin test again. This time she is convinced that the robot exists, particularly as the pin short-circuits its controls, send-ing it marching through the hotel spewing smoke and sparks. Finally it explodes into small pieces, much to the horror of the scientist who has arrived at the hotel just in time to see the demise of his invention.

The Perfect Woman was a moderate success in Britain but flopped in America despite an extensive publicity build-up. Critics thought it rather crude compared to other British comedy imports like the Ealing series, and the public stayed away for reasons of their own, ignoring even the giant cut-out of the scantily-clad Ms Roc that was erected on Broadway at the time.

Nigel Patrick and Stanley Holloway struggle with what they presume is a robot (Patricia Roc) in The Perfect Woman.

4 Boom! (1950–55)

The Second World War was one of the main causes of the boom in science fiction that took place at the start of the 1950s. Not only did the war induce a great technological leap forward, particularly in the field of weaponry and rockets, but more significantly it gave birth to the atomic bomb. Prior to Hiroshima and Nagasaki talk of splitting the atom was, to the man in the street, just another esoteric subject for egghead scientists to indulge in, but after the war the general public quickly realized that atomic power could destroy not only cities but the whole world. Almost overnight the assumed permanency of life on earth had vanished, and people were forced to live with the traumatic awareness that total, worldwide obliteration was a strong possibility in the near future. This came as a shock to most people, but science fiction readers had been entertaining such concepts for years. H. G. Wells, for instance, had described atomic warfare as far back as 1914 in his novel *The World Set Free*; his pilots, though, dropped atomic bombs over the sides of their bi-planes by hand after activating the fuses with their teeth, but he was still relatively accurate about the destructive power of such weapons, and he even included a mention of poisonous radiation created by the bombs. In 1944 the editor of *Astounding* magazine, John W. Campbell Jr, was questioned by the FBI after publishing a story by Cleve Cartmill called *Deadline*, which dealt with the development of the atomic bomb, a description that came a little too close to reality. Suddenly all that 'crazy Buck Rogers stuff', as science fiction was popularly referred to in the 1930s, didn't look quite so crazy anymore.

The public's attitude towards scientists also changed swiftly after the war. In the 1930s men who experimented with rockets and talked of one day firing them at the moon were regarded as harmless cranks but, with the arrival of the V2, these men became dangerous cranks and therefore important. Most important of all was Wernher von Braun, who had been instrumental in the development of the V2 and who had, at the end of the war – in a fast-thinking action Fu Manchu or Dr No would have been proud of – quickly offered his services to the American army, arriving at their lines a step ahead of the Russians with a team of his own technicians and a tanker-load of rocket fuel. His services were, of course, gratefully accepted. And Albert Einstein's cuddly public image of being the harmless absent-minded professor had been shattered by the realization that his quaint theories had led to the atomic bomb. Thus the 'mad' scientist was no longer restricted to the cinema screen, where he spent his time collecting spinal fluid or shrinking people, but had become a living entity at large in the real world.

The Cold War, basically an extension of the Second World War, also helped to creat a climate that generated interest in science fiction. The rivalry between the USA and Russia in rocket development brought home to the public the reality of space-age technology, particularly when newsreel shots showed a fast-receding earth photographed by automatic cameras from missiles fired from the White Sands testing site, and, later, white rats and monkeys floating in space. The Cold War also produced an atmosphere of anxiety and paranoia: anxiety mainly caused by the ever-present possibility of atomic war between the two super-powers and the resulting global destruction; paranoia caused by the fear of communist subversion, an invasion from within by people who looked like ordinary Americans but who were actually the pawns of an alien power.

Another factor in the climate of paranoia that existed in America during the late 1940s and the 1950s was the 'flying saucer' scare that began in 1947 and continued for well over a decade. Whether this was a genuine cause of the paranoia or merely a psychological side-effect of the Cold War is still a matter for debate. 'Flying saucers' are still being seen by people today, and the whole subject is going through one of its periodic flare-ups, especially since the release of Spielberg's *Close Encounters of the Third Kind*.

As a result of these fears most of ths sf films of the 1950s reflect a number of basic themes: the atomic bomb and its after-effects; the effects of atomic radiation; alien invasion and possession by aliens; and world destruction. Yet though the boom in sf magazines and sf cinema coincided in 1950, the two media rapidly diverged thereafter. Written sf moved on to new themes, new styles and new approaches, while the sf cinema more or less stayed stuck in the same rut for the remainder of the decade and beyond. After the first few years, during which all the major sf cinema themes were established – alien invasion in *The Thing, War of the Worlds, It Came from Outer Space*; alien possession in *Invaders from Mars, Invasion of the Body Snatchers*, and *I Married a Monster from Outer Space*; the effects of atomic radiation in *The Beast from 20,000 Fathoms, Them!*; world destruction in *When Worlds Collide*; and a bit of everything in *The Day the Earth Stood Still* – the film genre endlessly repeated itself with cheaper and less impressive variations on the same themes. By the mid-1950s Hollywood had completely lost touch with written sf, one of the few exceptions being *Forbidden Planet*, which could have been written by A.

E. Van Vogt for *Astounding* in the 1940s and was one of the few examples
of real space opera produced during the 1950s (the inferior *This Island
Earth* being another one).

Movies concerned with space travel weren't very successful, despite
the fact that the sf movie trend was sparked off by two such productions:
Destination Moon and *Rocketship XM*, both made in 1950 (*Destination
Moon* was the first to go into production but *XM*, cheaper and more
quickly made, reached the cinemas first). *Destination Moon* didn't reflect
many of the darker fears given form in subsequent sf films; it was
basically a pseudo-documentary about a journey to the moon, though the
reason for the trip is to prevent an 'unfriendly foreign power' from getting
there first and turning the moon into a military base. Although it was
based on a juvenile novel by Robert Heinlein called *Rocketship Galileo*,
written in 1947, it had little to do with the original story, which concerned
three boys and their scientist uncle building a spaceship virtually in their
backyard and travelling to the moon where they discover a Nazi
establishment. The film begins with inventor Dr Cargraves (Warner
Anderson) and General Thayer (Tom Powers) watching as their
experimental rocket crashes after take-off. The Army orders a stop to the
work but they then discover that enemy saboteurs were responsible for
the crash and they decide to continue. As the government won't supply

*A successful
touch-down on
the moon in the
1950* Destination
Moon.

them with further funds they approach a rich industrialist, Jim Barnes (John Archer), and ask for his help. He agrees, saying: 'The government always turns to private enterprise when they're in a jam.' The huge spaceship is built in the Mojave desert but, as the 'unfriendly foreign power' has succeeded in manipulating public opinion against the project, the government bans the take-off. However, despite the protests of the local sheriff, the pioneers do take off and are accompanied by radio technician Joe Sweeney (Dick Wesson), whose prime function is to provide comic relief, an assignment in which he fails miserably. The most dramatic moment on the trip to the moon occurs when Cargraves, who goes outside to repair a damaged radar antenna, loses his magnetized footing and drifts off into space. He is rescued by General Thayer, who uses a spare air tank as a miniature rocket. They land safely on the moon, at which point Cargraves announces: 'By the grace of God and in the name of the USA I take possession of this planet for the benefit of mankind.' Fortunately Neil Armstrong, nineteen years later, had a better script-writer.

When the time comes to take off the group discover that they have only enough fuel to bring three people back to Earth and for a while it looks as if one of them must remain behind, but by stripping everything except the bare essentials from the rocket they all return safely.

Unlike later sf movies of the 1950s, *Destination Moon* is scientifically accurate given the date it was made. Not only did Heinlein himself act as technical adviser on the film, but so also did German rocket expert Hermann Oberth (who had also worked on *Woman in the Moon*), and great care was taken with all the scientific details, including the recreation of the lunar landscape (astronomical artist Chesley Bonestell providing the backgrounds). But Hollywood producers quickly realized that it didn't matter whether their sf movies were scientifically accurate or not, since the number of people who knew or cared was relatively small. Film critics were among those who didn't consider such things very important. The London *Daily Mail* critic wrote in his review of the film: 'The temptation to populate the moon with pretty girls has been resisted. As a boy's magazine thriller it is fine. And a scientific man assured me that the scientific chatter is not too foolish – if you're interested.' In an article on the film published in the *Spectator*, Peter King wrote: 'It is said that a rocketship to the moon would be similar to the V2 rocket but the fuel in these allows only a slow escape of exhaust gases and, consequently, a slow forward speed. The German V2 had nearly 60,000 pounds of thrust or about 10 times the power of a jet engine. It reached a height of 60 miles at a top speed of something like 3,600 miles per hour. But a rocket to make some impression on stellar distances would need to travel about ten times as fast or somewhere near the velocity of light [*sic*]. No known fuel is capable of firing off a rocket at these speeds. Work is being done on chemical, chiefly liquid, propellants, and, less hopefully, on atom power. But "science fiction", which is the pretentious successor to the imaginative stories of Wells and Verne, has its own solutions. One of the most attractive is the "hyper drive" which cuts swiftly through the 4th dimension of "hyper space" and makes the comic strips fascinating reading.' But not as fascinating as Mr King's own writing, which is a perfect example of 'hyper journalism' that cuts swiftly through the logic barrier and goes where no man has gone before. For years now 'sophisticated' journalists writing for prestigious publications have picked on science fiction from time to time as a means of getting easy laughs; but invariably they end up making fools of themselves. Even the lowliest sf hack should have known that 10 times 3,600 mph is somewhat less than the speed of light, and he would not have confused interplanetary distances with interstellar ones. He might even have included a mention of something called 'escape velocity'.

No wonder, then, that producers quickly decided to banish science from their films, and along with the science went the authentic science fiction stories that provided the basis for several early 1950s movies such as *The Thing*, based on a story by John W. Campbell Jr; *The Day the Earth Stood Still*, based on a story by Harry Bates; *When Worlds Collide*, on a novel by Edwin Balmer and Philip Wylie; *The Beast from 20,000 Fathoms*, on a story by Ray Bradbury, and so on. In the years that followed, however, Hollywood ignored science and turned out its own brand of hokum.

Destination Moon, produced by George Pal (a former special effects expert from Hungary) and directed by Irving Pichel (an ex-actor), was rather unique among 1950s sf films in having an actual sf writer work on the screenplay. Together with writers Rip Van Ronkel and James O'Hanlon, Robert Heinlein himself was employed to work on the script, and it was thanks to him that the more sensational elements were kept out of the proceedings. 'For a time,' he wrote later, 'we had a version of the script which included dude ranches, cowboys, guitars and hillbilly songs on the moon . . . combined with pseudo-scientific gimmicks that would have puzzled even Flash Gordon.'[13] Perhaps, though, this version might have been a little more entertaining than the film that actually reached the screen because, unfortunately, *Destination Moon* turned out to be incredibly dull despite its scientific authenticity.

Heinlein worked on another space film in 1953, a cheap little production called *Project Moonbase* which was originally supposed to be the pilot for a television series until the producer, Jack Seaman, decided to expand it to feature film length. Richard Talmadge, the former stuntman who became one of Hollywood's top second unit/action directors, directed and the screenplay was written by both Heinlein and Seaman

(Heinlein wrote the first version which was then 'embellished' by Seaman). Set in 1970 it starts with the first orbital flight around the moon being organized from a United States space station in orbit around the Earth. The pilot of the spaceship is to be a female officer called Colonel Briteis (a typical Heinlein touch) and she is to be accompanied by two males – Major Moore and Dr Wernher. Little does anyone realize. however, that the Dr Wernher who arrives at the space station is not the real one but an enemy imposter. The ship leaves its base on schedule but during its trip to the moon Moore discovers the truth about Wernher; they fight and in doing so activate the wrong set of controls which sends the ship hurtling out of its orbit. With their fuel almost gone they are obliged to crash-land the rocket on the moon's surface. They survive the landing but are stranded on the moon. Relations between Moore and the false Wernher do not improve and, during the erection of a television aerial on the summit of a moon mountain, Wernher falls to his death. This leaves Briteis and Moore alone on the moon, something that the American public finds very disturbing, and when communication with the space station is established again one of the first things their commanding officer does is to order them to marry – to appease public opinion. Their marriage is subsequently performed – via television – by Madame President of the USA and the American public is able to breathe more easily.

Unsurprisingly, it's not a very good film. The cast deliver their lines with all the conviction of a jury giving their verdict on an open-and-shut case, and the script itself is incredibly trite, leading one to believe that not much remained of Heinlein's original. (But despite the cheap budget the special effects involving the models, created by Jaques Fresco, are impressive.) One of Heinlein's abilities as an sf writer was to make space travel grittily real – he could make his readers feel what it might be like to live and work in a spaceship. He was able to achieve this on the printed page, but to recreate it on the screen demanded resources far beyond those available to sf film-makers in the 1950s. It wasn't until many years later that Arthur C. Clarke, who concentrated on themes similar to Heinlein's, was to see his work given cinematic flesh by the genius of Stanley Kubrick (plus MGM's money), but Kubrick's equivalent didn't exist in the early 1950s.

George Pal is the film maker most associated with sf films during the 1950s, but he never really grasped what science fiction was all about. His main interest was in pure fantasy. Prior to his first feature film, *The Great Rupert* (1949), which concerned a unique squirrel, he had made his name with a series of short films called 'Puppetoons' featuring puppets animated by stop-motion photography. He shrewdly jumped onto the science fiction bandwagon before most other Hollywood producers even knew there was one, and his background in special effects ensured that his films were at least spectacular in that area, but his inability to choose good scripts was a serious handicap which persisted right through to the 1970s (as the abominable *Doc Savage* demonstrates).

Pal's early films, such as *When Worlds Collide* and *War of the Worlds*, though considered lavish epics at the time, were actually made on fairly small budgets, even for those days. Skilled use of special effects and various economic short-cuts allowed them to appear spectacular. *Destination Moon* cost just over $600,000 to make; but even more remarkable was the cost of its rival, *Rocketship XM* – a mere $94,000. According to Jack Rabin, the special effects man who conceived the idea, he had planned to make *Destination Moon* two years before Pal started his version, but the deal fell through. When he heard of Pal's version he went to Robert Lippert, who specialized in financing and distributing cheap exploitation films, and suggested they make a quick rocket-to-the-moon movie and beat Pal to the cinemas. Lippert agreed and *Rocketship XM* was shot in three weeks, reaching the cinemas a few months ahead of the Pal production. To save money their rocket-ship never reached the moon but ended up on Mars instead. This way they didn't have to build expensive moon sets within a sound-stage but could make use of real desert scenery in the Mojave Desert and around Palm Springs. Written and directed by Murray Lerner, *Rocketship XM* concerned a group of astronauts (led by Lloyd Bridges) who blast off from a secret base with the object of landing on the moon. Their ship goes a little off-course en route and they find themselves on Mars – the sort of mistake anyone can make. On the red planet they discover the remains of a human civilization that had destroyed itself with atomic warfare. The few remaining humans have reverted to primitive savagery and the earth explorers are attacked. Only three of them manage to escape back towards earth in the spaceship but due to the inevitable fuel shortage they crash and all are killed: a surprisingly downbeat ending, but presumably a crash was cheaper to film than a successful landing. Despite its cheapness it is more entertaining than the ponderous Pal movie and also a little closer to the magazine science fiction of the time. The special effects, created by Jack Rabin and Irvin Block, are of a high standard considering the circumstances. The film made money and even attracted some good reviews, prompting Rabin and Block to make a whole series of cheap sf films. First was *Unknown World* (1950) which they produced as well as providing the special effects. Directed by Terrell O. Morse, it features a giant mechanical mole used by scientists to investigate beneath the Earth's crust, with the object of seeing if there are any caverns suitable for a large portion of the American population in the event of nuclear war. They locate a huge cavern complete with oceans and deserts but discover that its atmosphere renders animal life sterile. Less downbeat, and even cheaper, was Rabin's 1954 production *Cat-Women of the Moon*, now considered a classic by connoisseurs of bad movies. Directed by Arthur Hilton it was shot in five days on sets left over from MGM's *Marco Polo*. Rabin and Block, along with fellow effects expert Gene Warren, worked on many other sf movies during the 1950s, mostly of the incredibly cheap variety though some, like *Kronos* (1957), were more impressive than others. Irving Block will always be remembered for writing the original story of *Forbidden Planet*.

Movies like *Destination Moon* that dealt realistically with the possibilities of space travel were rare. One such, made in 1954, was *Riders to the Stars*. It was produced by Ivan Tors whose various sf movies and subsequent TV series, such as *Man and the Challenge* and *Sea Hunt*, usually demonstrate an interest in actual working technology and avoid the more sensational elements endemic to the medium. However on this particular film he had as his writer Curt Siodmak – someone who has never shown any empathy for science – with the result that the basic idea of the film is completely illogical. The assumption is that meteors don't burn up in the Earth's atmosphere while steel objects, like rocketships, do. The idea is to try and capture a meteor before it enters the Earth's atmosphere to discover just what this mysterious protective quality consists of, and then to try and duplicate it on the hulls of spaceships (meteors, of course, *do* disintegrate when they hit the air, and it's only the remains of the very large ones that reach the ground). The film carefully and soberly documents the various attempts by a team of astronauts (played by William Lundigan, Richard Carlson, Robert Karnes and King Donovan) to capture a meteor by means of special scoops attached to their spaceships. After various mishaps and one or two fatalities they finally succeed and discover that meteors are protected by a layer of carbon and diamond dust which burns away as the meteor hurtles through the atmosphere, leaving the inner core untouched. Another breakthrough for pseudo-science! Directed by Richard Carlson, an actor who appeared in many sf movies during the 1950s, *Riders to the Stars* is, like *Destination Moon*, very dull when seen today, the only interest being provided, as usual, by the special effects.

George Pal returned to the subject of 'serious' space travel in 1955 with *Conquest of Space*, a film so bad it effectively killed off the genre until Kubrick's *2001*. Not as dull as *Destination Moon*, it is certainly one of the most embarrassing sf films ever made, for which James O'Hanlon's script must take a major share of the blame. Set in the 1980s, the story begins in a space station in orbit around the Earth. The commander of the station, Samuel Merritt (Walter Brooke), has been supervising the construction of a huge spaceship which is now complete and moored nearby. Officially the ship's destination is the moon, but it's been built with a large pair of wings attached to it – obviously a useless modification in a vacuum. Yet,

An unfortunate encounter with the surface of Mars in the 1955 Conquest of Space.

amazingly, the commander has refrained from asking his superiors on Earth *why* he has been asked to build the wings. No wonder he doesn't register much surprise when he receives the following curt message just before the mission is due to start: 'Moon trip cancelled. Your destination is now Mars.' As simple as that. Also on board the station is Merritt's son Barney and a team of highly-trained astronauts destined for the moon. They're a pretty hilarious bunch of characters and act like a group of lustful sailors from a mediocre Second World War navy movie. This is apparently the scriptwriter's method of establishing that, despite being highly-trained spacemen, they're not stuck-up but simple down-to-earth people just like the members of the audience. However this doesn't quite work and we're left with the impression that they wouldn't even be safe in control of a rowing boat, much less capable of handling a spaceship.

The reason for going to Mars is to see if it contains valuable raw materials; this explanation is put forward by a Japanese astronaut called Imoto (Bensong Fong) who, in a bizarre speech, suggests that the Japanese attack on Pearl Harbor and the war in the Pacific were caused by Japan's lack of steel and good food. The shortage of steel forced people to live in paper houses and eat with chopsticks, while poor nutrition made them stunted, unhealthy, and consequently very envious of the rich, healthy and handsome Americans. But, says Imoto, if Japan can obtain all its necessary raw materials from Mars it's unlikely that war between America and Japan will ever occur again.

The director, Byron Haskin, was well aware at the time that he had a dud on his hands. 'The picture was a flop,' he said years later, 'because the personal story was too intrusive. Our co-producer, Macrea Freeman Junior, insisted that we have this incredible father and son neurosis – the father [who commands a space station] loses his cool and his son has to kill him. Now a person chosen to be an astronaut is not going to blow his stack. He's long since been tested to prove that he's not the kind of guy that would succumb to that kind of pressure. Also we had another crewman killed earlier on and his body is sent off towards the sun . . . if anything the whole film was a series of impressive funerals.'[14]

Unlike most of Pal's other sf films, the special effects in this one were often ambitious but, on the whole, badly executed. Early in the film, for instance, there is an elaborate effects set-up showing a space shuttle arriving next to the space station and then a number of space-suited figures 'swimming' from the ship to the station while the Earth revolves below them. Thick matte lines around the various images – spacemen, ship and so on – completely destroy the illusion. The other major flaw is the model work. The models themselves are very unrealistic, with no surface detail, and so badly lit they look no bigger than their actual size; nor are they well animated, sometimes resembling spacecraft from a Flash Gordon serial. There were high spots in the effects though, such as the sequence mentioned above in which Ross Martin's space-suited corpse is pushed off towards the sun, and also the actual landing on Mars. For its day, though, the film was technically accurate in its description of how a trip to Mars might be carried out, which was to be expected considering that the technical adviser was Wernher von Braun, whose book *The Mars Project* provided the inspiration for the film.

That film-makers suddenly became interested in ways of leaving Earth is not surprising since, at the time, it didn't seem likely that the Earth would be around for much longer. But in true Hollywood fashion film-makers preferred not to face the threat of atomic war head on but to reflect it indirectly. Thus no film showing what actually might happen *during* an atomic war was ever made in the 1950s; instead the Bomb was represented by various euphemisms such as giant beasts, activated by atomic radiation, that rise out of the sea and trample down cities. Films like *When Worlds Collide* and *War of the Worlds* are also indirect reflections of a reality too awful to contemplate. In the former the world is destroyed not by atomic warfare but by collision with another planet, and in the latter the world is almost destroyed by an omnipotent force from Mars (both these properties had been bought by Hollywood in the 1930s but it wasn't until the ultra-paranoid 1950s that they were filmed).

Several films made during the 1950s did show the aftermath of atomic war, the most famous being *On the Beach* (1959) from the novel by Nevil Shute, but with this single exception they tended to be either safe warnings that showed none of the true horror or cheap exploitation productions like Roger Corman's *The Day the World Ended*. One of the first in this genre falls into the former category. Called *Five* it was written and directed in 1951 by Arch Oboler, who was famous for his radio plays. Five survivors of an atomic war, each one a living symbol, gather together in a cliff-top mansion and wonder 'where it all went wrong'. The five include an attractive pregnant woman (Susan Douglas), a murderer (James Anderson), an embittered idealist (William Phipps) a dying man (Earl Lee) and a token black (Charles Lampkin). For a time the five live together peacefully but conflicts predictably arise between them, and soon 'World War Four' breaks out, leaving only two survivors in its wake – the girl and the idealist. The 'profound' message of this pretentious little film is that people should learn to live in peace together if unpleasant happenings are to be avoided. It's a message oft repeated down the ages but the vital information on how this is to be achieved is always missing.

There was no attempt to answer such a profound question in *World Without End*, a 1955 Allied Artists production in which four astronauts, after orbiting Mars, return to Earth via a time warp and find themselves in the year 2508. Earth has been devastated by an atomic war and its surface is now inhabited by grotesque mutants and giant spiders, while below ground live the few remaining human survivors. The astronauts (played by Hugh Marlowe, Rod Taylor, Nelson Leigh, and Shawn Smith) join forces with the latter and assist them in the overthrow of both mutants and spiders. This old and familiar plot still recurs on TV today, Roddenberry's *Genesis II* and *Planet Earth* being recent examples. But the script, by Edward Bernds, who also directed, is not as bad as might be expected, and special effects man Milton Rice achieves some interesting visuals despite the cheap budget.

Even more cheaply made was *The Day the World Ended* (1955), the first of many sf/horror films to be directed by the now legendary Roger Corman. Written by Lou Rusoff it was really no more than a down-market variation on *Five*. Once again only five people have survived an atomic war, and they gather in a mountain sanctuary designed by a scientist (Paul Birch) to withstand atomic radiation. An argumentative lot, they include such disparate types as a gangster and a stripper (Mike Connors and Adele Jergens). A giant, three-eyed mutant has designs on the scientist's daughter (Lori Nelson) and eventually succeeds in kidnapping her. But before he, or 'it', can have his evil way with her body he is destroyed by a cleansing rain that washes away all trace of radioactivity. The hero (Richard Denning) and heroine are then able to leave the sanctuary and go forth into the world.

With few exceptions, humans are presented very badly in these films. No sooner is there a whiff of impending doom than the average citizen reverts to a cowardly, greedy, selfish and lustful animal. This was particularly so in George Pal's *When Worlds Collide* (1951) which, though it ends on an optimistic note, suggests that whatever catastrophe may befall mankind will be well and truly deserved. The atomic bomb symbolized for many people a vengeful God of the Old Testament, the idea being that if there was to be an atomic war it would be God's punishment on his wayward children. This trend reached its cinematic peak with *Red Planet Mars* in 1952, which was based on a play by John L. Balderston and John Hoare. Directed by Harry Horner it concerns a young American scientist (Peter Graves) who picks up TV transmissions from Mars and learns that utopia exists on the red planet, ruled over by a Supreme Authority who turns out to be God Himself. The world is thrown into confusion by this revelation, which enables the forces of righteousness to overthrow the godless communists in the various Iron Curtain countries. In Russia the Soviet government is defeated by a group of aged revolutionaries who restore the monarchy, making a priest the new Tsar.

In *The Day the Earth Stood Still* (1951) the world was warned by a superior force to mend its evil ways or face total destruction. This time the warning came from a community of interplanetary busybodies. The film is regarded by many as one of the few real sf film classics. Admittedly it is more sophisticated in style than most 1950s sf movies – with slick direction by Robert Wise, polished screenplay by Edmund North, an above-average cast of Michael Rennie, Patricia Neal, Hugh Marlowe and Sam Jaffe – but the basic story and theme are badly flawed. The film begins with a flying saucer landing in Washington DC. From it emerges a humanoid alien, promptly shot by one of the nervous troops who have swiftly surrounded the craft. At this a ten-foot tall robot appears, which disintegrates a number of guns and a tank before being verbally deactivated by the wounded alien (Michael Rennie). The alien is then taken to a military hospital but escapes and, in disguise, hides out in a boarding house where he develops a friendship with a young widow (Patricia Neal) and her son (Bobby Benson). We learn that his mission on Earth is to deliver a warning to all the world leaders, but first he has to arrange a demonstration of the power at his command. He does this by shutting down all electrically powered machinery across the world for one hour (the sequence that provides the film's title).

When the soldiers and scientists arrive on the scene the alien delivers his message which concludes with the words: 'Soon one of your nations will apply atomic power to rockets. Up to now we have not cared how you solved your petty squabbles. But if you threaten to extend your violence this Earth of yours will be reduced to a burnt out cinder. Your choice is simple. Join us and live in peace. Or pursue your present course and face obliteration.' In his book *A Pictorial History of Science Fiction Films* Jeff Rovin describes this speech as 'the finest soliloquy [sic] in sf film history'. But as the alien's civilization is supposed to be peace-loving it hardly seems logical or morally acceptable that it should threaten the natives on Earth with an even greater act of violence. Nor is their solution to our problems very attractive – namely that we should submit ourselves to the rule of a group of implacable, authoritarian robots like the one which has accompanied the alien to Earth. For the robot, we discover, is not the alien's servant but his supervisor – one of many built to keep law and order in the universe. The idea of placing our basic human rights in the custody of a machine, or any 'superior force', is not only an admission of defeat but also one which smacks of totalitarianism. Besides, in an sf film made eighteen years later, we see what happens when a machine is allowed to take over (see *The Forbin Project* in Chapter 8).

The gimmick of the robot turning out to be in charge was the *raison d'être* of the original story *Farewell to the Master* by Harry Bates, published in *Astounding* magazine in 1940, but it wasn't the plot that attracted 20th Century-Fox producer Julian Blaustein to the idea so much as the scene where the flying saucer lands and the alien emerges to receive a dose of human hospitality. 'The thing that grabbed my attention,' said Blaustein, 'was the response of people to the unknown. Klaatu (the alien) holds his hand up with something that looks unfamiliar to them and he is immediately shot. It was a terribly significant moment for me in terms of story.'[15] Blaustein had started reading sf stories in 1949 when he became aware of the booming circulation figures of sf magazines. He decided, on the basis of these, that he would be able to persuade Darryl Zanuck, the studio's head, about the feasibility of making a sf movie. One of the reasons he chose the Bates story was that it was set on Earth and would be relatively cheap to make.

As noted earlier, very few sf films made in the 1950s were based on the work of sf writers, and when they were, little remained of the original in the finished film. This is certainly true of *The Day the Earth Stood Still*, though Bates' story is a hoary piece of work when read today and Edmund H. North's screenplay was a great improvement on it. Bates, who was editor of *Astounding* magazine between 1930 and 1933, can best be described as a 'pre-Campbell' sf writer, and his work displays all that was wrong with magazine science fiction in the 1930s before John W. Campbell Jnr imposed his personality on the genre. Still, Bates deserved more than the $500 which was all he received for the sale of the film rights. The rights were actually sold to the film-makers by the copyright-holders Street & Smith Publications for $1,000 without their bothering to inform Bates of the sale. When film historian Steve Rubin recently tracked down the ageing author he found him still bitter about it. He did say that he thought the movie was very good but 'it had nothing to do with my story'.[16]

Technically the film stands up very well today and the scenes involving the landing of the flying saucer and the subsequent events around it possess an eerie quality assisted by Bernard Herrmann's marvellously alien-sounding electronic soundtrack. The flying saucer itself, designed by Lyle Wheeler and Addison Hehr, looks on the outside exactly as one would expect a real one to look though its interior was a disappointment and showing it destroyed the essential mystery of the craft. The giant robot Gort, though he tended to look a little rubbery behind the knees, was also impressive. Inside the suit, which consisted of rubber sprayed with metallic paint and a head made of sheet metal was Lock Martin, doorman at Grauman's Chinese Theater, chosen for the part because he was the tallest man in Hollywood.

Though often threatened with total destruction, the world rarely experienced such a fate in sf films of the 1950s. One exception was the George Pal production of *When Worlds Collide*, directed in 1951 by Rudolph Mate, the Polish-born ex-cameraman whose film career had begun back in the silent era. Based on the book by Edwin Balmer and Philip Wylie it had originally been bought by Paramount for Cecil B. DeMille; since it's basically a modern biblical epic one can see why. In Pal's version, with a screenplay written by Sydney Boehm, the film begins with pilot Dave Randall (Richard Derr) being assigned to fly a set of photographic plates from a South American observatory to one in the United States. The photographs reveal that a wandering star called Bellus, accompanied by its captive planet Zyra, has entered the solar system and will eventually collide with the Earth. The world is doomed, but a small portion of humanity has a chance of survival, according to scientist Dr Hendron (Larry Keating) who has designed a spaceship capable of reaching Zyra (which, it appears, is habitable). The building of the spaceship, as in *Destination Moon*, is achieved by private enterprise, the money being provided by an unpleasant, wheelchair-bound billionaire called Stanton (John Hoyt) whose reasons are purely selfish. A nation-wide lottery is organized to determine who should have the opportunity to escape destruction (only those who are young and capable of breeding being eligible, with the exception of Stanton) and those who don't get a winning number quickly give way to despair. There are outbreaks of rioting and riotous living as the rogue star approaches, bringing with it earthquakes and floods. The take-off proves successful and, despite the strains of acceleration, the ship's passengers survive to reach Zyra some hours later, their journey punctuated by the sight, on the ship's TV screens, of Bellus' collision with Earth.

Gordon Jennings and his team of special effects men justifiably won an Oscar for their work on *When Worlds Collide*; the model work showing the space ark taking off and the flooding of New York were of a very high standard. But strangely enough the event that gives the film its title is never shown – we never see the 'worlds collide'. We do see the passengers watching the collision but the audience itself misses the sight. (Perhaps this omission will be put right in the remake of the film that Paramount is currently planning.)

While Klaatu, the alien in *The Day the Earth Stood Still*, was landing his flying saucer in the middle of Washington DC another alien was being thawed out in his saucer near the North Pole. Unlike Klaatu this one didn't have humanity's best interests at heart. In fact, he didn't even have a heart, being nothing but a walking vegetable, albeit an intelligent and very powerful one. He made his appearance in *The Thing* (also known as *The Thing from Another World*) and his attitude towards mankind was to typify that of most extra-terrestrial visitors on the screen during the 1950s. As with so many of the films that established the main trends in sf cinema, *The Thing* is much superior to the various imitations that followed it. Though the directing credit is officially Christian Nyby's it is more or less common knowledge that the film was directed by one of Hollywood's film-making aristocrats – Howard Hawks (apparently Nyby, who had been the editor on many of Hawks's films, wanted a directing credit for union reasons and Hawks kindly gave him this one). The film contains all the Hawks trademarks, in particular the overlapping dialogue of the actors. 'We all kind of fell in love with his style,' said the film's star Kenneth Tobey in an interview years later, 'and, as it happens in dramas, you get a camaraderie and a sense of jollity and fun that comes across very clearly. Of course we rehearsed a great deal on that picture. It takes a lot of rehearsal to get that unrehearsed quality.'[17] Another major asset is the Charles Lederer screenplay; Lederer's ability to write smart, crackling dialogue hadn't diminished since he'd worked on the first screen version of *The Front Page* in 1931. All the characters in *The Thing*, stock ones though they may be, breathe with a certain life of their own – a quality so often missing from other 1950s sf films. Even the 'love interest' is handled with a certain amount of wit and style, its clichés made painless by an unusually talented director and writer.

Serious sf fans tend to regard the film with disapproval and consider it a typically Hollywood treatment of an sf masterpiece – John W. Campbell's short novel *Who Goes There?* published in *Astounding* magazine in 1938. While Hawks's film may not be perfect science fiction, it's certainly a better-than-average sf film, and excellent cinema.

The film begins with army pilot Captain Hendry (Kenneth Tobey) flying, with a group of his men, to a remote Arctic base where a number of scientists are holding a secret conference. En route his plane is diverted to a mysterious area in the snow where a great deal of magnetic activity has been detected. Investigation reveals a saucer-like object buried in the ice, but when an attempt is made to thaw the ice by using thermite bombs the 'saucer' explodes and the group are left with nothing but smoke until one of the men notices another, smaller, shape in the ice. A block of ice containing the 'thing' is chipped out and flown to the camp where it arouses great excitement among the scientists, who divide into two opposing groups, one of which, led by Dr Stern (Eduard Franz), wants to defrost the creature immediately, while the other warns that it may contain organisms dangerous to man and should be kept frozen for the time being.

However the creature is inadvertently thawed due to a mistake with an electric blanket and immediately crashes out of the nearest window into the snow, where it is attacked by a pack of sled dogs. By the time the men reach the scene it has vanished, leaving behind one arm that has been torn off by the dogs. Examination of the limb reveals that the 'thing' isn't an animal but a humanoid vegetable. 'You mean we're dealing with a walking carrot?' exclaims reporter Ned Scott (Douglas Spencer). The scientists also discover that in the palm of the thorny 'hand' are a number of seeds which, if planted, will produce more 'things'.

Various attempts to destroy the monster fail miserably and the 'thing' successfully invades a section of the camp, turning its hot-house into a breeding ground for its seedling offspring, which it nourishes with human blood. Eventually, despite being hindered by Dr Stern and his followers, who want to establish communication with the creature, Hendry and his men manage to destroy the alien by tricking it into standing on a high-voltage grid; like one of the monsters from earlier 'mad scientist movies', it is consumed in flames. Mankind is saved – but only for the time being, claims Ned Scott in a broadcast at the end of the film. 'I bring you a warning . . . to everyone of you listening to the sound of my voice . . . tell the world . . . tell this to everyone wherever they are . . . watch the skies . . . watch everywhere. Keep on looking! *Watch the skies!'*

In retrospect one wonders exactly what people were supposed to be watching for – flying saucers or Russian planes? With the 'early warning' associations of the Arctic setting the film can easily be interpreted as a parable of anti-communist vigilance. Some critics have accused it of being a piece of pro-military, anti-science propaganda, a view which is not justified as neither the military nor scientists come out of it well. Hendry, who is ultimately triumphant over the monster, only succeeds when he abandons the army rule book and uses his own common sense and that of his men (after it's been destroyed he receives a message from his superiors ordering him not to harm the creature). Some of the scientists are made to look foolish because they too are bound by a scientific rule book of their own; as the 'thing' is intelligent they believe there has to be some common ground between it and them, but there isn't. 'Its' race may be capable of building a spaceship, but that doesn't automatically make it 'reasonable' in the human sense of the word. If the film is anti-anything it is anti-dogma.

As it happens, Campbell's original concept would have made a more effective reflection of Cold War paranoia since his 'thing' was able to change its shape, becoming a perfect replica of its victims. Thus in his story the human survivors in the claustrophobic Arctic camp were unable to detect who was real and who wasn't, something that had a real-life political counterpart in the minds of many people at the time. Even so, the film possesses a certain real horror of its own – the monster may have been made more solid and less insidiously subversive, but thanks to Hawks's skilful handling (and some ruthless editing later to remove a number of sequences that too clearly reveal it to be James Arness in a padded suit) it is still a frightening creation. Early in the film a door is opened to reveal, briefly and unexpectedly, the snarling 'thing'. From then on, whenever a door opens (and Hawks ensures that throughout the film doors are opening constantly), the spectator instinctively flinches; the resulting build-up of tension is very effective. The monster is also disturbing because it is intelligent. It is one thing to be faced with a rampaging mindless beast, but to be threatened by something superior yet utterly hostile to man induces a profoundly unsettling feeling akin to that which a child experiences when he realizes an adult is actively hostile towards him. It is also an insult to the ego – we like to think that a superior intelligence from Out There would at least give us a condescending pat on the head in recognition of our meagre achievements, instead of contemptuously tossing us aside as the 'thing' does with Dr Stern when he approaches it 'scientist to scientist'.

The Martian war machines in action in George Pal's version of War of the Worlds. *Various rays were added optically to the film later but unfortunately the wires remained in view in many shots.*
(Right) *A technician adjusts the cobra-head attachment on one of the war machines.*

Just as contemptuous of humanity were the Martians in *War of the Worlds*, produced by George Pal in 1953. No sooner had three friendly locals approached their craft with a cry of 'Welcome to California!' than they were blasted to fine dust. Later in the film, when a priest tries the religious approach, walking towards the Martians with a Bible held high in his hands while he recites the 23rd Psalm, he receives the same treatment. All man's efforts to deal with the Martian invaders, including the use of the atom bomb, prove fruitless and it's only through the intervention of God Himself that the world, or what's left of it, is saved. The Martians, for all their seeming omnipotence, had failed to take into account the effect Earth's bacteria might have on them – bacteria which, as the narrator Sir Cedric Hardwicke puts it, are 'the littlest things God in His wisdom put on the Earth'. So much for mankind.

War of the Worlds, the most spectacular of the alien invasion movies of the 1950s, first began it long journey to the screen in 1925 when it was bought by Paramount's top film-maker Cecil B. DeMille. Over the years various plans were made to film this classic H. G. Wells novel, but such were the problems involved, mainly in the area of special effects and cost, that nothing ever came of them until George Pal joined Paramount in the

early 1950s. While the finishing touches were being applied to *When Worlds Collide* he began searching through Paramount's collection of properties for another suitable science fiction story and eventually decided on *War of the Worlds*. He then looked for a suitable writer to handle the project, and chose Barre Lyndon, a writer under contract to Paramount who had just worked with DeMille on *The Greatest Show on Earth*. 'I conferred with many writers,' said Pal later, 'But Barre came off best. He had written a very suspenseful film called *The House on 92nd Street*, a realistic semi-documentary detailing the arrest of Nazi agents in Washington DC and on that basis I felt he would do well with *The War of the Worlds*.'[18]

Next came the hiring of a director, who turned out to be Byron Haskin, a Hollywood veteran whose film career had begun in 1919 as an assistant cameraman to Louis J. Selznick. He made his directorial debut in 1927 with a Warner Brothers production called *Matinée Ladies*; then in 1930 he accompanied British film-maker Herbert Wilcox to England as his production executive. For a couple of years he was active in the British film industry but reaped few of the expected financial rewards, so he returned to Hollywood and Warner Brothers in 1932 and began a new career as a special effects cameraman, soon becoming head of the effects department. In 1947 he went back to direction with *I Walk Alone*, a Hal Wallis Production, then went on to direct Walt Disney's first live action feature *Treasure Island* in 1950. His knowledge of special effects made him an apt choice to direct a film as technically complicated as *War of the Worlds*.

The first problem for Pal, Lyndon and Haskin was to decide on their approach. The budget allotted by Paramount was a relatively limited one, and one way of saving money was to update the story and switch the setting from England to modern-day California – a transposition that upset a number of fans of the book. In an interview in 1975 Byron Haskin said: 'A recent writer on science fiction films said it was bad to have removed the story from its identifiable background, but it was identifiable to Americans, and that's who we were making the picture *for*. In making our choice we did as Orson Welles had done. We transposed it to a modern setting, hoping to generate some of the excitement that Welles had with his broadcast.'[19] 'With all the talk about flying saucers,' Pal himself recalled, '*War of the Worlds* had become especially timely. And that was one of the reasons we updated the story.'[20] But the story was also updated in a much less justifiable way – with one of Hollywood's dreaded 'love interest' sub-plots. Pal maintains that it wasn't his idea but the fault of Don Hartman, then Vice-President in charge of production at the studio, who felt that the picture had to contain a boy-meets-girl story to ensure box-office success. Boy-meets-Martians wasn't a sufficient attraction in his opinion.

The other main problem was a technical one: how do you put Wells's Martian war machines on the screen in the way that he described them? The answer was that you don't. In the book the war machines are hooded platforms mounted on top of three long mechanical legs, but for a special effects man to recreate one of these, and make it move realistically, would be a nightmare. How does a walking tripod move – like a one-legged man on crutches, or one leg at a time? As Haskin later said: 'Although we were afraid to desert the Wells concept entirely we eventually decided anything he may have written about water tanks on towers walking slowly across meadows in rural England was now ridiculous in a film sense.'[21] The alternative, designed after much trial and error by art director Al Nozaki, was something shaped like a cross between a flying saucer and a Manta Ray that floated on three beams of energy. The result, copper-coloured with green frontispiece and wingtips, was an impressively sinister creation, but what really gave it visual impact was a cobra-like appendage that protruded from the top (in the film the 'cobra heads' contained the Martians' deadly heat-ray projectors). Each of the three war machines was 42 inches across, but so heavy and complicated were they that each had to be supported by fifteen piano wires, connected to overhead tracks in the studio ceiling. Unfortunately these wires are often visible on the screen, particularly during the sequence when the war machines first emerge from their crater and engage the army in battle.

Much less successful was the design for the Martians themselves. Wells described them as resembling octopuses, consisting simply of over-developed heads, a pair of eyes, a beak-like mouth and a clump of tentacles, but Nozaki's version made them look like one-eyed mushrooms on legs. Only one of the Martians was built (the work of a small make-up man called Charles Gemora who, because of his diminutive size, found himself wearing the costume in the film) and it was only used briefly in one sequence, where a Martian leaves its war machine and enters the ruined farm house in which the hero and heroine are hiding. But even that brief scene was a mistake: it would have been best never to have seen what the Martians looked like, thus maintaining their basic mystery. Doubts arise as to whether Haskin was really the best choice for the film when one reads his following comments: 'I'd originally intended to use more of the creatures but Charlie Gemora had tied up more than sufficient time and expense with his one Martian. We spent six months building that thing. We called him Louis Lump Lump. Charlie worked him from the inside and could handle any number of movements, including veins that pulsated and eyes that flickered. He was on the screen for eighteen seconds and was very important.'[22]

More effective was the single Martian arm that emerges from beneath the crashed war machine at the end of the picture. Watched by the survivors in a devastated Los Angeles city street, the three-fingered, suckered hand painfully gropes its way down the hatch-cover, its distended veins rhythmically pulsating for a time, then suddenly stopping. This is a powerfully dramatic moment of cinema which is spoilt only when the hero (Gene Barry) picks up the Martian wrist between his thumb and forefinger and, after a pause, announces superfluously that 'It's dead!'

But for all the absurdities of the dialogue and a deadening performance by Anne Robinson as the heroine, *The War of the Worlds* remains an impressive movie and probably George Pal's greatest achievement, mainly because of the special effects (Gordon Jennings and his team won their second Oscar in a row for them) which succeed in creating the necessary excitement as well as a sense of awe and wonder essential to most good science fiction – elements not exactly obvious in the script. One curiosity about the film, remarked on at the time, was that, while we hear reports of how other countries are faring against their own Martian invaders (England puts up a 'magnificent but vain struggle', Sir Cedric Hardwicke informs us), we never hear about the Russians or any of the other communist countries. Are we to assume from this omission that the Russians and the Martians were somehow in league with each other? If so, the term 'red planet Mars' takes on a whole new meaning.

The alien invaders in *It Came from Outer Space* (1953) operated on a much smaller scale, nor were they really invaders in the strict sense of the word. Based on an original screen treatment by Ray Bradbury called *The Meteor*, the film concerned a group of aliens whose spherical spaceship crash-lands in an Arizona desert. To repair the vehicle they are forced to impersonate a number of people in a nearby town in order to obtain the necessary materials, and while they may perhaps bear humanity no real malice they are quite willing to destroy anyone who gets in their way. With its eerie desert setting the film, directed by Jack Arnold, creates a vivid atmosphere, and in place of the barrage of special effects used in *The War of the Worlds* the nature of the aliens is suggested through visual ingenuity. Much of the action is seen from their viewpoint, the camera becoming the alien as it moves through the desert or closes in on some terrified human. The aliens themselves are briefly glimpsed at times, one of the most effective moments occurring when a man driving along a lonely desert road at night suddenly picks up in his headlights something moving into the middle of the road. We receive a quick shot of what appears to be a huge eye, and little else, staring directly at us through the windshield.

According to Jack Arnold, who went on to direct a number of above-average sf/horror movies during the 1950s, many of the visual gimmicks

A typical 1953 advertisement for It Came from Outer Space.

in *It Came from Outer Space* were put in to make use of the 3D process. 'The film started,' he said, 'because Universal had bought a story from Ray Bradbury and they thought it could be successfully adapted to make a 3D picture. 3D had just come out and Warner Brothers had released a picture called *The House of Wax*, which was hurriedly put together in order to throw objects at people in three dimensions.' Even so, seen in merely two dimensions, it is still very effective and creates a genuine feeling of creepiness that lingers after the film has ended. 'I think the only way you can get an audience to accept the impossible is to get them involved in an atmosphere,' said Arnold, 'a mood, a feeling of what you're trying to do. That's why I made a lot of use of actual physical locations: I make them work for my story. Most of *It Came from Outer Space* was shot out on the desert; only the interiors were shot in the studio, and also the scenes in the little town which was on the Universal backlot. Everything else was filmed out in the desert in an area about ten or fifteen miles to the north of Hollywood. The spaceship was, of course, a model. We built a full-scale section of it and a crew went out into the desert and dug a big crater for it. Then we matched shots of it with miniatures in the studio for scenes of the actual spaceship.'

In the same year that *The War of the Worlds* and *It Came from Outer Space* were released there appeared a strange little film from the man who directed *Things to Come*, William Cameron Menzies. Called *Invaders from Mars*, it concerned a small boy (Jimmy Hunt) who one night sees a flying saucer land on the hill behind his home. The saucer burrows into the ground and disappears completely from view, and when the boy tries to tell his parents what has happened they ignore his story. In the days that follow the boy becomes aware that the aliens are slowly taking over the town, turning people into their puppets by implanting crystals in their brains. When the boy's parents are also taken over in this manner he goes to the police for help, only to find that they too have fallen victim to the aliens. Finally he succeeds in convincing a woman doctor of the truth and she calls in the army. They locate the aliens in a labyrinth of tunnels under the town: there is a battle and the invaders are destroyed, including their ruler who proves to be a disembodied head in a glass sphere. The boy wakes up and realizes that it was all a dream – but then sees the flying saucer landing once again behind his house.

The film was the realization of a childhood nightmare, a world where all the adults become frightening enemies, even one's own parents. A sort of catharsis occurs when the army moves in and fights the Martians but at the end of the film, when the whole terrible dream starts again, this proves to be illusory, and one realizes that the character is trapped in his nightmare for ever (a similar 'endless cycle' device was used in the classic horror film *Dead of Night*). The film was made on a very small budget but

(Below) *William Cameron Menzies' subtly distorted sets added to the atmosphere of paranoia in* Invaders from Mars; (left) *the Martian ruler in the same film.*

this handicap actually worked in favour of maintaining the dream-like atmosphere striven for by Menzies. The landing of the saucer on the hill was all done in the sound stage, the hill being nothing but a mound of sand made to appear larger through forced perspective. But the eerie atmosphere was chiefly created by the sets, all of which were subtly distorted, suggesting menace in every angle and shadow. In many ways, with its child's view of a frightening world, the film is reminiscent of *The Night of the Hunter*, directed by Charles Laughton in 1955. *Invaders from Mars* can hardly be described as a great sf film, but enough originality went into its making to lift it out of the category of simple hackwork.

The year 1953 was a good one for archetypal sf films. It saw the arrival of the first film about a giant monster being awakened by atomic radioactivity and causing havoc before being finally overcome. Called *The Beast from 20,000 Fathoms*, and directed by Eugene Lourie, it obviously owed a lot to *The Lost World* and *King Kong*, but the topical gimmick of radioactivity made it seem fresh and new. As noted earlier, the monster in this and subsequent imitations really represents the atom bomb itself as well as a form of divine retribution. The message is that man's technological tampering with nature will only result in nature striking back and destroying him (the biblical connotations reached their extremes with another Lourie film *Behemoth* in 1959, which took its title from a passage in the Bible) – the same message propounded by the 'mad scientist' films of the 1920s, 1930s and 1940s. The 1950s, however, had the atom bomb itself to show what form that destruction might take.

Based very loosely on a Ray Bradbury story called 'The Fog Horn', which was about a lighthouse foghorn being answered by the mournful cry of the last prehistoric monster left alive, *The Beast from 20,000 Fathoms* begins, like *The Thing*, in the Arctic regions where a nuclear bomb has just been detonated. Investigating the site of the explosion, a scientist called Professor Elson (Cecil Kellaway), accompanied by a number of army men, sees briefly what appears to be a large reptile moving through the blizzard. At first he believes he is mistaken, but later other sightings of the creature are reported and it is discovered that the explosion has revived a prehistoric monster buried in the ice for countless years. The giant reptile, it transpires, is not only infected with highly dangerous germs but is also heading for New York, which happens to stand on the site of the monster's old breeding grounds. Eventually the beast arrives there, causes the expected amount of damage, and is finally trapped and destroyed in an amusement park, consumed in flames amid a tangle of wreckage after being shot in the throat by a radioactive harpoon.

Despite its early similarities to *The Thing*, *The Beast* lacks the style, wit and excitement of of the Hawks film (the screenplay was by Lou Morheim and Fred Freiberger), its most interesting aspect being the special effects by Ray Harryhausen. Harryhausen had decided to specialize in the model animation techniques perfected by Willis H. O'Brien and had worked on a picture with O'Brien in the late 1940s. Called *Mighty Joe Young*, this was a small-scale remake of *King Kong* and concerned a fifteen-foot-tall ape captured by cowboys in Africa and taken back to America, to be put on display in a night-club. The film was well reviewed but wasn't a box-office success, coming out at the wrong time in 1949 – too late for the horror film boom of the early 1940s and too soon to take advantage of the sf/monster boom of the 1950s; but at least it earned O'Brien a well-deserved Oscar. 'We'd started a new film right after *Mighty Joe Young*,' said Harryhausen. 'O'Brien had written a story about a bull, a boy and dinosaur and Jesse L. Lasky Snr was interested in the project for Paramount but there was some difficulty in raising the finance and after many months of preparation it was finally called off. After that I went back to making animated fairy-tales for a time.' During this same period Harryhausen was also trying to launch a film version of *War of the Worlds* using the model animation process. 'I did a number of drawings and took them all over Hollywood. This was long before George Pal produced it for Paramount. Again Jesse Lasky was interested and he tried to get MGM to do it but nothing happened. I still have the drawings and would like somebody one day to remake *War of the Worlds* – the way Wells wrote it rather than modernizing it as Pal did.'

Harryhausen hadn't long been back to his fairy-tales when an acquaintance introduced him to a producer called Hal Chester who wanted to make a movie about a monster from the sea. 'That resulted in *The Beast from 20,000 Fathoms*, the first film where I was in sole charge of the special effects. It was also the film for which I first developed a simplified technique of combining animated models with live back-grounds. The film had a very low budget, only around $200,000, so I couldn't afford the complicated and expensive technique of using glass paintings combined with miniature rear projection in the manner of *King Kong* and *Mighty Joe Young*.'

Despite its small budget the film turned out to be one of the top money-grossers of 1953 and immediately began a trend. Soon atomic radiation was spawning all manner of monsters – giant reptiles, giant ants, a giant spider, a giant praying mantis, giant scorpions, and even giant people. Warner Brother, who had released *The Beast from 20,000 Fathoms* and subsequently made a fortune from it, followed it up with *Them!* in 1954, the first of the giant insect films. Directed by Gordon Douglas from a screenplay by Ted Sherdemann, it was set in the desert of New Mexico where recent H-Bomb tests had produced a species of giant ants. After a series of mysterious incidents the police and the FBI, in the guise of Ben Peterson (James Whitmore) and Robert Graham (James Arness – the 'thing' in *The Thing*), are called in to investigate and, with the help of a scientist, Dr Medford (Edmund Gwen), and, inevitably, his attractive daughter (Joan Weldon), they locate a huge underground nest containing the giant ants. The nest is destroyed, but not soon enough to prevent a queen, laden with eggs, from flying away in the direction of Los Angeles. She deposits the eggs in the city's underground drain system, and it's here that the film's final, and most exciting, confrontation with the insects occurs – a battle in which one of the heroes is destroyed along with the ants.

By now Hollywood science fiction films had left science far behind. While it might be conceivable for a vegetable species on a distant planet to evolve into humanoid form, as in *The Thing*, or for a superior civilization on Mars to be capable of all but destroying the human race as in *War of the Worlds*, a giant dinosaur, frozen but still alive after millions of years, was taking things too far – and giant ants were completely out of the question, scientifically speaking. One of the reasons insects have never evolved past a certain size is that they are limited by their breathing system; since they don't possess lungs, air is circulated through their bodies by air pressure alone via a number of holes on each side of the thorax – an effective method in small bodies, but not sufficient to oxygenate an animal the size of a dog, and certainly not adequate for ants the size of elephants as in *Them!*

Scientific quibbles aside, *Them!* is an above-average sf/monster movie and the ants themselves are convincingly handled. Unlike the monster in *The Beast from 20,000 Fathoms* they were not small models animated by stop-motion photography and then matted into the scenery but full-scale models manipulated manually. This gave them added realism in some shots but greatly restricted their movements in comparison to animated models. There were only two main ants built for the film, one complete and one consisting only of a head and forequarters. The latter was mounted on a boom which gave it some mobility, and this model was used for most of the close-ups of the ants' heads. It was also capable of moving its head, mandibles and antennae by means of a series of levers and knobs operated by the film crew (it was between the mandibles of this model that James Whitmore was 'crushed' during the climactic battle with the ants beneath Los Angeles). The complete model was used for long shots as well as a few overhead shots where the ant appeared to be walking but was actually being towed along on a camera dolly. A motor in its body moved its legs back and forth, but it was incapable of walking on its own. There were also a number of other model ants built for 'crowd' scenes, and while they weren't fitted with any motors their heads and antennae were constructed in such a way that a carefully positioned wind machine could move them to and fro. The ants were built by Warner Brothers' prop man

Dick Smith and the various special effects were handled by Ralph Ayres. *Them!* received an Academy Award nomination for its effects in 1954.

Though also set in a desert the style and approach of *Them!* make it very different from *It Came from Outer Space*. This was an exercise in almost pure atmosphere whereas *Them!* has the hard-boiled, realistic feel of the tough 1950s crime thrillers – pseudo-documentary films like *Pickup on South Street*, *Detective Story* and *I Was a Communist for the FBI*, which is not surprising since Douglas directed the latter film himself (a former comedy writer for Hal Roach, his directing career has produced only a few high spots, *Them!* being one of them, along with *Rio Conchos* in 1964 and *The Detective* in 1968). Apart from mentioning the atomic bomb tests, *Them!* doesn't seem to possess any of the darker connotations hinted at by other sf/horror movies of the period, but when it was released *Twentieth Century* magazine accused Warner Brothers of making a vicious allegory really calling for the extermination, not of giant ants, but of communists.

While the notion of Stalinist ants may be stretching things a little, the theory that the giant, and inevitably radioactive, monsters which spent their time knocking down cities in the 1950s were euphemisms for the atomic bomb has particular relevance in the case of Japan's contribution to the genre – Godzilla, the biggest euphemism of them all. It seems oddly masochistic of the Japanese that they would, a mere nine years after experiencing the real thing, take so much pleasure in watching on their cinema screens a vast monster, with radioactive breath, systematically levelling their cities. Called *Gojira* in Japan, it first appeared in 1954, a Toho Studio production directed by Inoshiro Honda who also co-wrote the screenplay (based on a story by Shigeru Kayama). Godzilla himself was the creation of special effects man Eiji Tsuburaya; basically the monster was a man in a very complicated suit but in many shots sections of a small mechanized model were used.

Over the years, as the fear of an imminent atomic doom has receded from the minds of most people, Godzilla has changed from being a threat to becoming Japan's unofficial champion, defending the country against the threat of smog monsters, etcetera. The films have also become increasingly juvenile, to the extent where Godzilla has now developed a voice and taken to conversing with his various monster friends. He was much more interesting as a character when he was knocking down Tokyo.

The same year (1954) saw another Ray Harryhausen monster emerging from the sea to knock down a city. This time the monster was a giant octopus and the city was San Francisco. The city authorities, however, weren't too happy about the idea and forbade the film crew from filming any of the city's real-life landmarks, which made Harryhausen's task even more difficult. Directed by Robert Gordon, the film was based on a screenplay by George Worthing Yates and Hal Smith and produced by Charles H. Schneer (Schneer and Harryhausen have been associated ever since). It was relatively cheaply made – the live action, starring Kenneth Tobey and Faith Domergue, was shot in one week – but Harryhausen's spectacular effects and a certain amount of stock footage give it an expensive gloss. The limited budget did mean, though, that Harryhausen could only afford to provide his octopus with six tentacles; to animate eight would have taken more time and more money.

Hollywood producers quickly realized that it was the monsters in science fiction films that chiefly attracted the public so subsequently the emphasis was placed on them at the expense of the science fiction elements. Why bother with costly special effects when all you need is a monster, which can be achieved quite simply by a man in a suit? Thus the sf film boom in the early 1950s led to the revival of Gothic horror films in the late 1950s, headed by the Hammer Film company which scored its first notable successes with sf/horror films.

Along with *The Thing* (whose monster, significantly, had a liking for human blood) the film that most accurately foreshadowed the direction the sf film boom was ultimately to take was *The Creature from the Black Lagoon* (1954). Theoretically it is a science fiction film – the monster is the last remaining member of a sub-human, aquatic species that evolved before man – but in style it is pure Gothic cinema. Directed by Jack Arnold it concerns the efforts of a group of scientists to capture the creature in its swampy home, located deep in the Amazon river basin. But the scientists soon become the hunted as the creature foils their various attempts and picks them off one by one. In a way this film can be described as the prototype for *Jaws* (itself an sf/horror film) since it involves people in a duel to the death with a powerful underwater monster. And *The Creature* also contains a number of evocative sequences that foreshadow similar ones in *Jaws*: as when the heroine goes for a swim in the lagoon, unaware that the monster is lurking in the depths watching her, obviously fascinated by the movements of her long legs. Speaking of this sequence Arnold later said: 'It plays upon a basic fear that people have about what might be lurking below the surface of any body of water. You know the feeling when you are swimming and something brushes your legs down below – it scares the hell out of you if you don't know what it is. It's the fear of the unknown. I decided to exploit this fear as much as possible in filming *The Creature from the Black Lagoon* but I also wanted to create sympathy for the creature – or my little beastie as we called it.' The film's original idea was conceived by film writer Maurice Zimm and the screenplay was by Harry Essex, who had worked on *It Came from Outer Space*, and Arthur Ross. The film proved a big financial success for Universal and spawned two sequels – *Revenge of the Creature* in 1955 and

The gill-man demonstrates his feelings towards modern technology in Revenge of the Creature.

The Creature Walks Among Us in 1956.

Science fiction films from the period 1950 to 1955 that didn't fall into the main categories detailed above were rare. One such was *The Twonky*, made in 1952 by Arch Oboler (producer/director of the sanctimonious *Five*), which was based very loosely on a story by sf writer Henry Kuttner, under the name of Lewis Padgett, and concerned a creature from the future who invades a television set, bringing it to animated life. The set is soon controlling its owner's life, scuttling about the building doing household jobs by means of an electronic beam and hypnotizing those who attempt to stop it. The idea is a good one, suggesting the contemporary fear of television's increasing power over people's lives (it was certainly an apt choice of subject for Oboler, whose success had come from radio) but Oboler's script was far too whimsical and revealed a lack of empathy with science fiction.

Ivan Tors and Curt Siodmak's association, which produced the sober but boring *Riders to the Stars* in 1954, had begun in 1953 with *The Magnetic Monster*, a curious little film in which the monster of the title is an expanding isotope that threatens to absorb the world's energy. It is finally destroyed in a cyclotron – a sequence that made use of footage from the 1934 German film *Gold*. Directed by Siodmak himself it purported to be more factual than the other sf/monster films of the period, but if anything its 'monster' was more fantastic than, for instance, *The Thing*'s carrot from out space. It also started a minor trend of its own – films that concerned an inanimate object getting out of control and destroying everything it touches. One of these was *The Monolith Monsters* in 1957 about giant silicon-absorbing crystals brought to Earth in a meteor (directed by John Sherwood, the film was based on an original treatment by Jack Arnold and Robert M. Fresco), and another was *The Night the World Exploded* (1957) directed by Fred F. Sears and written by Luci Ward and Jack Natteford, which had an 'element' from below the earth's crust emerging after the inevitable atomic test. Contact with the air causes it to explode with force into a number of pieces, each one of which quickly expands, absorbing the nitrogen from the air, until it reaches the size where it too explodes and the process begins again. As in *The Monolith Monsters* the menace is finally subdued with water.

The year 1953 also saw Curt Siodmak's novel *Donovan's Brain* being filmed for the second time. Directed by Felix Feist, a former director of comedy shorts, and adapted from the novel by Hugh Broke and Feist himself, it was no improvement on the 1944 version (*The Lady and the Monster*). This time Lew Ayres plays the scientist who keeps the brain of ruthless millionaire Tom Donovan alive after a plane crash and then falls victim to its evil influence. Once again the enormous potential of the subject was ignored in favour of a mediocre story of revenge mixed with pseudo-science and the supernatural.

Probably one of the best of the science fiction films made between 1950 and 1955 not to deal with monsters from outer space was Walt Disney's production of *20,000 Leagues Under the Sea*. Unlike George Pal, who had updated *War of the Worlds*, Disney decided to keep Verne's novel in its original late-nineteenth-century setting, which was something of an imaginative breakthrough for an sf film; yet the film is very much a product of the 1950s. It not only falls into the 'sea monster' category but also reflects the widespread fear and concern over the effects of a runaway technology that man may not be able to control. Significantly, it ends with what is clearly supposed to be an atomic explosion.

Considered purely as a science-fantasy adventure story it is an almost

The second, and successful, attempt to film the attack of the giant squid on the Nautilus.

perfect film, possessing that intangible 'sense of wonder' that sf fans maintain is the most important ingredient of the genre. Disney and his team succeeded in creating an atmosphere of evocative mystery; the film makes the familiar unfamiliar, as well as strange and exciting.

The film's plot, which has little to do with Verne's original, concerns a scientist, Professor Arronnax (Paul Lukas), and his two companions, Conseil and Ned Land (Peter Lorre and Kirk Douglas) who board an American warship to take part in a search for a mysterious sea monster that has been plaguing shipping in the area. The sea monster, a long, reptilian form with jagged scales and large glowing eyes, is sighted and fired upon by the warship with the result that it turns and rams the ship with tremendous force. The Professor, Ned and Conseil escape from the sinking ship in a lifeboat and eventually find themselves alongside the sea monster, which turns out to be a man-made vessel.

They go inside the craft and are then surprised by the master of the vessel, a Byronic character called Captain Nemo (James Mason) who, we later learn, is a scientist far ahead of his time and who, with the aid of his underwater ship the Nautilus, is conducting a campaign of destruction against the manufacturers of gunpowder by ramming and sinking their ships whenever he can find them. Nemo wants to force the nations of the world to abolish war, but at the same time he is seeking revenge on those who killed his wife and child, both of whom died at the hands of arms manufacturers attempting to force Nemo to give them his scientific secrets.

The film is undoubtedly the best of Disney's live-action features. Disney himself was fascinated with technology, and possibly the character of Nemo – both a technological genius and a loner who deliberately flaunts his individuality in the face of the establishment – had some special appeal for him. He poured a great deal of money into the project, ensuring not only that the special effects were top-class but that the film contained much expensive location and underwater footage. To direct the film he chose Richard Fleischer, who was then 37 years old and had been directing films since 1946, when he made *Child of Divorce* followed by a number of small-budget but impressive little films, such as *Trapped* (1949), *The Armoured Car Robbery* (1950) and *Arena* (1953), which established his reputation as an above-average film maker. But Disney's choice is a strange one, seeing that Fleischer is the son of Max Fleischer, a pioneer animator who was one of Disney's greatest rivals in the 1930s. It was a paradox that also puzzled Richard Fleischer at the time.

'He had called me out of the blue,' said Fleischer, 'and had asked me to come and see him. I did so and he presented the project to me, asking: "Well, what do you think?" And I said: "It looks marvellous and I'd be very interested in working on it but . . . do you know who I am? More to the point, do you know who my father is?" And he said: "Yes, I do." "Well," I said, "I'd love to do the picture but I don't want to offend my father. He might feel I was betraying him by working for you. I wouldn't want to take this assignment without his blessings." And Walt said: "You phone your father tonight and tell him what you want to do, then phone me tomorrow with the answer." So I phoned my father and he said: "Oh, that's absolutely fantastic. Your career is your career and you must do that film. Tell Walt that I think he's got very good taste in choosing you." And after that my father and Walt became very good friends after years of animosity. My father, who had retired by then, lived in New York and from then on, whenever Walt went to New York, he would always phone my father and arrange to have lunch with him. It was a marvellous thing to have happened, that these two giants of animation finally buried their differences and became friends.

'When Walt first asked me to his studio and showed me the material he had so far on *20,000 Leagues* the project hadn't really got very far. There was no script, there wasn't even a storyboard, it was just a collection of production ideas and illustrations showing what the submarine would look like and what some of the episodes would be about. But it looked a very fascinating subject and I'd always been interested in the book since I was a child. The thing that was most interesting to me, and was the real challenge of the story, was just how to get the wonder of a submarine across to modern-day audiences for whom a submarine was no miracle but a familiar piece of technology. At the start I wasn't sure whether or not it could be done but when I saw the sketches and plans I knew it was a very good and worthwhile project.

'I spent a year preparing the film. I worked on the screenplay with the writer Earl Fenton right from the start because, to begin with, there was no actual story. You can't make a story out of the book because it doesn't have one. The book really consists of a series of unrelated incidents with a few clues as to what might be a story about Nemo. There are all sorts of allusions as to what he is doing under the sea and why, allusions to what his politics are and what happened to his family and so on. So Earl Fenton and I found it very interesting to try and reconstruct a story from what was hinted at in the Jules Verne original. The odd thing is that now *20,000 Leagues* is always thought of in terms of our story, the story of the film, instead of what is in the actual book. Our trick was to retain the basic incidents that people always remembered from the book but not necessarily in the same way or the same order. For instance, everybody remembers the underwater burial and the fight with the squid, so we had to include those two incidents, but our motivations for them were quite different from the book. I must say that it was Earl Fenton who came up with a way of approaching the whole thing. He decided, and I fully agreed, that the only way you could tell this story, and make it work as far as suspense was concerned, was to make it a prison-jailbreak story, and that is basically what we did. The three men were captured by Nemo and kept in the submarine and we treated them as if they were in a prison story – all their time was spent planning an escape, and making several abortive attempts along the way, before finally succeeding at the end.

'I loved working with Walt Disney – there were no difficulties at all. One example of working with him: I'd got into the big sequence involving the fight with the squid in the studio. It was written to happen at sunset on a calm sea and the special effects people had this giant, mechanical thing which had very little animation to it – it was stuffed with kapok and pulled around with wires and I must say it gave me a lot of trouble because the damn kapok in the tentacles kept soaking up the water and getting heavier and heavier to the point where all the wires kept breaking. It kept getting soggier and soggier and would slowly submerge from view and it all looked very artificial. I just couldn't make it work. I tried for about a week and it just looked terrible. In fact, it looked very funny. So Walt came to me and said: "Stop shooting the squid sequence, go and shoot something else. There's something terribly wrong with that thing." I said: "I know there is. The squid is just no good." And he said: "Well, we'll just have to rebuild it." "But it's not just the squid," I told him, "there's something basically wrong with the whole sequence."

'So I talked over the situation with Earl Fenton, the writer, and again he came up with a solution. He said: "The problem is that you can see everything too clearly. This should be a sequence in a storm at night with big waves, lots of spray, so that you can't see the wires and all the other mechanical deficiencies." It was obviously the correct solution but it was going to be very expensive – it would mean putting in dozens of wind machines and all kinds of extra special effects that we hadn't budgeted for and would be a much more difficult thing to shoot. But I went to Walt and told him Earl's solution and he said: "You're absolutely right. That's the way we'll do it. We'll build a new squid that will be very flexible and we'll shoot it in a storm." Now that cost him a lot of extra money but there was no argument from him over it. Walt knew when things were right – he had a great instinct for that. But the new monster alone must have cost a quarter of a million dollars – each tentacle of the squid had eight or ten wires attached to it with one man on each wire. We must have had fifty or sixty men acting like a mammoth crowd of puppeteers moving this thing. Some made the tentacles move up and down and some made them move laterally. The squid also contained a complicated hydraulic system that moved some of the parts.

'I think our Nautilus also improved on Verne's description of the submarine in his book. That was the work of Harper Goff who designed the picture as a whole as well as the submarine. He also designed the submarine for me in *Fantastic Voyage*. The idea was to make the Nautilus look as menacing as possible, which is why he gave it those big eyes. We built the whole top section, from the water-line up, full-scale, and it rested on a float. We also built some full-scale underwater sections, such as the hatch for showing people coming in and out. Harper Goff was a great designer and he did something in that picture that was absolutely fantastic – we were shooting it in Cinemascope with anamorphic lenses and because the process was all very new (it was one of the first pictures to be done in Cinemascope) the lenses were quite slow. This was causing the special effects people a lot of difficulty with the shooting of the model stuff because a lot of the sequences involving the submarine underwater had to be over-cranked two or three times the standard speed and the submarine had to be a certain size so that it wouldn't look like a toy, but due to the slow lenses we needed a lot more light and couldn't get it underwater, even in the well-lit studio tank. And they weren't only having trouble with the lighting but also with the size of the model – the one they were using was about five or six feet long, so they could get some detail on it – which had to make a couple of sharp bends around rocks, and if they turned it too sharply then the wires would break. They had reached an impasse with it but then Harper Goff came to the rescue and designed a *squeezed* version of the submarine – it was built squeezed to anamorphic proportions so that it could be shot with a standard camera, a Mitchell with a fast lens, but when it was projected through an anamorphic lens onto a screen it was stretched out absolutely perfectly in the correct proportions. It's in the film and you can't tell when the compressed model is being used and when an ordinary one is.

'The Disney special effects and technical people were really fantastic on that film. One of the things they devised was the first real underwater camera. It didn't exist before that film. The idea of putting a Mitchell underwater was all theirs . . . it was designed and developed at the studio. We spent ten weeks doing the underwater work in the Bahamas, then we went to Jamaica, where we did the cannibal island sequence, for about a month. Then we came back to the studio and did the rest of the picture inside. which was really the bulk of it.

'Of all my films I think it's one of my best efforts though I haven't seen it recently. The Disney people re-release it every once in a while and it had an enormous success in Paris this year [1977] . . . it got great reviews from the French critics. It's a kind of a thrill for me to feel that a film I made over twenty years ago is still a successful film for modern audiences.'

5 British SF in the 1950s

British science fiction films in the 1950s followed a path similar to the American, though on a much smaller scale: during the first half of the decade they tended to reflect the underlying fears of the Cold War and it was during this period that the better films were produced. Then from 1956 onwards the cycle degenerated into ever cheaper and more perfunctory variations on the monster theme.

The atom bomb figured prominently in the British public consciousness just as it did in the American, but whereas Hollywood treated the subject indirectly in the early 1950s British film-makers faced it head-on in *Seven Days to Noon* made in 1950. Produced and directed by John and Roy Boulting, who became best known for their series of satirical comedies later in the 1950s, it concerned a scientist (Barry Jones) who, while working on a British atom bomb project, goes insane through a mixture of overwork and guilt. A deeply religious man, he writes to the Prime Minister demanding that the government destroy its stockpile of atomic weapons within seven days or he will explode an atomic bomb somewhere in London. He then calmly places one of the small bombs he has helped to develop in an ordinary shopping bag and vanishes in the busy streets of London. At first the government thinks it's a hoax, but when they discover that both the scientist and one of his bombs are missing they are forced to take his threat seriously. A desperate hunt is launched but as the deadline draws nearer without the bomb being found the city has to be evacuated. In a climax of nail-biting suspense the scientist is tracked down in the nick of time and the bomb defused.

Made in the semi-documentary style that British film-makers perfected in the late 1940s and early 1950s the film is very effective in its build-up of tension, but what makes it even more disturbing when seen today is that its theme has become more relevant now than when it was released nearly three decades ago.

The screenplay was by Roy Boulting and Frank Harvey, a British playwright who turned to scriptwriting and collaborated with the Boultings on several of their film projects, but the original story was written by Paul Dehn and James Bernard. Dehn, who shared an Academy Award with Bernard for *Seven Days*, was a film critic, and this marked his first entry into film writing. Later he went on to write the screenplays for such films as *Goldfinger* (1964), *The Spy Who Came in from the Cold* (1965), *Beneath the Planet of the Apes*, *Escape from the Planet of the Apes* and *Conquest of the Planet of the Apes* (1970, 1971 and 1972). James Bernard, his collaborator on the story and long-time friend, is the film composer best known for his music in many of Hammer's horror movies. (Also to be found among the credits for *Seven Days* is cinematographer Gilbert Taylor, who later photographed *Star Wars*.)

Another typically British sf film of the early 1950s was *The Man in the White Suit* (1951). Again it concerns a scientist and his invention, but being produced by Ealing Studios, the company that produced the best of the British post-war comedies, its treatment of a familiar sf plot – of the laboratory-created 'thing' that causes nothing but trouble – is in the inimitable Ealing style rather than that of a conventional sf film. Alec Guinness plays a scientist who invents an artificial fibre that neither wears out nor gets dirty. To prove its unique qualities he makes himself a shining white suit that retains its pristine condition throughout the film. His invention causes alarm to both the clothing manufacturers and their workers, who fear its effects on their industry. Various attempts are made to suppress the new material, all of which are resisted by the inventor, until finally he is cornered by an angry mob in a street and his suit – suddenly and symbolically – begins to disintegrate. Everyone is relieved that the material isn't the perfect substance it was believed to be, with the exception of the disillusioned inventor. But he is only momentarily dismayed and the film ends with him happily planning a second attempt. Basically a satire, what makes this sf film unusual is that it is not really anti-science: neither the scientist nor his creation is the target for the film's gentle ridicule, but rather the people around him, who react to something new with fear and ignorance. Directed by Alexander Mackendrick, the screenplay was by Roger MacDougall, John Dighton and Mackendrick himself and was based on an original play by MacDougall (the play, however, was never performed but adapted straight into a screenplay).

As in Hollywood not many of the sf films were based on the work of actual sf writers, but one of the British exceptions was a cheap little production called *Four-Sided Triangle* made in 1952. Produced by a small company called Hammer Films, it was taken from the novel by William F. Temple and concerned two scientists in love with the same girl. Having invented a matter duplicator they come up with the bright idea of duplicating the girl after she declares she loves only one of them – Robin (John Van Eyssen). The duplication process proves successful and there are now two girls (both played by Barbara Payton) but instead of falling in love with the other scientist, Bill (Stephen Murray), the new Lena is *also* attracted to Robin, much to the consternation of both men (it shouldn't really have come as a surprise, since she was supposed to be an exact duplicate of the original Lena). But the awkward situation is resolved by the inevitable laboratory fire that destroys both Bill and the fake Lena, leaving Robin and the first Lena to their own devices. Directed by Terence Fisher, who wrote the screenplay with American writer Paul Tabori, the film had an interesting premise but was too restricted by the tiny budget to be a success.

Also off the beaten sf film track, and as cheaply made, was *Space-ways*, another Hammer production. Terence Fisher was again the director (the assistant director was Jimmy Sangster who, like Fisher, was to become well-known through his involvement with Hammer's later series of horror films) and the screenplay, by Paul Tabori and Richard Landau, was based on a radio play by British writer Charles Eric Maine. Howard Duff starred as a scientist suspected of murdering his wife and placing her body in the nose cone of a rocket which was then blasted into orbit around the Earth. To prove his innocence, and to uncover the real killer, he has to smuggle himself on board another rocket and make a similar trip.

Nearer the American sf movies of the time was the strangely titled *Immediate Disaster* (1954): it was really a cheap remake of *The Day the Earth Stood Still* and even had Patricia Neal playing a similar role as the girl who befriends an extraterrestrial. Austrian actor Helmut Dantine played the man from Venus who arrives in a small English village to deliver a warning to mankind – stop setting off atom bombs or else! The Venusians' main concern is that if the inhabitants of Earth succeed in blowing up the planet they'll upset the 'balance of the Universe' and wipe out a number of other worlds as well.

Like the American sf films the British ones were also taken over by monsters at the expense of other sf elements. The film that did most to establish this trend in Britain was *The Quatermass Experiment* (US title: *The Creeping Unknown*) made by Hammer Films in 1955. It was based on a BBC-TV serial written by Nigel Kneale, a writer with an uncanny knack for combining contemporary sf themes with both mythology and traditional elements of the supernatural to produce stories that tend to bypass the forebrain and work directly on unconscious fears. 'It's the art of creating a state of unease,' says Kneale (for more information on the *Quatermass* TV serials and Kneale himself, see Appendix)[23]. It was Hammer's usual method to adapt proven successes from both radio and television and as the first *Quatermass* serial had been such a nation-wide success in 1953 they naturally chose to make it into a film in 1955. Their budget was as small as ever but they did have the advantage of an American distribution deal. This meant that a minor or fading American star had to be included in the cast to ensure that American audiences would have some kind of emotional 'focus' on the screen and not be alienated by all the strange accents. Chosen for this task was Brian Donlevy, a former Hollywood leading man and later character actor, who played the central role of Professor Quatermass. The American distributor was Robert L. Lippert, who had already been involved in a number of cheap exploitation sf films, such as *Rocketship XM* and *Project Moonbase*.

The film begins with a rocketship hurtling out of the night sky and burying itself nose-first in a field behind a farm house. Police, firemen and sightseers quickly arrive at the scene of the crash, among them Professor Quatermass, the man in charge of Britain's first attempted flight into space. He takes control and orders the firemen to aim the hoses around the hatchway so that the astronauts will have some protection from the heat of the ship's hull when they emerge. The door is opened by remote control and a figure slowly emerges – one of three astronauts inside the ship. He stumbles and falls, and is quickly placed on a stretcher and taken to an ambulance. Quatermass and the others find no sign of the other two men, but they do find their spacesuits. However, both of them are empty, yet linked up in such a way as to suggest that the men disappeared within them.

After this effective beginning the film continues its build-up of unease. The surviving astronaut, Victor Carroon (Richard Wordsworth), is apparently in the grip of a strange disease. After saying just two words in the ambulance ('Help me!') he can no longer communicate with anyone, even his wife Judith (Margia Dean), and his skin is beginning to undergo a transformation. Even his bone structure is changing, and in the hospital the process of change enters a new phase: he absorbs a cactus plant into his arm which takes on the appearance of a large, shapeless mass covered with spikes. He escapes from the hospital and staggers off into the night, an emaciated tortured figure who is still partly human and terrified by what he knows he is becoming.

When he is finally tracked down in Westminster Abbey the metamorphosis is complete and he has become a large, pulsating octopus-like creature, totally unrecognizable as a human being. Quatermass arranges to have him electrocuted before he can discharge a number of spores into the air, and no sooner have the 'thing's' screams died away than he announces that he is going to launch another rocket as soon as possible.

The Quatermass Experiment was directed by Val Guest, a former actor turned journalist who has been active in the British film industry as writer, director and producer since the 1930s. The first film he directed for the Hammer company was *Life With the Lyons*, a comedy based on the popular radio series, in 1953. 'I got involved with *Quatermass* through Tony Hinds, who was then a producer at Hammer,' said Guest. 'I was just

Richard Wordsworth, wearing his cactus make-up, as the astronaut who returns from space with an unwelcome social disease in The Quatermass Experiment.

going on holiday to Tangier and he called me and asked if I would read a breakdown of a thing called *The Quatermass Experiment* which had been a great success on television. I hadn't seen the serial at all because I'd been away, and I had one or two other scripts to read, so I went off to Tangier leaving Hammer's story breakdown on my bedside table. When I came back I read it through and I said to myself: "I don't really want to do this. It may have been a big TV success but I can't see what there is in this." So I left it and then my wife read it and said: "What are you going to do about this Quatermass thing?" I said: "I don't think I want to do it." And she cried: "You're mad! Do it. Do something different!" So that's how I came to do it. I very nearly didn't.

'I didn't work with Nigel Kneale on the script. Hammer had already had his original BBC scripts broken down and condensed into a treatment. As somebody else had already done this I didn't go through his original scripts myself but I did occasionally refer to them when I wanted to check up on some of the technical stuff he'd written.

'The film, of course, was made on a very small budget and there are always problems when you're working on a small budget, but that sort of situation can be good for you because it makes you think. You dig a lot deeper into your creative recesses to see what you can pull out of the hat. The rocketship in the opening sequence, for instance, we built in the grounds at Bray Studio. It looked enormous but it wasn't really; we only built the bottom part of it, the rest was matted on afterwards. I used wide-angle lenses on it most of the time to give it a feeling of vastness. It was the

Brian Donlevy (right) as Professor Quatermass puzzling over the whereabouts of two of his astronauts (only their spacesuits remain).

same with Westminster Abbey in the final sequences; we built that in what is called the large stage at Bray but it's actually quite a small one. We needed every trick in the book for that one. Again we only built the bottom part of the set and matted the rest on làter. We built the exterior of the Abbey entrance on the Bray lot and again I used as wide a lens as possible to shoot it. There were no shots of the real Abbey in the film at all.

'There were quite a few attempts to construct the monster that appeared in the climax and eventually it ended up being made mostly out of pieces of tripe, as well as rubber solution. That was all the work of Les Bowie, the special effects man. I didn't have much to do with it. We didn't have it on the stage at all, it was all shot in the special effects department.

'I was the one who cast Richard Wordsworth as the infected astronaut. He was a very good character actor and he had the right sort of face for the part. He gave an incredible performance, I thought. Funnily enough, whenever I see Dickie Wordsworth now he always says that it was thanks to me that, in his very first film appearance, he had to get sprayed in the face by seven fire hoses. I used him again in another Hammer film, *Camp on Blood Island*, because, again, he looked right with his thin, gaunt appearance. He looked as if he had been in a Japanese prison camp. I don't know why his career never took off after *Quatermass* because he was so good in that film. Particularly in his scene with the little girl, who was Jane Asher, by the canal.

'I can't remember if Brian Donlevy was actually part of the Lippert distribution deal but Margia Dean was because, I think, she was Lippert's girl friend. But Donlevy was in it just because it was thought he would be a good star to hang the picture on. It was obviously important to have an American star from the American release point of view and, of course, he was well-known.

'He was a great guy and great to work with. He used to like his drink, however, so by after lunch he would come to me and say: "Give me a breakdown of the story so far. Where have I been just before this scene?" We used to feed him black coffee all morning but then we discovered he was lacing it. But he was a very professional actor and very easy to work with.

'The whole film was a very enjoyable experience. There was a lovely family atmosphere at Bray and everyone was busting their guts to make it look like the film was made on two shoestrings instead of just the one. At the time we had no idea it was going to be an important film in terms of Hammer's future as a company. It was also personally important for me in that it was my first science fiction picture – I'd done every other kind of picture up to then but never an sf one – and it started me thinking in terms of making other sf films.' Apart from directing other sf films for Hammer, Val Guest later wrote, produced and directed *The Day the Earth Caught*

Fire, in 1961, which is discussed in Chapter 7.

The Quatermass Experiment (also known as *The Quatermass Xperiment* in order to exploit associations with the British 'X' Certificate classification) proved successful in England on a level rather unexpected by the Hammer executives (it was also a minor success in America where it was released under the title of *The Creeping Unknown*), and this prompted them quickly to put other sf/horror films into production. One of the first of these was *X – the Unknown*, made in 1956, and though it had many similarities with *Quatermass* there were two important differences. In the first place it wasn't made by the same Hammer team but was directed by Leslie Norman from an original script by Jimmy Sangster, though Tony Hinds, the producer, had worked on *Quatermass*. The other important difference was that the monster in *X – the Unknown* was depersonalized and had none of the emotional impact of the doomed but dangerous astronaut in the first film. Basically it was nothing but an animated blob that oozed out of the earth after an atomic bomb test in Scotland. Hungry for more radiation, which serves as its nourishment, the blob makes a series of attacks on establishments harbouring radioactive materials. Despite the typically small budget the film is well-made and compares favourably with the similar 'scientific menace' type of films, like *Them!*, being produced in Hollywood at the time. There is a good build-up of suspense with shadowy and remote Scottish settings used to good advantage, and the monster itself is kept out of sight until fairly late (when it does appear it doesn't disappoint on the technical level, thanks to fine special effects by Les Bowie, Vic Margutti and Jack Curtis), but overall it lacks the memorable quality of the first *Quatermass*, probably because its basic idea wasn't as original.

The same year Hammer also made a sequel to *The Quatermass Experiment* called *Quatermass II* (US title: *Enemy from Space*), based on a BBC-TV serial of the same name transmitted in 1955. Donlevy again played Quatermass, who this time becomes involved with an alien invasion on a much larger scale. Now in charge of a British space project, he is trying to persuade the government to finance the development of a life-support complex that would enable man to live on the moon. The government pleads lack of funds, so a disgruntled Quatermass returns to his rocket installation where he is informed by his assistant Marsh (Bryan Forbes) that a number of mysterious small objects have been picked up on their radar. These appear to be falling in the direction of nearby Wynerton Flats. The next day, while checking the area, they find several small projectile-like objects, but to Quatermass's greater amazement they also observe, near the sea, an establishment that lookes exactly like his own proposed moonbase. Shortly afterwards the projectile that Marsh is holding explodes, leaving a strange scar on his face. At that moment

Hammer make-up man applies dry ice to Tom Chatto's suit in Quatermass II.

masked soldiers emerge from the establishment, surround them and take away Marsh.

Furious, Quatermass goes to London to find out who is in charge of the 'moonbase' establishment, but though he learns that it is a *bona fide* government project it has been classified Top Secret and no one will talk about it. He encounters a Member of Parliament who is also trying to find out what is going on at Wynerton Flats. The MP, called Broadhead (Tom Chatto), and Quatermass join a government-organized tour of the establishment where they are told by the coldly aloof 'guide' that it is a plant for manufacturing artificial food for the Third World. Not satisfied with this, Broadhead goes off alone to discover what one of the mysterious domes really contains – and reappears covered in a black, smouldering substance. Screaming with agony he warns Quatermass not to touch him, then dies.

Quatermass escapes and returns to London but his efforts to raise the alarm are in vain. He notices that all the government officials he meets have the same V-shaped scar on their skin and he realizes that the British government has been completely infiltrated by 'something'. Finally, with the help of a trustworthy police inspector and a crowd of workers who live near the base, Quatermass forces his way back inside, after first ordering his rocket installation to fire a missile at a mysterious object they have detected in orbit around the Earth. There is a fierce battle within the mysterious establishment between the guards and the workers, during which Quatermass manages to cut off the supply of the black substance to the domes, with the result that vast blob-like creatures break out of them. The substance, it seems, was food for the giant aliens dwelling within the domes and the establishment itself was the bridgehead for an invasion of Earth. But as the giant monsters converge on Quatermass and his men the missile hits the orbiting alien spaceship above and all the aliens die instantly. Once again Quatermass has saved the world.

As with *The Quatermass Experiment* and the later *Quatermass and the Pit*, Nigel Kneale cunningly mixes science fiction with traditional horror elements. The alien invasion may be a science fiction idea but it is presented with the trappings of Gothic horror, such as the V-shaped marks of the devil' which all the alien-possessed people display. The film, like the Hollywood sf movies, is also an interesting symptom of the state of paranoia that existed in the West in the 1950s, but the paranoia in *Quatermass II* is of a peculiarly British kind and reflects fears of government bureaucracy becoming all-powerful. This fear has long been a major one in Britain – a physically small country with a strongly centralized government – and regularly emerges as a topic in fiction, films and television, producing such works as Orwell's *1984* and the recent BBC-TV series *1990*, whereas in America, with its various States still retaining

some autonomy within the federal system, the same fear is less intense.

Val Guest was again the director on *Quatermass II* and also wrote the finished script which was based on Kneale's original. 'Whether Nigel gave us a draft script I honestly can't remember,' said Guest. 'I think it was probably the former, seeing as he has a script credit on the film with me, but I certainly didn't work with him on the script.

'*Quatermass II* was a little more expensive than the first one, mainly because we went on location. On *The Quatermass Experiment* the furthest we went on location was Whipsnade Zoo. We did everything else on the lot at Bray, though we did a couple of night shots in Windsor, for the scenes of the old chemist shop and things like that; otherwise it was all contained in the studio. But on *Quatermass II* we went down and filmed at the Shell Refinery on the coast and it was a major operation for a small company like us to take a whole unit down there. We also had a bigger cast including people like Bryan Forbes. I used to employ Bryan all the time in those days. Whenever I had a picture I would try and give him a part, even if I had to write him in especially, to help him pay the rent. I had a small stock company that I used from picture to picture. One of them was Sidney James, and another was John Van Eyssen who later became head of Columbia Pictures in England.'

The following year Guest directed another film based on Kneale's work. Called *The Abominable Snowman* it was adapted from Kneale's BBC-TV play *The Creature*, which was transmitted in 1956 and concerned the hunt by a group of men for the legendary Yeti of Tibet. As usual with a Kneale story all is not what it seems and in the film's dénouement it is revealed that the 'abominable snowmen' are actually the last survivors of a superior race that once existed on Earth and that the real 'monsters' are the men hunting them. It was an unusual Hammer film in several ways but mainly because it wasn't a very horrific film, though it did contain a couple of first-class shock sequences near the end. As such it wasn't as financially successful at the Quatermass ones. 'We did all right with it,' said Guest, 'but it was never really a big success. It was too subtle and I also think it had too much to say. No one was expecting films from Hammer that said anything, but this one did – it had a message. Nigel had put in a lot of good stuff about man's supposed superiority over other species and all that but audiences didn't want that sort of thing from Hammer.

'For a Hammer film of that period it was quite lavish. It was more expensive than normal because of all the location shooting. We went and shot a lot of that in the French Alps – about 8,000 feet up we worked, and all roped together a lot of the time. It was something of an adventure making that picture. The rest we shot at Pinewood Studios. We used the Studio's biggest stage and built an enormous set consisting of rocks, snow and a cave. There wasn't enough space to do it at Bray though I shot some small stuff there, and we also built the Tibetan temple set at Bray, or part of it anyway – the rest was matted in together with the scenery.'

That year, 1957, Hammer gave up science fiction films, contemporary ones at least, having decided that it was the monsters and not the sf elements that attracted audiences. So they went back to basics and remade *Frankenstein* (the prototype of modern sf) in all its Gothic, period splendour and, most importantly, in glorious gory colour. It proved a tremendous success and launched the whole series of Hammer's now-famous Gothic horror films.

Most of the other British-made sf films produced during the 1950s were of the monster-from-space variety, but one exception was *The Gamma People* (1956). A real curiosity of a film, it was directed by John Gilling and again reflected the British obsession with the possibility of government bureaucracy extending its power into the very minds of the people. Set in a mythical European country which is obviously communist-controlled it concerned two Western reporters (played by two actors better known for their comedy roles, Paul Douglas and Leslie Phillips) who uncover a bizarre experiment being carried out on children and elderly people. The government, in order to test a scientific theory, has been bombarding these human guinea-pigs with intense gamma radiation, the idea being to increase their brain power. While some of the subjects have been turned into near geniuses, others have been reduced to the level of morons (the film has many similarities with Joe Losey's more pretentious 1961 film *The Damned*).

Much more conventional in theme was *The Trollenberg Terror* (1958; known in the USA as *The Crawling Eye*) which, like the Quatermass films, was based on a TV serial. The author this time wasn't Nigel Kneale though Peter Key's script certainly attempted to imitate Kneale's usual plot-line and build-up of atmosphere. Set in an Austrian ski resort called Trollenberg it concerns a scientist who becomes increasingly suspicious about a number of mysterious disappearances in the area. He realizes that all the missing people were last seen in the vicinity of one particular mountain, whose summit is always covered in cloud no matter what the prevailing weather conditions. Eventually it is discovered that the mountain top has been taken over by a number of grotesque alien creatures who use the manufactured cloud to conceal their activities. As they come from a planet with a very low atmospheric pressure they are at first restricted to the top of the mountain, but then they succeed in creating a force-field which will enable them to extend their influence. The cloud begins to move down the mountain until it covers the village, and with the cloud come the creatures, which resemble giant turnips with tentacles. But all is saved when a squadron of United Nations planes arrive and bomb the monsters to pieces.

Though an Eros Production, the film adaptation featured the work of a couple of Hammer regulars, one of them being the scriptwriter Jimmy Sangster who wrote the screenplay, the other being special effects man Les Bowie. 'It had an awful lot of effects in it,' said Bowie, 'and there was one shot of a cloud on the mountain that was really terrible. I squirm when I see it on TV now and I squirmed when I filmed it, but we were in a mad hurry at the time. We did the cloud with just a piece of cotton wool – we stuck it on a photograph of a mountain with a nail and then filmed it. And they used that photograph time and time again during the film : every time a character looked out of a window they'd cut to this photograph and we'd have stuck the cotton wool in a new position. Awful!' But the film itself was superior to many of that type.

It was certainly better than *Strange World of Planet X* (1958), another Eros Production which was also adapted from a British TV serial and based on the novel of the same name by René Ray. Directed by Gilbert Gunn, and again starring Forrest Tucker, it concerned a mad scientist called Dr Laird (Alec Mungo) whose experiments with magnetism have caused an aberration in the earth's magnetic field. One of the side-effects is to make the insects in the area increase in size. It was the sort of cheap film made purely for exploitation purposes that helped to give 'science fiction' movies such a bad name towards the end of the 1950s.

In the same category was *First Man into Space* (1959), one of two pictures Amalgamated Films made in Britain in the late 1950s, both of which pretended to be set in North America. Both starred American actor Marshall Thompson, and in this one he plays an Air Force officer in charge of a base where experimental flights into space are being carried out in a rocket-plane called the Y-13. The pilot involved in these flights is Dan Prescott (Bill Edwards) and after one such mission he come back covered in a repulsive, crusty substance that has turned him into an inhuman, blood-drinking monster. As in *The Quatermass Experiment*, the film it imitates, there are some moments of pathos, but overall it's an inferior film with a script of crippling banality. Written by John C. Cooper and Lance Z. Hargreaves from an original story by Wyott Ordung, it was directed by Robert Day.

A different team were responsible for the other Amalgamated production, *Fiend Without a Face* (1958), a rather more interesting film. Directed by Arthur Crabtree (who, like Robert Day, was a former cameraman turned director) it was written by Herbert J. Leder and based on a short story, *The Thought Monster*, by Amelia Reynolds. It involved a scientist whose experiments with a machine that can amplify thought waves accidentally bring into being creatures which consist of pure energy. Invisible at first, they commit a series of murders by sucking out

Bill Edwards as yet another astronaut who returns to Earth with a skin problem (make-up by Michael Morriss) in First Man Into Space.

Gorgo's mother at work on one of the many London landmarks she destroys at the climax of Gorgo.

their victims' brains through holes punctured in the base of their necks, but in the final sequences, when they have trapped the protagonists in a remote house, they gradually take form, revealing themselves to be disembodied brains trailing writhing spinal cords and twitching tendrils. The climax, where the brains smash their way into the house and attack the occupants, has a genuine nightmarish quality, and the special effects, featuring some clever stop-motion photography by Puppel Nordhoff and Peter Nielsen, are first-rate.

By the late 1950s the monster cycle in sf films had come to an end but, typically, one of the last major sf films made in Britain in that decade attempted to exploit the giant-monster-knocking-down-a-city type of story, a sub-category in the genre that had already run its course years before. Directed by Eugene Lourie, who had directed the prototype *Beast from 20,000 Fathoms* and the subsequent cheap imitation *Behemoth the Sea Monster*, it was called *Gorgo* and differed from its predecessors only in having a more lavish budget which enabled it to be shot in colour. The script, by John Loring and Daniel Hyatt, was full of the usual banal dialogue that seemed endemic to this type of production, but it did contain a couple of unusual twists, the main one being that the giant reptile captured off the coast of Ireland and then taken to London to be put on display turns out to be only a baby of the species in spite of being over twenty feet tall. He has an anxious mother looking for him back in the Irish Sea – a mother over 200 feet tall. Eventually mother Gorgo follows her kidnapped offspring to London and wrecks most of the city before returning to the sea with her reclaimed son.

According to the producers, Frank and Maurice King, the story had been suggested by their own mother and so they made the film as a tribute to 'mother love'. They were subsequently annoyed when the British censors declared it a 'horror film' and slapped an 'X' certificate on it.

On the technical level it featured some skilful optical effects by Tom Howard. The monsters were of the man-in-a-suit variety as opposed to animated models and occasionally looked a little unconvincing, but some of the scenes of destruction were very well staged, in particular one sequence where a long shot shows the giant creature methodically crashing through the city in the background while in the foreground frightened people flee from Piccadilly Circus. But for all its technical expertise the film was not a major financial success, and it marked the end of the giant monster genre for many years to come. The science fiction film was about to move off in a different direction.

6 Burn-out (1955–60)

Midway through the 1950s it seemed as if the Hollywood sf film was about to develop in an interesting new way when two films appeared: *This Island Earth* (1955) and *Forbidden Planet* (1956). Both contained all the ingredients of sf magazine 'space opera' – intergalactic adventures, dying or dead alien civilizations, vast, incredible machines and a great deal of super-science – a genre that had been popular with sf readers since the 1930s but until then hadn't been transferred to the screen. However, because of the need for plenty of special effects and elaborate sets, both films were very expensive to produce, and though they proved financially successful they weren't profitable enough to persuade other film companies to invest large amounts of money in similar films. So this development came to an end before it properly got started, and didn't surface again until the 1970s. After 1956 the Hollywood sf product, like the British sf films, took for the most part a major nose-dive in quality and the same period saw the take-over of the genre by the exploitation producers, who desperately began to wring what dollars they could out of the apparently fading sf boom by making films as cheap and sensational as possible. It was a time when film-makers like Roger Corman, Bert I. Gordon and Herman Cohen flourished on mindless productions, most of them made on tiny budgets. It was thanks to people like them that the sf film developed the bad reputation it is only now beginning to shed.

The crumbling surface of the doomed planet Metaluna in This Island Earth.

Of the two big 1950s space opera movies *Forbidden Planet* is by far the best, having a superior story, screenplay, cast and special effects, but there's no denying that *This Island Earth* possesses an absurd grandeur all its own. Produced at Universal by William Alland, who also produced Jack Arnold's sf/horror films, it was directed by Joseph Newman with a screenplay by Franklin Coen and Edward G. O'Callaghan based on the novel by science fiction writer Raymond F. Jones. Rex Reason starred as scientist Cal Meacham who receives a mysterious package in the mail containing a set of blueprints from some kind of electronic device. When he puts the bits and pieces together he ends up with a futuristic television set, the screen of which comes to life to show the face of a man with an unusually high forehead and white hair. Via the device the man (Jeff Morrow) informs Meacham that he has been selected, as a result of his

The cast of This Island Earth, *Jeff Morrow, Rex Reason, Faith Domergue and Lance Fuller, relax on the flying saucer set between takes.*

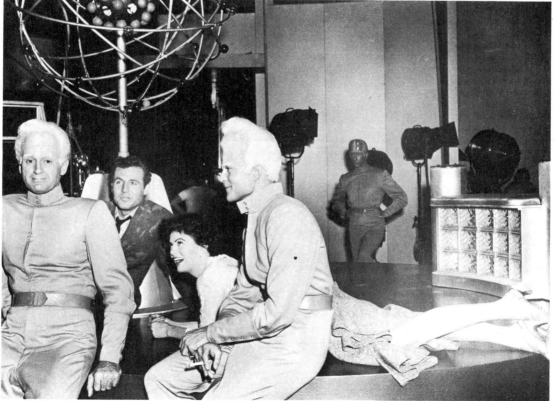

ability to construct the device, to take part in a secret scientific project of great importance. A remote-controlled plane then takes the scientist to an isolated mansion where he finds a number of the world's top scientists, including an old college friend Dr Ruth Adams (Faith Domergue) with whom he soon strikes up a tedious romantic relationship. He also meets the man who brought him there, Exeter, and his assistant Brack (Lance Fuller). Meacham, being a scientifically trained observer, notices that Brack has the same high forehead and white hair as Exeter and cleverly reasons out that there's 'something strange about those two'. After a lengthy build-up he and Dr Adams find themselves on a huge spaceship bound for the planet Metaluna, a world involved in the final stages of interplanetary war. Metaluna is nearing total defeat and in danger of being completely destroyed unless its defensive force-field can be maintained. Exeter and Brack had been sent to Earth to recruit fresh scientific talent, but by the time Meacham and Adams are brought to the planet it is already too late.

These sequences, showing the huge flying saucer arriving at the ravaged planet, and the subsequent scenes of alien ships guiding giant meteors in from space to crash down onto the surface, are the most spectacular in the film – a psychedelic light-show impressive for its spectacular artificiality, created by a combination of model work, matte paintings and superimpositions, all the work of special effects men Clifford Stine and Stanley Horsley (Stine was also the cinematographer on the film).

After the spaceship has landed Meacham and Adams are taken to meet the ruler of Metaluna, an incredibly old creature who tells them that the planet will soon be destroyed and that they are obliged to stay and share its fate. But as the force-field crumbles and the city begins to disintegrate Exeter has a change of heart towards the two Earthlings and rushes them back to the spaceship. It takes off just in time to avoid being obliterated with the rest of the planet but, unknown to all, with an unpleasant stowaway lurking below – one of a race of giant mutants created by the Metalunians to serve as their slaves. The mutant (actor Eddie Parker wearing a $24,000 costume) manages to wound Exeter fatally before being destroyed, but the alien succeeds in piloting the ship back to Earth. Meacham and Adams escape in an aircraft and the dying Exeter then sends the spaceship on its last journey – a spectacular sweep over the ocean which ends with the saucer, trailing flames, crashing into the sea.

This Island Earth may be seriously handicapped by a poor screenplay and by the long delay in the story before the action moves into outer space, but is saved by its truly amazing visuals. It deserves an important place in the history of the sf film for bringing to the screen for the first time familiar scenes that had previously only existed in the minds of sf pulp writers and in the lurid imaginations of their readers. (*Forbidden Planet* would do the same thing, as would *2001* and *Star Wars*.)

One reason why *Forbidden Planet* has a better story than *This Island Earth* is that it was originally written by William Shakespeare. Shakespeare's *The Tempest* happened to be special effects man Irving Block's favourite play and it was Block who, along with writing collaborator Allen Adler (nephew of the actor Luther Adler), wrote the original screen treatment for *Forbidden Planet*. The screenplay itself was written by Cyril Hume, who embellished the story but retained the basic Shakespearean plot-line. But whereas *The Tempest* was set on an island where the magician Prospero lives with his daughter Miranda, a hunch-backed witch-child called Caliban and the spirit Ariel, *Forbidden Planet* is set on a remote planet far in the future; the magician has become a scientist, Caliban a robot and Ariel an invisible monster created from a mixture of human lust and super-technology.

Directed by Fred McLeod Wilcox (best known previously for directing *Lassie Come Home* in 1943) *Forbidden Planet* begins with a spectacular display of special effects, foreshadowing the similar opening scenes in *Star Wars* two decades later. The credits, accompanied by the evocative electronic music of Louis and Bebe Barron, are presented against a backdrop of stars from which a space craft suddenly appears. This is United Planets Cruiser C-57D on a mission to trace an expedition from Earth that has been missing for years within the planetary system of the star Altair. A faint radio signal had been received from one of the planets, called Altair 4, and it is to this world that the spaceship is heading. The ship enters the Altair system – a sequence involving some magnificent special effects that are nearly as convincing as some of those in *2001* and *Star Wars* (particularly memorable is a shot where the enormous sun, Altair, is blocked by a planet, leaving only the spaceship silhouetted by the corona of the eclipse – the sort of imaginative detail usually only found on the covers of sf magazines at the time). The special effects and model work showing the saucer first skimming over the arid surface of Altair 4 and then landing in a cloud of dust were also of a very high standard, and the cut from miniature saucer to full-size set was deftly handled. Three model space cruisers were built: one six feet in diameter; one four feet and one only a foot and a half wide.

The spacemen, led by Commander Adams (Leslie Nielsen), discover that only one survivor of the original expedition remains – the coldly aloof scientist Dr Morbius (Walter Pidgeon); all the others mysteriously died shortly after arriving on the planet, including Morbius' wife. But the scientist is not alone; living with him in his luxurious home, which he built from the remains of the original spaceship, is his teenage daughter Altaira, born on Altair just before his wife died. Altaira (Anne Francis) is

a sexual innocent and, until the Earth ship arrives, had never seen another man apart from her father. The pair of them have apparently been living a life of idyllic ease, waited upon by their robot servant Robby, a miraculous piece of machinery that can manufacture almost anything from star sapphires to Bourbon (the robot was a complicated shell which contained over 2,600 feet of electrical wiring – needed for all the flashing lights and whirling gizmos in his head – and weighed over a hundred pounds; it was worn by a series of people during the making of the film, and its voice was provided by Marvin Miller).

The spaceship from Earth lands on the planet Altair IV in Forbidden Planet.

Morbius claims to have built Robby himself, a feat Commander Adams finds suspicious as Morbius wasn't an electronics expert but a specialist in languages. Finally Morbius is obliged to reveal the truth to the Earthmen: beneath the surface of Altair 4 lies the remains of a super-technological civilization belonging to an extinct race called the Krel. At the rear of his laboratory is a secret corridor that leads down into the bowels of the planet where the Krel machinery, built on an awesome scale, is still functioning automatically despite eons of activity. 'Prepare yourselves, gentlemen, for a new scale of physical scientific values!' announces Morbius as he prepares to show the Krel technological marvels to the Earthmen. They are then treated to a breathtaking series of sights, including an underground Krel railway, gigantic generators and the interior of an atomic furnace; most amazing of all is the dizzying view down into a generator shaft, full of moving electrical equipment, that is supposed to extend a total of 7,900 levels into the planet and actually looks as if it might. This effect was created by the team headed by A. Arnold Gillespie who filmed horizontally into a 'miniature' set nearly 150 feet long with a mirrored backdrop at the end of it. A further impression of size is created by a shot of the men walking across a ramp spanning the chasm and looking very small compared to everything around them. This was achieved by filming the actors from as high above as possible and then matting them into the miniature sets.

Naturally Commander Adams, surrounded by all this evidence of technological superiority, asks what happened to the Krel. Morbius is unable to answer, but his investigation of their records (decoding some of which enabled him to build Robby – basically just a Krel toy) shows that whatever did happen to them took place very suddenly, possibly in the space of a single day. He is unable to explain what all the energy produced by the Krel generators is for.

Meanwhile strange things are happening at night around the Earth spaceship – someone or something enters the ship, undetected by the guards, and destroys vital pieces of equipment. Suspicion naturally falls on Morbius and his robot, yet Morbius wants the Earthmen off 'his' planet as soon as possible. However, Altaira now falls in love with Commander

The Earthmen encounter Robby the Robot.

Adams and decides she wants to return to Earth with him. Morbius grudgingly admits that staying on Altair alone with him is hardly ideal for a young woman and gives his consent. But the following night there is another attack on the Earth ship, despite the erection of a radiation fence around the craft, which results in the death of two crewmen. The attacker is invisible but can be detected by the large footprints it creates in the soil. During the final attack the 'thing' is caught in the radiation from the fence and the blasts from several large ray projectors, and is revealed in the form of a fiery red outline (which resembles something out of a Walt Disney cartoon, unsurprisingly since it was created by Joshua Meador, a Walt Disney animator on loan to MGM). When it seems as if all the Earthmen are doomed the film cuts to Morbius asleep in the Krel laboratory, obviously in the grip of a nightmare, while in the background several of the Krel energy gauges register activity. A sudden cry from Altaira wakes Morbius up, and as he awakens the gauges fade out, while back at the spaceship the monster suddenly vanishes.

All becomes clear when Adams arrives at the Morbius house soon afterwards – there was no way, he tells Morbius, that the creature could have existed within the onslaught of deadly rays unleashed by him and his men unless it consisted of pure energy, and the source of the energy had to be the Krel power system. At last Morbius realizes the truth, and at the same time discovers what destroyed the Krel. They had built the vast underground energy complex in order to materialize from thin air whatever they desired. It was to have been the crowning achievement in their technical development, but instead it destroyed them for the device, once activated, gave substance to all the sadistic, vicious and murderous desires that still existed in the subconscious mind of each member of the Krel race, despite their high level of civilization. 'My poor Krel!' cries Morbius, 'destroyed by monsters from their own Ids!' At that moment his own Id monster makes a reappearance, knocking over several trees in the garden outside, then punching its invisible way through the steel shutters that automatically spring up around the house to bar its way. Morbius' subconscious is determined to prevent his daughter from being taken away from him by these young male invaders, even if it means destroying her as well. Only when Morbius faces up to this final truth does his monster from the Id disappear, just as it breaks through the final door into the Krel laboratory where he, Altaira and Adams had taken refuge. As the monster dies so does he (it isn't clear why), but before he expires he has time to give his future son-in-law instructions on how to blow up the planet. The film ends with Adams, Altaira, Robby and the surviving crew members watching from the spaceship en route to Earth as Altair 4 explodes into a nova-like flare of light. 'Lets hope when the human race reaches the same level of development as the Krel it will be better equipped to handle it,' says Adams.

The sophistication of *Forbidden Planet's* underlying Freudian themes was unusual for an sf film at that time, as was the subtlety with which they were handled. Block himself takes much of the credit for this: 'The idea of a bug-eyed monster is pretty childish,' he said, 'but there are real monsters and demons that exist within us that we know nothing about. We're capable of doing the most horrendous things and we're often shocked at this truism. The Monster from the Id is nothing more than the invisible demonic spirit of Morbius. That's why the monster is invisible.'[24] But the idea of an invisible monster didn't appeal to the MGM executives, and when Block was first describing the story to producer Nicholas Nayfack he was asked: 'How can you see an invisible monster?' Block replied: 'You can't. That's the point. It's very scary. When you see something it's not half as frightening as your imagination.' To which the producer said: 'But how will you know it's there?'[25] Block managed to convince the producer that it was a practicable idea but the other MGM executives couldn't accept a totally invisible monster, so they hired the Disney studio to give substance to the subconscious mind and of course they failed miserably. (Ironically, the film provided the Australian film censors of the 1950s – who ruthlessly butchered countless films – with their one instance of actually improving a film by their indiscriminate cutting; fearing the effect on children they removed the Disney creature from the film, thus making the sequence much more horrifying.)

At least MGM didn't insist that the extinct Krel be revealed as well. The only hint in the film comes from the shape of their doorways, all of which are triangular, yet the Krel presence remains a strong one. This is one of many examples of how *Forbidden Planet* doesn't treat its audience condescendingly, unlike so many sf films. It also takes for granted that the audience will be familiar with written sf, as it incorporates a number of traditional sf concepts and devices into the story. One example is the use of Isaac Asimov's 'Three Laws of Robotics' in the programming of Robby, which prevent him from any action that may cause harm to a human being. When given a direct order to kill, Robby simply short-circuits instead – a gimmick cleverly made use of near the end of the film when the robot is ordered to stop the invisible monster but is unable to move, thus providing further proof that the monster is Morbius himself. (Robby was designed by the Japanese draughtsman Bob Kinoshita, who also designed the interior of the space cruiser and the underground Krel machinery.)

That excellent science fiction writer Bob Shaw once said, when describing the way sf appealed to him as a youth, that good sf produced a mind-stretching effect: 'In those days you read certain authors and you could feel your mind opening. A. E. Van Vogt was very good at doing this. The first adult sf story I ever read was one of his in *Astounding*. It was one in his series about the "Mixed Men", man-made humans who had double brains and could switch their IQs up to 800 in an instant when the need arose. In the opening sentences of that particular story there was a whole bookful of ideas and it literally blew my mind.' It is very rare for an sf film to produce such an effect, but *Forbidden Planet* did so when it was first released. Other sf films that have revelled in ideas – in playing with audacious concepts and cosmic themes – in the same way as much of written sf does can probably be counted on the fingers of one hand: *Things to Come*, perhaps, can be included; *2001: A Space Odyssey* certainly, and *Quatermass and the Pit* (*Close Encounters of the Third Kind* and *Star Wars* definitely don't qualify in this area).

While *Forbidden Planet* remains for most sf fans the favourite sf film of the 1950s, movie buffs usually prefer to cite *Invasion of the Body Snatchers* as the best sf film of the period. Made in 1956 it was directed by Don Siegel, who has now acquired a cult following, and written by Daniel Mainwaring and Sam Peckinpah. Based on a novel by Jack Finney it is basically a variation on the old possession theme which had already been used in several 1950s sf films like *The Quatermass Experiment, Invaders from Mars* and *Quatermass II*. The film begins with a doctor (Kevin McCarthy) returning to his small Californian town after attending a medical convention and noticing that a lot of the townspeople have

King Donovan examines his 'pod' double, with Carolyn Jones, Kevin McCarthy and Dana Wynter looking on, in Invasion of the Body Snatchers.

'changed' in some way while he was gone. After resuming a relationship with his one-time fiancée Becky Driscoll (Dana Wynter) he learns that she too is aware of something wrong in the town. Later, during a visit to mutual friends Jack and Theodora Velichec (King Donovan and Carolyn Jones), a pod-shaped object is found growing in the Velichecs' greenhouse. When it opens it reveals a half-formed human figure in the exact likeness of Jack Velichec himself. Eventually it is found that there are many of these pods about and that they represent an alien invasion of Earth; the pods adopt the appearance of people, then replace or incorporate them when the victims are asleep. Finally the whole town is taken over with the exception of the doctor, who escapes to give the alarm to the rest of the country. Originally the film ended with him vainly trying to persuade passing motorists to stop and listen to his warnings, but the production company, Allied Artists, decided this was too downbeat an ending and insisted that further footage be shot showing him convincing the police of the danger.

Invasion of the Body Snatchers is now regarded by film scholars as a masterful piece of political allegory, though just which end of the political spectrum the pods are supposed to represent is difficult to say. Siegel himself doesn't give much away: 'People are pods. Many of my associates are certainly pods. They have no feelings. They exist, breathe, sleep. To be a pod means that you have no passion, no anger, the spark has left you . . . of course there's a very strong case for being a pod. These pods, who get rid of pain, ill-health and mental disturbances are, in a sense, doing good. It happens to leave you in a very dull world but that, by the way, is the world that most of us live in. It's the same as people who welcome going into the army or prison. There's regimentation, a lack of having to make up your mind, face decisions . . . People are becoming vegetables. I don't know what the answer is except an awareness of it. That's what makes a picture like *Invasion of the Body Snatchers* important.'[26]

No doubt Roger Corman could claim a similar importance for *It Conquered the World*, which he produced and directed in 1956, as it too is about people being taken over by an invader from outer space. Lee Van Cleef, who later followed Clint Eastwood into the world of Italian westerns, stars as a scientist who is seduced with promises of fame and fortune by a Venusian who needs some assistance in conquering the Earth. This Venusian needs all the help it can get as it resembles Humpty Dumpty and is just about as manoeuvrable. Living in a cave, it sends out little flying-bat creatures which fasten on people's necks and plant electrons in their spines, making them puppets of the alien's will. Eventually the scientist has a change of heart after his wife falls victim to the thing, and he decides to destroy it. In the film's hilarious climax we first see the creature ignoring a fusillade of army bullets and bazooka shells and then being

One army officer doesn't seem too worried by this threat from outer space in the 1956 Roger Corman film It Conquered the World.

overcome by the scientist, who wields a simple blow-torch. (Inside the Venusian 'costume' was Paul Blaisdell, who also handled the special effects on the picture.)

Mind-control is one of the themes in *Earth vs. the Flying Saucers* (1956), but this film, directed by Fred F. Sears and featuring the special effects of Ray Harryhausen, is much more polished and entertaining than Corman's cheap little disaster. Written by George Worthing Yates and Raymond T. Marcus from a story by Curt Siodmak, it was one of the few sf movies to live up to its title and accompanying posters, being full of spectacular sequences involving huge flying saucers, ray guns and weird aliens, and ending with an exciting battle between the Earth forces and the UFOs over the city of Washington DC during which a number of famous landmarks are destroyed by falling saucers. It is a silly film but great fun to watch, thanks mainly to Harryhausen's superbly animated UFOs. 'A prime fascination to me,' wrote Harryhausen later, 'was the challenge of seeing just how interesting one could make an inanimate object such as a rounded metal spaceship. Although the variations were limited for stop-motion they did provide the potential for doing something a little different than the other "saucer pictures" of the time.'[27]

An alien invasion of a different nature was the subject of *The Twenty-Seventh Day* (1956) directed by William Asher from a screenplay by John Mantley based on his own novel. Gene Barry (of *War of the Worlds* fame) starred in this typically 1950-ish morality tale about an alien who gives each of five people, in five different countries, a box of capsules which are capable of destroying all human life on any one continent. It appears that the aliens want to take over Earth but are prevented from direct aggression by a somewhat curious moral code, so they are trying to arrange for the various leading nations to wipe each other out. As the capsules will only respond to the telepathic commands of the actual recipients of the boxes the governments of the five countries each insist that their 'chosen one' use his/her power to destroy their enemies. The five people refuse and all go into hiding. Eventually it is discovered by one of them that the aliens are only using the capsules as a means of testing mankind's 'maturity'. In a climax which is chilling in a way the makers didn't intend the capsules selectively kill off 'every enemy of human freedom' in the world.

One wonders what George Orwell would have said about such an idea, but if he'd been alive in 1956 he would no doubt have seen the film version of his novel *1984*, and that doesn't bear thinking about. Directed by Michael Anderson, who later made such turgid genre films as *Doc Savage* and *Logan's Run*, it was scripted by William P. Templeton and Ralph Bettinsom and starred a totally miscast Edmund O'Brien as Winston Smith, the clerk in the Ministry of Information who decides to rebel against the totalitarian nightmare of 1984 where the TV sets do the watching. Together with his lover Julia (Jan Sterling) he creates a private world of his own for a brief time away from the ever-present gaze of Big Brother (the State's symbol of power) but is betrayed by a government official called O'Connor (in the book the character was called O'Brien), played by Michael Redgrave giving the best performance in the film, posing a a revolutionary in order to uncover potential dissidents. Two different endings were shot: one for the American market and one for the British. The former followed the book by having Winston and Julia successfully brainwashed and turned into devoted supporters of Big Brother, whereas the British version, incredibly, had them overcoming their conditioning and dying, hand-in-hand, in a hail of bullets while defiantly shouting 'Down with Big Brother!', an ending which completely vitiates Orwell's theme.

The year 1957 proved a tepid one for sf films, with only a few bright spots. AIP's *Invasion of the Saucer Men* was a pure exploitation movie designed for teenage audiences at drive-ins and based on the story 'The Cosmic Frame' by sf pulp writer Paul W. Fairman.

Monsters were still crawling out of the sea in 1957 and among the most unusual were the giant snails in *The Monster That Challenged the World*, a small-budget exploitation movie that nevertheless contained a few memorable sequences. Directed by Arnold Laven (who later directed such films as *Slaughter on Tenth Avenue, Geronimo* and *Rough Night in Jericho*) it was written by Pat Fielder and David Duncan. As with *The Creature from the Black Lagoon* and *Jaws* the horror comes from the idea of something monstrous lurking below the surface of the water, and one of

Bestiality appears to be raising its ugly head in this publicity shot from The Monster That Challenged the World.

the most effective sequences takes place when a pair of young lovers go for a midnight swim. As in the similar sequence in *Jaws* the girl disappears but later, when two frogmen are searching the gloomy bed of the sea, a sudden close-up exposes her white, contorted face amid the flowing underwater weeds – a shock effect that was also repeated in *Jaws*.

Attack of the Crab Monsters was a film with a similar theme but a banal script, wooden acting and cheap special effects – a typical Roger Corman film of the 1950s. The most unusual menace from the sea appeared in *Kronos*, another cheap sf film devised by special effects men Irving Block and Jack Rabin. Directed by Kurt Neumann from a screenplay by Lawrence L. Goldman (Block wrote the original story) it concerned a giant machine, under the control of aliens, that rises out of the sea off the coast of California and then moves inland, its aim being to absorb energy

A typically absurd-looking Roger Corman monster in his Attack of the Crab Monsters.

from American power stations and transmit it to the energy-starved aliens above. Kronos itself resembles two giant cubes joined together and moves by means of two giant piston rods that stamp up and down beneath it. Block later described how the final design had come about: 'I wanted it to be anthropomorphic, to look like a robot, but at the same time I wanted it to look like a piece of machinery. I spent a lot of time on it, it didn't come just like that! It was a long process . . . at one time it looked more like a construction by Picasso, but I reduced it down a whole series of steps until it ultimately became just a black box.' Describing the problems of making an sf film on such a low budget Block said: 'Some of the big scenes in the desert were nothing more than a white sheet with sand thrown on it, but it looks pretty damn good with the airplanes zooming in on it. Some of the scenes were paintings and some were models. There's a scene where a helicopter lands on Kronos. Well, we couldn't do anything like that. So we had the helicopter land on top of Hansen Dam, then we just took the dam and everything out of the scene and put Kronos in its place and did a blend with the sky. The actors had no idea what was going on. They were just standing on top of the dam moving around. Sometimes they'd get very confused. At times in the film, aside from the fact that they're maybe not the greatest actors, or they don't have the greatest direction or time, their acting is a littly corny. Well, you can't blame them because they're just acting to something which isn't in existence. They were always surprised to see the finished film.'[28]

No doubt the same applied to the actors in *20 Million Miles to Earth*, another predictable Charles H. Schneer and Ray Harryhausen production featuring the latter's model animation skills. Directed by Nathan Juran from a screenplay by Bob Williams and Christopher Knopf, it starred William Hopper (Hedda Hopper's son, who became best known for his rôle as the private detective in the long-running TV series *Perry Mason*), Joan Taylor, Frank Puglia and Thomas B. Henry and concerned a creature brought back from Venus that breaks loose in Italy. Called a 'Ymir' the thing looks like a humanoid dinosaur with a distinctly feline face, but its most unusual feature is that it won't stop growing and by the end of the picture becomes a giant.

That same year Harryhausen's mentor, Willis H. O'Brien, was also working on an sf/monster film. Called *The Black Scorpion* it had many similarities to the earlier, and superior, film *Them!* and concerned a horde of giant scorpions which emerge from a cavern beneath the Mexican desert to devour cattle, horses, people and anything else available. They are, of course, mutations created by atomic radiation, and as with the Harryhausen film the special effects provided the only interest.

Probably the most interesting sf film of 1957 was Jack Arnold's *The Incredible Shrinking Man*. After passing through a radioactive cloud (what else?) while on a motor boat, the man begins to decrease in size, slowly at first, and then much faster. By the time he's a mere three foot tall it's become obvious to both his wife and himself that things are never going to be the same again. Believing that the shrinking has stopped he strikes up a relationship with an attractive midget girl he meets in a park, but the affair comes to an end when he realizes that he is growing still smaller. Reduced to living in a doll's house he makes a brave attempt at coming to terms with things but suffers a further disaster when his pet cat, which gets into the room while his wife is out shopping, attacks the doll's house and attempts to eat him. Fleeing the cat he falls down the steps into the cellar and enters a whole new world of nightmare where a leaking boiler seems like the Niagara Falls and an ordinary spider is like a Volkswagen on legs. He finally overcomes all the threats to his survival but still continues to shrink, and we last see him preparing to leave the cellar (he is now small enough to pass through a fly-wire screen) and go into the garden. 'To God there is no zero. I still exist,' we hear him say as he disappears completely.

Scientifically it's nonsense (it ignores the problems of mass), but it is still good science fiction because its central protagonist undergoes a science-related experience which fundamentally alters his perception of the universe. It is also a multi-layered film, its underlying theme being not so much concerned with the physical problems of a man who shrinks but with the basic psychological fears that his bizarre situation stands metaphor for, such as the fear of ceasing to exist as a separate entity – of dying, in fact – and of sexual inadequacy. The 'shrinking man' first becomes as a child compared to his adult-sized wife, then reaches the point where he is kept by her in a doll's house – the ultimate sexual humiliation. Basically the film is an exercise in paranoia in that it concerns a man who realizes that all his familiar and comfortable surroundings, including his wife and neighbours, are becoming increasingly threatening – that his world is not the safe place it seemed but one of pure nightmare. The author of the book on which the film is based and the screenplay itself was Richard Matheson, a writer who has based his career on exploring aspects of paranoia (his novel *I Am Legend*, which has been filmed twice, is probably the ultimate paranoia story, though his script for the film *Duel* comes a close second).

On the technical level the film was also above-average with intelligent direction by Jack Arnold, fairly convincing special effects by Clifford Stine (the matte and split-screen work is very good), and the cast deliver capable performances, especially Grant Williams as the shrinking man and Randy Stuart as his wife.

The success of *The Incredible Shrinking Man* produced the inevitable cheap imitations, one of the first being *The Amazing Colossal Man* produced and directed the same year by Bert I. Gordon, a film-maker so determinedly crass in his work that he makes Roger Corman look by comparison like the genius many people say he is (Gordon is currently enjoying a comeback, thanks to the sf boom, and is doing his best to destroy the reputation of H. G. Wells with such films as *Food of the Gods* and *Empire of the Ants*). Glenn Langan starred as an army officer who is caught in yet another atomic explosion which causes him to grow into a giant. Unable to cope, he goes insane and starts on a rampage of destruction, demolishing cardboard buildings and equally cardboard characters before being destroyed himself (the clumsy special effects were also the work of Bert I. Gordon).

Even worse was *Attack of the 50 Foot Woman* made the following year by Allied Artists and directed by Nathan Juran (who had himself credited as Nathan Hertz) from a screenplay by Mark Hanna, who had also written *The Amazing Colossal Man*. Allison Hayes, whose first leading role was in one of the Francis the Talking Mule movies, starred as Nancy Archer, the woman who sees a flying saucer land in the desert shortly after she has been released from an insane asylum. Unwisely, she attempts to tell the police and then her husband, but no one believes her. Her husband, however, is pleased by this evidence of continuing insanity because it will enable him to have her recommitted and thereby leave him free to carry on his affair with Honey Parker (Yvette Vickers). But before the men in the white coats arrive Nancy flees into the desert where she encounters a monster from outer space, who promptly zaps her with a mysterious ray which turns her into the 50-foot woman of the title. Eager for revenge on her two-timing husband she returns to town and starts demolishing houses in her efforts to locate him, prompting the following conversation between two of the characters: 'She'll tear up the whole town until she finds Harry.' 'Yeah – and then she'll tear up Harry.'

In 1958 there was little to recommend in the way of sf movies, being the year of *The Blob* and *The Fly*. About the most interesting thing in *The Blob* was Steve McQueen masquerading as a typical movie teenager, but his natural screen presence and his age (he was then 26) worked against him, as did the script by Theodore Simonson and Kate Philips, the special effects by Barton Sloane, the title song by Bert Bacharach and Mack David, and so on.

More impressive as far as special effects were concerned was a Japanese film with a similar theme called *Bijo To Ekitain-in-Gen* (roughly translated, it means *Beautiful Women and the Hydro-man*), made by the same Toho Studio team responsible for *Godzilla*. Released as *The H-Man* outside Japan it begins with the crew of a fishing boat encountering a drifting freighter in a thick fog. A search of the vessel reveals no sign of life, but the nervous fishermen find several piles of empty clothing with the underwear inside the outer garments. Green slime runs up the leg of the nearest fisherman and dissolves him on the spot. Once again atomic radiation is the culprit; the monster reaches Tokyo where it slithers in and out of drains, under doors and through windows, dissolving and absorbing anyone it can catch. The 'blob's' various activities are well-staged by effects man Eiji Tsuburaya, and the high point comes when it invades a strip club and dissolves a couple of dancers, leaving nothing behind but their G-strings. Many scenes involved the use of full-size, inflatable dummies filmed at high speed as the air was let out. The film was directed by Inoshiro Honda and written by Takeshi Kimura and Hideo Kaijo.

Another effective movie monster made an appearance in 1958 in *It! The Terror from Beyond Space*. Though a low-budget, exploitation production it was scripted by science fiction writer Jerome Bixby and was a little more ingenious than others of its type. Set in 1972 it concerns a spaceship sent to Mars to find out what happened to the first Mars expedition that took place in 1968. Just before the ship takes off for the return trip to Earth a large, shadowy figure enters through one of the hatches, unknown to the men on board. After a battle of wits between the Martian and the Earthmen, and just as the monster starts to smash its way through the final hatch-cover and enter the nose-cone, someone has the bright idea of donning space suits and letting the air out of the ship. The ploy works, and no sooner has 'it' emerged into view than it expires through lack of oxygen.

As with *The Thing* the monster in *It* works best when it is a shadowy shape but loses all its menace when it comes into plain view at the end of the film, looking very much like a man in a costume (played by Ray 'Crash' Corrigan). Though he doesn't receive any credit, the plot is suspiciously close to A. E. Van Vogt's 1939 story 'The Black Destroyer', which later became incorporated into his novel *Voyage of the Space Beagle* and also concerned an alien monster which invades a spaceship and stores the bodies of its victims in the ventilation system, laying eggs in them as a wasp does with caterpillars. The same story, again uncredited, seems to have been used as the basis for Ridley Scott's 1978 sf movie, *Alien* (the original treatment was by Dan O'Bannon of *Dark Star* fame).

The year 1958 also saw *From the Earth to the Moon*, scripted by Robert Blees and James Leicester. Like the other 1950s Jules Verne adaptation, *20,000 Leagues*, they rightly set it in Victorian times, but whereas Fleischer and his scriptwriter managed to improve and build on Verne's original, Blees and Leicester reduced Verne's story to one of the most boring sf movies ever made. A good cast, including Joseph Cotton, George Sanders, Henry Daniell and Debra Paget, struggled bravely with the script but eventually fail to invest the proceedings with any semblance of life.

In a different kind of trouble was Gloria Talbot, co-star of *I Married a Monster from Outer Space*, which was produced and directed by Gene Fowler. If *The Incredible Shrinking Man* reflected male sexual fears, then Fowler's film represented female ones – the ultimate feminist nightmare that lurking behind the handsome facade of one's husband is a foul monster whose only interest is the exploitation of the female body. Anyway, that's what Gloria Talbot as Marge Farrell discovers about her handsome husband, Bill Farrell (played by Tom Tryon, now better known as a novelist), shortly after their wedding day. After being inexplicably late for the wedding he turns up acting like one of Siegel's Pod People, cold and emotionless, causing her to grow increasingly worried about him.

As in *Invasion of the Body Snatchers* it turns out that the whole town, including Farrell, has been infiltrated by these doppelgangers. Political implications, as well as feminist ones, can be read into the film, particularly as the title is similar to the earlier *I Married a Communist*, but the film succeeds purely on the level of creepy sf/horror film with the emphasis on horror rather than sf. No doubt if the film is remade it will be titled *I Married a Male Chauvinist Pig from Outer Space*.

A woman whose husband undergoes an unpleasant change was also the theme of *The Fly*, directed by Kurt Neumann, the German film-maker whose previous sf films had been *Rocketship XM* and *Kronos*. Despite an unusually absurd story *The Fly* turned out to be the surprise financial success of 1958, mainly because of the cunning approach adopted by Neumann, who also produced it. Instead of making another cheap, exploitation movie he hired a good scriptwriter (James Clavell) and a good cast and shot the film in colour. He also insisted that the cast play it absolutely straight, though it must have been difficult at times and

Tom Tryon confronts an alien over the question of just who is really married to Gloria Talbot in this publicity still from I Married a Monster from Outer Space.

Vincent Price has his usual trouble keeping his tongue out of his cheek. Patricia Owens played Helene who, at the start of the film, has been arrested for crushing her husband's head to a pulp in a giant steam press. In flashback we learn of the events which led her to take this extreme action. It seems that the husband (Al Hedison, who later changed his name to David) was a scientist engaged in experimenting with a matter transmitter in the basement of their house and one day had a nasty accident. She starts suspecting that something is wrong when he won't come out of the basement and starts asking for bowls of milk to be left outside the door. When she finally persuades him to let her in he greets her by draping a napkin over her head and then, via a series of notes, asking her to track down a certain fly that's loose in the house: a fly with curious white markings. We discover that, during an experiment, the scientist had become physically mixed up with an ordinary house fly which had got into one of the transmitter cabinets; the result is that he now has the head and arm of the fly while the fly has his head and arm. But how is it that the scientist still seems to have his brain within the fly's head now firmly established upon his shoulders? At the end of the film, after his wife has done the right thing by crushing him in the steam press, we see a close-up of a fly caught in a web complete with tiny human head and arm and squealing: 'Help me! Help me!' (His brother, played by Vincent Price, promptly hits him with a rock.) So what happened to the fly's brain? And why do the doctors, who perform the autopsy on the scientist's full-size body, fail to detect that the crushed parts belonged to a large fly?

Apart from grotesque husbands 1958 was also a good year for children in sf films, seeing the release of *The Space Children* and *The Invisible Boy*. The former was a Paramount production made by the same producer and director (William Alland and Jack Arnold) responsible for most of Universal's sf/horror movies during the 1950s, and it included in the production team such Hollywood veterans as John P. Fulton (*The Invisible Man* special effects), art director Hal Pereira (*War of the Worlds*) and cameraman Ernest Laszlo (*Fantastic Voyage*). Yet the film itself was a small-budget entry about a group of children whose parents work for a nuclear-missile development complex on the Californian coast. The children discover a brain-like organism in a cave on the beach, which is actually an extra-terrestrial super-being. It takes over their minds and uses them as tools to sabotage the missile programme which it regards as a threat to life on Earth and in outer space. According to one film historian the film deals with 'alienation between adults and children' and even John Baxter, in his book *Science Fiction in the Cinema*, describes it as 'restrained and thoughtful . . . containing the best of Arnold's mature work', but it's a dull and rather pretentious children's film in which a 'superior' alien comes to Earth to demonstrate to the natives that, basically, Might is Right (in this case the alien proves his point by killing one boy's father when the latter attempts to beat him).

Much more fun was MGM's *The Invisible Boy*, not a later instalment in the Invisible Man series but a kind of sequel to *Forbidden Planet* in that it was produced by Nicholas Nayfack and scripted by Cyril Hume, both of whom had performed similar functions on *Forbidden Planet*. It also starred Robby the Robot. Based on an original treatment by Edmund Cooper, it was aimed purely at kids and had a freewheeling plot that involved a young boy (Richard Eyer) assembling his own robot from pieces of equipment brought back from the future by a time-travelling uncle. Robby falls under the influence of an evil super-computer that is trying to take over the world by inserting transmitters into the brains of government and military officials, but he finally saves the day by refusing an order to kill his juvenile creator and instead destroys the computer. Even though a children's film, *The Invisible Boy* was much nearer pulp magazine sf with its way-out storyline than many sf movies of the 1950s.

Fear of the atom bomb was still, at the end of the 1950s, being reflected in the Hollywood product. In 1958 *The World, the Flesh and the Devil* was released, an MGM film written and directed by Ranald MacDougall (a writer whose previous film work included *Objective Burma* in 1945 and *Possessed* in 1947) and based very loosely on Matthew Phipp Shiel's novel *The Purple Cloud*. Similar to Arch Oboler's 1951 production *Five*, in this case the film reduces the number of survivors in a nuclear-bomb-ravaged America to three – a girl played by Inger Stevens, a black man played by the charming Harry Belafonte, and a cynical, world-weary adventurer played by Mel Ferrer. Compared to Oboler's talkative and dreary film, MacDougall's post-atomic war vision is superior in both script and direction. The plot is simple: black man finds white girl, white male racist finds both, and trouble develops. However, the film ends with all three of them walking off into the sunset together – the first post-nuclear war *ménage à trois*.

The final word on the atom bomb in the 1950s came from Stanley Kramer, whose 1959 production of *On the Beach* was based on the novel by Nevil Shute. The film is set in Melbourne ('the perfect place to make a film about the end of the world,' said one of the stars, Ava Gardner) in 1964 after an atomic war has destroyed life in every part of the world except for the southernmost parts of Australia. As the deadly radioactive shroud moves slowly down from the north the people of Melbourne attempt to live their lives as normally as possible, despite the ever-present knowledge that they will all soon die hideously of radiation sickness. Also stranded in Melbourne is an American nuclear submarine, and one of the film's most memorable sequences involves a voyage it makes to California to investigate the source of a radio signal, only to discover that this has

Ava Gardner and Stanley Kramer (right) on location in Melbourne, Australia, which provided the setting for the end of the world in On the Beach.

been caused by a window shade blowing against a morse code key. The crew realize that, as they feared, America is totally without life.

As the radiation reaches Melbourne the people are offered the choice of taking suicide pills, but some prefer alternative methods of dying. Racing-car enthusiast Fred Astaire prefers to go via carbon monoxide poisoning, while the crew of the American submarine decide to head out to sea on a voyage to nowhere. Despite its flaws of mawkish sentimentality and pretentiousness it remains a chillingly realistic portrayal of doom and despair in the face of an implacable force.

7 New Directions (1960–65)

Thematically science fiction films in the 1960s at last began to diversify and to get away from the bug-eyed monsters that typified the genre during the 1950s. There is no sf film made between 1960 and 1970 which can be said to be a typical 1960s sf film, though the new decade did see a small trend in satirical sf films such as *Dr Strangelove, Barbarella, The President's Analyst, The Day the Fish Came Out* and *The Bed Sitting Room*. The 1960s also blurred the edges between sf films and other cinema genres, a trend that began with the James Bond film *Dr No* in 1962, which assimilated traditional sf elements (mad scientist, futuristic laboratory, mysterious rays, rocketships) into the framework of an ultra-slick, contemporary action/thriller. Since the early days of cinema melodramas had often incorporated futuristic inventions into their storylines but the James Bond films helped make science fiction paraphernalia respectable. Suddenly the crazy Buck Rogers stuff was trendy, and as a result science fiction became an up-market commodity. This upward move was reflected by the sort of people who made sf films during the 1960s: in the previous decade the genre failed to attract big-name film-makers (except for Stanley Kramer) but in the 1960s directors like Hitchcock, Kubrick, Godard, Frankenheimer, Brook, Truffaut, Losey, Lumet, Schaffner and Sturges were all associated with sf cinema. This trend has now, in the late 1970s, reached its peak, since most of Hollywood's recent major productions have been science fiction films.

The 1960s also saw a move by the film-makers back to written sf as a source of original material, though Hollywood scriptwriters continued to 'adapt' and 'mould' the material into a state suitable for the screen, with the usual dire results. Once again the work of the old masters, Verne and Wells, was mined for filmable stories, along with the work of other sf writers like Conan Doyle, John Wyndham, Ray Bradbury, Arthur C. Clarke, and Robert Sheckley. *Journey to the Centre of the Earth* (actually made in 1959) began this new cycle of films adapted from sf classics and was a moderately entertaining production despite the presence of Pat Boone in the lead role. Fortunately James Mason was also present and contributed his usual quota of style and charm. He played a Scottish professor by the name of Lindenbrook who is given a paperweight and discovers that it contains a message from a man who had reached the centre of the Earth. He immediately decides to launch a similar expedition, taking with him his daughter (Diane Baker), one of his students (Pat Boone), the widow of a colleague (Arlene Dahl), and an Icelandic guide (Peter Ronson) and his duck, Gertrude. Scriptwriters Walter Reisch and Charles Brackett (the latter also produced the film) turned Verne's somewhat gloomy and claustrophobic novel into a tongue-in-cheek romp with plenty of colourful sets and special effects, but the overall tone of the film can best be demonstrated by the ending, which has Pat Boone blown out of a volcano, losing his clothes in the process, and landing in a tree where he is discovered by a couple of passing nuns. The director was Henry Levin.

Among those who have kneed science fiction in the groin Irwin Allen must rank high. A former literary agent, he began producing films for RKO in 1951, and in 1953 won an Academy Award for a pseudo-documentary called *The Sea Around Us* which he wrote and directed. In 1956 he made a similar film called *The Animal World* which included animated dinosaur sequences created by Willis H. O'Brien and Ray Harryhausen, and in 1957 he made the bizarre *The Story of Mankind*, in which Cedric Hardwicke played a godlike figure sitting in a cloud and holding a heavenly court to decide whether mankind should be destroyed by an atomic war, and in which Harpo Marx played Sir Isaac Newton. Then, in 1960, Allen discovered science fiction and the genre has never been the same since, particularly since a few years later he began producing the first of many sf television series and went on to dominate the medium with his particular brand of sf during the rest of the 1960s. Allen's approach is appallingly juvenile: he ignores logic, scientific facts, characterization and story construction, and simply concentrates on producing as many spectacular special effects sequences as possible. It is a formula that has worked well for him over the years, more recently with *The Poseidon Adventure* and *The Towering Inferno* (his latest production is *Swarm,* about a horde of killer bees).

His first sf film was a remake of *The Lost World* in 1960, and his attitude towards the genre was obvious from the start in this lifeless, mechanical and clumsy version of Conan Doyle's story. The special effects, supervised by L. B. Abbott, are adequately colourful but unlike the 1925 version the various dinosaurs are portrayed by photographically enlarged real-life lizards, whose death throes, when the plateau is engulfed by the inevitable volcanic fires, are alarmingly realistic.

A more successful variation on the same theme was the Schneer/Harryhausen remake of *Mysterious Island* produced the following year. It took the usual liberties with the Verne original in order to incorporate Harryhausen's model animation, but the result was a

Not *a giant chicken, but a prehistoric Phorohacos, one of the creatures in* Mysterious Island.

modestly entertaining fantasy-adventure film, primarily aimed at children. Not only do the castaways have to cope with a giant crab, giant bees, a giant octopus and a giant bird ('It was a prehistoric Phorohacos,'[29] said Harryhausen, 'but owing to script deletions its antediluvian origin was discarded. Most reviewers and audiences assumed it to be an overgrown chicken'), but they also encountered the famous Captain Nemo and his submarine, the Nautilus. They learn that it was Nemo (a fine portrayal by Herbert Lom) who was responsible for all the giant animals; they were the result of his experiments on forced-food growth, the benefits of which he intended to pass on to mankind when a volcanic eruption (what else?) traps him in the Nautilus and once again he goes down with the ship. Good, tight direction was by Cy Endfield and a better than average script (for a Schneer/Harryhausen production) by John Prebble, Daniel Ullman and Crane Wilbur.

George Pal made one of his best sf films in 1960, a version of H. G. Wells's *The Time Machine*. Rod Taylor starred as the Victorian inventor who builds a time machine (beautifully designed by the film's art directors George W. Davis and William Ferrari) and zooms off into the future, pausing along the way to watch London destroyed in an atomic war, before finishing up in the year 802,701 AD. As in the Wells story he finds a world divided into two distinct groups: the child-like Eloi who spend all their time playing games, eating and drinking; and the monstrous Morlocks who tend their machines below the ground and who are in reality breeding the Eloi for food. But whereas Wells's time traveller was a

The menacing Morlocks in George Pal's The Time Machine.

somewhat passive observer the Pal character takes positive action, and he saves the Eloi in spite of themselves. He may dress like a Victorian Englishman but Rod Taylor's time traveller is actually an all-American, two-fisted hero who brings to the Eloi the profound message that a good punch on the jaw will solve anything. His example finally jolts them out of their fatal lethargy and within moments they are all gleefully committing acts of violence. With their assistance the time traveller manages to set fire to the Morlocks' underground establishment and everyone lives happily ever after, providing the Morlocks from neighbouring districts don't move in (are all the Eloi and Morlocks in the world restricted to one small area?).

Though the film drastically simplified Wells's original story, visually it almost makes up for its thematic short-comings. The time-travelling sequences are especially evocative, with nice use being made of a shop window dummy to suggest the passing of the years by rapid changes in fashion, thanks to cameraman Paul C. Vogel and effects men Gene Warren and Wah Chang; and make-up man William Tuttle produced some suitably ugly Morlocks. The script was by David Duncan.

After the many pleasures provided by *The Time Machine* Pal's next film, *Atlantis, the Lost Continent* (1961), came as a severe let-down. Even the MGM special effects team were unable to produce much entertainment, though their model Atlantean submarine, in the shape of a large

Berry Kroeger as an Atlantean scientist performing some bizarre surgery on an unamused victim in Atlantis, the Lost Continent.

fish, had a lot of charm and moved very realistically. The scenes of destruction at the end of the film also suffered from the shoe-string budget, despite being padded out with footage of Rome burning from *Quo Vadis?* (Oddly enough, in the final shots of Atlantis sinking into the sea, the tall mountain ranges in the background disappear from view *before* the city in the foreground does.)

The unlikely writing team of Jules Verne and Richard Matheson collaborated, despite a gap of over fifty years between their working lives, on AIP's *Master of the World* in 1961. Theoretically it incorporated material from two of Verne's novels *Robur the Conqueror* and *Master of the World*, but its plot seemed to be based on Disney's version of *20,000 Leagues Under the Sea*. Like the Nemo character created by Earl Fenton and Richard Fleischer for the Disney film, Robur (played by Vincent Price) doesn't bear much resemblance to Verne's creation but is an anti-war fanatic who uses his flying machine, the Albatross, as a weapon against the nations of the world in an attempt to force them to renounce war. As in the Disney film, *Master of the World* concerns a group of people captured by a mad genius, who keeps them imprisoned in his mysterious vehicle while he travels the world wreaking havoc and destruction. Finally Robur's captives succeed in sabotaging the flying ship and make their escape just before it blows up and hurtles out of control across the sea in a death dive, giving Vincent Price time to give his loyal, though doomed, crew a morale-boosting lecture along the same lines as the one James Mason delivered in the Disney film.

The model of the Albatross is quite impressive – it resembles an airship with a forest of windmills on top – but the special effects have an air of desperation about them. Effects men Tim Barr, Wah Chang, Gene Warren, Pat Dinga and Ray Mercer had to use every trick in the trade to stretch the available money, and this included using as much stock footage as possible: in one sequence the Albatross is supposed to be hovering over mid-19th-century London but the shots of the city reveal a medieval skyline – no wonder, considering that this footage dated from the 1944 production of *Henry V*. The director was William Witney and the cast, apart from Vincent Price, included Charles Bronson and Henry Hull.

The dread Irwin Allen made his own version of *20,000 Leagues* in 1961 under the title *Voyage to the Bottom of the Sea*. Setting his story in contemporary times, Allen packed a group of hackneyed characters into a glass-nosed submarine called the Seaview, loaded them with every plot cliché known to cinema audiences and sent them off to save the world. The film begins with the crew of the experimental submarine, while on a test run in the Arctic Sea, discovering that the Van Allen radiation belt is on fire. Fortunately the sub's inventor, Admiral Harriman Nelson (Walter Pidgeon), is on board and he also happens to be the world's foremost scientific genius. His solution is to fire a nuclear missile into the radiation belt from a certain point on the Equator. Not everyone agrees with him, however, and the United Nations send two submarines to stop him, but both implode when they attempt to follow the Seaview on a deep dive into the depths of the sea. Other objectors to the scheme include Dr Susan Hiller (Joan Fontaine), resident lady scientist on the Seaview, and Miguel Alvarez (Michael Ansara), the ship's resident religious fanatic who believes the fire in the sky is God's judgement, but Admiral Nelson wins out over all obstacles, including a giant octopus that happens to be passing, and fires his missile into the Van Allen belt. The film, though sneered at by critics and sf fans, was a financial success and spawned a long-running TV series of the same name.

There was fire in the sky in another 1961 sf movie – the British-made *The Day the Earth Caught Fire*, which was produced, directed and written (with assistance from Wolf Mankowitz) by Val Guest. It begins with strange weather conditions being experienced all over the world, the reason for which is a complete mystery until the science editor of the London *Daily Express* (played by Leo McKern) uncovers, with the help of another *Express* reporter (Edward Judd), the truth that the governments of the world are trying to hush up: two atomic detonations, one at the North Pole and one at the South, have pushed the world out of its orbit and set it on a course towards the sun. When the news is released there is,

The 'wrecked' front of the Daily Express *building in Fleet Street as it appears in* The Day the Earth Caught Fire.

predictably, panic across the world, but the film centres on events in London. As the temperature rises and the Thames dries up, forcing people to queue for water rations, rioting and looting break out. The film ends on an ambiguous note: four nuclear bombs are to be exploded simultaneously in different parts of the world with the intention of pushing the planet back into its right orbit. The final shot shows two *Daily Express* headlines already prepared: one reads 'World Saved'; the other 'World Doomed'.

'It was entirely my own idea,' said Guest. 'I'd been reading about all these people writing to *The Times* and saying how all these atomic tests were changing the atmosphere and the weather, and other people were saying: "What absolute rubbish!" but I suddenly thought: "What if these tests did do that? What could happen?" And these days I'm amazed when I see headlines practically the same as the ones we had printed for the *Express* in our film, such as "Incredible Summer!", "Floods Sweep Europe!"; "New Ice Age On The Way!" Everything that was in that picture has been happening recently. I read something about an enormous amount of ice melting at the North Pole that had made a displacement of water and caused the Earth to shift, very slightly, on its axis. And this is not very far off reversing the Poles, as I did in my picture.

'Actually I wrote the treatment for the film seven years before anyone would let me make it. Whenever I had a successful film the company concerned would say: "What would you like to do next?" And I would say: "Well, I'd like to do this science fiction story I've got." And they'd immediately say: "No one wants to know about the Bomb." And so the treatment got pushed aside and pushed aside. Eventually I found a producer here called Steven Pallos who was interested and between us we rustled up the money. I had made a lot of money from *Expresso Bongo*, a film I'd made in 1960, so I ploughed it into the film and Pallos and I became partners in producing it ourselves. Then I got hold of Wolf Mankowitz and said: "Do you want to come in on this? I can't afford to pay you yet but read it and let's do it together." So we wrote the script together, based on my treatment, and we both made an enormous amount of money on it, along with Steven Pallos. The money is still coming in.

'A lot of it was actually shot in the *Daily Express* offices. We were allowed to do that because I brought Arthur Christiansen, who had been the paper's greatest editor, into the picture (he played himself in the film) and he organized it with the paper's owner, Lord Beaverbrook. But it was an enormously difficult picture to make and we had to pull every known trick in the book to get some of the scenes we wanted in London. For instance I had to show Fleet Street completely deserted and desolate with windows boarded up, overturned buses and cars and an enormous layer of dust over everything, and I was told by the police: "No way can you do this to Fleet Street!" Well, we argued and argued. We went to see the top people at Scotland Yard, Chris called the Home Office, the Prime Minister . . . everyone, and finally they agreed to give us Fleet Street for three minutes at a time providing it wouldn't hold up traffic at peak periods. So we worked it out like a battle and timed it all perfectly: we would rehearse the scene when all the traffic was going by – the police had put up 'No Parking' signs all the way along the street from the *Express* building up to the Law Courts – and when we had our three minutes a whistle would be blown and they'd hold the traffic up at the Law Courts end. Then two motor-cycle policemen would tear up the street knocking down all the 'No Parking' signs followed by our prop van with about four guys shovelling out all this Fuller's Earth onto the road, so we then had Fleet Street covered in a haze of dust and dirt . . . and then we'd shoot our scene, all within three minutes. And if we didn't get the take we wanted then we had to let the whole thing go for at least a quarter of an hour. We had other props lying around as well, girders and things, and we had the front of the Express building so that it looked as if it had been shattered. One day the old man himself, Beaverbrook, went by and saw this and was aghast. He called up and cried: "What in Christ's name has happened to the *Express*?" Later he said to me: "I don't care what you do with the offices or the building but the day the *Daily Express* doesn't come out you're finished.''

'We also had terrible trouble getting Trafalgar Square for the sequence where we had a demonstration and a fight in the square. We had to book it months in advance with the police because they rent out the Square to various groups. Our big problem was money, of course. We didn't have a very big budget – we made it for under £300,000, though today to make the same film you'd need a ridiculous amount – so we had to use a lot of money-saving effects. Les Bowie did the special effects for me; I gave him a lump sum of money to do them and, of course, he did a hell of a good job. But we had terrible trouble with the sequence where the fog was supposed to come up the Thames and cover everything. We were shooting in Battersea Park beside the river and we had fog machines all over the place – we'd also emptied Battersea Bridge and put all our stuff on it, including a queue of people waiting for water rations – and it happened to be the day that the Queen was opening the Chelsea Flower Show, and the wind suddenly changed and all our fog drifted into Chelsea. Very embarrassing! The police came down and told us to turn off our machines but while my unit and location manager was saying to the police: "Yes, yes, we'll turn them off!" we just continued shooting as quickly as possible.'

While some sf film-makers were attempting to diversify others were still trying to exploit the old 'giant monster' formula. One such was Herman Cohen who, in the 1950s, had made *I Was a Teenage Frankenstien* and *I Was a Teenage Werewolf* for AIP. In 1960 he produced *Konga* (originally to have been called *I Was a Teenage Gorilla*) about a mad scientist (Michael Gough) whose wife turns a chimp into a giant ape. When asked why he had an innocent girl killed in the film, Cohen replied: 'I wanted to use my carnivorous plants. She was a very pretty girl and very sexy, and I thought the audience would get a big kick out of seeing her killed rather than Margo Johns or Michael Gough.'[30]

Another monster left over from the 1950s lurched into view above Copenhagen in the Danish-made 1961 film *Reptilicus*, which was produced, written and directed by Sidney Pink. Also involved in the screenplay was Ib Melchior, the Danish-born screenwriter who has long worked in Hollywood and who has written scripts for several low-budget sf movies, such as *Angry Red Planet* (1959), *The Time Travellers* (1964), both of which he directed, and *Robinson Crusoe on Mars* (1964). The film started off with an oil survey team discovering that their drill bit is full of flesh and blood, which has come from something hundreds of feet below the ground. It turns out to be the tail of a buried dinosaur, which then grows a new body after being struck by lightning. Reptilicus itself was the silliest-looking dinosaur ever to be fired on by an army. It looked more like a dragon and even had a pair of tiny wings that enabled it to soar shakily through the air.

A much more down-to-earth sf film was made in England in 1960 by Wolf Rilla. Called *Village of the Damned* it was based on the novel *The Midwich Cuckoos* by the British sf writer John Wyndham and concerned a small English village that is mysteriously cut off from the outside world for several hours by an electro-magnetic field. When the field disappears the military quickly move in. They find that all the inhabitants are unharmed but can't remember anything that happened. Then twelve of the village women inexplicably become pregnant, including the wife of the protagonist Dr Gordon Zellaby (George Sanders). Each of the women gives birth to an apparently normal child, but it is soon apparent that these children are anything but ordinary. As they grow up at a phenomenally fast rate they demonstrate above-average intelligence and uncanny telepathic powers. By the time they reach the equivalent age of ten years it is clear that all twelve of them – six boys and six girls – have the same 'father' as all possess the same striking features: blonde hair, high foreheads and large, piercing eyes. They have also formed themselves into a tight, exclusive group that will have nothing to do with the other village children. And as Dr Zellaby discovers, the group is actually a *gestalt* – all the children are telepathically linked and together form an 'overmind' that is vastly superior to, and more powerful than, any human mind. By now Dr Zellaby has worked out the truth – that the children represent an alien invasion, but an invasion with a difference. The aliens, in some far-off world, have invaded the Earth by proxy; by the use of an electronic beam they have fertilized the Earth women by long-distance manipulation, inserting their genetic information into the human eggs via the 'radio' beam.

Zellaby is unable to discover whether the children represent an attempted alien take-over of the world or an attempt by a dying civilization to ensure the survival of its race, mentally at least. At first he is willing to give them the benefit of the doubt, but he soon recognizes that the children are a threat to the human race purely because of the 'overmind's' strong survival instinct – something made clear when a number of villagers who have displayed aggression towards the children are willed by them into committing suicide. Sooner or later, reasons Zellaby, the children and the human race will clash on a major scale, and if the 'overmind' reaches maturity by the time this happens the human race will be the loser. So, in a supreme gesture, he packs a briefcase full of explosives, attaches a timing device to it and goes into the children's classroom. They suspect something is wrong but by the time they break down his mental defences (represented on the screen by a crumbling brick wall) it is too late.

The Village of the Damned succeeds mainly because of its unsensational, low-key approach to its subject – the horror is given extra impact by being so carefully understated – and also because of the eeriness of the children themselves. Credit for this must go to Rilla and also to the make-up man Eric Aylott, who created much of their subtly weird appearance by means of special wigs that suggested slightly bigger foreheads than normal children have. (In prints of the film released outside England the children's eyes glowed whenever they used their powers, but the English version of the film is shown without this extra detail, presumably because of pressure by the censor.) Another asset of the film is its above-average cast, including George Sanders, Barbara Shelley, Laurence Naismith, Peter Vaughan and Martin Stephens (the last of whom played the children's spokesman and in 1962 gave another memorable performance in *The Innocents*), and the excellent screenplay was by Stirling Silliphant, Wolf Rilla and George Barclay.

The film proved to be a financial success and led to a sequel (*Children of the Damned*) made in 1963, though this time the director was Anton M. Leader and the screenplay was by John Briley. It was more of a remake than a sequel in that the story was similar: a group of women give birth to children with strange powers, and once again it is discovered that aliens 'out there' are responsible. But the theme is less satisfactorily handled than in the Rilla film. *Children of the Damned* is concerned with the activities of two UNESCO scientific investigators (Alan Badel and Ian Hendry) as they work their slow way to the unsurprising conclusion. The children are no longer 'unknown quantities' but benign entities who want to be left in peace. The film ends with a confrontation in an old ruined church between the children and the military. Just as it seems they have convinced the authorities that they represent no real threat, the children are accidentally fired upon and killed.

More highly regarded is *The Damned* (also known as *These Are the Damned*) made in 1961 but not released until 1963 in Britain and 1965 in America. It too concerns a group of unusual children but has nothing to do with Wyndham's novel, though no doubt it was inspired by the success of *Village of the Damned*. It was directed by Joseph Losey, the expatriate American director and self-declared Marxist who has worked in Britain since the early 1950s (he now resides in France) and who could film the phone book and still have the result acclaimed by most critics. *The Damned*, based on the novel *The Children of the Light* by H. L. Lawrence and scripted by Evan Jones, is very pretentious. The story concerns an American (Macdonald Carey) who, during a visit to an English seaside town, becomes involved with both the sister of the leader of a local gang of young thugs and a scientist in charge of a secret project being carried out at a nearby military installation. His relationship with the girl (Shirley Ann Field, giving the worst female performance in an sf film since Ann Robinson in *War of the Worlds*) is bitterly resented by her brother (Oliver

Reed looking his most murderous) and finally they have to flee from him and his gang. They take refuge in a cave under the military base and discover a group of children living there – children who are incredibly cold to the touch. It turns out that they are human guinea-pigs being used by the scientist (Alexander Knox) to create a race of humans who can withstand atomic radiation and thus be able to survive an atomic war. The one drawback is that they themselves are so radioactive that they will eventually kill anyone who comes in contact with them. Not realizing this the American and the girl attempt to free the children from their subterranean prison but by doing so became fatally contaminated themselves. The children are recaptured while the dying couple drift out to sea in their boat, shadowed by a vulture-like helicopter which is waiting for them to die.

For all Losey's striving to transform the material into an important statement on the moral corruption of Western technocracy, embellished with evocative imagery, the film's basic message seems to be that sustained exposure to atomic radiation drastically lowers one's body temperature and is likely to be harmful in the long run.

Another of John Wyndham's novels, *The Day of the Triffids*, was adapted into a film in 1963. Directed by Steve Sekely and Freddie Francis from a screenplay by American writer/producer Philip Yordan (who also produced the film) it can best be described as an interesting disaster. Wyndham's story about a species of mobile plants that take over the world after radiation from a shower of exploding meteors has blinded most of the world's population is presented in a very disjointed way. This is mainly because some of the sequences, involving Kieron Moore and Janette Scott besieged by Triffids in a lighthouse, were shot separately a year later (by Freddie Francis) and tacked on because the financial backers thought the original film, directed by Steve Sekely (a Hungarian director who has worked in Hollywood since the mid-1930s), lacked sufficient punch as well as running time. Lack of money was also a problem, as the cut-price look of the special effects betrays. The Triffids themselves vary in quality and appearance from scene to scene and rarely look very menacing in any of their manifestations, with the exception of one sequence where a large number of them smash their way through the windows of a ruined country mansion. In some scenes they look positively comical, particularly when they pursue an ice-cream van down a road. Howard Keel starred in the Sekely-directed section of the film and later claimed that the dialogue was so sparse in the script that he had to write his own in order to have something to say.

As noted at the beginning of this chapter the first James Bond film, *Dr No*, had a tremendous influence on science fiction's spread to a wider audience during the 1960s. This movie starts off as a fairly straight-

Mad, and also very annoyed, scientist Dr No (Joseph Wiseman) attempts to push James Bond (Sean Connery) into his private atomic reactor.

forward thriller (though in 1962 its mixture of 'graphic' violence and black humour was unusual) with secret agent James Bond being sent to Jamaica to find out why two British colleagues stationed there have mysteriously disappeared. By the end of the film the audience has been led into a world straight out of an old sf movie serial, complete with oriental super-villain and underground headquarters full of weird and wonderful gadgets. The difference was that most of the sf devices in the film were only a step or two ahead of contemporary reality, whereas when the serials were made they were still fantasies. In 1962 the space race was in full swing and audiences were willing to accept things that they would have scoffed at as too far-fetched only a decade previously. The villain, who sabotages American rockets as they take off from Cape Canaveral by means of a powerful radio transmitter, also had a contemporary relevance which his cinematic forebears, such as Fu Manchu, lacked. One of the most important scientists in America at that time was Wernher von Braun, whose value to the nation's efforts to win the race to the moon was so great that he had been given the ultimate accolade – a Hollywood movie based on his life called *I Aim at the Stars* (1960), in which his former 'misdeeds' are given an amazing cosmetic job. (At the end of the film one of the characters, whose children had been killed in a V2 raid, has been so entranced by this paragon of brains and virtue that he says: 'Goodbye, von Braun, and good luck with the universe.') Doctor No, significantly, is half-German, and when James Bond asks him if he works for the Russians he replies aloofly: 'East . . . West . . . mere points of the compass, Mr Bond. I offered my services to both and they refused. Now they will pay.' Stanley Kubrick took this parallel to its ultimate conclusion in his film *Dr Strangelove*, which ends with the German scientist, who works for America, so excited at the outbreak of nuclear war that he lurches out of his wheelchair (like Dr No he also has a mechanical hand) screaming: 'Mein Führer . . . I can walk!.'

Doctor No represents the end of a long line of mad scientists and as such incorporates many of their characteristics: like Fu Manchu, he is oriental; like Rotwang in *Metropolis*, he has an artificial hand (two of them, in fact); like Captain Nemo, he has an obsession with the sea (No's underground headquarters have a large glass wall enabling him to observe life below the waves); and like both Dr Moreau and Dr Thorkel (*Dr Cyclops*), he enjoys toying with people – inflicting pain for its own sake.

But unlike the character in the book the film's Doctor No (played icily by Joseph Wiseman) also has control over the world's most potent post-Second World War symbol: atomic power itself. Bubbling away beneath its water-shield in the centre of his laboratory is an atomic reactor which he uses to provide energy for his giant transmitter (his hands had become contaminated and had to be amputated) and, significantly, it's the reactor that kills him at the end of the picture. In a fight with James Bond on a catwalk above the reactor he falls onto a platform that is descending into the pool and after his mechanical hands fail to get a purchase on the wet, slipperly metal he is slowly boiled alive in the reactor's water-shield. (There is a small but important scientific error here: the reactor runs wild when the control rods are inserted whereas, in reality, the removal of the rods would cause this to happen.)

Dr No, directed by Terence Young and written by Richard Maibaum, Johanna Harwood and Berkely Mather, was a tremendous financial success and quickly become a trendsetter. By the time the third Bond film (*Goldfinger*) was being made in 1964, imitations were already beginning to flood onto cinema and television screens, most of which contained plenty of overt sf elements within their story-lines. On television came such series as *The Man from Uncle, Amos Burke – Secret Agent, The Wild, Wild West* and *The Avengers* and in the cinema came the Matt Helm series of films, *Our Man Flint*, etcetera. As the Bond series continued it became increasingly sf-orientated and increasingly successful, and in 1977, fifteen years after *Dr No*, the Bond film *The Spy Who Loved Me*, using more or less the same formula, made more money than any of them. (The latest Bond film, *Moonraker*, is based on Fleming's most overtly science fictional novel.) *Bona fide* science fiction writers, on the other hand, are still claiming they're not being paid enough for their services.

Science fiction elements were also incorporated into John Frankenheimer's oddly prophetic 1962 political thriller *The Manchurian Candidate*, based on the novel by Richard Condon. A group of American soldiers are captured in Korea and subjected to an elaborate brainwashing programme by the Chinese as part of a plot to have an agent of the Chinese elected President. Laurence Harvey plays the American officer conditioned to become a killing machine whenever one of the people working for the Chinese (who include his own mother) gives the right command. Frank Sinatra plays his friend who has also been brainwashed but who succeeds in overcoming his own conditioning and eventually disrupts Harvey's programmed actions. The film's climax at a Party Convention, where the character shoots his mother and her lover instead of the Presidential candidate he's been programmed to assassinate, is a masterpiece of direction. It is probably Frankenheimer's best film to date, though a great deal of the credit must go to George Axelrod's excellent, multi-layered script.

Foreign-language science fiction films also became more prevalent during the 1960s, and one of them was a Russian production made for children called *Planeta Burg* (*Storm Planet*). Directed by Pavel Klushantsev at the Leningrad Studio of Popular Science Films, it concerned two Russian astronauts who crash-land on Venus accompanied by a robot obviously inspired by Robby. While they wait for a rescue mission they have to cope with the Venusian environment. There are seas, lakes, abundant plant-life and even animals, including pterodactyls, but no sign of intelligent life. Another group of astronauts descend from the large mother ship in orbit round Venus leaving the ship in the control of a lone female astronaut. Subsequent radio conversations between her and the ground party provide opportunities for plenty of uplifting homilies about the Soviet way of life. The two groups link up and continue the search for intelligent life despite hazards such as volcanic eruptions and attacks from the local wildlife. They finally give up and leave, unaware that their departing ship is being watched by an intelligent Venusian lurking below the surface of a lake. The special effects and Venusian settings are interesting but basically the film is slow-moving, over-talkative and rather dull.

Ikaria XB-1, a 1963 Czechoslovakian film, had its title changed to *Voyage of the End of the Universe* when it reached America; it was cut from 81 minutes to 65, and one brief shot was added at the end. Directed by Jindrich Polak it was set on a giant spaceship during a long exploratory mission. Attention is centred on the daily routines of the ship's inhabitants, and the stock situations which one would expect in an American or British film with a similar setting are almost completely avoided. The ending is predictable: the spaceship reaches an alien planet which we recognize to be contemporary Earth. Not expected, however, is the loving shot of the Statue of Liberty, but this turns out to have been inserted by the American distributors.

A short French film, made in 1962, that has won a small cult following over the years is *La Jetée* (*The Pier*). Written and directed by Chris Marker, it is set after World War Three when a group of French scientists, living in the underground vaults at Chaillot, are attempting to send a man back in time. A particularly vivid childhood memory is used as a catalyst to send their subject (Davos Henich) back through time with the assistance of certain drugs. His most vivid memory concerns a time when, as a child, he had been watching a beautiful girl at Orly Airport at the moment when a man came running nearby and was killed. He is successfully sent back in time but falls in love with the girl and decides to remain in that period. When he attempts to escape with the girl at the airport he is shot dead by another traveller from the future, and we realized that, as a child, he had witnessed his adult self being killed. Composed almost entirely of still photographs the film is nearer in theme and approach to the 'New Wave' sf writings of the 1960s than to traditional time travel stories.

Time travel was also the theme of *The Time Travellers* (1964), a more obviously commercial film directed by Ib Melchior from his own screenplay. It starred Preston Foster, Philip Carey, Merry Anders and

Stephen Franken as four scientists who accidentally create a time portal in their laboratory. They go through this 'door' and find themselves in the future which, as usual, is represented as a world suffering the after-effects of atomic war with mutants on the rampage.

Roger Corman made what is probably his best sf film in 1963. Titled *The Man With the X-Ray Eyes* it starred Ray Milland as a scientist in a hospital who is trying to create a serum that will enable him to see through solid, opaque materials. His reasons are purely altruistic – he believes that such an ability would greatly improve medical diagnosis – but naturally everything goes wrong. No sooner does he start experimenting with the serum on his own eyes than he gets into an argument with a colleague and accidentally knocks him out of a window, killing him. Forced to go on the run from the police, he hides out in a small-time carnival where his powers are exploited by a sideshow manager (Don Rickles giving a splendidly nasty performance). His girlfriend Diane (Diana Van Der Vlis) catches up with him and together they go to Las Vegas where for a time he has fun breaking the bank in a casino before his unusual winning streak attracts the attention of the police. Pursued by them into the desert he crashes his car and then stumbles into the tent of an evangelical preacher. His eyes have now become black discs; he stares into the air and tells the audience that he can see into the very centre of the Universe. When the preacher asks him what he sees there he replies that he can see a huge eye watching him – watching all humanity. 'If thine eye offends thee, pluck it out!' suggests the preacher helpfully. The scientist does just that, and there is a brief shot of him looking like Oedipus with gaping eye sockets and blood running down his cheeks. Directed by Corman himself from a screenplay by Robert Dillon and Ray Russell, the film is mainly interesting because of its visual inventiveness, though Corman's usual lack of a sufficient budget prevented the possible permutations of the idea being fully realized. The film's message is the same one that has echoed down sf cinema since the beginning, except in this case it's not so much 'There are some things Man was not meant to know,' as 'There are some things Man was not meant to see.'

The year 1963 wasn't an auspicious one for British sf films. It saw the release of yet another remake of *Donovan's Brain*, called simply *The Brain*. Director Freddie Francis provided the film with some visual verve (before turning to directing, he was an Oscar-winning cameraman) but the familiar story was as tired as ever despite a couple of plot twists. Peter Van Eyck, Anne Heywood and Bernard Lee starred and the screenplay was by Robert Stewart and Phil Mackie.

Rather more interesting was *Unearthly Stranger*, a low-key, unpretentious and very cheaply made film about a man who gradually discovers that his wife is an alien, one of many who have infiltrated the world. She is ordered by her superiors to kill him but cannot, having fallen in love with him. Her emotional involvement with a human destroys her ability to survive undetected on Earth, and one of the film's most indelible images is of her tears leaving corrosive tracks down her cheeks as she admits the truth to her husband. She later dies in his arms, leaving nothing behind but a bundle of clothes. The hackneyed plot is handled with a certain amount of style and intelligence by director John Krish. The screenplay was by Rex Carlton and the cast included John Neville, Gabriella Lucudi, Jean Marsh and Warren Mitchell.

Alternative world stories have long been a popular sub-genre in science fiction but are rare in the cinema. The British film *It Happened Here* (1963) is one exception, showing what might have happened if Nazi Germany had successfully invaded England. Shot in a realistic, documentary-like style, it is a remarkable film, especially since it was made over a period of years by two young amateurs, Kevin Brownlow and Andrew Mollo, working mainly at weekends and using non-professional talent.

Alfred Hitchcock's sf/fantasy *The Birds*, based on the story by Daphne du Maurier was also released in 1963. Scripted by Evan Hunter, the film leads up to the day when ordinary birdlife suddenly turns against mankind in a series of murderous attacks. The centre of the phenomenon is located in a small American seaside town called Bodega Bay, which is also the hometown of a handsome young lawyer played by Rod Taylor (the Australian actor who had also starred in *The Time Machine*). He has been pursued there by an impetuous heiress ('Tippi' Hedren) who has fallen in love with him after meeting him in a bird shop. The arrival of the heiress apparently initiates the first bird attack, though Hitchcock and his scriptwriter deliberately avoid revealing the real reason for the birds' behaviour. The basic mystery behind the attacks is maintained even at the climax of the picture, when a vast horde of birds, which only moments before had been engaged in a violent onslaught upon the lawyer's home, quietly allow him and his companions to escape. The final shot is of his retreating car dwindling in size until it is lost from sight in an endless sea of motionless birds.

The actual bird attacks are the film's main setpieces and they are suitably spectacular, achieved by a combination of real birds, model ones and process work by Ub Iwerks, a colleague of Walt Disney's. Other effects in the film were created by Lawrence A. Hampton.

The apocalypse in the form of atomic war remained a popular theme in the early 1960s. Ray Milland directed and starred in *Panic in the Year Zero* in 1962, based on a script by Jay Simms and John Morton. Milland played a middle-class father, Harry Baldwin, who is taking his family on a camping trip into the hills outside Los Angeles. No sooner do they leave the city then it is destroyed by atomic missiles (suggested simply by flashes of light). Harry is only momentarily dismayed before starting to act as if he's been waiting for this to happen all his life. He breaks into a gun shop and steals a number of firearms. 'It's going to be the survival of the fittest,' he tells his shocked family, which includes his wife (Jean Hagen), his daughter (Mary Mitchel) and his son (Frankie Avalon). At first his family are alarmed at his cold-blooded attitude towards other people, but when the daughter is kidnapped and raped by a gang of thugs they see the error of their ways, and Mom is quite happy when Pop and Son catch up with Sis's captors and shoot them all dead in cold blood. Milland's message seems to be that if you happen to survive World War Three shoot first and ask questions later, which is exactly the sort of attitude that is likely to cause World War Three.

The best film to date on the subject of nuclear war is *Dr Strangelove, Or: How I Learned to Stop Worrying and Love the Bomb* (1963), written and directed by Stanley Kubrick. (Terry Southern and Frank George, whose novel *Red Alert* the film was based on, also contributed to the screenplay.) The plot concerns a demented US Air Force general who sends his squadron of B52s to drop their cargoes of H-bombs on Russia. The pilots are under the impression that World War Three is underway, and they ignore all attempts by the President and his military advisers to recall them, thinking these are part of a Russian trick. Eventually the renegade general's secret recall code signal is obtained and transmitted, causing all the planes to head back to base with the exception of one B52 that has had its communication system knocked out by a missile hit.

The War Room in
Dr Strangelove.

Commanded by a neanderthal Texan called Major Kong (Slim Pickens), it successfully penetrates the Soviet defences and reaches its target. We last see Major Kong, stetson in hand, riding his H-bomb like a rodeo performer as it plummets towards the Russian industrial complex. The subsequent explosion sets off World War Three, and the film ends with shots of mushroom clouds accompanied by Vera Lynn's voice singing 'We'll meet again.'

Originally Kubrick had planned to film Peter George's novel as a serious suspense story: 'As I tried to build the detail for a scene I found myself tossing away what seemed to me to be very truthful insights because I was afraid the audience would laugh. After a few weeks I realized that these incongruous bits of reality were closer to the truth than anything else I was able to imagine. And it was at this point I decided to treat the story as nightmare comedy.'[31] The realism of the settings and the machinery, particularly the interior of the B52, gives an added impact to the horrifying absurdity of the action and characters. Kubrick is aided considerably by a fine cast that includes Peter Sellers in three roles: as the ineffectual President, a Royal Air Force officer and the President's German adviser, the mad scientist Dr Strangelove (who, as it happens, looks uncannily like Kissinger); George C. Scott as the hawkish, blustering General Buck Turgidson; and Sterling Hayden as General Jack D. Ripper, the insane officer who initiates the fatal action because he believes the Russians are polluting his 'vital bodily fluids'.

The same year saw the release of *Fail Safe*, directed by Sidney Lumet, which superficially appears like a serious version of *Strangelove*. A mechanical malfunction causes an American bomber to obliterate Moscow by mistake, and to avert a nuclear war the American government placates the understandably miffed Russians by dropping an H-bomb on New York. But as Julian Smith points out in his excellent book *Looking Away: Hollywood and Vietnam*, there is something very unhealthy about the film. '*Fail Safe*, a far more "serious" film than *Dr Strangelove*,' he writes, 'is ultimately weaker and shabbier because it turns disaster into an excuse for national pride. The disaster itself is blamed on a machine instead of on the men who put so much trust and pride in their toys; the hero of the piece becomes the brave American president who does what must be done, and the tragedy is that the Empire State Building becomes ground zero. The Eugene Burdick and Harvey Wheeler novel refers to the president's sacrifice of New York as "the most sweeping and incredible decision that any man had ever made", and ends on a patriotic and upbeat note as the president orders a Medal of Honor citation be prepared for the general who bombed New York.'[32] If Kubrick had got his hands on that story the resulting film might have been even funnier than *Strangelove*.

Films about space travel weren't in fashion during the early 1960s, but two exceptions were *First Men in the Moon* and *Robinson Crusoe on Mars*, both made in 1964. The former film was a Charles H. Schneer/Ray Harryhausen production and typically hasn't much to commend it apart from Harryhausen's impressive special effects. Despite being based on a Wells novel and a screenplay partly written by Nigel Kneale, creator of the Quatermass series, it was played strictly for laughs and obviously aimed at the juvenile market. Lionel Jeffries camps it up as Professor Cavor, the inventor who creates an anti-gravity material that enables him to fly to the moon in a spherical spaceship. With him go Arnold Bedford (Edward Judd) and his fiancée Kate (Martha Hyer), and once on the moon they encounter the insect-like Selenites who prove none too friendly. Arnold and Kate finally escape back to Earth in the anti-gravity sphere but Professor Cavor stays behind to see if he can establish friendly relations with the lunar inhabitants. The film's main twist was a contemporary prologue and epilogue; in the prologue we see a United Nations spaceship land on the moon and when the astronauts emerge they are amazed to find a British flag waiting for them. Back on Earth a very old man in a rest home tells reporters that he put the Union Jack on the moon in 1899. He is, of course, Bedford, and as he tells his story the film proper begins in flashback.

'The Wells novel had always been a favourite of mine,' said Harryhausen. 'I had wanted to make a film of it for many years but every time I mentioned it to Charles Schneer he would always bring up the argument, and rightly so, that there was not enough variety in it as it stood for a feature production. Also, space science had advanced to such a degree that it would be difficult to make it believable for today's audience. One day, while Charles was talking to writer Nigel Kneale, who is also an H. G. Wells enthusiast, Nigel came up with the brilliant idea that stimulated Charles into new interest in the project. Anyone who has seen it will agree that the prologue makes the whole thing work in a believable fashion.'[33] Though it may be a clever touch, it doesn't really enhance the original. There was more to the Wells novel than a story about two men flying to the moon and having trouble with the natives: Wells also used it as a means of exploring certain sociological concepts, but the Selenites' 'brave new world' society is ignored by the film-makers. The epilogue has the United Nations explorers finding the underground Selenite city empty and in a state of decay. Bedford remembers that Cavor had a cold on the moon and deduces that his germs must have wiped out the Selenite civilization. This black joke – a reversal of the ending in *War of the Worlds* – must surely have been another Nigel Kneale contribution.

Byron Haskin, who had directed several sf films for George Pal in the 1950s, returned to the genre in 1964 with *Robinson Crusoe on Mars*, a futuristic version of Defoe's classic novel. Written by Ib Melchior and

John C. Higgins it starred Paul Mantee as the survivor of a two-man spaceship that crashes on Mars. He struggles to survive in the alien, barren environment – his only companion a tiny monkey – and for months lives in a small cave renewing his air supply by heating Martian rocks that give off oxygen while being haunted at night by ghostly images of his dead colleague (Adam West). Up until this point the film is a relatively realistic and convincing study of one man's fight to overcome hostile surroundings and mental breakdown, but then an alien spaceship arrives and the film degenerates into pure hokum. Spying on the aliens the man observes that they keep slaves, and when one of them escapes he helps him to avoid the flying drones sent out from the alien mother ship. The slave, who looks like a South American Indian, becomes his Man

Byron Haskin (left) on location with his crew in Death Valley during the filming of Robinson Crusoe on Mars.

Friday and together they make a long trek to the Martian polar ice cap where they await rescue by another American spaceship.

'I consider that film the best thing I've ever done, said Haskin later, 'because it had basically one of the soundest stories ever written. Unfortunately the film did not become a hit because of the bad judgement of the producer and the releasing company. I fought like a tiger to get rid of the silly-ass title but to no avail.

'We filmed most of it in Death Valley. People have shot movies there before but usually down in the valley. We shot our stuff up on the ridges so that we'd have the sky in the backgrounds. Larry Butler, who later did the effects in *Marooned* over at Columbia, did the effects on *Crusoe* as a favour to me. He has an optical printer you wouldn't believe and he removed all our skies for us. We had to convince audiences dramatically that they were not seeing Earth. A blue sky would have been a dead give-away, so he matted in an orange red colour. The skies up in Death Valley were very blue and gave us good travelling matte outlines. So all that we shot there provided its own matte-line and we simply added the orange red.'[34]

The Earth Dies Screaming was the subtle title given to a small-scale 1964 sf film directed by Terence Fisher, who is best known for his Hammer horror films. In fact all the screaming had stopped by the time the film started. A test pilot (Willard Parker) returns from an experimental flight in space to find that everyone in London is dead, even the tourists. After a futile search to find out why, he encounters two more survivors in a small hotel (Dennis Price and Virginia Field) and all three begin a trek to see if anyone else is alive. They locate two more people (Thorley Walters and Vanda Godsell) but also come across two large robots who kill one of the women (Godsell) when she attempts to communicate with them. Retreating to the hotel they find two more survivors, one pregnant woman (Anna Falk), and later receive another shock when the dead woman makes a reappearance and kills Price. The others come to the conclusion that the Earth has been conquered by aliens and that they have the power to reanimate corpses. As usual with low-budget sf movies that try to handle a large theme the action is so localized as to be absurd. A Robert L. Lippert production, it was written by Henry Cross and Harry Spalding.

Another film set in a hotel after a worldwide cataclysm has destroyed most of human life was the Czech 1965 production *End of August at the Hotel Ozone*. Directed by Jan Schmidt and written by Pavel Juracek, it concerned a group of women survivors of a nuclear war who are desperately searching for a man to continue the human race. They eventually locate one living in a large ruined hotel, but he turns out to be too old to be of service. This bleak and depressing film was in direct contrast to another Czech film made in 1965, *Who Could Kill Jessie?*

Written and directed by Milos Macourek and Vaclav Vorlicek, this was the hilarious story of three comic-book characters who are inadvertently brought to life and cause chaos in a large Czech town. Originally it was conceived purely as a children's film but the makers soon realized its potential as satire. The film concerns an over-worked scientist who becomes obsessed with a newspaper comic strip featuring a voluptuous heroine called Jessie, who is constantly being pursued by two villains — a cowboy and a character similar to Superman. The man's wife, also a scientist, has invented a machine that can eradicate unwanted dreams, but its unsuspected side-effect is to give three-dimensional substance to the subjects of the dreams it removes from the brain. When she tries out the device on her sleeping husband, the three characters materialize in their apartment. They promptly wreck the place and then continue their anarchic chase across the city, to the consternation of the authorities who eventually capture them and put them on trial. The trial itself is a very funny sequence, particularly since the comic-book people can communicate only by speech balloons that form like circular billboards above their heads whenever they speak. (At one point the judge asks a clerk to swivel one of Jessie's 'balloons' round in his direction so he can read it more easily.) They are finally sentenced to death but the authorities find it impossible to kill something that isn't technically alive in the first place. The film ends with the scientist married to Jessie, the object of his fantasies, but realizing to his horror that she's beginning to sound exactly like his first wife. Unfortunately this exhilarating film hasn't had a wide distribution outside Czechoslovakia.

A major cause of embarrassment to the sf writer Robert Sheckley must be the film *The Tenth Victim*, a French/Italian co-production based on his story *The Seventh Victim* about a future world where, as a safety valve for latent aggression, the government has organized legal duels to the death. If a licensed 'hunter' can score seven kills he or she will be entitled to almost unlimited privileges. The story is one of Sheckley's typically cynical morality tales, but the scriptwriters inflated it into a pretentious showcase for the languid talents of Marcello Mastroianni and Ursula Andress. About the only memorable incident is the sight of Ursula Andress shooting somebody with her bra.

Whether or not Jean-Luc Godard's *Alphaville* (1965) properly qualifies as science fiction is a matter for debate. It concerns intergalactic secret agent Lemmy Caution (Eddie Constantine), who is sent to the planet Alphaville to deal with an evil computer used by Alphaville's rulers to control and suppress the people. Caution succeeds in his mission, at the same time winning the affections of the daughter (Anna Karina) of the ruler. Godard has transformed the pulp elements of the story into an ambiguous allegory of contemporary technology-dominated society.

Eddie Constantine, Jean-Luc Godard and Anna Karina during the making of Alphaville.

Alphaville itself is a thinly disguised Paris, and Caution doesn't use a spaceship to get there but simply drives his Ford through 'intersidereal space' which is an ordinary highway. *Alphaville* contains a maze of allusions culled from a wide variety of sources, including Hollywood 'B' films, comic books, thrillers, and even cartoons (two scientists introduce themselves as 'Dr Heckle and Dr Jeckle') as well as the tradition of sf.

Where Kubrick approached the subject of nuclear war with cold irony British film-maker Peter Watkins used anger and outrage bordering on the hysterical in his pseudo-documentary *The War Game* (1965), which showed a nuclear attack on England and then concentrated on the aftermath in a small town in Kent. Though clumsily made it is full of shattering images, including the glare and concussion of the bombs; the raging fire storms; the hideously disfigured casualties; the torment and slow death from radiation poisoning; mass cremations; buckets of wedding rings being gathered from the dead; and execution squads composed of English policemen shooting looters. For all its faults it creates a graphic picture of nuclear war and also demonstrates just how ineffectual civil defence organizations would be in such an event, all of which explains why the BBC refused to show it on British television even though it had been made especially for TV. 'It might disturb audiences,' explained a BBC spokesman at the time, which is exactly what the film was designed to do. However, the film did receive a theatrical release and even won an Academy Award.

Another film about atomic bombs made that year was *Thunderball*, the fourth in the increasingly popular James Bond series. The plot revolved around the hi-jacking by a criminal organization, SPECTRE, of a NATO bomber containing two H-bombs. Unless the West pays a vast ransom the bombs will be exploded in two major cities, the first being Miami, Florida. As the bombs in this film are merely part of the wide range of gadgetry that James Bond has to cope with in the course of the story, the atom bomb itself is thus defused and made safe in the minds of the audience – an interesting reflection on how the Bomb, the Damocles sword of the 1950s, was being transformed in the 1960s into just another technological toy.

James Bond makes a safe landing with his rocket belt after escaping from SPECTRE agents in Thunderball.

8 *We* Are The Martians (1965–70)

By the second half of the 1960s the Vietnam war had become a dark shadow over most aspects of American life, yet there is no reflection of this in any of the science fiction films of the period and Hollywood as a whole did its best to ignore the war. As in the first half of the decade, sf films continued to diversify in theme and approach. Most typical of this trend was *Fahrenheit 451* made in 1966 by François Truffaut and based on the novel by Ray Bradbury, one of the first major sf writers to gain respectability in the eyes of the intellectual establishment. Bradbury achieved this back in the 1950s when Christopher Isherwood announced that he wasn't just an sf writer but a poet. With one bound Bradbury was free of the sf ghetto.

Truffaut's film is a stylish and evocative adaptation of Bradbury's parable about a future world where all books are banned. The central character, Montag (Oskar Werner), is a member of the Fire Brigade, an organization whose function is not to put out fires but to start them – by burning illegal hordes of books whenever they are discovered. Slowly, however, Montag's attitude changes when he comes under the influence of a girl who is one of the rebel Book People. Compared to his vacuous wife (Julie Christie) the girl (also Julie Christie but with a different hair-style) is alive and stimulating and Montag is soon questioning not only his role in society but society itself. Eventually he rebels completely and on his next book-burning mission he incinerates the Fire Chief (Cyril Cusack) instead of the books. He escapes from the city and joins the Book People community, the members of which are each memorizing a book, word by word, in order to preserve them for posterity (Montag chooses a book by Edgar Allan Poe).

The film is much more ambiguous than Bradbury's original; Truffaut can't completely accept the clear-cut message of the novel. At the end the Book People plod about in the snow like zombies, creating a rather depressing picture. The Book People have become like robots, living memory banks whose only function is to store words. The books may be preserved in this manner, but literature as a living art form is dead. Perhaps Truffaut might have become more emotionally involved in the theme if films had been the subject of the ban instead of books.

(Above) *François Truffaut demonstrates to his actors, Anton Diffring and Oskar Werner, the way he wants them to use the fireman's pole in* Fahrenheit 451. (Right) *The firemen speed off to another book-burning assignment.*

That same year, 1966, John Frankenheimer made his most overt sf movie – *Seconds*. Based on a novel by David Ely it featured a middle-aged businessman (John Randolph) who is approached by a mysterious organization and offered the chance of living most of his life over again – for a price. He pays the required sum, which is huge, and undergoes a series of operations that restore his youth and leave him looking like Rock Hudson (who takes over the role at this point). He is also provided with a whole new life-style, becoming part of a community of wealthy, young, bohemian swingers who live in a series of luxury dwellings on a Californian beach (and who are all, it is suggested, recipients of the 'Youth Treatment'). He enjoys his new life at first but then begins to feel guilty about his abandoned wife, who is under the impression that he is dead. He has been told that it is forbidden to have any contact with the people from his former life, but he disobeys the rule and pays a visit to his wife, though he doesn't reveal who he really is. The visit so affects him that he asks for the process to be reversed, but 'they' inform him there's no going back. The film ends with him being killed in an operating theatre, knowing that his body will be used as a replacement corpse for some new client.

Frankenheimer's cold and calculating direction, along with James Wong Howe's atmospheric black-and-white photography, creates an effective mood of ever-increasing paranoia which culminates in the operating theatre sequence, all of which helps to rejuvenate and disguise what is basically an old and worn sf plot. Amusingly Frankenheimer and his scriptwriter Lewis John Carlino seem to be under the impression that youth can be restored merely by what appears to be a series of operations amounting to little more than extensive face-lifts.

More traditional in approach was *CYBORG 2087*, a low-budget 1966 movie directed by Franklin Adreon and written by Arthur C. Pierce, which starred the late Michael Rennie playing a character very similar to his famous Klaatu in *The Day the Earth Stood Still*. Rennie plays Garth, a cyborg (part-human, part-machine, the trendy term for which is now 'bionic') from the future who has returned to 1966 in order to prevent a scientist, Professor Marx (Edward Franz), from building a device that will later be used as an instrument for mind-control by a totalitarian government in the year 2087. The film is hardly a masterpiece and its threadbare production values are evident, but it is well-made of its kind and at least logically self-consistent. The best sequence shows two government cyborgs tracking Garth through the town, never deviating from the invisible trail they are following even if it means pushing cars to one side or going straight through a house with a party in progress.

Another cheap, small-scale 1966 sf movie was the British-made *Invasion*, which was based on a story by Robert Holmes and directed with nice build-up of tension by Alan Bridges (who works mainly as a TV director). Edward Judd, a veteran of sf movies, plays a doctor who knocks down a mysterious girl with his car while driving one night to his small, isolated country hospital. He takes the unconscious girl to the hospital where an examination reveals that she's not quite human in the places where it counts. The girl is, of course, an alien from outer space and soon her friends – two pneumatic Asian-looking girls in skin-tight costumes – come to rescue her.

The 1960s' contribution to the 'shrunken man' cycle was *Fantastic Voyage*, the most spectacular one yet. (1977 was supposed to have seen the release of Harry Saltzman's multi-million dollar 'shrink' epic *The Micronauts*, but financial problems caused the project to be shelved.) In *Fantastic Voyage* not only are a group of people shrunk but so is a submarine, which is then injected into the bloodstream of a man. As usual with these films the problem of mass is completely ignored: if it were possible to shrink five people and a submarine to the size of a human cell, the combined mass would be so concentrated that it would immediately fall through the floor and end up in the centre of the Earth. In the novel he wrote based on the film's script, sf writer Isaac Asimov did his best to rationalize some of the story's most obvious scientific idiocies but without complete success.

The screenplay was based on a short story by Otto Klement and Jay Lewis Bixby and adapted by sf writer David Duncan, who had already written a number of sf film scripts (including *The Black Scorpion, The Time Machine, The Monster That Challenged the World*). The film was directed by Richard Fleischer: 'I was attracted to the project because it had a unique idea – something that I had never seen before. I was fascinated with the whole idea of going on a trip through the human body and presenting it from such an unusual perspective. What also attracted me was the possibility of being able to inspire young people to some understanding of the incredible complexity of the human body, and the sheer *wonder* of it. It's such a fantastic mechanism but we often take it for granted and don't think of it as being anything special, so I tried to get that across in the film. Of course, a lot of the sets representing various internal parts of the body were stylized but even so much of the film is completely accurate in the way things really look. For instance, our portrayal of the molecular structure of the body is astounding in its accuracy; it's an amazing abstract creation in itself so we didn't have to stylize it. We did an enormous amount of research on it – a whole year beforehand in fact – so it's all completely authentic. We had doctors come round and inspect our sets and they'd always know exactly what they were looking at. As a matter of fact we built a model of the heart which was the largest working model of a heart ever built – it was about 40 feet wide and 30 feet high and all of it moved! Usually in a case like this one would have used miniatures

Suspended perilously by wires, the cast of Fantastic Voyage hover in the giant lung set.

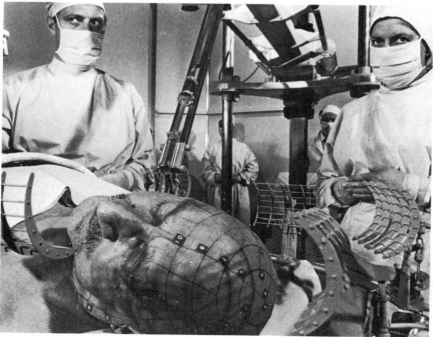

Miniature radar scanners ludicrously 'track' the tiny submarine within the scientist's brain.

but we chose to use giant-scale models. But that film was so difficult in many ways because there were so many technical problems: for instance we were shooting three times normal speed in reverse with the camera sometimes upside-down or on its side, and one had to visualize how it was all going to appear on the screen.

'One of the biggest problems was the wires. It was all supposed to be happening underwater so everybody was 'flying' on wires. It was a big wire job and also a rather dangerous one because sometimes the actors would be 20 or 30 feet off the stage floor and held up by only about four wires, and if only two of the wires broke the actor could fall. We broke wires all the time but luckily it was only ever one at a time, never two. Once we heard a wire go we brought them down immediately, of course. You see, one of the main problems when you're using wires is to hide them – to prevent reflections on their surfaces, etcetera. One way is to paint them so that they blend in with the background but that wasn't a feasible solution in our case because our backgrounds had so many varied colours, and if we'd painted them black you would have seen a black line somewhere in the shot. So the best thing we could do was to make the wires as invisible as possible by keeping the light off them, which, of course, we couldn't always do – so we wiped the wires with acid which corrugated their surfaces and prevented them from reflecting back light. But naturally the acid weakened the wires and that's why they kept breaking.

'It was a very hard picture to make, and a very boring one to make. It was a very slow and laborious job because for one thing we had that big submarine to manipulate and shoot; and getting all those people wired up and rehearsed for each shot. Then a wire would break and we'd have to start all over again. And in a lot of shots we had to use blue backings for the travelling mattes and blue backings are always difficult to light. We'd hopefully get one set-up done in the morning and one in the afternoon and the rest of the time one just waited. The whole film took about a year to make – there were hundreds of days of actual shooting on it. But even so I still love making big films: they're a strain but then making *any* film is a strain.'

Despite the basic absurdity of the plot, which concerns a group of miniaturized doctors making their way through the body of a very important scientist to perform an operation in a section of his brain that can't be reached by normal procedures, the film is a visual feast full of memorable images – like the submarine hurtling down a Niagara Falls of liquid through the needle of a hypodermic syringe and into one of the patient's arteries; the sight of red corpuscles transferring their precious cargoes of oxygen to the cells lining the wall of a blood vessel; the journey through the heart and the arrival within the brain itself, which resembles a network of giant spiderwebs pulsating with electrical flashes. The art directors on the film were Jack Martin Smith and Dale Hennesey, and the special effects were created by L. B. Abbott, Art Cruickshank and Emil Kosa, Jr.

Part of the visual feast that *Fantastic Voyage* provided was an early glimpse on the screen of Raquel Welch. Clad in a white, skin-tight wet suit she kept her male colleagues (including the late Stephen Boyd, Donald Pleasence, Arthur Kennedy and William Redfield) aware of the fact that the human body can be a pretty amazing mechanism when seen from the outside as well. But even more of her was seen in another sf film made that same year – Hammer's remake of *One Million Years B.C.* Apart from Raquel Welch its other main attraction was the work of Ray Harryhausen. 'Hammer had bought the rights from Hal Roach,' said Harryhausen, 'and they approached me to do the special effects. Michael Carreras (who wrote the screenplay and also produced it) and I worked pretty closely together on it. We tried to keep fairly close to the original story-line of the old 1940 version but, of course, in the earlier one they didn't use animation, they used live lizards and for one sequence a man in a dinosaur suit. But it had some good things in it. The live action in our film was shot in the Canary Islands and the animated creatures were matted into real scenery.'

Harryhausen provided a host of monsters for the film, including a giant turtle, a family of pterodactyls and several dinosaurs. Most impressive among the latter was a young Tyrannosaurus Rex that invades the seaside camp of a tribe of cavemen and kills a few of them before being spectacularly despatched by the film's hero (John Richardson) – a marvellous example of Harryhausen's skills at their best. He was even obliged to animate a small model of Raquel Welch for a series of shots of her being snatched up and carried off by a pterodactyl.

Like Raquel Welch, Jane Fonda found her body being exploited by male chauvinist film-makers the following year (1967) in *Barbarella*. At the time she didn't seem to mind too much but even then she looked rather miscast as a dewy-eyed, dumb blonde who travels about space bringing sexual salvation to any male she happens to encounter. Based on the French comic strip by Jean Claude Forest the film is a tongue-in-cheek space opera about a female intergalactic secret agent and her search for a missing scientist and his doomsday weapon, which leads her to the planet of Sogo. The latter part of the film is set in the Black Queen's (Anita Pallenberg) decadent city which is built over a vast, writhing organism called the Matmos. Here Barbarella is installed, by the Queen's evil Prime Minister (Milo O'Shea), in the Excessive Machine which is designed to kill through an excess of sexual pleasure; but Barbarella's capacity is such that she causes the machine to explode instead. The film ends in an orgy of destruction as the Prime Minister, who is really the missing scientist, destroys everything in sight with his super-weapon before the Matmos erupts and consumes the city and all its inhabitants – with the exception of Barbarella whom it can't bear to touch because of her innate goodness.

Directed by Roger Vadim, the film had eight writers – Terry Southern, Jean Claude Forest, Vittorio Bonicelli, Brian Dagas, Claude Brule, Tudor Gates, Clement Biddle Wood and Vadim himself. Most of the humour is heavy-handed and falls very flat, except for a sequence where Barbarella encounters an inefficient revolutionary (David Hemmings) and they make love, via her sex pills, simply by touching fingertips – an experience which Hemmings finds literally hair-raising. Also on the credit side are Enrico Fea's suitably bizarre sets, August Lohman's special effects and Claude Renoir's stylish photography.

Terence Fisher, who had made *The Earth Dies Screaming* in 1964, returned to the genre in 1966 and 1967 with two low-budget, sf pot-boilers which he directed for a company called Planet Films. The first was *Island of Terror*, which was written by Alan Ramsen and Edward Andrew Mann and concerned giant mutated viruses – the result of cancer research gone wrong – that resemble large piles of old porridge and get loose on a small island where they destroy their victims by sucking the bones out of their bodies.

From giant piles of porridge Fisher turned to giant fried eggs, which is what the alien invaders resembled in *Night of the Big Heat* (also known as *Island of the Burning Damned*). Based on John Lymington's novel, it was written by Ronald Liles and Pip and Jane Baker and starred Patrick Allen as the owner of a small hotel on an island off the English coast which is experiencing a freak heat wave, caused by the aliens. They have come to Earth in search of energy sources and are apparently so desperate for the stuff that a simple car battery will attract them; nevertheless they are finally dissolved in a rainstorm.

These two films, with their monsters-on-the-loose plots, were out of step with most sf films being made in that period. Nineteen sixty-seven, for instance, saw the release of such films as *Privilege, The Day the Fish Came Out, The President's Analyst* and *The Power*, all of which differed greatly from each other yet can still be classed as science fiction.

Privilege was directed by Peter Watkins, who made *The War Game*, and is a typically paranoid film about the Establishment. It concerns a rock star (Paul Jones) who is used by the British government both to control and to mould the opinions of its youthful citizens. The singer is forced to change his image to suit the sinister plans of the government officials, but when he finally rebels he is destroyed by his own teenage followers who don't want the truth, only fantasy. Watkins's usual inability to avoid overstatement detracts from the potential interest of the theme. The screenplay was by Norman Bogner and based on a story by Johnny

Speight, creator of the TV series *Till Death Us Do Part* (which became *All in the Family* in the US).

The Day the Fish Came Out was a black comedy written, produced and directed by the Greek film-maker Michael Cacoyannis and based on a true incident when an American bomber, carrying two H-Bombs, crashed into the sea off the coast of Spain. The film is set, sometime in the near future, on a small Greek island which becomes the centre of frenzied activity when a similar incident occurs in the sea nearby. The bomber is carrying not only two nuclear bombs but also a mysterious 'Doomsday' weapon. To prevent this knowledge becoming widespread the NATO recovery team, led by Sam Wanamaker, arrive on the island disguised as garishly dressed holiday-makers. However, this creates the impression that the island has suddenly become the 'in' place of the Jet Set and soon, to the islanders' amazement, the arid, unattractive little island is swarming with trendy tourists, including the enigmatic Candice Bergen. Meanwhile a poor fisherman has recovered a strange metal box from the sea which he believes contains valuables of some kind but which resists all his attempts to open it. Finally he succeeds with some stolen acid, but all he finds inside are a number of sponge-like objects which his wife angrily throws into the nearby reservoir. The box, which the fisherman hurls back into the sea, contains deadly viruses and the film ends with all the fish in the sea starting to die – a sign of what is to come on a worldwide scale.

The film is a strange mixture of slapstick (the two pilots from the crashed bomber – Tom Courtenay and Colin Blakely – spend the whole film hiding on the island in a state of undress), trendy sexual posturing and grim satire, but it doesn't work successfully. However the final shots of the dead fish floating belly up in the black sea while the tourists, oblivious to their impending doom, dance with frenzied abandon on the beach have an undeniable impact. Also memorable are the music by Mikis Theodorakis and Candice Bergen's costumes.

Much more successful as satire was *The President's Analyst*, written and directed by Theodore J. Flicker, which starred James Coburn as a psychoanalyst who is hired to listen to the President's troubles but soon crumbles under the strain. When he realizes that his house is bugged, that he is under constant surveillance and that even his girlfriend (Joan Delaney) is working for the FBI, he flees Washington DC and takes refuge with a 'typical' middle-class American family who describe themselves as 'militant liberals' (the father has a vast collection of guns, the mother is taking karate lessons and their young son is into wire-tapping). Pursued by the FBI (short men in suits), the CIA (college graduates with pipes and tweed jackets), the Russians and the Chinese, Coburn avoids death by inches several times before discovering who the real villain is, and who really runs America. This turns out to be the vast Telephone Company which is manned by bland, smiling robots who want to link the whole world into their system by planting miniature telephones into the brain of every human being alive. A witty and literate script by Flicker and a good cast, which includes the late Godfrey Cambridge, make this a better-than-average sf comedy.

The Power saw the teaming-up again of producer George Pal and director Byron Haskin, but it wasn't a happy occasion for either of them. 'The personal friction between MGM and George Pal, the hatreds between them you just wouldn't believe, were allowed to operate on that film's economy. It wasn't released with any fanfare. It was grudgingly left to escape with everybody at MGM hoping it would flop because they were trying to get rid of Pal,' said Haskin later.

'I don't think the film is too bad although you could get confused unless you paid very close attention. I came onto the project when it was fully prepared. I assisted the writer (John Gay) in polishing one or two points but I had no authority to change anything further. I felt that a few things could have been changed but I didn't go into it because I was glad just to be doing *something*.'[35]

The Power is a fairly interesting adaptation of a minor novel by sf writer Frank M. Robinson about a scientist (George Hamilton) working at a space research laboratory who discovers, through an experiment in telekinesis, that one of his co-workers is a mutant with awesome mental powers. The film concerns the attempts to identify who is the one. Though the script is

George Hamilton is faced with the sight of his own drowned body in The Power.

disjointed and the film rather sluggish in places, it's not a complete failure. With today's vogue for films dealing with telekinetic powers – such as *Carrie*, *The Medusa Touch* and *The Fury* – the time is ripe for *The Power* to be reissued.

The year 1968 saw the release of two films whose stories concerned the discovery of alien artefacts. These lead to the realization that mankind's development has resulted from alien manipulation dating back millions of years into the past. One of these films was, of course, *2001: A Space Odyssey*, which remains the greatest sf film ever made despite more recent contenders like *Star Wars* and *Close Encounters*; the other was Hammer's production of *Quatermass and the Pit* (called *Five Million Years to Earth* outside Britain), which was based on Nigel Kneale's 1958 BBC-TV serial – the third in the series involving space expert Professor Quatermass. Though the film telescopes the original story the plot basically follows that of the serial (the screenplay was also written by Kneale). It begins when the remains of an ape-man are discovered while a new underground railway station is being excavated under a London street called Hob's Lane. An anthropologist (James Donald) and his assistant (Barbara Shelley) arrive on the scene and uncover more primitive remains, as well as a large cylindrical object which appears to be made of metal and which is thought to be an unexploded German bomb. The Army soon realize that it is more likely to be a German rocket. This brings in rocket expert Professor Quatermass and his military counterpart, the arrogant, narrow-minded Colonel Breen (Andrew Keir and Julian Glover respectively).

When the object is completely free of the surrounding clay Quatermass has profound doubts as to whether it has anything to do with the Second World War, particularly when one of the strange fossil skulls, which date back over five million years, is found *inside* the object. To the amazement of Quatermass and the others the object is also found to contain the bodies of several large, insect-like creatures which begin to putrefy rapidly as soon as the air reaches them. Quatermass believes them to be aliens from outer space but Breen maintains that they represent part of a Nazi propaganda campaign that never got properly under way.

Quatermass deduces that the creatures originated from Mars and when, millions of years ago, they realized their planet was dying they invaded Earth. But it was an invasion by proxy; not being able themselves to live on Earth they captured a number of primitives apes, took them back to Mars and altered their genetic structure, turning them into Martians *mentally*. The ape creatures were then returned to Earth and let loose to breed with others of their species. The implications stun Quatermass as he realizes that the human race didn't evolve naturally but as a result of Martian interference. 'Gentlemen!,' he cries, '*we* are the Martians!'

Despite Quatermass's objections Breen arranges for a TV crew to film

The astronauts prepare to examine the Black Monolith found buried on the moon in 2001: A Space Odyssey.

the object. But as soon as the power cables for the TV equipment are laid through the pit and into the interior of the object there is an outbreak of psychic activity with objects flying in all directions. The area of activity rapidly increases and before long groups of people roam the streets in a form of trance, hunting down people who don't possess the 'power' and killing them with a barrage of telekinetically propelled objects.

Barricaded in a pub, Quatermass explains that the Martian strain in the human species remained dominant genetically. The Martians had programmed their altered creatures periodically to conduct a cull of the species in order to remove any human mutations who might have been born with the Martian genes. Over the years this programming had faded, with the result that a great number of 'non-Martian' people had evolved naturally. However, the object in the pit, which was organic in nature, was not merely a space vehicle but also designed to reinforce the programming. It had lain dormant for eons, except on occasions when seismic activity had slightly activated it and produced ghostly manifestations. Now that it had an enormous supply of energy it was fully activated and spreading its influence farther and farther afield.

The huge form of one of the Martians then appears; with its triangular face and its horns it looks exactly like the devil. The anthropologist saves the day by mixing an old law of the supernatural (about a demon being unable to survive cold iron) with science; he sacrifices his life in swinging the steel boom of a crane round to penetrate the Martian shape, thus effectively grounding it and dissipating its energy. The second Martian invasion is over.

With this story Kneale created one of the most ingenious alien-invasion plots of all time. In a nod to Wells's Martians he gives his Martian 'insects' three legs, and as with the other Quatermass sagas it is the cunning mixture of contemporary science with deep-rooted myths and super-stitions that gives the work its extra resonance. In this Kneale is exploring themes similar to those of sf writer Arthur C. Clarke. The idea of the devil becoming implanted in the human racial memory as a result of contact with a horned alien species figured prominently in Clarke's 1953 novel *Childhood's End*, and the idea of an alien artefact being discovered underground was the subject of Clarke's 1950 short story *The Sentinel*.

The Sentinel provided the basis for Stanley Kubrick's *2001: A Space Odyssey*, which also incorporated elements of *Childhood's End*. In the novel the human race in its present form is discovered to be the equivalent of a caterpillar in terms of its cosmic evolution, and the book ends with all the children of the world forming a super *gestalt* which flies off into space

(Left and right) *Scenes from* 2001: A Space Odyssey.

to join others of its kind. Clarke is often thought of as a pure technology buff, but much of his work deals with people encountering a profound and almost absolute Mystery presented in a form that borders on the religious. Writing about *Childhood's End* Brian Aldiss observed that the story 'is expressed in simple but aspiring language that vaguely recalls the Psalms, even down to the liberal use of colons; when this is combined with a dramatized sense of loss, Clarke's predominant emotion, the result has an undeniable effect.'[36] In another age Clarke's religious urges might have led him to become a theologian, but having been seduced by science at an early age he has been forced to rationalize his need to believe in a superior being by clothing the concept in scientific terms. Thus 'God' becomes an alien race so incredibly evolved that it is beyond the comprehension of mere human minds. Von Daniken is trying to say much the same thing, though in a more pedestrian way.

In Stanley Kubrick Clarke found the perfect collaborator. Both men are technology-fixated, have high energy drives, are perfectionists, and are insatiably curious, and both share similar ideas on God. 'I will say that the God concept is at the heart of *2001*,' said Kubrick, 'but not any traditional, anthropomorphic image of God. I don't believe in any of Earth's monotheistic religions, but I do believe that one can construct an intriguing *scientific* definition of God.' Whether one considers *2001* as a religious epic or as a science fiction film that deals with religious concepts scientifically one has to admit that it succeeds in creating a sense of awe and wonder around the basic mystery of the Universe, as well as producing in the viewer a feeling of vague optimism – a rare thing in most sf films.

The 'plot' of *2001* is simple: it begins in prehistoric times with the arrival of an alien artefact, in the form of a black monolith, that triggers a number of primitive ape-men into becoming tool-users. The film then jumps to the year 2001 where we join a passenger (William Sylvester) on a spaceship heading for the moon. We learn that he is a government official on a mission to the moon to supervise the handling of a remarkable discovery in the American sector. Buried beneath the moon's surface has been found what appears to be a 'man'-made object – a black monolith. When the official and his companions arrive at the excavation and examine the object it suddenly emits an incredibly powerful radio signal. The film then cuts to a huge spaceship called the 'Discovery' on its way to one of the moons of Jupiter – the target of the radio beam transmitted from the monolith. (The idea of an object on the moon acting as a 'cosmic burglar alarm' when Man arrives was the basis of Clarke's *The Sentinel*.) In the spaceship are five men, three of whom are in suspended animation, and one intelligent computer called HAL 9000 which controls the ship. The two conscious astronauts, David Bowman (Keir Dullea) and Frank Poole (Gary Lockwood), later realize that HAL is malfunctioning, but the computer kills Poole and traps Bowman outside the ship. Then it shuts down the life support systems of the hibernating astronauts. Bowman finally succeeds in forcing his way back into the ship and then enters HAL's computer core where he proceeds to deactivate him.

When the 'Discovery' arrives at its destination Bowman sets off in one of the pods and encounters another black monolith floating in space. As he approaches it he is suddenly bombarded with a stream of visual and physical sensations – in actuality he has entered a 'star gate' and is travelling, via another dimension, over unimaginable distances. Finally he and the pod end up in an eerie, completely white room where he is prematurely aged by the unseen entities and then transformed into a new type of being.

2001: A Space Odyssey.

The final shots are of a embryo-like form staring with an unreadable expression down upon the Earth. It's the 'star child', the next step in Man's cosmic evolution, though what will happen now to all the unchanged millions on Earth is a question that receives no answer.

Reaction to the film on its initial release was hostile; critics described it as confused, pretentious, disjointed, boring, baffling, dull and banal. The chief complaint was that it was difficult to understand what it was all about, and Kubrick was accused of being deliberately enigmatic in order to disguise the fact that the film wasn't really about anything at all. Yet to any regular reader of science fiction most of the film was perfectly clear and so it was younger audiences, more familiar with sf, who first appreciated *2001*, subsequently ensuring its financial success and, at the same time, forcing many critics to re-examine their original opinions. Much of the film is deliberately ambiguous, revolving as it does around a giant question-mark concerning Man's relationship with both the Universe and the mysterious beings that have been manipulating his development. If these mysteries were explained the film would lose most of its magic and wonder; yet people conditioned to having films provide clear-cut answers to everything persisted in asking Kubrick what the 'message' of *2001* was. In a *Playboy* magazine interview Kubrick replied: 'It's not a message that I ever intend to convey in words. *2001* is a nonverbal experience; out of two hours and 19 minutes of film, there are only a little less than 40 minutes of dialogue. I tried to create a *visual* experience, one that bypasses verbalized pigeonholing and directly penetrates the subconscious with emotional and philosophic content. . . . You're free to speculate as you wish about the philosophical and allegorical meaning of the film . . . but I don't want to spell out a verbal road map of *2001* that every viewer will feel obligated to pursue or else fear he's missed the point.'[37]

Yet even a number of established science fiction writers reacted with hostility towards the film. Ray Bradbury, for instance, wrote in a review: 'Clarke should have done the screenplay totally on his own and not allowed Kubrick to lay hands on it . . . the test of the film is whether or not we care when one of the astronauts dies. We do not . . . The freezing touch of Antonioni, whose ghost haunts Kubrick, has turned everything here to ice.'[38] Then he later told an interviewer: 'I think it's a gorgeous film. One of the most beautifully photographed pictures in the history of motion pictures. Unfortunately there are no well-directed scenes, and the dialogue is banal to the point of extinction.'[39]

What upset some of the older sf writers who disliked the film was Kubrick's treatment of humanity. It had long been the tradition in the old school of sf to present Man as a plucky little creature who faces the Universe with a slide-rule in one hand and a blaster in the other and soon has it cowering in fear. Kubrick, on the other hand, treats the human race with cold irony – presenting Man as an impotent, rather pathetic, helpless pawn of forces far beyond his comprehension. To many sf writers this was a step backwards to a time when religion ruled Man by fear – a time before science enabled Man to break free of his bonds and put to rest all the old 'superstitions'. Lester Del Rey, who once wrote a story where Mankind declares war on God and wins, was particularly incensed by *2001*.

An even bigger crime on Kubrick's part, in their eyes, was his condescending attitude towards technology. In the old school of sf, technology was to be the means whereby Man conquers the Universe, but when Kubrick jump-cuts from the ape-man hurling his bone-weapon into the air to the shot of the satellite (actually a weapons platform) he is suggesting that, for all the advances in technology that lead from the bone to the satellite, nothing has changed fundamentally. Man is still an ape creature playing with his toys; he hasn't developed one iota in the cosmic sense.

Despite the breathtaking technological wonders revealed on William Sylvester's trip to the moon – the spaceships, the space station, the gadgetry – the overall effect of gleaming white interiors is to suggest a feeling of sterility. Cocooned in his marvellous machines Man has come to a dead end. This feeling is reinforced by all the people we meet during the film – they are bland and lifeless and their conversation consists of nothing but exchanged banalities. The nearest thing to an 'emotional' character is the computer HAL 9000 who breaks down under the strain and goes insane. He, or it, represents another dead-end. Man had fashioned him in his own image but he wasn't up to the job and, like Man, couldn't cope with concepts beyond his programmed powers of comprehension.

The film, of course, wasn't a drama about people in the accepted sense of the word. It wasn't *about* the various individual characters – it didn't matter whether they lived or died, which is why we don't care very much when Poole and the others are killed – it was really about the human race as a whole and its position in the Universe. Kubrick's aim was to force his audiences to look afresh at these questions – to re-examine their own perceptions of the Universe – all of which would have been obscured by the presence of emotionally involving, *real* characters.

Whatever games of interpretation one may play with *2001* one has to admit that it is a stunning visual and auditory experience, right from the first shots of the Earth, moon and sun in alignment, accompanied by the 'Dawn' passage of Richard Strauss's *Also sprach Zarathustra*. Kubrick's choice of music throughout the film shows a touch of genius, like his idea of accompanying the shots of the Pan Am space shuttle moving towards the space station with *The Blue Danube*.

On the technical level *2001* has yet to be surpassed. The special effects, supervised by Kubrick himself and created by a large team of experts headed by Wally Veevers, Tom Howard, Douglas Trumbull and Con Pederson, are amazing in their realism. Eighteen months were spent shooting them at a cost of $6,500,000 (the total cost of the film was $10,500,000). 'I felt it was necessary to make this film in such a way that every special effects shot in it would be completely convincing,' said Kubrick, 'something that had never before been accomplished in a motion picture.' Nor has it been since, despite the publicity for *Star Wars*. The model work and associated effects in *Star Wars* are certainly spectacular – more so than those in *2001*, perhaps, and certainly more ambitious in scope – but technically the model shots in *2001* are far superior, as a careful comparison will readily show. The reason is that Kubrick rejected the use of any automatic matting process, such as the blue screen system, which invariably produces matte lines and thus destroys the illusion of reality. Instead he insisted that all the various components of each effects shot be combined on film by means of hand-drawn mattes. This meant, for instance, that a scene showing a spaceship passing against a background of stars involved each shot of the spaceship being meticulously rotascoped frame by frame onto animation cells which were used to produce mattes to blank out the corresponding areas on the star-background footage. Much of *2001* was put together in the manner of an animated cartoon, the main difference being that all the image components had to appear as realistic as possible, thus making the task much more difficult than that faced by cartoon animators who only have to combine drawings.* These methods produce the best results but they are very time-consuming and expensive, and if the *Star Wars* technicians had followed the same path the film probably wouldn't have been released until late 1978, having cost twice as much as it did. Because the makers of *Star Wars* wanted to use many more model shots than in *2001* they were forced to utilize an automatic matting process, with the result that matte lines are visible in some scenes whereas *2001* is flawless in this respect.

Most of the sf films that followed *2001* were something of an anti-climax, particularly those that involved space travel. The fifth film in the James Bond series, *You Only Live Twice*, suddenly looked awfully weak in its outer space sequences, the special effects appearing almost amateurish compared to those of *2001*. With its plot concerning SPECTRE's attempt to start World War Three by using its shark-like spaceship to capture American and Russian space vehicles it was the most sf-orientated Bond film up until that time. Most of the attention centred on the villains' secret rocket base, which was situated within an extinct volcano on a island off the coast of Japan. The interior of the huge set was built on the backlot at Pinewood Studios at a cost of over a quarter of a million pounds and was

*For a more in-depth look at the effects in *2001*, see *Movie Magic*.

The vast volcano set under construction at Pinewood Studios, England, and (below) the completed set as it appeared in You Only Live Twice.

certainly impressive, but its use in a key sequence in the film – when a full-scale mock-up of a spaceship, spouting flame from its tail, lands through the crater opening – was spoilt by the very obvious sight of the crane cable attached to the nose of the rocket. The special effects at the end of the film, involving the destruction of the volcano, were also rather poor, with several embarrassing shots of rigid little dummy men being bounced up and down on the volcano floor with each explosion. The director was Lewis Gilbert and the screenplay was by Roald Dahl.

Also something of a space dud was *Marooned*, directed in 1969 by John Sturges, who is best known for westerns like *The Magnificent Seven*. *Marooned* was the first space soap opera. Written by Mayo Simon and based on a novel by Martin Caidin, it concerned a space mission that goes wrong, trapping three American astronauts in orbit around the Earth. The scenes involving the three wives waiting anxiously back at the base were particularly mawkish, but the dialogue wasn't much better up in the space capsule. The exchanges between the astronauts were so trite that they made the deliberate banality of the dialogue in *2001* seem almost scintillating. Each of the three actors playing the astronauts (Richard Crenna, James Franciscus and Gene Hackman) was saddled with a pure stereotype, and even Hackman couldn't manage to invest his role with any substance. Nor were the special effects, again in comparison with *2001*, very special, and the most impressive visuals in the film came from footage of an actual Saturn rocket launch. Just as dull was the similar film *Countdown*, directed in 1976 by Robert Altman, which had lone astronaut James Caan stranded on the moon.

Superior in the area of special effects was a 1969 British film called *Doppelganger* (*Journey to the Far Side of the Sun*), directed by Hollywood veteran Robert Parrish, but the script was a mixture of pseudo-science at its most illogical and sheer pretentiousness. It was written by Gerry and Sylvia Anderson, the British equivalents of Irwin Allen, and the film was based on the old idea of a planet on the opposite side of the sun from the Earth which can therefore never be detected by Earth astronomers. Unfortunately the Andersons lose control of the plot en route and the film degenerates into pure confusion.

The special effects were supervised by Derek Meddings, who had been in charge of the effects in the Andersons' popular puppet TV series *Thunderbirds*. 'It was terribly complicated from the effects point of view,' said Meddings. 'We had to simulate a rocket take-off from Cape Canaveral because we couldn't use any existing stock footage, as our rocket was supposed to look more futuristic than any existing rocket and also much bigger. So we had to build a miniature Cape Canaveral in the studio, which we did, and it was very successful. So was the rocket take-off itself; for that we built a model six feet high, and all around it we had

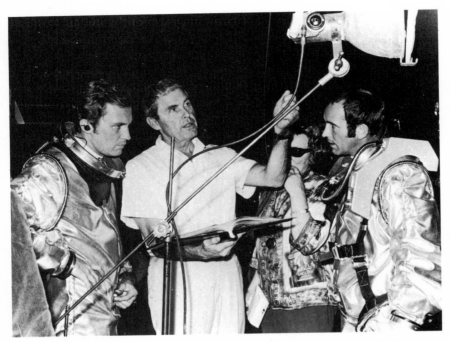

Director Robert Parrish (centre) with Roy Thinnes (left) and Ian Hendry (right) on the set of Doppelganger.

the miniature launch area — including the gantry, the tower and other buildings as well as little vehicles running around. Later in the film we had to wreck all that for the sequence where the rocket comes back out of control and crashes into the launch site.

'It was quite a large miniature because we had to be able to track right through it with a very low camera — between the buildings and so on — to provide back-projection footage for scenes where the characters are supposed to be in vehicles driving through the base. I think we spent over £100,000 on the effects in that film — at that time the company was riding high because of the success of *Thunderbirds* etcetera, so it was able to get finance for whatever it wanted to do. We were put up to be nominated for an Effects Oscar that year but unfortunately didn't even get the nomination. The film that won the Effects Oscar was *Marooned*.'

Neither *Marooned* nor *Doppelganger* was a great box-office success and the blame was put chiefly on the real moon landing that took place that year, an event that tended to make the cinema's space age activities look rather out-of-date. The same excuse was used to explain the failure of Hammer's 1969 space opera *Moon Zero Two*, but the sheer looniness of the project can't have helped. In that it was a space western it was a forerunner to *Star Wars*, but there all resemblance ends. 'It's all just about bad enough to fill older audiences with nostalgia for the inspired innocence of Flash Gordon, or even the good old days of Abbott and

Costello in outer space,' said the British *Monthly Film Bulletin*. Directed by Roy Ward Baker, this exercise in pure camp is set on the moon in the year 2021 AD. The moon has become the equivalent of the Old West, complete with saloons, gunfights and moustache-twirling villains. James Olson stars as the down-on-his-luck-but-basically-honest space pilot/cowboy who is forced to work for the villainous, money-grasping J. J. Hubbard (Warren Mitchell) and assist him in his search for a 6,000-ton asteroid of pure sapphire which will enable Hubbard to rule the solar system. But, with the aid of the beautiful Clementine Taplin (Catherina von Schell), who has been swindled out of her inheritance by Hubbard, he does the right thing in the end and foils the villain's evil plans.

Ironically, one space film that did relatively well that year was a throwback to the old monster-from-outer-space variety. Called *The Green Slime* it was an American/Japanese co-production directed by Kinji Fukasaku and starred Robert Horton and Richard Jaeckel in a story about a space station in the future invaded by an alien organism. The more interesting sf films during this period were, with the exception of *2001*, the non-space ones such as *Charly* (1968) directed by Ralph Nelson (whose most recent sf entry was *Embryo*), scripted by Stirling Silliphant (who wrote the screenplay for *Village of the Damned*) and based on the highly regarded story, which was later expanded into a novel, by Daniel Keyes called *Flowers for Algernon*. Many actors would jump at the chance of playing a character who, within the time-span of one film, ranges from a subnormal 30-year-old to a super-genius and then back again to

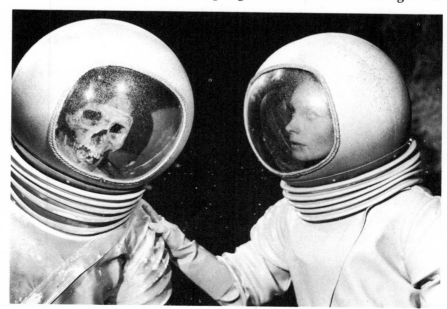

'You don't look well,' Catherina von Schell *seems to be saying to her companion in this scene from* Moon Zero Two.

subnormal; Cliff Robertson, who starred in *Rod Brown of the Rocket Rangers* – a children's sf TV serial – back in 1953 and played John F. Kennedy in *PT-109* in 1963, did more than jump – he formed his own production company and, after various setbacks, succeeded in obtaining the necessary finance to make the film. It was a gamble that paid off in more ways than one and his performance in *Charly* won him an Academy Award that year. But apart from being an effective showcase of an actor's talents the film also retains some of the evocative pathos of the original. As in Keyes's story we follow Charly's tortuous progress from amiable idiot to intelligent innocent (the result of an experimental brain drug), his discovery of love and sex with a woman doctor (Claire Bloom), his further development to the level of genius, and then the horror of his regression back to his former self when it is learnt that the effects of the drug are only temporary.

Less successful was the overly pretentious *The Illustrated Man* based on Ray Bradbury's anthology of the same name. As a connecting framework for the book Bradbury used the device of a completely tattooed man each of whose tattooes represents a different story. But the formula doesn't work in the film. Only three of the stories from the book are used and although the tattooed man (Rod Steiger) serves as an introduction to each there is no obvious connection between them (apart from Steiger and Claire Bloom playing different roles in all three). Best of the three stories is *The Veldt*: two children in the future use one of their playroom 'toys' – which can create a three-dimensional image of an African setting, complete with lions – as a means of disposing of their parents.

Equally pretentious was *Je T'aime, Je T'aime* (1969), written and directed by Alain Resnais and starring Claude Rich, Olga Georges-Picot and Anouk Ferjac. With this film the French film-maker continued along the cinematic road that he established with his innovatory *Last Year at Marienbad*. When a failed suicide is discharged from hospital he is abducted by a group of scientists who place him in a very organic-looking time machine. They intend to transport him back one year in time but the machine malfunctions and he begins to oscillate back and forth in time. The remainder of the film consists of fragments of his previous life (presented by Resnais in the deliberately disorientating *Marienbad* manner) that slowly build up to produce a picture of humdrum monotony as well as a suspicion that he may have murdered his dreary girlfriend. The film ends with another suicide attempt by the protagonist, the implication being that this one will be successful.

A reflection of the short-lived hippy/youth culture boom of the late 1960s was *Wild in the Streets*, a 1968 AIP production directed by Barry Shear and written by Robert Thom. (AIP has had an eye cocked at the teenage market since the mid-1950s when such films as *I Was a Teenage*

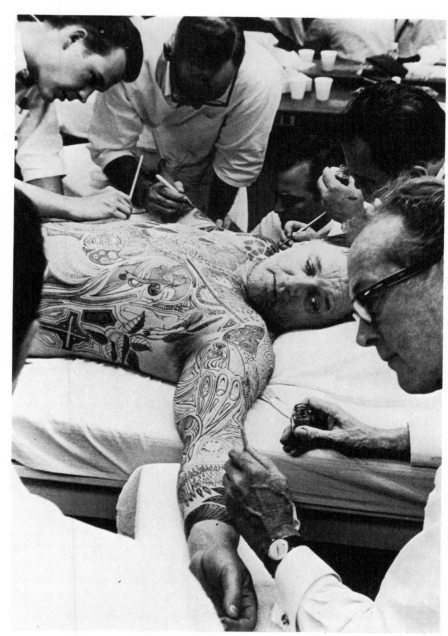

Rod Steiger's 'tattoos' are supplied by a team of make-up artists for The Illustrated Man.

Frankenstein helped establish the company's financial security.) The plot concerns a young pop star, Max Frost, who lends his support to a Kennedy-style senator in California and subsequently wins the election for him. Frost immediately demands, as his price, the lowering of the voting age to 14. Compromise is reached on 18 but Frost and his group take over the country, putting everyone over 35 in concentration camps. The teenagers and the 20–30 age-groups create a permissive society and enjoy themselves hugely, but by the end of the film the sub-teens are muttering rebellion and another revolution seems imminent.

The ever-present threat of atomic war reared its cinematic head again in 1969 in Richard Lester's *The Bed Sitting Room*. A sort of postscript to Kubrick's *Dr Strangelove*, the film is an absurdist black comedy set in England after World War Three. A number of dazed survivors try desperately to pretend that everything is normal, even when some of them start mutating into wardrobes, bed sitting rooms and parrots. The play on which it was based, written by Spike Milligan and John Antrobus, was a free-wheeling, much-improvized piece of slapstick, and what remains of the original material in the screenplay (Charles Wood provided additional material) clashes awkwardly with Lester's chillingly bleak settings showing the aftermath of an atomic war : the shattered dome of St Paul's Cathedral protruding from a swamp ; a line of wrecked cars in a permanent traffic jam along a disconnected length of motorway ; a grim expanse of landscape dominated by great piles of sludge and heaps of discarded boots, broken plates, false teeth. 'The really awful thing,' said Lester, 'is that we were able to film most of those things in England without having to fake it. All that garbage is real. A lot of it was filmed behind the Steel Corporation in Wales and it really is a disgusting area. Endless piles of acid sludge and every tree is dead. And there's a place in Stoke where they've been throwing reject plates since the war and it has become a vast landscape of broken plates.'

A real oddity was *The Most Dangerous Man in the World* (also known as *The Chairman*) which starred Gregory Peck as a scientist who has a transmitting device implanted in his head and is then sent to China to seek an audience with Chairman Mao. The object of the exercise is to convince Mao that he has defected and thus to obtain the secret of a new enzyme which the Chinese have developed to enable crops to be grown under any conditions anywhere in the world. The transmitter in his brain automatically passes on everything he hears and sees to the intelligence people in London, but they haven't told him that there is also a small bomb in his head – and that they intend to detonate it by remote control if anything goes wrong. The film was based on a straight novel by Jay Richard Kennedy, but director J. Lee Thompson and his writer Ben Maddow wisely decided to approach the subject with their tongues firmly in their cheeks.

As mentioned earlier the Bond films began the trend in which science fiction elements were increasingly incorporated into thrillers during the 1960s – a trend which reached boom proportions in the latter half of the

The last remaining churchman in England after World War 3 is forced to hold his services underwater in Richard Lester's The Bed Sitting Room.

The British Prime Minister and a BBC interviewer discuss the country's future after World War 3: a scene from the same film.

decade. Foremost among the Bond imitators were the Matt Helm series of films (*The Silencers, Murderers Row, The Wrecking Crew*) starring Dean Martin; the two Derek Flint films, *Our Man Flint* and *In Like Flint*; and the various 'Man from Uncle' feature films (created by combining TV episodes and adding extra footage) like *The Spy With My Face, One of Our Spies Is Missing, One Spy Too Many* and *How to Steal the World*, all of which became progressively more far-fetched. But the most way-out sf/spy film of all was *Casino Royale* (1967), a bizarre concoction that had nothing to do with the Ian Fleming novel of the same name. The cast included Peter Sellers, Ursula Andress, Orson Welles, David Niven, Deborah Kerr, William Holden and Woody Allen, and the plot, if such it can be called, ranged between surreal black comedy and pure slapstick and ended with Woody Allen, playing the would-be master of the world, swallowing a pill-sized atom bomb and blowing himself, and everything else, to bits. The disparity of styles within the film is understandable given the horde of writers and directors who each contributed something to the proceedings. The man behind the film was the late Charles K. Feldman, a Hollywood agent turned producer, and one of the people he hired to work on the film was writer/director Val Guest. 'Charlie called me in right at the beginning,' said Guest, 'and he said: "Look, I'm going to give you six scripts of *Casino Royale* and I want you to try and get *one* out of them all." And they were as widely varied as you could possibly get; there was one by Ben Hecht, there was one by Terry Southern, one by Dore Schary, and so on – all top writers – but eventually we didn't use any of them. It was a psychedelic nightmare – he had to start shooting on a certain date because he'd signed Sellers up to start then and he didn't want to lose him. So we virtually started shooting without a script; then Charlie flew Woody Allen over and I worked with Woody on the script for a long time, which was great – he's fun to work with – but Charlie would go through the stuff we'd beaten out and would cut out all the gags and just leave the build-ups.

'The main problem was that we were shooting in three different studios and we used to commute from MGM at Elstree to Pinewood to Shepperton. We had standing sets in each studio . . . it was a nightmare because Charlie would call me up in the middle of the night and say: "Look, I can get Bardot next Wednesday. Which set are we on then? Well, write her in." That was the way he got those eighteen or so international stars in the film. He started off by conning Sellers into doing it by saying that Niven was going to do it, then he called Niven and said Sellers is going to do it and so then he got Niven. I used to sit in Charlie's office while he conned people on the telephone. He got Bill Holden because he used to be his agent at one time, but I remember we had a terrible time getting Jean-Paul Belmondo. We told Ursula Andress: "You've got to persuade Belmondo to come in,"

and she said: "He doesn't want to know about it." But we made her keep pestering him until he gave in. It was all a nightmare but it eventually made money – a lot of money.'

In 1969 two sf films were released aimed primarily at children. The first was *Captain Nemo and the Underwater City* directed by James Hill and written by R. Wright Campbell and Pip and Jane Barker. It starred a tired-looking, and very miscast, Robert Ryan as Captain Nemo, who is trying to establish a utopia within his underwater city but, as usual, is betrayed by human greed. The second film was the Schneer/Harryhausen production *The Valley of Gwangi*. Based on an old project of Willis O'Brien's it concerned a group of cowboys in modern-day Mexico who find a lost valley inhabited by dinosaurs. Despite the worn-out old plot Harryhausen was surprised when the film wasn't a success and blamed it on the vogue for sex films. 'A naked dinosaur just wasn't outrageous enough,' he said.

The big sf movie success of the late 1960s, apart again from *2001*, was *Planet of the Apes*, directed in 1968 by Franklin J. Schaffner. Based on the novel *Le Planète des Singes* by Pierre Boulle, it was scripted by Michael Wilson and Rod Serling and starred Charlton Heston as an astronaut whose spaceship goes through a time warp and hurtles thousands of years into the future. When he and his companions crash-land on what appears to be an 'alien' planet they discover it is ruled by English-speaking apes and that human beings are relegated to the position of lowly animals. One of the three astronauts is shot dead (we later see him stuffed and mounted in a museum) and the other two are captured by the apes. Heston manages to avoid the fate that befalls his surviving companion – who is given a frontal lobotomy – by persuading two ape scientists, Di Zira (Kim Hunter) and Dr Zaius (Roddy McDowell), that he is actually an intelligent being (he achieves this by speaking English at them), and they finally help him escape from the ape city in the company of one of the local human females. The film ends with Heston encountering the half-buried form of the Statue of Liberty and realizing – surprise! – that he is still on Earth.

As a piece of action-adventure cinema *Planet of the Apes* is very slick and competent, but as science fiction it's illogical rubbish. The plot revolves around the fact that the astronaut doesn't realize, until the very end, that the ape world is really Earth in the future – a future where the apes have evolved to become the dominant species – despite the fact that he had heard them speaking English. Nor are the apes unduly surprised when they hear him speaking English: they're only surprised that he can talk at all. Yet the film became one of the most popular sf ones of all time, spawning a whole series of sequels and a TV series, and its success demonstrates that despite the increasing sophistication of sf movies during the 1960s the general public still didn't understand what science fiction was all about.

9 Boom Two (1970–73)

In the early 1970s diversification within the science fiction film genre continued. The year 1970, for instance, saw the first sf musical since *Just Imagine*, though not many people have had the opportunity of seeing it. The film was called *Toomorrow* and was the brainchild of Harry Saltzman, the Canadian-born producer who, with co-producer Albert R. Broccoli, had launched the James Bond series of movies. 'When I joined the project,' said Guest, the film's writer and director, 'Harry had all sorts of ideas about the film, but the script hadn't yet been written. He brought in David Benedictus to do the script but after about thirty pages he called me in and said: "This isn't right, is it?" And I said, "No, but we can make it right." It was very well-written but a little bit too "high-faluting" – obviously not the sort of musical that Harry wanted to make. So Harry said: "Well, don't say anything to him. Let him go on and finish but you start writing the script from scratch now. I'll take care of him." So I went ahead and did as he said, but it wasn't until I'd finished my script that Benedictus found out that there was another script apart from his. Apparently Harry had never told him, and as a result I made a great enemy of Benedictus – he wrote me the most ghastly letter.

'*Toomorrow* was to be the first space musical. The basic plot was that there was a galactic shortage of sound and these aliens send an emissary to Earth to locate the type of sound that contains the certain vibrations they lacked "up there". And the aliens pick on a group of poor, struggling musicians mainly, I think, because one of them has a home-made moog synthesizer. So these kids get transported up into a space craft to teach the galactic people how to make this sound. Anyway, I think that was the plot. But working with Harry was similar to my experience with Charlie Feldman on *Casino Royale* – it became a vast project and Harry spent a lot of money on it, about eight or nine million dollars altogether. He was never satisfied, he was always wanting to do a scene or rebuild a set in a different way. He went into partnership with Don Kirshner, who was "Mr Music" in America, but Don, halfway through the film, backed out because he couldn't get on with Harry.

'Eventually the film was finished and it was delivered over to Rank, the distributors, who opened it at the London Pavilion cinema in London. It

Dr Forbin is dwarfed by his creation—the super computer Colossus.

only ran for two weeks because I put an injunction on it and they had to take it off. The reason I did that was because I hadn't been paid. And I haven't been paid to this day even though I later won a High Court case against the company that had made it – Sweet Music. So the film has never been shown at all since then, anywhere. Perhaps Rank will say one day that it's probably worth paying me just to be able to screen it somewhere, though it's way out of date now. I think it could have been a success at the time. It was a lot of fun, it had some great visuals and very good special effects [by John Stears, who later handled the physical effects in *Star Wars*], and it had a good score written by two guys who wrote all the stuff for the Monkees – Don Kirshner had brought them over. And what's more it launched a new young singer called Olivia Newton-John. It should have made money.'

But whether it would or not, those critics who managed to see it didn't like it. A typical comment was that of the *Monthly Film Bulletin*, which called it 'a corny blend of pop and science fiction. Extravagant sets and a fresh-faced, embarrassingly ingratiating pop group light years removed from the real thing.'

Another film that few people have seen is *The Forbin Project* (also known as *Colossus: The Forbin Project*), mainly because its distributor, Universal, didn't show much faith in it. Directed by Joseph Sargent and based on the novel *Colossus* by D. F. Jones, it's a slick and well-constructed film about a computer designed to take control of the US defence network, since the decision whether or not to launch a nuclear attack is clearly too important to be left to mere people. Once it's activated the computer reveals personal ambitions of its own which have little to do with the wants of human beings, including those of its creator Dr Forbin (played with a suitable machine-like brittleness by Eric Braeden). Unlike the neurotic HAL in *2001*, who was more human than the astronauts, Colossus is a computer of the old school – emotionless, arrogant and practically omnipotent. When the authorities are slow to give in to his commands Colossus takes direct control of various missile sites and threatens to destroy American cities. He links up with his Russian counterpart and the two of them hold the entire world to nuclear ransom. The film then becomes a battle of wits between Colossus and Forbin as Forbin, the machine's designer, is the only man who possibly possesses the necessary knowledge needed to overcome the computer. Colossus realizes this but, because he holds his creator in high regard, he doesn't have Forbin killed; instead he attempts to isolate him from all outside contact and keeps him under constant surveillance with his electronic eyes and ears.

To solve this problem Forbin pretends that his female assistant, Cleo (Susan Clark), is his lover and he insists to the computer that to preserve his sexual well-being she must be allowed to visit him. 'How many visits from her a week will you need?' asks Colossus. 'Oh, at least five,' replies Forbin. 'I said *need*, not want,' says Colossus. The sequences where Forbin and Cleo carry out their romantic act (he embarrassed and she enjoying herself) under the watchful eyes of the computer are well-handled and amusing (never before has the 'love interest' been so ingeniously incorporated into an sf movie). The suggestion is that to outwit the machine the cold and unemotional Dr Forbin will have to become less like a machine himself: he will have to learn how to become a human being for the first time in his life.

An attempt is made to render Colossus powerless by removing all the warheads from every missile – under the guise of normal maintenance – but the computer discovers what is going on and has the ringleaders executed, though once again sparing Forbin. The film ends with Colossus still in control and promising that a new age is about to begin on Earth. He will end all wars, all disease, all poverty – but things are going to have to change. Forbin declares his continuing defiance, but the impression remains that Colossus is here to stay.

The Forbin Project successfully communicates the feeling that something immensely powerful has got out of control – a mood chillingly established in the opening sequence when the vast interior of the computer comes alive section by section (these shots, created by effects man Albert Whitlock, are reminiscent of the Krel machinery in *Forbidden Planet*) and it is then irreversibly sealed off within the bowels of the Rocky Mountains. One recalls the famous short story by sf writer Fredric Brown that ends with a group of scientists asking their first question to the super computer they've activated: 'Is there a God?' 'There is now,' it replies.

Easier to encounter in the cinema was *Beneath the Planet of the Apes*, the sequel to the highly successful *Planet of the Apes*. Once again the producer was Arthur P. Jacobs, the man behind the whole ape project. He had bought the rights to Boulle's novel back in 1965, mainly because he wanted to remake *King Kong* but couldn't obtain the rights to that property. 'Then I spent about $3\frac{1}{2}$ years of everyone refusing to make the movie,' said Jacobs in a 1971 interview. 'First, I had sketches made, and went through six sets of artists to get the concept, but none of them were right. Finally, I hit on a seventh one and said *that's* how it should look. Then I showed the sketches to the studios, and they said, "No way." Then I got Rod Serling to do the screenplay, and went to everybody again – absolute turndown. I went to Rank in England and Samuel Bronston in Spain. Everyone said no. So then I figured, maybe if I got an actor involved; and I went to Charlton Heston who, in one hour, said yes. Then Heston suggested Franklin Schaffner as director, and he also said yes. Now I have Heston, Schaffner and a screenplay, and all the sketches. I go right back to everybody and they throw me out again.

'I finally convinced Richard Zanuck to let me make a test, and I got Heston and Edward G. Robinson, with Schaffner directing it. I showed it to Zanuck who really got excited about it. The test consisted of a conversation between Heston and Robinson as Dr Zaius in ape make-up. Everyone thought that no one would believe an ape talking to a man . . . we packed the screening room with everyone we could get hold of, and Zanuck said: "If they start laughing, forget it." Nobody laughed, they sat there tense, and he said, "Make the picture." '[40] (One wonders if anyone *dare* laugh in the presence of Mr Zanuck.)

The second film contains the same implausibilities as the first. In *Beneath the Planet of the Apes*, directed this time by Ted Post and written by Paul Dehn and Mort Abrahams, another astronaut (James Franciscus), a friend of the first one, travels through the same time warp in his spaceship, ends up in roughly the same year, crash-lands in the same area of the world, encounters the same primitive girl, Nova (Linda Harrison), as Heston did, and then becomes involved with the same friendly ape, Zira (Kim Hunter). Like his predecessor he doesn't realise he's on Earth for some time until he discovers some underground ruins which he recognizes as parts of New York.

He and the girl are captured by a race of telepathic mutants who live in the ruins (actually dressed-up sets left over from *Hello Dolly!*) and who are the survivors of an atomic attack on New York that took place 2,000 years in the past. They now worship an object in their subterranean church which turns out to be a Doomsday Bomb, and chant such things as: 'Glory be to the Bomb and the Holy Fall-out; As it was in the beginning and always shall be,' and singing 'All things bright and beautiful, the Lord Bomb made us all.'

The film ends in a violent battle between apes, humans and mutants, with Heston making a cameo appearance just in time to see his friends die, get shot himself and finally fall on the button that detonates the Bomb that destroys the world. To 20th Century-Fox's surprise the film made as much money as the first (around $15,000,000). This resulted in the scriptwriter Paul Dehn receiving a telegram in London from Fox which said: 'Apes exist. Sequel required.' Having blown up the whole world this put him in something of a quandary, but he came up with an ingenious solution and *Escape from the Planet of the Apes* begins with three of the apes arriving in present-day America having escaped the holocaust by travelling back in time, via the same time warp, in the astronauts' salvaged spaceship. The three intelligent apes, Zira (Kim Hunter), Cornelius (Roddy McDowall) and Milo (Sal Mineo), are at first fêted by society and treated as celebrities, but when it is learned that Zira is pregnant they come to be regarded as a possible threat, and these fears are exploited by an ambitious

Presidential candidate (Eric Braeden, who played Forbin). After Milo is accidentally killed, Zira and Cornelius decide to hide out from the authorities and are given refuge by a kindly circus owner (Ricardo Montalban). Zira gives birth to a son but she and Cornelius are later tracked down and killed by the authorities. However, their offspring is rescued by the circus owner and the film ends with the little ape saying: 'Mama . . . mama!'

The fourth film in the series was entitled *Conquest of the Planet of the Apes* (1972) and was directed by J. Lee Thompson, the British director whose previous credits included *The Guns of Navarone*, the Wernher von Braun fiasco *I Aim At the Stars* and *The Chairman*. The scriptwriter was again Paul Dehn and the story concerns Zira's son Caesar as a young man, or rather young ape (played by Roddy McDowall), and his struggle to lead a revolution by apes against their human oppressors. Throwing science out the window, Dehn explained the sudden access of intelligence on the part of the world's ape population by saying that a plague had wiped out all humanity's usual pets, so the apes were used as substitutes: 'It was found that they could be taught to do simple things . . . and being apes they were far more intelligent than dogs, so very soon they began to do very much more difficult things like bed-making, cooking, sweeping . . . and they become the servants of mankind – the slaves,' said Dehn.[41] In other words he is suggesting that, if you take a gorilla out of the zoo and set him pottering around the house, in a few years he's going to be doing the *Times* crossword and striking for higher pay.

Caesar and his ape revolutionaries win their fight and end up ruling the world, but when his old friend the circus owner commits suicide Caesar has a change of heart and prevents his people from destroying the humans, telling them that the human race will eventually destroy itself in a nuclear war. Even as social satire or political allegories Dehn's ape stories leave a lot to be desired, and they operate on a very juvenile level.

That level dropped even further in the fifth and last film in the series *Battle for the Planet of the Apes* (1973), which was written by John William Corrington and Joyce Hooper Corrington and directed by J. Lee Thompson once again. Established in their own Ape City after the expected destruction of mankind in the Third World War the apes, still led by Caesar (Roddy McDowall), become involved in a war with a group of mutants who have joined forces with militant gorillas. The battle sequences are well-handled but there's an air of pointlessness about the whole film – as if everyone knows that this is the last attempt to wring a few remaining dollars out of the Ape phenomenon. (It wasn't quite, though: in 1974 a *Planet of the Apes* TV series began, but only lasted thirteen episodes.)

In 1970 former box-office idol Cornel Wilde directed *No Blade of Grass*, based on John Christopher's excellent novel *The Death of Grass*. In the novel the castastrophe that wipes out most strains of cereal across the world is caused by a form of mutated virus, but in the film chemical pollution is the suggested reason. The film vaguely follows the plot of the novel, concentrating on one family, led by the quick-thinking father (Nigel Davenport) who has foreseen the disaster. The family journeys across an England that has collapsed into anarchy and mob rule and reaches sanctuary at a relative's farm in the Lake District. With its suggestion that the fall of civilization tends to bring out the worst in people and that such qualities as compassion had better be put in mothballs until more comfortable times return, the film is very similar to *Panic in the Year Zero*. However, *No Blade of Grass* is crude and rather disjointed; as one English critic observed: 'The mood changes violently from one scene to another, the visual quality and the colour flash from shot to shot as though it had been photographed by different crews and the actors seem unsure of what kind of film they are supposed to be making.' Some of the blame for the film's lack of cohesion rests with the distributors as a number of sequences were cut by them at the last minute. However, there are some memorable sequences, such as the attack on the straggling column of refugees by a horde of armed motorbike 'Huns' wearing horned helmets, and the scenes early in the film when quantities of rich food are consumed by well-fed patrons in a restaurant, all of whom are oblivious to the pictures of Third World misery being shown on a TV screen above them. Wilde's heart may have been in the right place; it's a pity his cameras weren't.

No Blade of Grass was a signpost towards two contemporary public

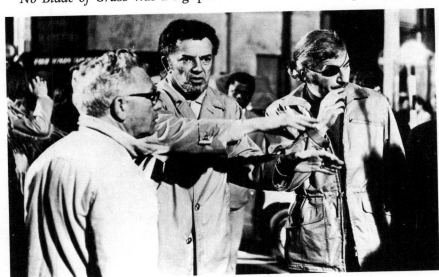

Cornel Wilde at work on the set of No Blade of Grass.

obsessions that were often to surface in sf films during the 1970s: pollution, and the possibility of germ warfare, both of which tended to replace the Bomb as a source of exploitable material. One of the best films dealing with the threat to humanity posed by microscopic organisms is *The Andromeda Strain* (1971), based on the best-selling novel by Michael Crichton and directed by Robert Wise, who had directed the classic *The Day the Earth Stood Still* twenty years previously. *The Andromeda Strain* is unusual among sf films in that real science is one of the most important factors in the development of the plot – in fact the recreation of scientific procedure *is* the plot – which makes a pleasant change from most sf films, where the scientific content is arbitrarily thrown in along with the 'love interest'. Wise and his scriptwriter Nelson Giddings (who also worked with Wise on *The Haunting*) decided to follow the book as closely as possible and therefore reproduced its authenticity on the screen. The author, Michael Crichton, has a solid medical background. After graduating in anthropology from Harvard University he took a degree in medicine and later joined the Salk Institute. Not only a prolific author, he is now also a highly-regarded scriptwriter and director. (*Coma* is his latest film.)

The Andromeda Strain concerns a dangerous, virus-like organism brought to Earth on a returning space probe. The probe lands near a small American desert town where it is later opened by the local doctor. The result is instant death for everyone in the vicinity, with the exception of one baby and the town drunk. The government acts quickly and isolates the two survivors within a vast underground laboratory complex, called Wildfire, built to cope with any future outbreak of germ warfare. Sealed in with them is a team of scientists whose job is to discover the true nature of the alien organism, code-named Andromeda, and then to find a way of overcoming it. Things go wrong – there are personality clashes between the scientists (played by James Olson – star of *Moon Zero Two* – Arthur Hill, David Wayne and Kate Reid) – and by the time Andromeda's secrets have been analysed it has mutated into a new organism with a whole new set of characteristics.

In a way the film is an updated version of an old 1950s monster-from-outer-space, but there is more to it than that. It can be argued that the villain in the piece isn't Andromeda but technology itself. It is technology that brings the virus to Earth, but proves useless in the attempts to combat the organism while at the same time remaining a threat to the human characters. Once sealed within Wildfire the scientists are totally at the mercy of its gleaming, electronic innards, their every action monitored by the laboratory's computer; they are themselves alien organisms within a 'superior' host body. When Olson penetrates the ventilation shaft at the end of the film the computer activates the lasers because it presumes that one of the laboratory test animals has escaped. For all its apparent celebration of technology the film conceals an entirely different message.

Be that as it may, the electronic gadgetry in the film certainly looks impressive, as it should considering that the budget topped $6,500,000. Much of the equipment actually functioned too, such as the powerful microscope system that included a built-in TV camera behind the lens, and to enable the film cameras to record what appeared on the TV monitors on the set a special television unit had to be built with a 2,000-line resolution (the normal resolution is around 600 lines). Most of this equipment was designed and constructed by technical effects man Douglas Trumbull, who had been one of the effects supervisors on *2001*.

Germ warfare also provides the theme for *The Omega Man*, a 1971 production based on the novel *I Am Legend* by Richard Matheson. The screenplay was written by John William Corrington and Joyce Hooper Corrington (who later wrote *Battle for the Planet of the Apes*), and it was directed by Boris Sagal, a former TV director (a previous sf film of his was the made-for-TV version of *Hauser's Memory* based on the Curt Siodmak novel). The Matheson novel is one of the most paranoid works ever written, dealing with a man whose house is surrounded every night by a crowd of vampires who, if they aren't trying to break in, spend all their time calling him by name. During the day he tries to find as many of them as possible, all of whom he despatches in the traditional way, with hammer and stakes, while they are asleep. They aren't real vampires, however, but victims of a plague that produces vampire-like characteristics. Eventually the protagonist is captured by the 'vampires' who tell him, before they kill him, that they represent the new race that will inherit the Earth, and that he is now the aberration in the scheme of things – the 'vampire' that must be destroyed for the common good.

It's a powerful, haunting novel but unfortunately little of it remains in *The Omega Man*. The vampire element, so crucial to the story, is missing altogether and instead the protagonist (Charlton Heston) is hounded each night by a group of hooded albinos who are apparently suffering from terminal eczema. They prove to be the survivors of a bacteriological war that has wiped out most of human life on Earth, the Heston character escaping a similar fate because he was able to inject himself with the last few drops of an effective antidote just in time. Some of the atmosphere from the novel is present in the scenes where Heston is isolated in his penthouse fortress while the hooded creatures harangue him from the street below, but the film changes direction a third of the way through and tries to become a James Bond-style action-thriller with spectacular chase sequences, motor-bike stunts and so on. At this point Heston encounters an attractive black girl (Rosalind Cash) and her group of young companions who are so far unaffected by the plague. To protect them

Heston manufactures more of the serum from his own blood, but before he can escape with them he is killed by the crazed albinos. He dies leaning against the base of a fountain, his pose subtly suggesting that of the Crucifixion. He's dead, but his blood will save the world.

This was the second time *I Am Legend* was filmed – the first being a Robert L. Lippert production made in Italy called *The Last Man on Earth* and starring Vincent Price – but Matheson was very disappointed with both versions. 'The first one was very poorly done,' he said, 'but at least it followed the book. *The Omega Man* bore no resemblance at all to my book so I can't comment on it . . . I don't know why they bothered really. I still think the book would make an interesting film.'

Another film dealing with germ warfare which was much less pretentious than *The Omega Man*, much nastier and also more fun was *The Crazies* (1972), written and directed by George Romero (who had made the successful cult horror film *Night of the Living Dead* in 1968). A small American town is suddenly invaded by hundreds of white-suited, masked troops who begin herding the townspeople into the local high school. It seems that a government plane carrying an artificially-created plague virus has crashed the previous week outside the town and the virus has invaded the town's water supply. The plague causes a severe mental breakdown in its victims before killing them, and there is no known cure for it. The town quickly collapses into chaos, and the townspeople violently resist the troops. Like *Dr Strangelove* the film is really an attack on the military itself, since it is the army which developed the virus in the first place, didn't act fast enough after the plane crash, and provoked the bloody gun fights with the local inhabitants through a failure of communication, and it is army red tape which prevents the one scientist who discovers a cure from passing on the information. The film ends with everyone in the town either dead or insane and the army commander on his way to another town where a plague outbreak has also been reported.

Film-makers were wary of tackling another major contemporary problem – over-population – no doubt for fear of stepping on religious toes. One film that did deal with the subject was *Zero Population Growth* (1971) directed by Michael Campus and written by Max Ehrlich and Frank DeFelitta. (The latter made several award-winning documentaries for American TV in the early 1960s; his most recent success was his novel *Audrey Rose*, which he also adapted into a screenplay for Robert Wise.) 'Zero Population Growth' is the term which refers to a society where the population remains at a constant figure – neither increasing nor decreasing. To achieve this state the birth-rate has to match the death-rate, which means ensuring that most married couples are restricted to having only two children, but for some inexplicable reason Ehrlich and DeFelitta thought ZPG would mean having no children at all and so wrote their screenplay accordingly. Strictly speaking the film should have been called *Zero Population*.

The film is set in a future world where the air pollution is so bad that a yellow smog covers the whole planet and everyone is obliged to wear face masks. So great is the over-population that all births have been banned for 30 years. People who disobey this law are publicly executed in a novel way: a glass dome is lowered over the guilty pair and their child and then sprayed with black paint, those inside being left to suffocate. If the executions are supposed to be public, it may be thought curious that the domes are sprayed with paint, but this, it turns out, is to enable the film's hero and heroine to escape unseen with their baby down a convenient man-hole.

The hero and heroine are played by Oliver Reed and Geraldine Chaplin, with Reed looking as murderous as ever, even during the love scenes. Dissatisfied with the state-provided alternative to real children – horrible-looking dolls that stagger around croaking 'Momma . . . Dada . . . !' – they decide to break the law and have a secret baby. After a quick do-it-yourself course in obstetrics Reed delivers the baby himself, and for a time they successfully keep it hidden until a jealous neighbour (Diane Cilento) discovers their secret and betrays them to the authorities. But after cleverly arranging for their death dome to be placed over the man-hole, Reed and family journey by rubber raft down a huge sewer to freedom – leaving the audience to wonder how, in such an overpopulated and polluted world, there can be anywhere left to escape to.

In an interview in *Films and Filming* DeFelitta put the blame on the film's director, Michael Campus, claiming that he hired an English writer to rewrite their script with the result that 'their serious story on over-population became comedic.'[42] But no other writer's name appears in the credits, and the film still takes itself very seriously indeed, which is what makes it so amusing. The film was shot in Denmark with a mainly Danish technical crew supervised by a number of British technicians. Among the latter was special effects man Derek Meddings, who said: 'I got involved with that film because the production designer, Tony Masters, knew my work and asked me to join him on it. So I went to Denmark and did all the "floor effects" on ZPG which included creating all the mist and fog that was constantly covering everything in all the exterior shots. We didn't have much of a budget for the effects and the worst thing was that I also had to start training the Danish technicians. I wasn't allowed to take any British technicians with me and having always worked with a great crowd of assistants around me it was a bit of a shock to have to do everything myself, make all the models and everything from scratch while the Danish boys watched to see how it was done. The biggest problem was those dolls. They were awful. I didn't make them myself, they were made by a company in England and they were built very quickly without much thought being given on how they would look. I didn't see them until I arrived in Denmark and it took a lot of work on my part to make them look convincing. The worst thing, of course, were the eyes and mouths. Having been involved with puppets [he was the effects man on *Thunderbirds*] I was able to change both the eyes and the mouths until they worked convincingly. At least I *hope* they worked convincingly.'

The best film to date dealing with overpopulation is *Soylent Green*, directed in 1973 by Richard Fleischer, whose previous sf films were *20,000 Leagues* and *Fantastic Voyage*. The film was based on the novel *Make Room! Make Room!* by one of science fiction's most successful writers, Harry Harrison. The novel itself is primarily a grim warning about what will happen if the problem of overpopulation is ignored and the rampant exploitation of Earth's dwindling resources continues unabated. As such it's an exercise in futility and despair – the world that Harrison describes is past saving – and we can only watch as civilization goes down the plug-hole. The basic plot of the novel concerns a New York detective, called Thorn, who is assigned to investigate the murder of a racketeer once his corrupt superiors decide that it is the work of an out-of-town conspiracy. Thorn struggles to track down the murderer while at the same time having to cope with all his other duties in the overcrowded New York of 1999 where the population has reached 21 million and the city's facilities are collapsing under the strain. He becomes involved with the late racketeer's ex-mistress, Shirl, who moves into his small two-room apartment which he already shares with friend Sol, an old man of over 70 who remembers a time when things were different and much better. For a time all three are as happy as anyone can be under the circumstances, but then Sol contracts pneumonia after being injured in an old people's demonstration and dies. His room is taken over by a large, obnoxious family and the pressure of having to live with them forces Shirl to leave. Thorn succeeds in finding the murderer but he turns out to be a scared teenager who had killed the racketeer in a moment of panic when discovered robbing the apartment. Thorn is forced to shoot him dead – an act which gets him into trouble with his superiors who have already forgotten about their conspiracy theory. The book ends with Thorn demoted to being a uniformed policeman again and completely alone, yet still determined to do what he can to preserve what remains of law and order. His refusal to give in no matter how bad things become is the only positive note in the book's closing description of a city where the food and water rationing is reaching the point where it will barely support human life and the rioting is becoming more violent and widespread. Despite the efforts of Thorn and perhaps others like him, the suggestion is that the end is near.

An effective method of riot control in Soylent Green.

Edward G. Robinson enters the suicide parlour in the same film.

The film, scripted by Stanley R. Greenberg, preserved much of the grimness of the future New York (though the date is moved to 2022) but made the foreground action determinedly more up-beat and action-packed. For one thing Shirl (Leigh Taylor-Young) doesn't have to experience the squalor of Thorn's apartment – she remains in the luxury apartment (in the film she is classified as 'Furniture' and therefore goes with the apartment) and consequently remains in love with Thorn (Charlton Heston). Nor does the film Sol (Edward G. Robinson) die in his bed; instead he signs himself into a suicide parlour and dies a happy death surrounded by cinemascope images of vanished earthly pleasures such as fields of flowers, bubbling brooks and clean beaches. But the major change involves the non-existent conspiracy plot in the book: in the film it becomes a real conspiracy to cover up the true nature of 'soylent green', the world's most abundant form of artificial food. The racketeer of the novel becomes, in the film, a government official (Joseph Cotten) who is killed because his colleagues fear that the guilt and remorse he feels over his connection with the manufacture of the stuff will cause him to reveal publicly the truth. Sol, who works as Thorn's police researcher in the film, uncovers the secret of soylent green and it's this that causes him to register for suicide. He passes the information on to Thorn before he dies, but the detective doesn't believe him until he sneaks into the soylent green plant and sees dead bodies being converted into food. The film ends with him badly wounded after a fight with the conspirators' hired killer and being carried away shouting: 'Soylent Green is people!' The cinema audiences are left to decide for themselves whether he will be believed by anyone, so the ending is ambiguous.

Harry Harrison, despite all the changes imposed on his finely textured and evocative novel, was relatively happy about the film. 'Overall I think it succeeds as a film. I think the worst part of it was the screenplay. It just about qualifies as a second-rate thriller . . . well, maybe, with hindsight, it isn't *that* bad in that it was supposed to be a commercial product and it certainly proved successful, but it lost a lot of the feeling of the book. Originally it was even worse but the people who were really involved with the idea – the producers, Walter Seltzer and Russ Thatcher, and the star, Charlton Heston – managed to improve it some. The technical people helped too – obviously the art director had actually read *Make Room!* because he [Edward C. Carfagno] used all the background apparatus from the book in his sets. And, of course, the background is what it's all about – the background is the foreground. In the book, which appears at first just to be an adventure story, I didn't draw attention to the setting – I just let it sink in slowly. When the reader is about two-thirds into it he suddenly becomes aware of the horrible reality of this terrible New York of the future and then it becomes obvious as to what the book is really about.

Happily, it's the same with the movie – no one cares, or *should* care, about the dumb little story rattling around up front – no one cares what soylent green is either as it's pretty obvious from the beginning, but what they're really looking at is that terrible world. A lot of people, youngsters in particular, will see it and not like it at first but they keep thinking about it and maybe a week later it suddenly hits them – "My God, will it really be like *that*?" The dumb story has been forgotten and the reality of the extrapolation comes through – so on that level I think it succeeds. It certainly succeeded as a commercial picture because it was the only film MGM made money on in 1973. By July 1974 Charlton Heston had made a million dollars out of it.

'I heard later that it was all Heston's doing that the film ever got made. He'd read the book and had been trying for five years to set it up. He got the producer, Walter Seltzer, involved in the project early on as well and they both kept trying. The size of the budget was one of the problems – it was almost $4,000,000 – and MGM, the studio they were both working for, would not do it. But they persisted; they invested a good deal of their own money and had a screenplay written and drawings made but the MGM chiefs kept saying that they didn't think the subject of overpopulation was important enough. So when they came up with the plot-twist of cannibalism MGM finally decided it was a viable theme for a film – which gives you some idea of how the film industry thinks!

'But at least Heston was emotionally involved in the film. He's a very politically involved guy – the president of the actors' union or whatever; he's a little too right-wing for me in his politics but he *is* involved – he really cares about the overpopulation problem, pollution, ecology and so on and that's why he wanted to film *Make Room!* Seltzer was involved because he wanted to make money but he's a good producer in that he gets the thing rolling and then steps aside and lets the director take over. Richard Fleischer is a very strong director and like Heston he got involved in the theme. He runs a very taut ship. At the start they'd shot about a week's material and he decided he didn't like it, so he fired the cameraman on the spot and got a new one.

'I wasn't able to write the screenplay myself – the contract was very adamant about that – they just wanted to buy the rights of the book, period! They wanted to be able to change the title, write their own script and do whatever they wanted while I was to have nothing to do with it all. I just had to sign the contract and fade away into the woodwork. I talked it over with my agent and decided to sign it because I *did* want to get involved with the making of a major motion picture. And despite the contract I did start pressuring them afterwards – I wrote them lots of nasty letters. First I asked if I could rewrite the script and they said no, so I sent them little notes suggesting various things, along the lines of: "Gee, what a *fine* script but the reason you bought this book is that, though it takes place several decades in the future, it connects with *today*. People alive today will be alive then too but for some reason, perhaps due to an oversight on the part of your *excellent* screenwriter, that fact has been eliminated. There is no connection with the present world at all." So they went and got somebody to do that opening sequence with the series of stills. The guy's name is Chuck Braverman and he's very good – he started with shots of pioneers chopping down trees and railroads being built, and the stills slowly built up to the opening scenes of the future New York. That way the audience then sees that it *is* the USA and not some fantasy-limbo world. That was very important to the film, but if I hadn't pointed it out they would have just had it opening in the future.

'I made a lot of other suggestions, many of which were never acknowledged. For instance, in the book I had invented about forty new words because slang changes very quickly – perhaps every five years – and so thirty years in the future they're bound to use words that are unfamiliar to us now. But the scriptwriter hadn't used *one*, so I wrote and pointed this out. I think they finally did put one new slang word into the screenplay.

'But they did incorporate a lot of my suggestions into the screenplay and on the basis of that I rang up Walter Seltzer one day and said I'd like to come down and watch the shooting, and he said: "Oh, any time you like, Harry." So I went down to the set and took a lot of copies of the book with me and gave one to everyone I could think of – the actors, the cameraman, the technicians – all of whom seemed to appreciate meeting me. I mean, they don't care about screenwriters but authors of *real* books are something different. They don't get to see many real books in Hollywood, only rotten screenplays. So I was handing out these books and being taken around by the co-producer, Russell Thatcher, and treated rather well, so I got the feeling that all my suggestions had been valuable. The first feeling I had of this was when Walter Seltzer clapped me on the back and said: "Harry, you're costing us a lot of money."

'Later on I was watching a scene with Edward G. Robinson being shot – it was a closed set but they let me stay – and I heard Robinson complain to Fleischer that he didn't know what his role was supposed to be, so I got him aside and said that I was the guy who wrote the book and gave him a copy, and I said: "Do you mind if I explain a bit about what your role is supposed to be?" And he said: "Sure, come to my dressing-room and have some lunch." So, over a sandwich I told him: "Very simply, you are *me* in this story. I'll be your age at the time when all the events of the film are taking place. You are the only living connection with the old world – you are the only person in the whole film who lived in a world of plenty – you are the link that connects our world with the world in the film." And he said: "Thank you very much for your help." And once he knew what he was doing he put a lot of colour into his scenes, inventing lots of bits of extra business. Heston was the same – he embellished his role in the same way. Like the eating scene where they're both eating some horrible cracker made of seaweed – in the original scene they just ate while they were talking but both of them invented little schticks as the scene was shot so that in the finished sequence you see Heston actually enjoying the stuff because that's all he'd ever known, he'd been eating it all his life, whereas Robinson was looking disgusted because he could remember real food. And this sort of building upon the original by the actors went on right through it.

'I was on the set when they filmed the scene with the girl and the bodyguard going to buy illegal meat from the meat-legger and I saw, on the side of the set, a large pile of plastics bags. So I asked where the bags were supposed to come from. I said: "Remember that there isn't supposed to be any petroleum left, and plastic is made out of petroleum." "Really?" they said, "we never thought of that." I said: "Well, *I* did so throw them away. The girl brings her own bag to put the meat in, the way they do in Europe now." "Gee," they said, "we didn't think of that either."

'There was one thing during the making of the film that I found very ironic – the final sequence which is supposed to take place in the plant where human bodies are converted into soylent green was actually filmed at the Monarch Sewerage Plant which is situated at the end of the runway at Los Angeles airport. So while the filming was going on I was talking to an engineer who worked there and I learned an amazing thing – this monstrous sewerage plant, which cost a fortune, was built to convert all the crap from the residents of Los Angeles into dry fertilizer. A wonderful thing, right, seeing as there's a world fertilizer shortage? But it turns out that there's a fertilizer monopoly in the USA which is in the hands of the big meat-packing plants who grind all their old bones up into fertilizer. So when the sewerage plant started selling their fertilizer at a slightly cheaper rate the meat packers' monopoly cut the price of fertilizer to the extent where it became unprofitable for Los Angeles to sell it at that price – they would have lost about $4 per bag – so they just stopped selling and now there is a 30-inch-wide pipe that bypasses this $80,000,000 sewerage processing plant and dumps the crap straight into the ocean. It's been doing that for years now. I couldn't believe it when I heard it. What rampant stupidity, yet it was the perfect place to shoot a movie about a world where the natural resources have been totally wasted.

'But watching the film being shot was mainly a lot of fun. I'd never seen a major film being shot before, the only other films I'd seen being made were Grade C $30,000 pieces of schlock, but this was the big time – a big film with a decent budget made in the old traditional way on the MGM back lot with some of the best technicians in the world involved, like Gene Marowitz, the first assistant director; Joe Canutt, who handled the action sequences; Bud Westmore, who did the make-up; the cameraman Richard Kline and the cutter Sam Beetley. They cut the film very well, I thought. They cut from five to ten minutes out of the film – stuff that looked good at the time they shot it but which they had enough sense to throw out when they saw it all in one piece. Whole sequences went, like one where you see the girl and the bodyguard on their way out to go shopping and they're jumped by three or four guys and the bodyguard earns his keep by chopping them up. It was a very expensive sequence, what with the cost of the stuntmen, but it didn't have any real relation to the rest of the picture. You didn't have to *show* Chuck Connors being a bodyguard for the audience to get the message that he was one – he just had to *look* like one, which he did. So they cut it out, which was good.

'And of course Dick Fleischer is a damn good professional director, so it was an education for me on how to make a film. I also learned a great deal about screenwriting and how they turn a screenplay into a film. And overall I was happy with the way the film turned out, given that screenplay and such things as the "furniture" girls, which should have been thrown away as it was just nonsense. The ending was cornball too but everyone likes to see blood so I suppose it was a wise move on their part. And the suicide parlour sequence worked okay . . . I didn't put it in the book because I didn't want to use any of the old science fiction gimmicks, I wanted to keep it all as realistic as possible, but the scriptwriter obviously didn't realize that a suicide parlour is such a cliché sf device, so he put it in. And I've got to admit that in the film it took on a different aspect and worked very well – perhaps he wasn't such a dummy because certainly no one has ever put a suicide parlour in a film before – but a lot of the credit must go to Chuck Braverman again. In the original screenplay it just says: "They take Sol into the suicide parlour and show him scenes of his youth" – or something – "and then he dies." But Braverman inserted all these shots of beautiful landscapes with pure blue skies, virgin white snowscapes etcetera, and after sixty minutes or so of watching life in a claustrophobic New York where a green smog is covering everything and everyone is suffering from the heat and looking dirty, these shots have a tremendous impact. And of course you also had a fantastic actor like Robinson involved. The scriptwriter just says something like: "He looks up and dies." But Robinson and Fleischer worked from that and produced something very memorable.'

Harrison's comments make an interesting comparison with those of the film's director, Richard Fleischer: 'The story of *Soylent Green* concerned one of my favourite topics really – the pollution of the environment, what's happening to us and what will happen to us. It's a look into the future but I don't consider it science fiction – it's science fact. It was a bit of a commercial risk to show the future as being grim and depressing, but I don't think you can honestly show how wonderful the future is going to be when you know how terrible it will be. You hope that somebody will learn something when they see the film and that they will say to themselves: "My God, we can't let this happen," and then do something about it. I think what we showed was a very accurate extrapolation of our time because if we go on as we're going that picture will come true. But even though it was an honest look at the future it was also an entertaining one with some wonderful actors in it. I think Eddie Robinson in particular was marvellous, and Chuck Heston's performance was a different type of one for him.

'There are a lot of things in it that I like – what it has to say about police corruption, for instance, which in the film has become so commonplace it's no longer looked upon as corruption but part of their daily routine. When the Chuck Heston character goes to see his superior in the film he's asked: "What did you take from the apartment?" And he says: "Everything I could lay my hands on." And then he shares out the loot with his chief. That sort of thing is today extended just one more step but it isn't really taking things too far, and that's what I think is attractive about the film because everybody can already see this part of the future – it isn't beyond their credibility or beyond the range of their imagination or vision. Another thing I find interesting about the film is that it presumes a backlash against Women's Lib has taken place in the intervening years as the women in that society no longer have any status or power – they're simply referred to as 'furniture', they go with the apartment. The suggestion is that women are going to have to endure the worst role they've ever had in history due to the overpopulation.

'About the only futuristic thing in *Soylent Green* is the euthanasia sequence, but again it's relevant to what's happening today because the subject of euthanasia keeps coming up again and again in the media. And the whole business of going out that way – surrounded by pleasant images and beautiful music – I found very interesting.

'I think we're witnessing, at the moment, the start of a big climb in popularity of science fiction films. I think they're going to become part of our standard film fare, like westerns or thrillers. I'd certainly like to do another one – I've been approached to do a film on an Anthony Burgess novel called *The Wanting Seed* but nothing definite has been arranged yet. Actually I feel that a book like *Brave New World* should be filmed today – first of all because it's so close to us now, in fact we've passed some of the prophecies in that, and because it deals primarily with genetic engineering, a subject of rapidly growing importance. Anyway, it's always been a favourite book of mine.'

The shape of things to come provided source material for a number of other film-makers during the first half of the 1970s. A young Canadian by the name of David Cronenberg in 1970 made *Crimes of the Future* – a small-budget black comedy set in a future where all females have been killed by a disease created by a mad dermatologist, with the exception of one 5-year-old girl. The film's open bad taste, together with Cronenberg's apparent obsession with skin, plastic surgery and bizarre sexual practices, make it an obvious forerunner to his later, more accessible, films like *The Parasite Murders* and *Rabid*.

More serious was Peter Watkins's *Punishment Park*. Made in 1970 at a time when youthful protest against America's involvement in Vietnam was at its peak, this film can best be described as propaganda of the most blatant kind, yet at the same time it is clearly the work of an important cinema talent. The film concerns a group of young political dissidents who are forced to endure a government-controlled 'run-of-the-gauntlet' before they can attain amnesty for their political 'crimes'. Set loose in a desert they have to travel miles across the hostile environment and reach a pole flying the American flag, at the same time avoiding the army patrols who have orders to shoot on sight. What provides the film with an extra dimension is the presence of a TV camera crew who follow the group of dissidents in their dash for freedom across the desert, recording all that happens to them. As the TV team members become increasingly involved with the predicament of the people they are filming, Watkins's ingenious method of emotionally involving the audience in the situation too, by making them feel guilty for their voyeurism, becomes apparent. The film is too strident, too unremitting in its anger and rage to work successfully, but it's certainly an interesting and provocative piece of work.

Another 1970 film by a young film-maker was *THX 1138* – the work of George Lucas, who has earned a permanent place in the history of the cinema since then with his production of *Star Wars*, not only the most financially successful sf film ever made but also the most financially successful film of all time (at the time of writing). Lucas started work on *THX 1138* when he was still at the University of Southern California Film School. With the help of other students he made, in 1967, a 15-minute sf film called *THX 1138:4EB* which subsequently won a number of awards. He then won a scholarship to Warner Brothers to observe the making of the film *Finian's Rainbow*, which was being directed by Francis Ford Coppola, another young film-maker only a few years older than Lucas himself. The two became friendly and Lucas worked as Coppola's assistant on the latter's next film *The Rain People*. Coppola had persuaded Warner Brothers to allow him to set up his own production company, called American Zoetrope, with which he proposed to turn out high-quality, low-budget features. One of these was *THX 1138*, which Lucas based on his

(Above) *Two views of the menacing robots featured in* THX 1138. *(Right) Director George Lucas in the unsettling all-white set used in* THX 1138.

student film, but it did so badly at the box-office, despite some good reviews, that Coppola was faced with financial ruin until the success of *The Godfather* saved the day for him.

The plot of *THX 1138* will be instantly familiar to any sf fan. It concerns a totalitarian, and apparently subterranean, society of the future run by computers in which bland human technocrats act as both supervisors of the machinery and supervisors of each other. Everyone is fed a constant supply of sedative drugs (failure to take which results in prosecution for 'drug evasion') and any sign of individuality is forbidden. Everyone wears the same white clothing and all heads are shaven. This uniformity also helps to blur the differences between the sexes – a good thing as sexual intercourse is also forbidden (all breeding being done through artificial insemination). The film's central character is THX (Robert Duvall) who suddenly finds himself aware of the emptiness of his existence after his wife, LUH (Maggie McOmie), deliberately alters his drug intake. He also discovers sex and love (THX and LUH) and before long LUH is pregnant. They are both arrested by the robot policemen (tall, black-clad figures with chrome-plated heads), tried, and found guilty. LUH is 'terminated' and her code-name passed on to a bottled embryo while THX is thrown into a 'prison' which consists of nothing but an endless sea of white. In here he encounters another would-be rebel, SEN (Donald Pleasence, repeating a role he played in both the TV and film versions of *1984*), and eventually the pair of them escape, accompanied by a large black man who declares he isn't real but is just a three-dimensional hologram who decided to get out of the 'entertainment circuits'. The three of them later became separated; SEN makes it to the boundaries of the city but is so frightened at the thought of having to cope with the unknown world that lies beyond that he returns and lets himself be captured; the hologram man is destroyed in a car crash, and only THX finally succeeds in reaching the surface and possible freedom, though, as in *Zero Population Growth*, one wonders if there is still any place in the world to escape to.

Lucas begins the film, after a brief prologue consisting of scenes from the old *Buck Rogers* movie serial, with a sequence of apparently unrelated visual fragments accompanied by snatches of jumbled sounds and dialogue; a woman approaches her talking drug cabinet which tells her what pills to take; drugged technicians hunch over their control panels as they manipulate highly dangerous radioactive material; their monitors hunch over other control panels and blithely reel off the casualty rates from the latest industrial disaster, at the same time urging the people to work harder and 'avoid accidents' (the technicians are so drugged up that accidents are unavoidable, but if they weren't on tranquillizers they wouldn't dare do the work they're doing); and the robot policemen go about their own work – either politely arresting people or helping small children – all of which elements gradually coalesce to form a comprehensive picture of THX's world.

With hindsight *THX 1138*, with its grim, meticulous creation of an utterly depressing world, might seem an unlikely film to have come from George Lucas, who has since demonstrated that his cinematic forte lies with films that exude juvenile exuberance (*American Graffiti, Star Wars*), but on closer examination it's not really so. *THX 1138* has a lot in common with the other two films, as Lucas himself readily admitted: 'Absolutely, it's all the same story. *THX* was allegory with a touch of cubism, *Graffiti* was sociology plus nostalgia, and *Star Wars* is total fantasy, but all three films are really about me. I identify totally with THX struggling out from a benevolent and disintegrating environment; I used to cruise around like the kids in *Graffiti* and now, with *Star Wars*, I'm on an intergalactic dream of heroism. I'm telling the story of me.'[43]

Two-thirds of the way into *THX 1138* the whole mood of the film suddenly changes at the point where THX and SEN meet the hologram man, and from grim reality we are plunged into exhilarating fantasy as THX proceeds to outrun, out-drive and outwit his pursuers. Another *Star Wars* seed in *THX 1138* is the obvious fun Lucas has with robots. For all their apparent efficiency they're far from perfect, and their foibles provide the film's main source of humour, culminating in the final sequences where the robots are unable to continue chasing THX because they've exceeded the total budget allotted for his recapture: '*Please* come back,' cries a robot as the unheeding THX flees up the tunnel to the surface, 'we only want to help you.' *THX 1138*, like *Star Wars*, is fun but the difference is that it pretends to be profound as well.

In 1971 Stanley Kubrick presented a different type of futuristic nightmare in *A Clockwork Orange*, his third sf-related film in a row. A social, political and religious allegory, it was based on the novel by Anthony Burgess about a teenage thug, called Alex, who is turned off his violent way of life by a form of aversion therapy, thus becoming the 'clockwork orange' of the title. Burgess's message is that everyone must have the freedom to choose between good and evil and that it is an even greater evil to remove the freedom of choice from a person like Alex than it is to let him continue with his violently anti-social activities. In a way Burgess, who is apparently a religious fundamentalist, is reworking the old *Frankenstein* theme in warning that Man should not compete with God, except that he is also saying that it is just as wrong, in God's eyes, to unmake a monster as it is to make one. This opens up the question of the nature of freewill and how it fits in with predestination, but Mr Burgess doesn't provide any answers in his novel. It is the work of a total conservative, political as well as religious, who is against the idea of change *per se*, whether it be social, scientific or whatever.

Fortunately Burgess's simplistic message becomes rather blurred in Kubrick's film; perhaps Kubrick, like Lucas with *THX 1138*, was only interested in the story because of its interesting visual potential. No doubt the fact that music played an important role (Alex is obsessed with the work of Beethoven, which he associates with visions of violence, sadism and sexual lust, and it is later used against him as part of the aversion therapy) helped attract Kubrick to the project. As a film *A Clockwork Orange* is certainly a stunning *tour de force*. As in *2001* many of the electrifying images were given a greater impact by being accompanied by music which contrasted wildly with the visual content, such as Rossini's 'The Thieving Magpie' as the background for an attempted rape, and Alex's rendition of 'Singing in the Rain' while kicking in the ribs of Mr Alexander. Even Kubrick's self-indulgent little jokes were cleverly presented, as in the scene where Alex and his Droogs (futuristic slang for what are now called Punks: in fact the Punk 'culture' has appropriated a number of things from the film, particularly in the area of fashion) approach the old tramp sleeping in the underpass – back-lit and in the same formation as the astronauts in *2001* approached the black monolith; and the slow-motion sequence where Alex attacks the Droogs with his sword-stick, mimicking the movements of the ape-man at the beginning of *2001* when he discovers how to use the bone as a weapon.

The cast included Malcolm McDowell (as Alex), Michael Bates (as the prison officer), and Warren Clarke (As Dim the Droog). All were very good but particularly memorable was Aubrey Morris as the appalling social worker Deltoid and Patrick Magee as the fanatical Mr Alexander. Kubrick gave Magee his head and his incredible over-the-top-and-beyond style was perfect for the character and produced some memorable moments, as in the sequence were he reacts to the realization that Alex, who is singing 'Singing in the Rain' in his bathroom, is his wife's killer. Also in the film is David Prowse, playing the bodyguard called Julian, who is now famous as Darth Vader from *Star Wars*.

Two films made in 1971 concerned characters who become displaced in time and space: one was *Slaughterhouse Five* and the other was the less well-known and rather turgid *Quest for Love*. The latter was based on a story by John Wyndham and starred Tom Bell as a physicist who is caught in an explosion in his laboratory and then finds himself in a completely different life. Slowly he discovers that he is in a parallel world in which he is no longer a scientist but a successful playwright called Colin Trafford married to a beautiful woman (Joan Collins). However he realizes that the original Colin Trafford was obviously something of a creep, even to his wife. So the new Colin attempts to persuade her that he is now a different person in more ways than one. They fall deeply in love but three weeks later he wakes up in hospital, back in his own world. He tries to return to the parallel world but fails, so he tracks down the equivalent of his other-worldly wife living in this world. She turns out to be a Pan Am air hostess; he saves her life and all ends happily.

Slaughterhouse Five was slickly directed by George Roy Hill from the novel by Kurt Vonnegut Jr. It concerned a middle-class, middle-aged American man, Billy Pilgrim (Michael Sachs), who, vaguely dissatisfied with life in general, starts to experience sudden shifts back in time to when he was a prisoner-of-war in the German city of Dresden which was subsequently fire-bombed on a massive scale by the Allies. He then experiences forward shifts to a time in the future when he has become the prisoner of an alien race who keep him in a zoo on their planet of Tralfamador, and who provide him, for company, with a half-naked Hollywood starlet called Montana Wildhack (Valerie Perrine). But while the juxtaposing of the horrors of Dresden with the fantasies of Tral-famador worked effectively in the novel, the contrast between the grim reality of the Second World War and the ludicrous sequences in the alien zoo with Ms Perrine is unpleasantly jarring in the film. The Dresden sequences, however, are very impressive, and the film's other major asset is the performance by Michael Sachs, who convincingly portrays both a gawky adolescent of unusual innocence and a balding, pot-bellied middle-aged man who has given up trying to understand the world or the people in it.

Films about outer space and space travel were thin on the ground in the early 1970s, but one exception was *Silent Running* (1972) directed by Douglas Trumbull, the special effects man who had made his reputation working on *2001* and *The Andromeda Strain*. Made for a fraction of the cost of *2001* its scenes of vast spaceships cruising silently through space compare well with similar ones in Kubrick's film (Trumbull was assisted in the filming of the model effects by John Dykstra, who later created the effects in *Star Wars*), but there all similarities between *Silent Running* and *2001* end.

Silent Running is set in a giant spaceship called the 'Valley Forge' (many of the interiors in the film were shot in a decommissioned aircraft carrier of that name), which is part of a fleet of ships whose sole purpose is to fly about in space carrying all that remains of Earth's plant life. No explanation is given as to what happened to bring about the defoliation of the planet, nor as to why the Earth hasn't been reseeded. We know the planet is still capable of supporting life because there's plenty of evidence in the film to show that the human race is continuing to flourish. One of the characters mentions that there is no more unemployment, and you would certainly need an advanced technology to uproot whole forests and blast them into space. What is the human race doing for food now that all the vegetation is gone? We see the 'Valley Forge' crewmen eating

Bruce Dern and director Douglas Trumbull on the set of Silent Running.

'artificial' food, but that is no explanation.

The authorities on Earth, apparently going insane from lack of food and fresh oxygen, decide they need the space fleet for commercial purposes and give the order to jettison the domes containing the greenery and then blow them up. It isn't explained why they have to be blown up, or why the domes can't be left in orbit around the sun; there's no real reason for them to be attached to spaceships at all. The hero of the film, with the subtle name of Freeman, who is played by Bruce Dern looking and talking like a mad monk, turns out to be the last true conservationist left alive and refuses to obey the idiotic orders from Earth. His crew-mates, however, are quite happy to dump everything and get back to civilization, so Freeman murders them all and heads the ship in the direction of deep space, his plan presumably being to hang around on the fringes of the solar system until trees come back into fashion. He goes off, accompanied only by three cute little robots that look like walking TV sets and are called Huey, Dewey and Louie – the direct ancestors of cute little Artoo Deeto in *Star Wars*.

The three robots were actually amputees. Trumbull got the idea from watching Tod Browning's *Freaks*; he was impressed by one of the unfortunate characters who, though legless, could walk by using his hands and it occurred to Trumbull that by putting a small metal suit around such a person you could create a very effective robot. So armed with this idea he had three writers, Mike Cimino, Derek Washburn and Steve Bocho, assist him in the construction of a screenplay around this one main gimmick – and the result was *Silent Running*, an illogical, sentimental mess. The special effects, however, are superb and the film improves once Freeman has begun his lone journey through the solar system towards Deep Space, with the relationship between him and the robots becoming amusing and even touching. Absurdities still occur; for instance, Freeman is totally mystified when all the plants start dying, until he realizes that the lack of sunlight (the sun is now far away) might have something to do with it – a conclusion such an expert on plant life should have reached much sooner.

The other space film of 1972 was completely different. Called *Solaris* it was a Russian production, based on the novel by Polish sf writer Stanislaw Lem and directed by Andrei Tarkovsky. Like *2001* the film concerned an encounter between mankind and the basic mystery of the Universe, once again represented by an alien force beyond human comprehension. A research station has been placed in orbit around the planet Solaris to study the strange, ocean-like mass that covers its surface. As various shapes and patterns keep appearing in the fluid it is believed to be sentient, but the Russian scientists have been unable to find a way of communicating with it. Then, when it becomes apparent that all is not well on the space station, another scientist (played by Donatas Banionis) is sent to investigate. He finds both the station and its occupants in a state of chaos, and discovers that the station is being 'haunted' by phantoms, three-dimensional, substantial creatures that the scientists, due to the influence of Solaris, have created from their innermost desires; but, like Morbius and his monster from the Id in *Forbidden Planet*, they have no control over them.

The new arrival is soon plagued with a solid phantom of his own, in the form of his late wife (Natalia Bondarchuk) who had committed suicide some years before as a result of their unsatisfactory relationship. The film is at its best when dealing with the tortured scientist's efforts to cope with this artificial creature who, though she possesses some of his dead wife's characteristics – provided by his memories of her – including her love for him, is a totally alien being. His attempts to destroy her fail and even when he succeeds in trapping her in a rocket and shooting her off into space, a duplicate soon manifests itself in his room. And when 'she' begins to realize her true nature and attempts suicide (by swallowing liquid oxygen) to spare him any more pain, that too is a failure.

As by the very nature of its theme there can be no satisfactory resolution to the questions raised in the film, *Solaris* doesn't really have an ending but simply winds down and then comes to an enigmatic halt (as did *2001*). Though it has been described, with justification, as being too pretentious and too long, it remains an interesting and stimulating film in spite of its flaws.

10 The Boom Goes On (1973–76)

The old monster-from-outer-space type of sf film, so plentiful back in the 1950s, seems to have died out almost completely in the early 1970s. There were certainly none being made in either Hollywood or Britain, but in 1972 a Spanish producer came to the rescue with *Horror Express* (also known as *Panic on the TransSiberian*), which was directed by Eugeno Martin and written by Arnod d'Usseau. Its absurdities make it entertaining – it puts Christopher Lee and Peter Cushing on the Trans-Siberian express together with Telly Savalas as a murderous Cossack and a prehistoric ape-man that comes to life and turns out to be possessed by an alien.

A different kind of monster featured in *Duel*, written by that master of unease, Richard Matheson. Universal Studios were so impressed by this made-for-TV movie directed by the young Steven Spielberg (then only 24) that they had extra sequences added and released it outside America as a feature film. It subsequently attracted a great deal of favourable critical comment, particularly in Britain, all of which boosted Spielberg's reputation enormously and led to such films as *Jaws* and *Close Encounters of the Third Kind*; and it qualifies as sf because its basic theme is that of man versus machine.

A tightly constructed thriller, it displays well Spielberg's ability to create an atmosphere laden with nerve-jangling tension. It is also a typical Matheson piece of work, being another variation on the theme of paranoia: in this case the feeling every motorist experiences at sometime or other that all the other vehicles on the road are trying to kill you. Dennis Weaver plays a travelling salesman who is pursued by a mysterious oil tanker, the driver of which is never seen. The tanker slowly assumes all the characteristics of a living, malevolent animal, and when the salesman finally succeeds in luring it over a cliff the vehicle emits a dinosaur-like bellow of rage as it crashes to its doom.

The clichés of science fiction also began to provide the subject for a handful of comedy films, during the early 1970s, the best of which came from comedian/writer/director/actor Woody Allen. In 1972 he made *Everything You Always Wanted to Know About Sex (But Were Afraid to Ask)*, which was based very loosely on David Reuben's book of the same name. Consisting of short episodes satirizing various aspects of sex, the film includes two sections that can be described as sf satires. One involves a mad scientist (John Carradine, sending up a role he's played many times in the past) who creates a giant, mobile breast that breaks out of his laboratory and ravages the countryside drowning its victims in milk, until it is trapped by Woody Allen wielding a crucifix, who lures it into a giant bra cup. 'We'd better watch out,' he says. 'These things usually travel in pairs.' The other episode plays around with the old sf theme of the human body as some kind of vast machine populated by tiny people. Allen's version concerns what goes on in this NASA-like organization during a seduction attempt in the back seat of a car. Up in the brain room, which resembles a set from *The Andromeda Strain*, white-suited technocrats try to keep things running on schedule despite being hindered by the overworked proles in the lower regions. Allen plays one of the group of sperm cells – who look and act like a squad of paratroopers about to be dropped on enemy territory – and is the most nervously reluctant of them all. 'You hear rumours about this pill these women take,' he moans.

These episodes turned out to be a practice run for Allen's full-length science fiction satire called *Sleeper*, which he wrote and directed the following year. He uses the device of having a person from the present day finding himself in the future as a means of commenting on contemporary society rather than as a genuine way of speculating about the future. But apart from jokes on such early 1970s American obsessions as Nixon,

An unusual giant monster on the loose in Woody Allen's Everything You Always Wanted to Know About Sex.

health food, beauty contests and revolutionary politics, he also includes a number of pure sf gags involving robots, futuristic gadgets, ray guns, mechanized pets and a variety of artificial food that has to be beaten into submission before it can be served. One of the best sequences involves an attempt to clone a new body for the country's dictator, using the only part of him that remains intact after a successful assassination attempt – his nose. 'We're going to clone him right into his shoes,' says Allen as he puts the nose at one end of a table and the shoes at the other. It's not as polished as his more recent films and there's rather too much emphasis on slapstick, but as an example of that rare species – funny science fiction – it rates very highly.

It is certainly a lot funnier than *Flesh Gordon* (1973), which originally began as a cheap pornographic spoof on the *Flash Gordon* movie serial but slowly developed into a much more expensive production as the special effects took on a life of their own and became increasingly elaborate. Several of the effects sequences involved model animation of a high standard, in particular the climax which featured an amusing monster called the Great God Porno who, clutching the heroine (Suzanne Fields), scales a tall building with all the panache of King Kong while muttering a series of amusing asides about his various problems. Once on top of the building he begins to undress the girl, snarling: 'Let's see your tits.' Unfortunately the live action sequences don't equal the animated ones. It was directed by Michael Benveniste, Howard Ziehm and Walter R. Cichy and the screenplay was by Michael Benveniste and William Hunt. A host of Hollywood technicians were involved in the special effects, including Dave Allen, Jim Danforth, Jim Aupperle, George Barr, Joe Clark, Douglas Beswick, Ray Mercer, Bob Costa, Mike Hyatt, Dennis Muren and Russ Turner. Jason Williams played Flesh.

One sf film made in 1973 that doesn't fit into any easy category is *The Day of the Dolphin*, directed by Mike Nichols, scripted by Buck Henry and based on the novel by Robert Merle. It stars George C. Scott as a marine biologist who has succeeded in teaching dolphins to speak English. The first half of the film, which deals with this historic contact between two intelligent species, conveys a genuine sense of wonder found in the best science fiction, but instead of following up the implications of the breakthrough the rest of the film concentrates on the attempts made by various groups to use the dolphins for their own sinister purposes, including the planned assassination of the President. Despite its degeneration into a conventional spy-thriller *The Day of the Dolphin* remains, because of its initially serious approach to the subject of mankind's relationship with other forms of life that may be intelligent, an important sf film.

That year (1973) also saw Michael Crichton's début as a feature film director (he had previously directed a TV film called *Pursuit* in 1972 about a crazed politician who holds a city to ransom with a nerve bomb) with *Westworld*, based on his own original screenplay. 'Westworld' is the name of a section of a futuristic amusement park called Delos, the other two section being set in medieval England and ancient Rome. The park is populated with humanoid robots, as well as robot animals, designed to obey any order given to them and supervised by technicians in an underground control room. The film begins with the arrival of two male visitors (Richard Benjamin and James Brolin) who both enjoy themselves on the first day by doing such things as out-shooting the local robot gunman (Yul Brynner) and sleeping with the robot saloon girls. But things go drastically wrong the following day when the robot gun-slinger actually outdraws one of the men (Brolin) and shoots him dead, leaving his companion in a very frightening position. Up until this point *Westworld* seems as if it's going to be something out of the ordinary; the Wild West park obviously isn't based on the real Old West but Hollywood's recreation of it (a point emphasized by the fact that Brynner wears the same costume as he wore in *The Magnificent Seven*), and the film appears to be about a man who discovers that his *machismo* fantasies, created and nourished by Hollywood films and TV series, are somewhat redundant in the face of grim reality. But from here on *Westworld* becomes the sort of film that visitors to the park like to pretend they're part of – a film in

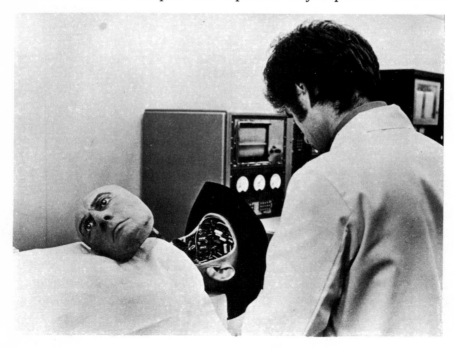

The Yul Brynner robot is repaired in Westworld.

which the hero overcomes all odds by blasting his way to victory. Though entertaining, the film is a disappointment since it fails to deliver what it promises. The screenplay is also rather vague on the reasons behind the robot revolt.

The theme of Crichton's novel *The Terminal Man*, which was filmed in 1974, concerned a human who is turned into a machine. Unfortunately Crichton himself wasn't involved with the direction or the screenplay this time; instead it was written and directed by British film-maker Mike Hodges (*Get Carter, Pulp*). Hodges is very adept at making gritty, off-beat thrillers, but his understanding of science fiction is less certain and Crichton's basic theme gets lost along the way. George Segal stars as a computer specialist called Harry Benson who suffers from violent black-outs as a result of brain damage sustained in a car accident. As his condition can't be controlled by drugs it is decided to insert a number of tiny electrodes into his brain, linked to a small computer surgically implanted in his shoulder. The idea is that when one of his seizures begins the computer will send soothing impulses into his brain and thus prevent the black-out from occurring. In practice his brain enjoys the soothing effect so much that it induces the black-outs to occur at an ever-increasing rate, causing Benson to escape from hospital and go on a rampage of violence.

One of the best, and most disturbing, sequences in the film is when the technicians coolly test the implanted electrodes by stimulating various areas in Benson's brain by remote control – causing him to experience pain, fear, pleasure, lust at the mere touch of a button. But the chilling implications suggested by these scenes aren't followed up, as Hodges is more anxious to concentrate on the thriller aspects of the story. Once Benson escapes from hospital the film degenerates into yet another murderer-on-the-loose movie. It's stylish, entertaining and often exciting but, like *Westworld*, it doesn't deliver what it promises. It was a box-office failure in America and hasn't yet received a release in Britain.

A slick throwback to the old monster days, though using the topical gimmick of pollution, was *It's Alive!*, written and directed by Larry Cohen in 1974 and featuring a mutant baby which is all claws and teeth and capable of leaping like a gazelle, the first of a new breed of human that has evolved to cope with life in an over-polluted world. Cohen has a nice line in black humour, best demonstrated in a scene where we see a milkman fall victim to the hungry little monster, and he wisely never shows the baby very clearly, instead presenting it in a series of fast, almost subliminal, shots. The model used to represent the baby is a genuinely nasty creation – the work of make-up designer Rick Baker (who worked on the 1976 remake of *King Kong*, designing the face and also wearing the ape suit in a number of sequences), with bulging forehead, large, unpleasant eyes and a vicious-looking set of teeth. Definitely not a film for expectant mothers.

Contender for the position of 'Most Pretentious and Self-Indulgent SF Film Ever Made' is *Zardoz*, written and directed in 1974 by John Boorman. In the year 2293, many years after the Great Collapse of Civilization, the world is divided into two regions – the Vortex and the Outlands, separated by an impenetrable force-field. Within the Vortex live the Eternals, immortal and decadent, while in the Outlands live the Brutals, who are ruled over by the Exterminators, themselves controlled by a giant, flying stone head which represents their god, Zardoz. When the Exterminators aren't killing the Brutals, with weapons supplied by Zardoz, they are forcing the Brutals to grow food which is given to the giant head. Zardoz is controlled by one of the Immortals, and so the food ends up in the Vortex. Eventually some of the Exterminators become suspicious about the whole set-up and one of them, Zed (Sean Connery), hides in a shipment of grain placed within the head and is thus able to penetrate the force-field and enter the Vortex. His presence causes consternation among the Immortals, a rather wishy-washy bunch of characters who spend most of their time running around in wispy, coloured underwear while trying to look superior. Despite their efforts to tame Zed he succeeds in destroying the computer, called the Tabernacle, that controls and sustains the Vortex, bringing the Immortals' society to an end. The Exterminators swarm in and massacre everyone, leaving Zed to escape with a reformed Immortal (Charlotte Rampling).

The message is a familiar one: Technology is Evil and Nature (or God) knows best. Zed represents the Primal Force that brings back to the Immortals such favourite human experiences as Fear, Hate, Love, Sex and Death, thus releasing them from their static, impotent way of life and allowing them to become part of the Natural Order of Things once again, that is: dead. Unfortunately Boorman overlooked one other powerful force – the Audience, which subsequently rebelled at having to put up with so much ludicrous posturing.

On the credit side, however, the film is a visual feast, thanks to both the Irish settings and the photography of Geoffrey Unsworth (who also worked on *2001*), and the special effects involving the flying head were also impressive. 'I'm very pleased with those,' said Boorman, referring to the various shots of the head. 'With only one exception they were all done in the negative, there are no process shots at all. The secret is that we used different sizes of Head according to the shot and the perspective, and from time to time we used differential focus – the big giveaway is always the focus. Where the Head lands for the first time I used bits of full-size sections, and by cutting all these things together, hopefully there's the illusion that you've actually seen the thing arriving . . . the Head actually

Sara Kestelman and Charlotte Rampling pose in front of the regeneration tank in Zardoz.

One of the 'Exterminators' from the same film.

started off looking like the mask from *The Wizard of Oz* film but stylistically it was too naïve. So then I based it on Blake's drawing, because Blake's kind of fantasy is something very close to me – that kind of nightmare world is something I find sympathy with. But the Head kept on changing . . . I had a modeller who was making it and it rather alarmingly became more and more like me. I used to go down and tell him each day what I wanted, I want more of this kind of look, and I'd show my teeth and he'd say great, just hold that for a minute.'[44]

Another less-than-satisfactory sf film made in 1974 was *The Final Programme* (called *The Last Days of Man on Earth* in America), written and directed by Robert Feust, a former set-designer who is best known for directing the *Dr Phibes* films. It was based on the novel by Michael Moorcock, one of Britain's most innovative sf writers (Moorcock prefers to think of his work as being speculative fiction rather than science fiction) and features Moorcock's most famous creation – Jerry Cornelius, a multi-faceted, multi-purpose character who embodies many of the prevalent myths of the mid-20th century. He's rich, he's a rock star, a mercenary, a mystic, a secret agent, a Christ figure and many other things beside. *The Final Programme* looks impressive but not much of Moorcock's unique creation remains. Cornelius' father had died, leaving behind some hidden microfilm on which is the mysterious 'final (computer) programme' that contains a number of profoundly important secrets. Apart from Jerry there are others involved in the hunt for the film, including his evil brother Frank, who has kidnapped their sister Catharine (whom Jerry loves in a way that exceeds brotherly affection), and the awesome Miss Brunner who has a tendency to consume her lovers completely, bones and all. In the book the 'final programme' serves to combine Jerry and Miss Brunner into a single creature – a bisexual Messiah who leads the population of Europe into the Mediterranean in a lemming-like rush to oblivion, but in the film their combined bodies form a shaggy neanderthal who winks into the camera and does a Humphrey Bogart imitation.

Jon Finch as the enigmatic Jerry Cornelius in The Final Programme.

Jon Finch fits the part of Cornelius visually but fails to reproduce the infinitely ambiguous character of the book; more successful is Jenny Runacre as Miss Brunner, who comes on like a Force 10 hurricane, tossing men around like rag dolls and absorbing her lovers, male and female, with casual ease. Least impressive is Derrick O'Connor as Frank Cornelius, who lacks the necessary rat-like presence. The film does capture some of the off-beat atmosphere of the novel, suggesting a world where reality is crumbling around the edges, but overall it falls far short of complete success. Michael Moorcock was indirectly involved with the making of the film, but unlike Harrison with *Soylent Green* he didn't find it a very enjoyable experience.

'What happened was that Sandy Lieberson of Goodtimes Enterprises was very keen on the book and as I'd admired what he'd done in the past, like producing *Performance* – and Goodtimes seemed a good company – I was very happy that he was involved, but he failed to get any finance for it so it went more or less fallow. I hadn't done a treatment or anything because at the time I was very suspicious about getting involved with film people because it is such a depressing business. So I thought, well, if they want to buy the book – great – if they don't buy it – fair enough – as long as they leave me out of it. I also felt that I didn't know enough about the film business then so I thought it was best to leave it to the professionals.' A script was written but as the result was something of a shambles Lieberson lost interest. Various attempts were made at Goodtimes to revive the project but it wasn't until Robert Feust became involved and succeeded in raising finance for the film that it finally got underway.

'Bob Feust was very keen to work on something,' said Moorcock, 'so he elected to do a script and talked EMI into putting up the usual front money. And he wrote a script which appealed to Nat Cohen (then the head of EMI), and in a sense the film would never have got made and I wouldn't have got any money apart from the orginal option money if Feust hadn't written such an idiot script that appealed to Nat Cohen. So the whole thing started going ahead but Sandy didn't like the script and asked me to come in on the script conference. I had a look at the script and – it was a bad script on anyone's terms. I began to realize that I knew more about scriptwriting than Feust did, and up until then I'd been saying, well, you're the experts, the professionals. So what I did was to take the script and I revamped it – I cut out all the reaction shots and tightened it up, and I put in a much clearer plot running through it – more than the book had because as a film it needed a stronger plot – and I added various visual scenes to amplify it.

'So then I took the script back to them – I only had one copy, all I'd done basically was to work on the original – and Sandy liked it, but Feust said: "Well, I'll take it away and read it." And Sandy was saying: "No, it's all right . . . we'll get it copied first so we can all read it." And there was this incredible egocentric thing going on all round the table. I didn't know what half the people there were supposed to be doing at this conference – it was just like an old-fashioned satire of a Hollywood script conference with everyone having their own axe to grind but nobody actually working towards a common end, which I innocently thought we were supposed to be doing. But they were all pissing about – though Lieberson wasn't, I have to admit. I have a lot of respect for him – a very hard man but he knows what he wants. Anyway, it was finally agreed that Feust would use my script, and Feust didn't like this but he said: "Super! Marvellous! We're all very excited here, Michael." And off he went. And when I went down to watch when he started shooting, it began to dawn on me that he was using his original script – he'd actually chucked mine and was using his own script. The result was that he ended up with about three hours of film, two hours of which were primarily reaction shots – all the stuff that I'd crossed out with a pen was back in there. When it came to editing it, of course, it was all out again but by then they'd spent thousands of quid shooting it. Unfortunately Lieberson wasn't around when it was being made – he was working on some other film. John Goldstone, his partner, was. I've worked with him since then and found him very reliable but that was his first film and he didn't really quite know what he was on about. None of the actors knew what they were supposed to be doing – and they had a lot of good actors in it. By the time the film was halfway through the actors were all coming up to me and saying: "Look, what the hell is it all about because *he's* not telling us." And the emphasis of the film kept shifting all the time, because the actors didn't know if it was supposed to be serious or a James Bond type of film, or a take-off or what. The final sequences were, by and large, the best ones – they certainly had a lot more of the spirit of the book largely because they gave up. Most of the good bits in it were the little cameo parts that the actors did themselves. For instance, that joke-fight sequence in the underground cavern between Finch and the villain where Jerry shouts: "Miss Brunner, I'm losing!" and all that sort of stuff – that all came about after Jon Finch and I talked about it.

'The cast was very good. Jenny Runacre was good as Miss Brunner but her sister had just died before they started shooting and she reckons she could have been a lot better if it hadn't been for that. It was quite a good performance but she was under stress at the time. I thought she was the best thing in it really. Jon Finch would have been a lot better if he'd had a clearer idea of what it was all about.

'As for the ending, it would have been all right in a TV sketch. There's nothing wrong with the idea but it had nothing to do with the rest of the picture. Feust was doing his best to shore it all up by sending up everything that had happened before because there was no sort of fundamental logic to the structure of the film. I think that's where a lot of films go wrong and when I was originally discussing the film with Feust I was talking about "prefiguring images" – I wasn't being pretentious, it's quite a simple thing. For instance, a film that I admire, and I suppose it's almost an sf film, is *Kiss Me Deadly*, the Mickey Spillane film, which is beautifully done because everything that happens in it is prefigured all the way through. There's a moment in the early part of the film where Mike Hammer's talking to a cop saying: "Well, nothing much can happen to me, can it?" And at that moment the lift doors open and lights suddenly hit him. There are all sorts of things like that. It's a very nicely constructed film, and when you reach that shock ending it doesn't feel wrong, it's all been led up to. And that's what I was trying to do with the script, put in little images that all finally add up so that the film, on its visual level, works. Feust didn't know what I was talking about and took the piss out of me for suggesting it. By the end of it all I was openly contemptuous of him.

'A fair amount of my suggestions *were* used in it, I suppose – odd jokes and things like that. I got about £20,000 for it which I wouldn't complain about, but in a sense I really paid dearly for that money. The film screwed me up for a good year, if not longer – the strain of it all and the disappointment at the shambles of it when it came out. There's something absolutely terrible about a bad version of your stuff, and it affected me very, very badly and quite fundamentally for a long time. When I saw it I sat there willing it to be better but the strain of watching it was just too much. There were one or two sequences involving scientific explanations which, when I first saw them, I literally laughed aloud, they were so ridiculous.

'I didn't want the film to do well. I knew it wouldn't do well. I mean my faith in the British public would have been badly shattered if it had done well. The thing that counts a lot is the attitude of the distributors towards a film and in this case they actually thought it would do well in the provinces but not in London. Well, it got praised in all the big, heavy weekly publications and got really good publicity in London, and if they'd kept it in London they would have probably made money out of it, but they released it first to the provinces and, of course, it did dreadfully. So they didn't have any confidence in it after that, and quite rightly. It even did badly in France.

'I was very glad it did badly but in a way I was also very bitter because they'd bought the rights to the sequels and obviously no one is going to film the sequels after that one was such a disaster. But the thing is they'd be very different films. It's possible to interpret *The Final Programme* in very trendy, daft terms in the way that Feust did but you're less and less able to do that with the later books.'

Yet another 1974 sf film that promised more than it delivered was *Phase IV*, directed by Saul Bass, written by Mayo Simon and starring Nigel Davenport, Lynne Frederick and Michael Murphy. The film is a beautifully photographed story about a species of ant which acquires intelligence, presumably as a result of an alien influence. The core of the film is the battle of wits between the ants and a fanatical scientist who has set up a dome-shaped experimental station in the heart of their territory. From the apparent security of the dome he carries out a series of tests on them – bombarding them with high-frequency sound waves and spraying their nests with insecticides – but the ants turn the tables on him every time and finally, when he refuses to accept the truth, they are obliged to destroy him. Unfortunately the script ignores both logic and science; the scientist admits from the beginning that the ants are intelligent – which is why he's there to study them – but each new manifestation of this intelligence takes him by surprise. Instead the emphasis is put on mysticism. The film tries too hard to emulate *2001*, even to the extent of having a similar ending with the two surviving humans being transformed, either by the ants or by the intelligence guiding them, into a new form of life. Bass originally filmed a spectacular, surreal montage lasting four minutes, showing what life would be like on the 'new' Earth, but this was cut by the distributor.

Phase IV represents Saul Bass's directing début. He was previously best known for his striking credit sequences, like those for *Walk On the Wild Side* and *Psycho*, and while he is a master of his craft when it comes to pure visuals, his handling of actors is less than satisfactory. The film falls into the 'interesting failure' category, and its main attraction lies in the superb insect photography by Ken Middleham rather than in its science fiction content.

Phase IV was a masterpiece compared to *Doc Savage: Man of Bronze* (1974), produced by George Pal and based on one of the 181 Doc Savage pulp novels written by Kenneth Robeson (real name Lester Dent). 'Research has proved that science fiction buffs, people who like camp, kids and original readers are snapping up the books,' said Pal during the making of the film. 'We think the same thing will happen with movie audiences. People of all ages will be interested in our movie. With luck it's possible we will film all 181 stories.'[45] The mind boggles, but as it turned out once was enough. The film was made in the same style as the 1966 TV *Batman* series, trying for the 'it's so bad it's funny' effect but failing completely. Michael Anderson's leaden direction conspires to make it very embarrassing and a great come-down for Pal, who had produced such films as *War of the Worlds, The Time Machine* and *The Power*.

Technically *Earthquake* (1974) counts as science fiction, since it concerns a future event that may or may not happen (and it also stars Charlton Heston, who seemed to be appearing in nothing but sf films at this time). Directed by Mark Robson and written by George Fox and Mario Puzo it follows the efforts of a small group of people to survive after Los Angeles has been devastated by a major earthquake. Genevieve Bujold aside, the special effects are the film's main attraction. Several of Hollywood's top experts had to be persuaded to come out of retirement to work on the project. One such was Clifford Stine, who was once the camera effects man at Universal during the 1950s and worked on most of their sf/horror films. Other effects men included Glen Robinson, Frank Brendel and Jack McMasters. The many complex matte paintings showing the ruined city were produced by British matte painter Albert Whitlock.

(Above) It may look like an expensive costume but Dan O'Bannon constructed it out of a second-hand asbestos fire-suit, hosing from a vacuum cleaner, a vacuform bubble, a cookie tin and some styrofoam packing sections from a typewriter case: typical of the ingenious

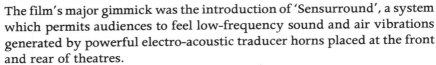

economic short-cuts taken during the making of Dark Star. (Below) The commander of the 'Dark Star' is dead but still conscious within his cryogenic freezer.

The film's major gimmick was the introduction of 'Sensurround', a system which permits audiences to feel low-frequency sound and air vibrations generated by powerful electro-acoustic traducer horns placed at the front and rear of theatres.

The same year (1974) also saw the release of an animated, Franco-Czech co-production called *La Planète Sauvage* (*Fantastic Planet*), which was directed by René Laloux (who also wrote the script with Roland Topor) and based on the novel *Oms En Serie* by Stefan Wul. The plot is over-familiar to sf readers, involving human beings on a distant planet who are kept as pets by a race of giant blue humanoid creatures. What makes the film interesting is the surreal and bizarre background in which various nightmarish creatures are seen going about their sinister business. Typical is the plant-like creature that spends its time swatting down small flying animals purely for fun. Unfortunately this ingeniously disturbing world, created by artist and writer Roland Topor, is completely at odds with the juvenile events taking place in the foreground.

The best sf film of 1974 was *Dark Star*, directed by John Carpenter, who also wrote the script in collaboration with Dan O'Bannon. The film is a funny satire on space films and sf in general. The 'Dark Star' of the title is a spaceship in which four men roam the universe on a boring and apparently endless mission, which involves locating 'unstable' worlds and destroying them with thermostellar bombs. Conditions in the ship have deteriorated – the computer is having difficulty in maintaining the life-support system; the crew members are in various stages of psychosis; the captain is dead but still partially conscious in one of the ship's freezers; and the ship's mascot – a rather nasty alien shaped like a beach ball with claws – is getting increasingly belligerent. But the most urgent problem involves one of the thermostellar bombs which is intelligent and has to be continually talked out of exploding prematurely.

Dark Star was originally a 45-minute film shot on 16mm by a group of students at the University of Southern California for $6,000. It was the brainchild of John Carpenter, who started planning it in 1970 and shortly afterwards interested Dan O'Bannon in the project (O'Bannon appeared in the film as the deranged Pinback, and he also designed the special effects). For the next three years they spent all their spare time working on the film, financing it out of their own pockets. They were influenced by *2001* for the interior design of the ship and many of the exterior shots, but O'Bannon maintains that the talking bomb, one of the film's most interesting devices, was not based on HAL 9000 but on an old idea of his own. Later producer Jack H. Harris provided the necessary money to enable extra footage to be shot and to transfer the whole film onto 35mm. Even so distribution remained very limited for years, but the success of *Star Wars* has given *Dark Star* a new lease of life. Perhaps it will now be recognized for the major achievement it is.

Another 1974 sf film that hasn't had wide distribution and wasn't released in Britain until 1978 is *The Stepford Wives*, a well-made, entertaining movie concerning a very topical subject – Women's Lib. There were also a number of major names behind it – it was based on a novel by Ira Levin, the screenplay was by William Goldman, and it was directed by Bryan Forbes – and the cast included such performers as Katherine Ross, Paula Prentiss, Peter Masterson and Patrick O'Neal. Despite this it flopped at the box-office.

Katherine Ross stars as Joanna, a happily married photographer whose husband, Walter (Peter Masterson), suddenly insists they leave New York and move to a rural residential area in Connecticut. Once settled there Walter becomes involved with a local club, membership of which is restricted to men only, while Joanna pines for her old life in New York. She then begins to realize that all the wives in the community act like the stereotyped 'housewives' that feature in TV commercials – interested only in cooking, keeping the house clean and looking attractive for their husbands.

Joanna's suspicions increase, particularly as her husband's attitude towards her has changed since he joined the 'Men's Club' which is presided over by the sinister Dale Coba (Patrick O'Neal). Eventually she realizes the awful truth – the women are being replaced by artificial duplicates. It's all the work of Coba, a former Disneyland technician, who has perfected the means of building humanoid automatons and has been offering the husbands in the town the opportunity of trading in their wives for new 'improved' versions, though his motives for doing this aren't very clear. 'Why? Because we can do it,' he tells Joanna at the end of the film before introducing her to her robot double.

On a certain level the film works successfully – building up an effective mood of paranoia and tension – but as science fiction, or even as an allegory about man's exploitation of women, it doesn't quite work. It is hard to imagine technology ever being able to build a machine that looks, acts and feels like a human being, yet we are expected to believe that a technician from Disneyland has accomplished this, practically on his own. It would have made more sense to have explained the artificial women as being organic replicas (clones) of the originals, but it would have been best of all if the men had merely discovered a way of mentally conditioning their wives to act the way they wanted them to. This would not only have been more scientifically feasible but also increased the feeling that the men were actually taking over their wives mind and body, thus giving an extra cutting edge to the film as an allegory about female exploitation. As it is the film's closing sequence showing Joanna and the other wives drifting contentedly around a vast supermarket lacks the impact it should have because we know these duplicates have no connection with the real women and thus the sense of tragedy is dissipated.

In 1975 violence made its presence felt in the sf cinema, most notably in Norman Jewison's slick but empty *Rollerball* based on a short story by William Harrison. As usual when a short story idea is stretched to fill over two hours of screen time the result is a lot of padding and fake profundity. 'Rollerball' is the name of a game played in the future in which groups of men on roller-skates attempt to beat each other's brains out with metal-studded gloves. The Corporations, which rule this future world, have devised the game as a means of keeping the population under control, the idea being that if people are able to watch men on skates beating each other up they won't want to indulge in any awkward political activity. The scheme goes wrong when one of the rollerball champions, Jonathon (James Caan), is so successful at the game that he becomes a cult figure throughout the world. Fearful of this dangerous display of individuality the Corporations attempt to eliminate him by making the game increasingly dangerous (they abolish the rules). He survives, however, and the film ends with him alone and triumphant on a body-littered track while the Corporations, represented by John Houseman, gnash their teeth with frustration as the crowds roar Jonathon's name.

The rollerball sequences are well-staged and exciting to watch, but off

James Caan (left)
in Rollerball.

the track the film is slow and boring – consisting mainly of seeing James Caan brood about What It All Means. As science fiction the film is unsatisfactory because we are told very little about this future world, which is only forty years away, apart from the fact that Corporations have abolished all individual nations and that war, poverty and disease no longer exist. The James Caan character's token search for information about the past only leads him to Sir Ralph Richardson doing an amusing cameo as the caretaker of a broken-down computer in which all historical records have been stored. The computer, called Zero, keeps wiping its memory banks by mistake ('We've just lost the 13th century,' murmurs Richardson. 'Oh well, there was only Dante and a few corrupt Popes') and isn't much help. As a result the events in the film are left suspended in a cultural and social limbo, yet according to Jewison his intention in the film was to issue a warning about the growing violence in popular sports and how this caters to the baser instincts of the spectators. His 'warning' would have had more relevance if he had set the film nearer our own times.

Less pretentious, and much more entertaining, was the Roger Corman-produced *Rollerball* rip-off *Death Race 2000*, written and directed by Paul Bartel, about a car race across America in the year 2000. The winner is not the fastest but the driver who can kill the most pedestrians. Any person on foot is a legal target but drivers score the most points by running down

One of the bizarre cars featured in Deathrace 2000, *Roger Corman's amusing imitation of* Rollerball.

children and old people. David Carradine plays the black-clad Frankenstein, the champion who has been in so many crashes that most of his body
has been replaced by artificial parts (this turns out to be a myth, however).
Another of the drivers, called Machine Gun Joe Viterbo, is played by
Sylvester ('Rocky') Stallone who gives a marvellous portrayal of pure evil:
he's such a fink he runs over his own service crew in order to score the
first points.

It has long been a tradition in Hollywood movies that when the hero is
pursued by a horde of villains he should be accompanied by a girl who
stumbles and sprains her ankle at a crucial moment. However in *The
Ultimate Warrior* Yul Brynner is saddled with a girl who chooses such a
moment to give birth to a baby – not that this slows down Brynner, who
plays the warrior of the title, for more than a moment or two. Not even
pausing to boil water he delivers the baby in about five seconds flat, then
calmly despatches several of his pursuers with the same knife he has just
used to cut the umbilical cord. In a way *The Ultimate Warrior* can be
described as the first Kung Fu sf film – though there's not really any Kung
Fu in the film, it does follow the usual formula of that genre: two opposing
groups, each with its own champion who, after a series of skirmishes,
fights it out to the death in the final reel. But *The Ultimate Warrior*,
written and directed by Robert Clouse (who previously made the Bruce
Lee epic *Enter the Dragon* and the more recent *The Pack* about a band of
killer dogs), is a very good sf film – hard, uncompromising, cynical,
unpretentious and excellently directed by Clouse, who moves the action
along at just the right pace.

In this film Brynner plays the same sort of implacable, irresistible force
as he did in *Westworld* – something he does so well and with such
assurance that one accepts the way he easily out-fights and kills some
twenty or thirty men during the course of the film. But whereas in
Westworld he was supposed to be a robot, in this he is a creature of flesh
and blood – a fact he graphically proves in the film's climax when he hacks
off his own hand with an axe to prevent himself being dragged to his death.
What is most refreshing about the film is its lack of sentimentality. Even the
so-called good guys are capable of great callousness, and a saintly plant-
lover turns into a raging killer when someone steps on his tomatoes.

A similar future world of chaos, anarchy and violence is created in *A
Boy and His Dog*, written and directed by L. Q. Jones and based on the
novella by American sf writer Harlan Ellison. Set in the year 2024 after a
nuclear war has laid waste to most of the world, the film concerns two of
the survivors who dwell in this bleak, Beckett-like landscape – a young
man called Vic (Don Johnson) and his canine companion Blood. The latter
is no ordinary dog but a mutation that possesses human intelligence and

telepathic powers. Much of the entertainment comes from the telepathic conversations between Vic and Blood (Tim McIntire), the latter having a nice line in weary cynicism and sarcasm.

Ellison's black little allegory about what a young man's fancy turns to when it comes to a choice between his girl and his dog has been faithfully transferred to the screen by actor-turned-director L. Q. Jones (he's appeared in a number of Sam Peckinpah's films and his directing style has been influenced by him). The film's only real flaw is that the underground sequences, which are stagey and artificial, contrast badly with the gritty realism of the surface scenes. Ellison himself takes the blame for that: 'It's my fault, it's not an inadequacy on L. Q. Jones's part, because I was being dishonest when I wrote that section of the story. I didn't really create a down-under section that was realistic, I did a kind of papier-mâché Disneyland because I wanted to poke fun at the middle-classes. But L. Q. was saddled with that when he came to write the script.'[46] Nevertheless the film remains a superior piece of science fiction cinema.

Even more violent was *They Came from Within* (also known as *Shivers* and *The Parasite Murders*) which was written and directed by David Cronenberg. The film begins with a mad scientist strangling a young girl, stripping her of her school uniform, cutting her stomach open with a scalpel, pouring acid into the cavity and then cutting his own throat with the same scalpel. From then on it's all downhill.

Some people have taken the film seriously, comparing it to *Night of the Living Dead* and *Invasion of the Bodysnatchers*, but Cronenberg, a former experimental/underground film-maker is having his own weird joke at the genre's expense. *They Came from Within* sends up the traditions of the old sf/horror films and as such is good clean fun.

Strange crawling creatures also featured in another 1975 sf film – *Bug*, one of the last films to be produced by the late William Castle, who made such films as *The Tingler, Strait-jacket, Project X, Rosemary's Baby* and *Shanks*. Directed by Jeannot Szwarc it was written by Thomas Page and based on his own novel *The Haephestus Plague* about the insect-like creatures which emerge out of the ground after an earthquake and create fire by means of rubbing two rear appendages together. William Castle, it seems, was trying to make an old-fashioned sf/monster film while Thomas Page was trying to produce a religious allegory, and neither succeeded in his aim. Castle, having a reputation for publicity gimmicks, had planned something special for *Bug* too. He declared: 'During the screening of the picture the roaches will seem to get loose in the theatre – we're working on something that will enable the audience to *feel* the roaches actually crawling over their legs! It will be similar to the vibrations in *Earthquake.*' The device was never used, which is probably just as well; it sounds like something that would empty a cinema rather than fill it.

In 1975 the Amicus film company, which had previously specialized in horror films, made *The Land That Time Forgot*, a lost-world fantasy aimed at family audiences. It proved a great success and has since spawned a number of sequels, such as *At the Earth's Core, People That Time Forgot* and *Warlords of Atlantis*. Directed by Kevin Connor, *The Land That Time Forgot* was based on an Edgar Rice Burroughs novel and concerned a strange land inhabited by dinosaurs and primitive tribes which is discovered during the First World War by a German submarine, crewed by a mixture of German and British seamen, and one American – the hero. It would have been an ideal subject for Ray Harryhausen's model animation but alternative methods were used to create the dinosaurs. Special effects man Derek Meddings explained why: 'Well, I'm a great fan of Harryhausen's work but there are some people who aren't, so I can't always say to a film company: "I think you should get Harryhausen!" Besides, he's always busy with his own films and Jim Danforth, the other animation specialist, is always busy too. With *The Land That Time Forgot* we couldn't get involved in animating models ourselves because it takes so long – it means spending a year of your life just animating models. And apart from Harryhausen there's not really anyone in England set up to do model animation. If you start on a medium-budget picture the company concerned just can't afford to set you up in such a specialist operation either, whereas Harryhausen can set himself up whenever he wants. He gets paid a lot of money to do it and he does it very successfully. There's no one to beat him really.

'So in *The Land That Time Forgot* we used model dinosaurs that were about three foot high on average and were manipulated either

A pterodactyl, full-size and suspended from a crane, in action in The Land That Time Forgot.

mechanically or like glove puppets with someone's hand inside them. They weren't made by my team or me but by Roger Dicken. We were involved in the filming of them and we also helped him operate them because obviously he couldn't operate them all at once. It was complicated because we had to make them move and attack people, but as they were basically puppets it was difficult to show them actually walking so we had to use a lot of tricks. To combine them in the same scenes with the actors we used front projection [supervised by Charles Staffel].'

One of the better sequences involved an aquatic dinosaur, consisting of a huge head and long neck, suddenly appearing next to the submarine and attacking the crew on deck. 'That head and its mechanism was built at Shepperton Studios,' said Meddings, 'and they did a fantastic job on it, but the funny thing was that it got full of water every time we ducked it under, despite having been made of water-proofed, non-absorbent material, and it got heavier and heavier. As you know it had to snatch a German sailor off the deck of the sub and plunge him underwater – well, we used an actor up to a certain point in the action and then we had to use a stuntman for when he actually went into the water, and inside the head was an aqualung so that the stuntman could breathe when the head was under the surface. We did the shot several times and each time it got harder to raise the thing because of all the water it had absorbed. It got so heavy we had to put a block and tackle on it and pull it up very gently. We had a mechanism inside, like a hydraulic arm, and everything started to pull against it as the material got more and more water-logged. But we got the shot we wanted, eventually.'

Less impressive was the pterodactyl used in the sequence where a caveman is snatched up and carried away. 'That we weren't very pleased with,' said Meddings. 'It worked all right in the film though. We built a full-sized model, which was suspended from a crane, for the shot where it swoops down and picks him up, and for the shot showing it flying off with the man in its mouth we used a smaller model. The man was a model in that shot too, and he contained a mechanism that moved his arms and legs.'

The best effects in the film involve the German submarine, which was a model over twenty feet long. 'There were four of us working on that,' said Meddings. 'We built the sub and filmed it in the largest tank at the studio. It moved on an underwater track and we were underwater ourselves a lot of the time shooting it. We lived like fish for about six weeks filming that thing.'

Surprisingly, one of the two scriptwriters who worked on the screenplay was none other than Michael Moorcock: 'I became involved when Edgar Rice Burroughs Incorporated slung out the first script that Amicus submitted to them – I've still got a copy of it somewhere and it's incredibly meaningless gibberish. ERB Inc said they wanted a new script, so the producer, Milton Subotsky, phoned my agent and asked if she knew of anyone suitable and she suggested me. Well, ERB Inc had heard of me and thought I was an ideal choice and I said, yeah, I'll do it if Jim Cawthorn could do the script with me because I knew that he's always wanted to work on an Edgar Rice Burroughs film. And because of the mess that had come about from me not being able to do the script on the *Final Programme* I thought – here is a chance to learn how to write a script and get paid for it at the same time. I knew Amicus would only be paying peanuts – I think I got paid a thousand quid – but it would only be a week's work, which is really all it was. And as ERB Inc were putting up half the money for the film they were insisting that the script be close to the original book, which is just how Jim and I wanted to write it. With them behind us we thought we were pretty safe but, of course, Amicus screwed it up and put in the volcano and all the usual stuff. None of that was in our script – we had what they would have regarded as a downbeat ending. It doesn't matter how many times you tell them that the most successful films, like *Frankenstein* and *King Kong*, have sort of tragic endings, they still feel you've got to have some kind of up-beat ending, like an exploding volcano. Our ending followed the book's pretty faithfully. It wasn't a profound book but it was the most interesting one, I felt, that Edgar Rice Burroughs had ever written. It was one of the few books of his that had an idea of some interest – the island as some sort of womb.

'Another problem that occurred during the filming was that the actor John McEnery, who played the U-Boat captain, did his whole part as a send-up and wrecked a lot of the tension of the film because in our version of the script the German was more or less the central character. We didn't want the usual Burroughs 1916 ranting Hun so we made him the philosophical core of the film. We gave him speeches and everything – we made him a "sensitive Kraut", But McEnery played the whole thing for laughs. They had to re-dub all his dialogue with Anton Diffring.

'Most of the action in the film came from our script up until two-thirds through. They improved on the beginning by making cuts – we made as many as we could because most of the book is all in that bloody submarine with them taking turns in taking it over.

'I try to be as professional as possible in whatever I do but I knew it would be silly to get too serious about a film like this. Anyway, before Jim and I started, as I wanted to do the best I could for the film I asked Amicus: "What's the budget? What can you afford to do?" Because if we knew what they could afford we could write the script accordingly. And they said: "Oh, don't worry about *that*." And they kept saying that, so in the end we just had to write the script in the dark as far as the budget was concerned, and as a result about 500 bleeding dinosaurs came down to one glove puppet.

'But working on that film was in no way as traumatic as the *Final Programme* experience had been because I had no personal involvement with it – none at all. I insisted at the beginning that we do one script – one version – and that would be it, and that was the way we did it. We delivered the script and we got the money, after some time. I think they finally paid us in monthly instalments.

'Actually I quite enjoyed the picture when I finally saw it completed. I took the kids to see it wherever it was on in the West End and I thoroughly enjoyed it. I love dinosaur pictures anyway. The dinosaurs themselves were something of a disappointment in some ways but there were certain static scenes that were quite good – like one long shot where you saw a dinosaur on a cliff – and there were similar shots I liked. Obviously the rest of it was a shambles but I can always go a long way with the helping of my imagination.'

Moorcock and Jim Cawthorn were supposed to write the script for the sequel, *At the Earth's Core*, also based on a Burroughs novel, but after a disagreement with one of the Amicus producers, John Dark, Moorcock pulled out of the project and the treatment that he and Cawthorn had written wasn't used. 'I'd hate to think anybody thought I was associated with *At the Earth's Core*,' said Moorcock. 'It was a *terrible* film even though it had the same director – Kevin Connor – who I think is quite a decent director. He's a lot better than Feust anyway. I was astonished by it, and I noticed in some places it got better reviews than *The Land That Time Forgot*. At least our film had some decent images, such as the ice-covered submarine.

'What happened with *At the Earth's Core* is that ERB Inc. pulled out halfway through when they saw what was happening. They had wanted Jim and me to do the script and presumably there were politics going on behind the scenes, but by that time I couldn't care less about it. But Jim got in contact with the Burroughs people for some reason and they said: "We've had it. We're pulling out." And they pulled their money out too. You'll notice the early sequences involving the giant mole look quite expensive and you think you're going to see a decent film, but I think most of the money went into these scenes – the first ten minutes. It looked as if there was less money spent on the rest of the film than on the average *Dr Who* TV series, and the script was just atrocious! But I liked those flying creatures, the Mahars, and again I think that Kevin Connor isn't a bad director because those Mahar sequences in particular were very well done. There was a nice atmosphere to those scenes and given a bit of time and money – and also a bit more respect for his subject – he could probably do quite a decent film.'

11 A Close Encounter With Star Wars (1977–78)

By the end of 1975 it had become apparent that a new science fiction film boom was about to start. All the major film companies were either making or planning to make sf films. At the beginning of 1976 sf films that were in various stages of production included *The Man Who Fell to Earth, Logan's Run, Futureworld, The Big Bus, Demon Seed, Damnation Alley, Food of the Gods, King Kong, Embryo* and *Star Wars.* But unlike the sf film boom of the 1950s this one didn't begin suddenly, nor is it as easy to explain its cause. There was no sudden boom in sf magazine sales, which was one of the main reasons for the 1950 sf film explosion; rather the opposite, in fact, since – though sf novels are as popular as ever – the magazines are dying out. Some of the film companies seem to have decided that science fiction was going to be the next big film trend after the disaster cycle and so began to buy sf properties and put them into production. Noting this, other companies anxiously followed suit.

One possible factor was the incredible success of *Jaws* which, while it wasn't strictly an sf film, followed the pattern of the old sf/monster movies of the 1950s, such as *Them!, It Came from Beneath the Sea, The Creature from the Black Lagoon, The Beast from 20,000 Fathoms* and many others, with the monster at first being an ominous, off-screen presence and finally appearing for an all-out confrontation with the human protagonists before being destroyed in an explosion of apocalyptic dimensions. The shark in *Jaws* is no ordinary shark; its intelligence and feats of strength border on the supernatural, and like the monsters in the old sf films it represents a primal force that symbolizes basic subconscious fears. Significantly the director, Steven Spielberg, chose an sf subject for his next film – *Close Encounters of the Third Kind.*

One of the first major sf films to be released in 1976 almost stopped the bandwagon in its tracks. Called *The Man Who Fell to Earth* it was directed by Nicolas Roeg, written by Roeg and Paul Mayersberg and based on the novel by Walter Tevis. But Tevis' evocative, almost impressionistic novel about an alien who cames to Earth in order to use the planet's resources to build a spacecraft large enough to save most of the inhabitants of his dying world, has been turned, by Roeg and Mayersberg, into a confused, self-indulgent film that alternates between pretentiousness and brilliance.

The overtly Freudian advertising artwork for Jaws, *the big film success of 1975 that utilized the old monster-from-the-deep formula so prevalent in the 1950s.*

A much less threatening aquatic creature surprises George C. Scott in The Day of the Dolphin.

The relatively clear-cut narrative of the book has been replaced by a non-linear structure that swings back and forth in time in a way that has become Roeg's trademark as a film-maker (*Performance, Walkabout, Don't Look Now*). Elements of the book which were perfectly straightforward, such as the reason for the alien's visit, have been deliberately obscured. In the book the alien tries to resist having his head X-rayed because he knows that his ultra-sensitive eyes will be permanently damaged, but in the film the X-rays, for some inexplicable reason, merely fuse his contact lenses to his eyes. Various unnecessary characters and incidents have been added, including some embarrassing sequences set on the alien's home planet when his wife and children totter about the sand dunes in what appear to be left-over costumes from an old Buck Rogers serial. There's also a tedious emphasis on the alien's sexuality (and every other character's sexuality too) that wasn't in the book and which results in some of the longest and most boring sex scenes ever filmed.

Clearly, like other prestigious film-makers before him (such as John Boorman), Roeg feels that he can only justify being involved in a science fiction film by making it as pretentious as possible. What he's trying to say is: 'Look, it might appear as if it's a science fiction film but really it's very clever.' In effect, he and Mayersberg destroyed all the elements in the novel that helped make it good science fiction. In an article for *Sight and Sound*, Mayersberg wrote: 'When Nicolas Roeg first showed it [the novel] to me, and when we subsequently talked about it, the adaptation looked like being a relatively simple matter, at least from the point of view of a screenplay. That's to say there didn't seem to be any major obstacles in the development of the plot. The characters looked essentially right, the mood was coherent, and so on. Later, as I wrote the first draft, I became aware that the eventual film was not going to be at all easy. Slowly I began to see why the book had not been filmed before. In an odd way it was *too much of a good thing*.' (My italics.)

Later in the article Mayersberg says: '*The Man Who Fell to Earth* is an extravagant entertainment. It has dozens of scenes that go together, not just in terms of plot, but also like circus acts following one another; the funny, the violent, the frightening, the sad, the horrific, the spectacular, the romantic and so on. We have clowns and lions and trapeze artists and dancing elephants and performing seals and ladies fired from cannons. ... Nic was unwilling to discard any scene, however clumsily written, if he thought it held an element which might be of value, although not perhaps in the form in which it was immediately expressed. The reason was that he believed any thought was worth examining because of what it might lead to . . . Curiously, I would be inclined to think of the finished film as I wrote, whereas in the early stages of writing, Nic would prefer not to think of the finished film at all.'[47]

Some of the extraneous 'circus acts' are quite impressive, but the film's main asset is the central performance by David Bowie as the frail, ethereal and vulnerable alien whose contact with the harsh world of humanity corrupts and ultimately dooms him. The other members of the cast are fine too, particularly Candy Clark as Mary-Lou, the crude and boozy girl who loves Thomas Newton (the alien's alias) no matter who or what he is. Rip Torn is as magnetic as ever in the role of the scientist Nathan Bryce who becomes the Judas who finally betrays Newton, but there are times when it seems that he's not exactly sure what he's doing in the film. *The Man Who Fell to Earth* lost 23 minutes when it was released in America and a lot of the 'circus acts' were cut, which led the *Time* magazine reviewer to describe it as 'pretty straightforward science fiction.'

A much bigger disappointment in 1976 was the long-awaited *Logan's Run* based on the novel by William F. Nolan and George Clayton Johnson. As *Cinefantastique* magazine commented on its release: 'The science fiction boom begins with a bomb.' The novel had combined all the old and familiar sf clichés, devices and traditions in such a way that it was basically a celebration of science fiction — a slick, inventive exercise in nostalgia, a glittering *tour de force*, a glorious soufflé of a science fiction novel. The film is none of these things and instead settles in the mind like a cinematic rock cake. The makers treat the clichés as new inventions, proudly trotting them out to amaze us with their cleverness. The producer, Saul David, who previously produced *Fantastic Voyage*,

Jenny Agutter and Michael York in Logan's Run.

explained: 'I don't know any more about the future than anybody else does. I have the same share in it that everybody else does but that's it. When you make this kind of film, depending upon your wit or your temperament, you extrapolate from what you've got in the present to what you think may happen in the future. In other words, you take all the tendencies you see around you now – juvenile delinquency, sexual licence, you name it – and you project those things to the future, simply exaggerating them.'[48]

The film is set in the year 2274 where the remains of the human race, after an atomic war, live in a large domed city. As natural resources are scarce the computer running the city has decided that no one can live past the age of 30. To disguise the grim reality a device called the 'Carousel' has been invented. When a person reaches 30 he must enter the Carousel and allow himself to be drawn up towards the ceiling of the dome where he then disappears in an explosion of colourful lights. People enter the arena willingly because they've been told that the process is a form of life-renewal, but, of course, the Carousel is an exterminating machine. Those who attempt to avoid this fate become 'runners' and are tracked down by government executioners called Sandmen.

The impeccable Michael York stars in the film as a Sandman called Logan who is ordered by the computer to pretend to be a runner in order to discover the meaning of 'Sanctuary', the place that all runners hope to reach. Chased by his former Sandman colleagues, Logan becomes involved with a girl called Jessica (Jenny Agutter) who has been helping runners to escape the city. After various predictable adventures they arrive at a vine-covered city which we recognize to be Washington DC in a bad state of repair. But instead of the mythical 'Sanctuary' all they find is Peter Ustinov, also in a bad state of repair, and his cats. As he is the first old man they have even seen they are amazed and take Ustinov back to the city to prove to the others that you don't have to die at 30 but can instead grow old, wrinkled, and senile. Everyone seems happy with the news and, after Logan zaps the computer with his blaster – causing it to blow itself up along with most of the city – they all go out to start a new life (the danger of radio-activity having been conveniently forgotten by the scriptwriter, David Zelag Goodman).

The film has very little to do with the novel but it might have been entertaining if it had been handled with the right light touch. Instead it moves with the grace and style of an arthritic elephant. It was directed by Michael Anderson, the British director who has made such films as *Around the World in Eighty Days*, *The Shoes of the Fisherman*, *Doc Savage*, *Orca*, *Pope Joan* and *The Quiller Memorandum*. But as with most sf films, the special effects are always watchable no matter how boring and silly the film itself may be. The ones in *Logan's Run* were mainly the work of production designer Dale Henessey (who had won an Oscar for his work on *Fantastic Voyage*) and veteran effects man L. B. Abbott. One of Henessey's jobs was to design and build the futuristic blasters used by the Sandmen: 'I decided to go for an entirely self-contained unit that would shoot flames out of the front,' he said. 'It was equipped to do fifteen shots before reloading is necessary. I then rigged the targets with explosive squibs so there would be sparks when they were "hit".'[49] But his biggest task on the picture was the construction of the miniature domed city. It covered 80 square feet of an MGM sound stage, one of the largest model cities ever constructed. It was built as big as possible in order to enable a special camera, fitted with a 'snorkel' – a mirrored lens on a long tube – to film the model at 'street level' and thus create a more realistic illusion of vast size.

L. B. Abbott was responsible for the visual effects, in particular the numerous matte paintings used in the film – each one costing between $4,000 and $7,000 to produce. 'Asking an artist to paint realistically, just from research and sucking it out of his thumb, makes matte painting extremely difficult,' he said. 'Fortunately, in *Logan's Run* we were able to use colour photographic enlargements as a base onto which the matte artist added the needed details, and this photographic base always came through to give it a sense of reality. In the case of the Washington DC shots, we sent one of the art directors there with a cameraman and they photographed the various monuments at the desired angles. We had enlargements made from their photos [it's only recently that printing paper has been manufactured in sizes large enough to allow this to be done] in the proper format and the matte artist, Matt Yuricich, then had to paint the ivy on them and age them. It worked perfectly.'[50]

Logan's Run cost over $9,000,000 to make (almost as much as *Star Wars*) yet it did relatively well at the box-office and actually made a profit; it also spawned a TV series.

Even *Futureworld*, the inferior sequel to *Westworld*, was more enjoyable than *Logan's Run*. Unfortunately *Futureworld* lacks the unified structure of Michael Crichton's original film, as the makers seem confused and take it in several logically conflicting directions before settling for one of pulp sf's oldest plots: a mad scientist creates robot duplicates of influential people in order to control the world (it was used every second week on *The Avengers* TV series). Though made on a fairly small budget *Futureworld* makes good use of a number of actual NASA settings filmed at the Houston Manned Space Center, which are complemented by Brian Sellstrom's and Gene Grigg's colourful special effects. The main flaw is a superflous dream sequence in which Blythe Danner is pursued through a house by Yul Brynner's robot gunslinger from *Westworld*, obviously the only way the makers could contrive to include the key image from the

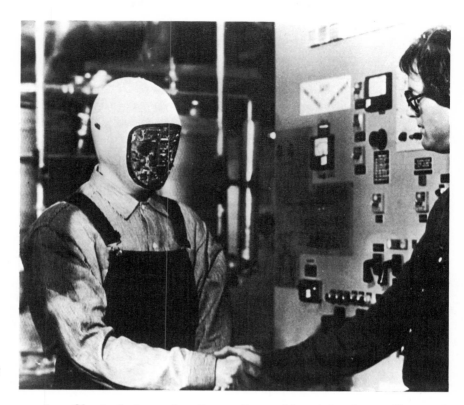

Peter Fonda (right) greets one of the inhabitants of Futureworld.

previous film in their version. It was directed by Richard T. Heffron and scripted by Mayo Simon (who wrote the screenplay for *Phase IV*) and George Schenck.

After being well-treated by film-makers in the 1930s and relatively well-treated by George Pal in 1953 and 1960, H. G. Wells finally got the Z-film treatment in 1976 with the production of *Food of the Gods*, based on a 'portion' of his novel. Producer, writer and director of the film was Bert I. Gordon, who did so much for the genre back in the 1950s with such cheap disasters as *The Amazing Colossal Man*. His production values have becomes a little slicker in the intervening years but his writing and directing abilities appear to have stayed in suspended animation. The film is set on an island off British Columbia where a mysterious substance, oozing out of the ground, is causing the local wildlife to grow very large indeed. A group of people become trapped in a farmhouse by a horde of giant rats but are finally saved when the hero dynamites the local dam and floods the area. The mixed cast includes Marjoe Gortner (former child evangelist turned actor), Pamela Franklin, Ida Lupino and Ralph Meeker. Not only did they have to cope with giant rats but they also had to endure Mr Gordon's dialogue. For example, in one scene Pamela Franklin has to say to Gortner: 'I shouldn't talk to you when you're doing your thing. 'What's that?' he asks. 'Facing danger,' she replies with a straight face. And later, when the rats are massing at the doors and windows, she says to him: 'This may be a bad time, but there's something on my mind.' 'What?' he asks. 'I want you to make love to me,' she replies.

The screws continued to be tightened on the ghost of H. G. Wells with the release of *The Island of Dr Moreau* in 1977, which had previously been filmed as *The Island of Lost Souls* back in 1932. According to the publicity hand-out that accompanied the movie: 'American International Pictures made it perfectly clear that they are not re-making that film but have decided to play *The Island of Dr Moreau* in 1911, immediately providing limitless opportunities to approach the film not as fantasy nor as science fiction but as if the film-makers believe that every bit of what happens on the Doctor's island can happen. This thinking called for a different approach – namely science fact.' No doubt it will come as a surprise to many sf writers and film-makers that it's only their personal conviction which separates their work from being either fiction or fact.

The Island of Lost Souls was far superior to this dull travesty directed by Don Taylor (whose previous sf film was *Escape from the Planet of the Apes*) and scripted by John Herman Shaner and Al Ramrus. *Lost Souls* wasn't completely faithful to the book but at least it had style and atmosphere and moved at a fast pace. More importantly, it retained Wells's original

Michael York grapples with an unwelcome passenger as Barbara Carrera looks on helplessly in **The Island of Dr Moreau.**

idea of Moreau achieving his humanoid-animal creations by means of vivisection and the literal grafting of flesh and bone onto his tortured subjects. Thus the description of his laboratory as the dreaded 'House of Pain' had a powerful relevance, and the beast men understandably regarded him with a mixture of terrible fear and awe. But in the new film the makers brought the Doctor's methods up-to-date and made him a genetic engineer (in 1911!) who creates his 'humanimals' by means of injecting his subjects with chromosomes; thus the references to the House of Pain lose all meaning and Moreau himself is diminished as a symbol of godlike power and cruelty.

As Dr Moreau Burt Lancaster doesn't try to repeat Charles Laughton's wildly over-the-top performance but instead plays him in a quiet, underscored way, and with a better script he might have succeeded in creating a memorable character. Michael York as the young man shipwrecked on Moreau's island is his usual blandly sincere self, and Barbara Carrera is suitably decorative as the vaguely feline Maria.

Not quite as funny was *The Big Bus*, written and directed by James Frawley, which was a spoof on the disaster film cycle and a number of other film genres too. The plot concerns the world's first nuclear-powered bus, called Cyclops, which has been built to make the journey between New York and Chicago non-stop. Not only is the bus nearly 100 feet long but it also contains such amenities as a swimming pool, bowling alley and

The passengers in the world's first atomic-powered bus find themselves taking an unexpected detour in the amusing spoof The Big Bus.

bar complete with pianist. Undaunted by sabotage attempts the bus begins its maiden trip complete with the usual collection of familiar stereotypes: the nymphomaniac, the alcoholic doctor (except he's a vet), the dying man, the priest who's lost his faith, the married couple who never stop arguing, the old lady having one last fling, and so on. There are a number of good black jokes in the film, such as the protective suits that drop from the ceiling of the cabin in the event of a radiation leak from the reactor and which have to be donned within ten seconds, and the sequence where the crew deal with a time bomb by looking in *Jane's Book of Bombs* for information on how to defuse it. Apart from the cleverness of much of the script the film is also impressive visually.

An odd throwback to the early days of sf cinema was *Embryo* (1976), directed by Ralph Nelson, whose only other sf film was *Charly*, and written by Anita Doohan and Jack W. Thomas. It stars Rock Hudson as a scientist experimenting with a process that will accelerate foetal growth. After some success with dogs he moves on to human beings, using a female embryo taken from a dying woman, and ends up, within the space of a few days, with an attractive, fully-developed woman (Barbara Carrera). But though physically mature her mind is virtually blank and it becomes the scientist's task to mould her personality. He falls in love with her while doing so, but the girl turns out to be irredeemably evil and murders a number of his relations. Finally he is obliged to destroy her, but before she dies she first gives birth to their baby.

For all its modern, scientific hardware *Embryo* is a reworking of the old Gothic theme about people who are created by artificial or unnatural means being 'tainted' with evil and therefore doomed to cause nothing but pain and misery before being, inevitably, destroyed. It has more in common with the old German films like *Homunculus* and *Alraune*, as well as *Frankenstein*, than with modern sf. Even the way the girl dies – by shrivelling up in the time-honoured manner of vampires (and Ayesha in *She*) – suggests that the film is not concerned with science but the supernatural.

With the success of *Jaws* a number of film-makers quickly rushed their own 'dangerous monster' films into production but one producer, Dino De Laurentiis, had the clever idea of remaking the most famous monster movie of them all – *King Kong*. Early in the film one of the characters points to the trail of damage left by the rampaging ape and asks his disbelieving companion: 'What do you think did all that – a guy in a monkey suit?' And here lies the rub, because Kong *is* just a guy in a monkey suit. The 1933 *King Kong* represents the art of model animation at its peak; in fact the name is synonymous with the process, and much of the film's attraction lies in seeing how skilfully Willis O'Brien and his team, by means of stop-motion photography, breathe life and personality

Spot the difference: (above) Rick Baker in his ingenious ape costume in King Kong; *(below) Carlo Rambaldi's mechanical ape used in the same sequence (despite the publicity to the contrary, this was the only sequence in which it appeared).*

into an 18-inch-tall collection of metal, rubber and fur. However, De Laurentiis went ahead with his animation-less *Kong* without a qualm, and even claimed that his film would surpass the original on a technical level because his giant ape would consist of a full-size model and thus appear more realistic. Even when the film was released the accompanying publicity blurb had the nerve to claim that 'The Kong that looms on the screen is an ingenious 40-foot mechanical monster, weighing $6\frac{1}{2}$ tons, able to cover 15 feet in a single stride, electronically controlled by a complex hydraulic valve system that can roll his eyes and give 16 separate movements to his hands. Yet the Kong we see on the screen is make-up expert Rick Baker in an ape costume. The 'mechanical' Kong does appear in the film but only very briefly (in the sequence where the ape is unveiled in his cage in the stadium and then breaks out), and it certainly didn't make any 15-foot strides though it did move its arms a bit. More important, it didn't even match up visually with Mr Baker in his ape suit – the most obvious difference being in the shape of the shoulders and the overall colouring. Yet this mechanical monstrosity, designed by Italian effects man Carlo Rambaldi, supposedly cost millions of dollars to make. Several critics accepted the publicity at face value and reviewed the film in a way that suggested the 40-foot model was used throughout. Much more effective were Kong's full-size mechanical hands; they were a genuine engineering marvel and appear amazingly realistic in all their movements during the film (they were used for close-ups). The optical effects, supervised by Frank Van Der Veer, involving travelling mattes and split-screen work, are also of a high standard. Rick Baker does an adequate job inside the suit but the suit isn't gorilla-like enough – it's too slim and the legs are too long – with the result that sometimes Kong resembles a giant ape-man rather than a giant gorilla. Reputedly the original costume was more ape-like but the director, John Guillermin, insisted on its being altered for fear of losing audience identification with Kong. It certainly bears no resemblance to the Kong pictured on the film's poster.

Apart from the special effects, how does the new version compare with the original? Not very well. On the credit side De Laurentiis has a director who is very good with big action subjects (Guillermin's previous films included *The Blue Max* and *The Bridge at Remagen*); he has a better cast and a better script (written by Lorenzo Semple Jr, who also wrote the *Batman* TV series); but his overall story is much weaker. Gone are many of the setpieces from the original, involving Kong's battles with the various prehistoric monsters that inhabit the island. All the remake can produce is one solitary, and very awkward-looking, giant snake.

In the new film many of the visual thrills have been replaced by pathos, the emphasis being on tragedy rather than spectacle and excitement. The original *Kong* had plenty of pathos too but it wasn't dwelt upon at the expense of the film's action. The makers knew that if you allowed your audience to start taking seriously a love affair between a girl and a 50-foot ape you'd be asking for trouble, but De Laurentiis and his team *do* make this mistake. They try to have it all ways: they want their film to be a spectacle, a spoof, a tragedy and an allegory about the 'rape of the environment by big business', but in the end they don't succeed properly in any of these categories.

Nevertheless the film is often entertaining. There are many funny lines and the cast is excellent, particularly Charles Grodin as Wilson, the cynical oil company executive who is determined to bring back 'the big one' at all costs, even though it's not exactly what his company had in mind. René Auberjonois is suitably off-beat as Bagley, Wilson's scientific adviser, and Jeff Bridges is fine as Prescott, Kong's rival for the girl (the role Bruce Cabot played in the original). Jessica Lange makes an adequate substitute for Fay Wray. She's an updated version, of course, in skimpier costumes, more calculatingly ambitious, and with a tendency to talk about astrology (she tells the bemused Kong that he's an Aries) but she has the obvious streak of vulnerability that all true damsels in distress need to be successful, even though she does, at one point, accuse Kong of being a 'male chauvinist pig ape'.

At the same time as *King Kong* was in production De Laurentiis started work on a more obvious imitation of *Jaws* – *Orca*, the story of a killer whale – and the result was very inferior to his remake of *Kong*. *Orca* stars Richard Harris as a fisherman working off the coast of Newfoundland who upsets a killer whale when he kills its mate while trying to capture her for an oceanarium. On the technical level it's a brilliant film. The underwater photography, including some shark footage by Ron Taylor who filmed the live shark scenes in *Jaws*, is most impressive, as are the special effects, but the script is confused and banal and Michael Anderson's direction typically flaccid. The story doesn't contain any real dramatic tension and there's no element of surprise or mystery in the whale's actions. It counts as science fiction mainly because it deals, like *The Day of the Dolphin*, with Man coming into contact with another intelligent species and having to reassess his position in the universe as a result of the experience.

Harder to justify as sf is Brian De Palma's *Carrie*, based on the novel by Stephen King. Though it concerns a girl with the power of telekinesis, which may or may not be explained 'scientifically' one day, a strong streak of the supernatural runs through the film, culminating in the sequence where her house descends into a fiery pit. Whether or not *Carrie* can be legitimately described as sf, De Palma himself is a director with a genuine feel for science fiction as a genre. Along with George Lucas and Steven Spielberg he forms part of a group of new, young film-makers who

The avenging killer whale vents his spleen on mankind in Orca.

grew up with sf as part of their cultural background and are thus perfectly comfortable working with its conventions and traditions; whereas many older directors are obliged to make a credibility jump in order to overcome their personal discomfort with the genre, and this accounts for the lack of conviction evident in so many sf films. With his latest film, *The Fury*, De Palma is still in *Carrie* territory with another story involving people who possess murderous psychic powers, but he hopes that his next production will be based on the sf classic by Alfred Bester, *The Demolished Man*.

One 1977 sf film that deserves to be called science fiction is *Demon Seed*, mainly because its various extrapolations have a solid base in scientific fact. It was directed by Donald Cammell, who was best known for co-directing *Performance* with Nicholas Roeg; both of them later chose to film sf subjects, though where Roeg chose to use sf as a springboard for his own fantasies Cammell made a disciplined, solid but thought-provoking sf film which is ultimately the more successful of the two. *Demon Seed*, scripted by Robert J. Jaffe, was based on a novel by Dean R. Koontz and stars Julie Christie as the wife of a scientist (Fritz Weaver) who has been supervising the construction of a super computer at a nearby laboratory complex. The switching-on of the computer, called Proteus IV, coincides with the break-up of their marriage. The marriage has failed, we learn, mainly as a result of their young daughter dying of leukemia, an event which has served to push Alex totally into his work while Susan has become increasingly distrustful of science and technology.

Like Colossus in *The Forbin Project*, Proteus IV displays signs of having a mind of its own, much to the alarm of its inventor. But unlike Colossus, Proteus doesn't want to conquer the world but to become a living, breathing part of the world. 'When are you going to let me out of this box?' it asks Alex, who chooses to ignore his moral responsibilities towards his creation; instead he attempts to inhibit Proteus even further by keeping a strict control on the various computer terminals open to it. But he has overlooked the terminal installed in the basement of his own house – a house that has also been fitted with a sophisticated electronic system called 'Alfred' that is capable of performing a series of domestic tasks.

Proteus invades the house via the terminal and finds in Alfred a ready-made electronic appendage. The computer takes over the system and then reveals itself to Susan, whose first reaction is to try and escape. As Proteus now controls the building's automatic security system she finds there is no way out, and her subsequent attempts to outwit the machine fail completely.

Proteus finally reveals to Susan why it is holding her prisoner – it wants her to be the mother of its child. Despite Susan's understandable resistance Proteus forcibly 'impregnates' her with its own electronically created genetic information, and she gives birth to a hideous 'thing' – a monstrous baby covered with what appear to be metallic, bulbous scabs. Susan wants to kill it but Alex prevents her, then peels off the metallic covering to reveal a human child who is the exact replica of their dead daughter. Only when she opens her mouth and says, in Proteus' voice: 'I'm alive,' does one realize that the computer has succeeded in getting out of its box, thereby fusing man with machine in a way never before achieved.

Many critics concentrated on the sado-masochistic aspects of the story at the expense of the science fiction elements, describing it as yet another rape fantasy in which a woman is exploited and degraded to provide titillation for males. That accusation may be levelled at the novel with some justification, but the film-makers are clearly more interested in ideas than in sensationalism. The so-called 'sex' scenes between Proteus and Susan in the film were handled tastefully but, as so often is the case, many critics based their reviews on the pre-publicity material rather than on the film itself. *Demon Seed* touches on many interesting concepts, such as the idea of a computer creating visual simulations on a TV screen that are so realistic they resemble real people, but the film's most successful achievement in terms of sf is to suggest something of how a sentient computer would perceive the universe. In an impressive sequence Proteus attempts to communicate to Susan just what 'seeing' is like when your 'eyes' – radar scanners, radio telescopes, etcetera – are sensitive to the whole range of the electromagnetic spectrum and you are being bombarded by an awesome sensory input.

Visually *Demon Seed* is also impressive. Proteus' tetrahedron manifestation, which ingeniously suggests a halfway point between a machine and an organic creature, is particularly well-handled in design and execution by art director Edward Carfagno and special effects man Glen Robinson. The only real flaw in the film is the uninteresting abstract visual patterns that accompany Proteus' words on his terminal display screens.

A film with little to recommend it is *Welcome to Blood City*, in which a group of people wake up to find themselves in the middle of nowhere with their memories wiped out and the only clue to their identities being a card in their pockets stating that each of them is a murderer. This world turns out to be a computer-induced illusion aimed at discovering who is suitable 'Kill Master' material, a breed of person desperately needed by the authorities in their efforts to keep control in an increasingly chaotic world. The film has some similarities to Michael Crichton's superior *Westworld*, but *Welcome to Blood City* is nothing more than a mediocre western with an sf story clumsily tacked on. It was directed by Peter Sasdy and written by Stephen Schenck and Michael Winder.

Canadian film-maker David Cronenberg continued to mine his obsession with the more unpleasant aspects of human physiology in *Rabid*, which he wrote and directed. Marilyn Chambers, former star of pornographic movies, plays a girl who becomes the unwilling carrier of a rabies-like disease after being given an experimental skin graft. The disease turns people into berserk monsters, dominated by a desire to eat raw meat – anybody's. Soon all Montreal is in a state of chaos as victims of the disease, drooling an unpleasant substance from their eyes and mouths (a recurring image in all of Cronenberg's films), strike without warning. Martial law is established and citizens who cannot produce proof of inoculation are immediately shot by troops and their bodies dumped into garbage trucks. Like Cronenberg's other films *Rabid* is basically a black joke – a mixture of clichés from sf and horror films and deliberate bad taste in the form of an exaggerated use of Freudian symbols (the girl spreads the disease by means of a needle-like organ that emerges from a vaginal-type orifice under her arm), though some critics have read serious political intent in his work.

At the beginning of the 1970s it seemed that the James Bond cycle of films had run its course. On a technical level the last Bond film made during the 1960s, *On Her Majesty's Secret Service*, had been far superior to its immediate predecessors, with a tightly constructed plot and some attempt at character development, but didn't do as well at the box-office. The presence of George Lazenby in the title role probably had much

James Bond is likely to turn up anywhere (from Diamonds Are Forever).

to do with its relative failure, but with *Diamonds Are Forever* (1971) the producers decided to return to the reliable old formula – as much spectacle as possible and to hell with logical plot development – though their wisest move was to persuade Sean Connery to return to the James Bond role. They also increased the science fiction gimmickry and as a result *Diamonds Are Forever* featured a space laboratory complex, a moon buggy, rocketships, missiles and a satellite capable of destroying whole cities with a powerful laser beam.

The next film *Live and Let Die* (1973), directed by Guy Hamilton, who also directed *Diamonds Are Forever*, concentrated on stunts rather than gadgetry, but old-fashioned sf came back in *The Man With the Golden Gun* (1975) in the form of a car that can turn into a plane and the villain's island headquarters containing a solar power laboratory that can produce a heat beam of great power. But it was in the next film, *The Spy Who Loved Me* (1977), that a return was made to the full-scale technical extravagance of *You Only Live Twice*. There were many similarities between the two films, including the fact that Lewis Gilbert directed both of them. The plots were almost identical. In *You Only Live Twice* the villain has a spaceship that swallows up American and Russian space vehicles in order to provoke World War Three; in *The Spy Who Loved Me* the villain has a giant super tanker that swallows up American and Russian submarines in order to provoke World War Three. In *You Only Live Twice* James Bond penetrates the villain's headquarters in disguise, is discovered but succeeds in freeing the captured Americans and Russians – there is a fierce battle and the villain's henchmen seal themselves off within a steel-shuttered control room, but James Bond succeeds in escaping and prevents World War Three in the nick of time by pressing a button that blows up the enemy spaceship; in *The Spy Who Loved Me* James Bond (Roger Moore) penetrates the villains's headquarters in disguise, etcetera – there is a fierce battle and the villains seal themselves off within a steel-shuttered control room, but on this occasion the film comes to a halt while Bond spends time defusing an atomic missile in order to extract its high explosive detonator. As soon as he uses it to blow up the control room the film starts moving again and Bond succeeds in preventing World War Three in the nick of time by pressing buttons and causing the two enemy submarines to blow each other up – all of which shows how far the Bond films have progressed in originality during the last decade.

But at least there has been progress in the special effects. In *The Spy Who Loved Me* they're impressively handled by Derek Meddings. There's an extensive use of miniatures in the film but it's hard to spot them. The villain's headquarters, Atlantis, is first seen rising majestically from the sea like some huge spider. 'It was quite a model,' said Meddings. 'We built it twelve feet across and it even had little figures on it, moving and walking, which were mechanically operated. We even had helicopters taking off from it – we used radio-controlled models combined with shots of a real 'copter.'

Probably Meddings's most challenging task was the building and operating of the giant super tanker that swallows up the submarines. 'The "model" was 63 feet long,' he explained, 'and the reason we built it so large was because we had to deal with submarines in the same shots, and subs are basically just featureless tubes with conning towers stuck on top – they don't displace the water realistically as models unless you build them to a reasonable size and even then you have to have all kinds of gadgets to disturb the water around them as they move along in order to create a realistic bow wave and wake. These devices are built into the model below the water line. Water is always a problem when you're dealing with miniatures because you just can't scale water, you've got to be clever enough to shoot it the right way. The American film industry has tried any amount of things to try and make water "heavy", for want of a better word, and they've never succeeded. As one has to shoot water stuff at a very high speed the secret is to make certain you don't create a splash which is, of course, going to produce big globules of water on the screen and immediately give the game away. Even though our tanker was 63 feet long it would only create a bow wave and wash that was in scale with a 63-foot-long launch, which is nothing like what a super tanker, with its vast displacement of water, would create, so again we had to have water disturbers and so on all along the hull under the waterline.

'All that tanker footage was shot in the real sea out at the Bahamas. We

Derek Meddings (centre) at work on the giant model super tanker used in The Spy Who Loved Me.

The super tanker in action—on the prowl for atomic submarines.

built the tanker at Pinewood Studio in three sections and flew it out in a cargo plane. It was put back together in Nassau. Our base was a place called Coral Harbour which had been the site for a planned luxury area with a hotel and everything, all of which was never completed and is now derelict – but they had built a number of channels leading into the sea and they proved ideal for us in launching the tanker, which weighed over twelve tons, though we had to build our own slipway.

'Shooting at sea is, of course, a lot more risky than filming in a studio tank and the big problem we had with the tanker was that it wasn't really very seaworthy, being mostly hollow in order to swallow a submarine. Only the aft section was actually built like a boat, the rest was like a catamaran built on two floats. We had a huge 175 hp marine engine in it which gave us a terrific wake, though, of course, nothing near a real tanker's. And something went seriously wrong on the first day we took it out to sea. We'd launched it in the canal and it looked beautiful, then we started to drive it up the canal and out into the open sea. I was on a barge ahead of it and just as it was coming out of the canal I noticed that it was getting lower and lower in the water. There were three men inside, one of whom was Peter Biggs, my right-hand man, but they weren't aware of what was happening because they had very little vision – they were looking down almost 60 feet of tanker deck and that was their only field of vision. When the bow doors were open they could look right through the tanker because we'd built a window for them but the doors weren't open on this occasion. We were in radio contact so I yelled over the radio: "Peter! You're sinking!" And he replied, very calmly: "Yes, I thought we were." Then he flung the engine in reverse and we managed to get it back into its berth just as the front of it went underwater. We had to dive down to it, sling straps under it and pull it up with a crane. What had happened was that one of the pontoons had started to leak and two of the six pumps had packed up at the same time. But after that we never had any trouble at all.

'When the tanker had to swallow a submarine it involved careful synchronization between the crew operating the tanker and the divers controlling the model submarine. The sub was motorized too but manipulated by a number of divers who had to follow a set pattern of movement. It all worked very successfully. Then we had to blow up the tanker for the sequences at the end of the film when there's that big battle inside. The interior battle sequences were filmed on the huge stage at Pinewood, but there are a number of cuts showing the explosions blasting through the hull and deck of the tanker. The whole thing continues to explode until Bond and his companions escape through the bow doors in one of the subs. We had to build a model of the tanker interior for that final sequence – it was 30 feet long with every bit of detail as in the full-size one. We blew it up with a series of explosions and finally we had the catwalk which spans the interior come crashing down just as the submarine leaves the berth – we had to do all that with a model because we couldn't bring down the catwalk in the full-size set, it would have been much too dangerous.

'We spent days blowing up the model tanker and then we had a controlled sinking showing it going under. It's still there – at the bottom of the sea in the Bahamas.'

Meddings also had the job of faking a shark attack for the sequence where the villain disposes of a female accomplice by sending her down a chute into his shark tank (in *You Only Live Twice* it was a pool full of piranhas). 'We shot a real shark in a pool in Nassau and then used a dummy shark for the shots where it actually gets hold of the girl around the waist and shakes her. Then we built another mechanical shark back here at Pinewood for the scenes where the villain's giant henchman "Jaws" has his fight with the shark at the end of the film. Our sharks were very simple mechanisms compared to the ones in *Jaws* – ours ran on wires attached to trolleys, but they looked very convincing. You see it swimming around the tank in the film and it appears completely realistic.

'We also did all the underwater stuff involving the Lotus car that turns into a submarine. We had quite a big underwater operation at Nassau – we built a special rig to fire the car down the jetty when it was being pursued by the helicopter and it was travelling at 50 miles per hour when it left the rig. When the film cuts to show the car sinking through the water we used a very convincing model with dummies representing Bond and the girl inside it. The change from car into submarine involved five underwater model cars with each one being used to represent a different part of the transformation process, such as the wheels retracting, the fins popping up, the motors coming out at the back etcetera, and there was also a full-size version that was completely drivable under water – it was full of engines and buoyancy compensators and took a two-man crew. It was quite fantastic.

'We also made the sequence where the rocket comes out of the back of the car, hurtles out of the water and explodes the helicopter hovering above. The 'copter was a radio-controlled model. And for the sequence where the Lotus sub approaches the base of Atlantis, which is like an oil rig in structure, we again used models.'

During the making of *You Only Live Twice* in 1966 Pinewood Studio was dominated by a huge structure built to contain the set representing the interior of the villain's artificial volcano, and similarly in 1976 a vast stage shaped like an airship hangar rose on the backlot to house the set representing the interior of the super-tanker. Both structures were created by production designer Ken Adam, but whereas the artificial volcano had to be torn down due to protests from local residents the new Bond building, officially called the '007 Stage', is to remain a permanent fixture at Pinewood (it isn't as high as the volcano) – a monument both to Ken Adam's grandiose vision and to the Bond phenomenon in general.

Star Wars, the big sf success of 1977/78, owes a lot to the James Bond films. But then it owes a lot to all sorts of movies, such as westerns, old serials, Errol Flynn swashbucklers, Second World War movies, *The Wizard of Oz*, and even *Snow White*. The story concerns a young man called Luke Skywalker who leaves his uncle's farm on a small, arid planet called Tatooine to help rescue a beautiful princess from the clutches of the evil Grand Moff Tarkin, who represents a decadent galactic Empire. Tarkin's henchman is a mysterious, black-clad giant called Darth Vader and their base is a vast space station called the Death Star which is the size of a small moon and capable of destroying whole planets. With the help of an old man called Ben Kenobi, who was once a member of an order of mystical warriors called the Jedi Knights that was later abolished by the Empire, a mercenary space pilot called Han Solo, and two cute robots – one resembling a mobile coffee pot, the other a humanoid with camp mannerisms and an English accent – Luke succeeds in rescuing the Princess and destroying the Death Star, but Darth Vader escapes into the void to fight another day.

The plot could have been lifted from a low-quality sf pulp magazine of the 1930s or 1940s, and its intellectual level is that of the old Flash Gordon serials, as George Lucas intended. He originally wanted to make a new film version of Flash Gordon but couldn't obtain the rights to the character: instead he wrote a script that incorporated many of the elements from both the Flash Gordon serials and the comic strip. 'The plot is simple,' said Lucas, 'good against evil – and the film is designed to be all the fun things and fantasy things I remember from the period when I was twelve. The word for this movie is fun.'[51]

Such a statement practically disarms serious criticism, which is probably what it's designed to do. The simple-minded dialogue is intentional (Harrison Ford, who plays Han Solo, said: 'There were times when I issued a threat to tie George up and make him repeat his own dialogue'). Gaping holes in the plot or credibility-stretching coincidences are explained away by the claim that it is all a fairy story set 'a long, long time ago in a galaxy far, far away'. There is no justification, therefore, in asking why this particular galaxy seems to be ruled by human beings (of the white variety only) despite the existence of other alien races, or why the Death Star has such a convenient flaw in its defences, or why the spaceships and the various explosions make sounds in the vacuum of space. And it seems like quibbling to point out that the space battles in the film, which were choreographed from footage of Second World War aerial

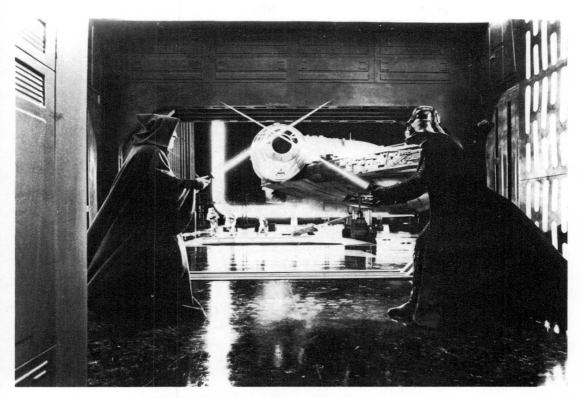

Alec Guinness and David Prowse (as the villainous Lord Darth Vader) cross light swords in Star Wars.

Mark Hamill, as Luke Skywalker, races to his hover car after learning that his family is in danger.

dogfights, are totally unrealistic because the spaceships would be moving so fast that such close manoeuvring would be impossible. It also seems like quibbling to wonder why there is no lack of gravity in any of the spaceships, large or small – there isn't even a token mention of 'artificial' gravity, that old stand-by of sf writers.

'I just wanted to forget science,' said Lucas. 'That would take care of itself. Stanley Kubrick made the ultimate science fiction movie and it is going to be very hard for somebody to come along and make a better movie, as far as I'm concerned. I didn't want to make a *2001*, I wanted to make a space fantasy that was more in the genre of Edgar Rice Burroughs; that whole other end of space fantasy that was there before science took it over in the 1950s. Once the atomic bomb came everybody got into monsters and science. . . I think speculative fiction is very valid but they forgot the fairy-tales.'[52]

As Lucas willingly admits, *Star Wars* has been cobbled together from a wide variety of different sources – movies, comic strips, serials and so on – so we get such favourite old western clichés as the scene where Luke returns to the homestead to find it on fire and his relatives massacred, prompting him to vow vengeance; and the sequence in the alien bar mirrors countless saloon scenes in Hollywood westerns, including even the traditional brush with the bounty hunter. Other ingredients of Luke's desert home world are inspired by Frank Herbert's *Dune* series of books, and several scenes seem directly based on sf magazine covers by such artists as Ed Emshwiller, John Schoenherr and Kelly Freas.

Movies about the Second World War also provide a great deal of visual inspiration. Apart from the dogfight footage used to choreograph the battles, the climactic 'bombing run' across the surface of the Death Star was based on movies like *The Dam Busters* and *633 Squadron*. The villain, Grand Moff Tarkin, is the embodiment of every evil Nazi officer to appear on the screen and his Imperial soldiers are called, significantly, Stormtroopers.

Other sources of material incorporated into *Star Wars* include Asimov's *Foundation* trilogy, with its vast and decadent galactic empire, and such films as *The Wizard of Oz* – the golden robot Threepio is an updated version of the Tin Man, and Chewbacca the Wookie (Han Solo's co-pilot) is really the Cowardly Lion – and Disney's *Snow White* (Princess Leia has a more than passing resemblance to Snow White, and the little robot Artoo could be one of her loyal dwarfs). Artoo and Threepio have also been compared to Laurel and Hardy. Darth Vader himself is a cross between the Black Knight, a James Bond villain and Marvel Comics' Dr Doom.

Lucas has mixed all the ingredients together very skilfully and as he intended the result is fun, especially since there's a nice line of clever humour running through the film; yet it's hard not to wish that all the magnificent sets, effects, technical expertise and talent hadn't been used to make something a little more substantial and original. Like most of the new generation of American film-makers Lucas seems obsessed with nostalgia; instead of making genuinely original films the trend is to remake all their favourite old ones.

The most serious criticism of *Star Wars* is that it embodies Nazi mythology. Several critics noticed that the film's closing victory ceremony might have been inspired by Leni Riefenstahl's *Triumph of the Will*. Was the mystical Force which figures so prominently in the film ('The Force is the energy field created by all living things,' explains Ben Kenobi, 'it binds the galaxy together') and which provides Luke with the power to destroy the Death Star, an expression of a basic Nazi tenet? Absurdly far-fetched though this may be, the film does reflect a growing tendency amongst the young to reject rationalism in favour of mysticism. 'Your eyes can deceive you,' Ben Kenobi instructs Luke. 'Don't trust them. Stretch out with your feelings . . . let go of your conscious self and act on instinct.' Alec Guinness, who plays Ben Kenobi, has found that some people have taken his mystical pronouncements seriously: 'I've been getting some strange letters from America. From married couples, not teenagers. They think because I play a wise man in the film I can solve all their problems. The letters say: "You've altered our lives. You must come and live with us." 'My wife and I are thinking of setting up a Maharishi office and charging 50 dollars for a couple of minutes of chat.'[53]

Though Lucas claims that it's purely a 'fun' movie aimed primarily at providing children with a 'rich fantasy life' of the sort that Lucas had when he was young, *Star Wars* is probably the most violent movie of all time. It's one long battle, beginning with a massacre on board a spaceship and ending in an orgy of futuristic destruction, while along the way a whole planet and its population are blasted into oblivion. All in all *Star Wars* racks up a higher body count than the Second World War and Vietnam put together. There's not much blood, of course, and no one actually suffers on screen, so that makes it good, harmless, clean fun.

Leaving aside these cavils, there is no doubt that Lucas has put the nearest thing to real space opera on the screen at last. Thanks to his familiarity with the traditions of sf, *Star Wars* is filled with the visual realization of things that had previously only existed in the imaginations of sf writers and their readers. There is a convincing simulation of what it might be like to enter hyper space in the sequence where Han Solo's spaceship hits faster-than-light speed to escape the Imperial cruisers. The special effects, especially the model work, are almost above criticism. For the first time since *2001* models have been used most impressively; all the space vehicles have a feeling of size, and the Death Star itself appears to have the dimensions of a moon. Apart for the occasional matte-line the only criticism concerns the sequences where the planet of Alderaan is

The Imperial Stormtroopers hunt for the inhabitants of the space capsule.

Our heroes, disguised as Stormtroopers, use the giant Wookie (Peter Mayhew) as a decoy to gain entrance to the bowels of the Death Star.

blown up, and later the Death Star is destroyed. In both cases the explosions occur much too quickly and therefore fail to convey the hugeness of the objects being exploded.

Lucas himself is not completely satisfied with the effects: 'On a technical level it can be compared to *2001* but personally I think that *2001* is far superior. *2001* had more time and money put into it and obviously it came out better. Most of the special effects in *Star Wars* were first-time special effects – we shot them, we composited them and they're in the movie. We had to go back and reshoot some . . . but because of the cost, much of our stuff we had to do as a one-shot deal. We did a lot of work but there is nothing that I would like to do more than go back and redo all the special effects.'[54]

Lucas had been working on the *Star Wars* script for several years – it began life as a planned sequel to *THX 1138* – but it wasn't until after making the successful *American Graffiti* that he began trying to launch the project in earnest. With producer Gary Kurtz (who had produced *Graffiti*) he approached big Hollywood companies like United Artists and Universal but was repeatedly disappointed (Universal, who had backed *Graffiti*, offered him $25,000 to write and direct *Star Wars*). He finally talked 20th Century-Fox into becoming involved, mainly, he feels, because of their previous success with the *Planet of the Apes* series of films. At this point *Star Wars* began its long and complicated journey from the page to the screen.

One of the first tasks was to find suitable locations. Originally it had been planned to make Luke Skywalker's home world a jungle planet and therefore the jungles of the Philippines were considered a possibility, but it was decided that shooting for months in a jungle would present too many problems, so Tatooine suddenly became a desert world. The deserts of Tunisia were chosen for the location sequences and in March 1976 the *Star Wars* production unit and cast descended upon Tozeur, a small town in Southern Tunisia where North Africa and Arabia meet and the Sahara desert begins. The construction crew worked for eight weeks to turn the desert and towns into another planet, aided by a landscape where, due to the many mirages, it was already difficult to separate real from unreal.

The man chiefly responsible was British production designer John Barry, whose previous sf films were *A Clockwork Orange* and *Phase IV*. To help create Tatooine, which is a mixture of the futuristic and the primitive, Barry and his crew took a load of scrap and junk which they utilized in ingenious ways. Parts of jet engines, drainage pipes and so on were incorporated into the scenery, becoming realistic background paraphernalia for such creatures as the Jawas – small, robed scavengers whose faces are never seen and who travel about the desert in a massive, tank-like vehicle called a 'Sand Crawler'. For long shots a model was used which was only a few feet long but for close shots Barry's team built a full-scale section complete with huge caterpillar treads: 'It was flimsily made from glass fibre and plywood but looked like something H. G. Wells might have dreamed up. One day we got a message that the Algerians were asking questions about what was the large military vehicle just across their border with Tunisia.'[55]

Another British technician involved was special effects man John Stears, who handled all of the 'physical' effects as well as being responsible for constructing Artoo, Detoo and the other robots (See Threepio was the work of Ralph McQuarrie, Norman Reynolds and Liz Moore, all of whom were clearly inspired by the robot in *Metropolis*). Stears, who worked on a number of the James Bond films, also had to create Luke's anti-gravity car – a vehicle that always appears to be hovering several feet in the air, even when stationary. For the latter shots several versions of the vehicle were used. Constructed out of fibreglass, each was supported from the ground in a different position; thus for a shot where the left side of the car was shown the support would have been off-camera to the right, and vice versa when the right of the car was shown; and the same technique was used when either the back or the front of the car was shown. In one scene where the whole of the car appears the support was concealed within some artificial rocks at the side of the car. And in the sequences were the car had to move an entirely different vehicle was used – one which had a wheeled undercarriage. To create the illusion that the car was skimming a few feet above the ground the undercarriage had to be matted out of each frame of film and replaced with hand-painted desert scenery beneath. Even the moving shadow beneath the car was the work of artists, and one shot where the car is seen hurtling into the distance at centre frame was created entirely by animation.

Many of the problems that occurred at the Tunisian locations involved the two robots, Artoo and Detoo. Artoo, the smaller of the pair, was sometimes manipulated by a 3-foot 8-inch-tall midget called Kenny Baker, and at other times it was represented by various radio-controlled models. These caused most of the difficulties, constantly ignoring their radio commands and running wild, but even the one with Baker inside often went out of control as he couldn't see where he was going due to the dazzling Tunisian sunlight. As for Threepio, the gold-plated one (a costume worn by British actor Anthony Daniels), he was practically melted by the hot sun. To add to Daniels' ordeal he also had trouble seeing out of Threepio's glittering aluminium and plastic head and as a result the two robots were continually bumping into each other.

After two and a half weeks of shooting in the heat of Tunisia the *Star Wars* cast and crew moved to England and the sound stages of Elstree Studio. It took all nine of the studio's sound stages to house the production as well as one at Shepperton Studio (Shepperton has one of the largest stages in Europe), which was needed for the sequence set in the vast rebel hangar containing the squadron of rebel fighters (which were all full-scale mock-ups). Elstree was chosen because it was the only studio in England or America that could provide nine large stages simultaneously as well as making available a big group of top British technicians. It was at Elstree that the sequences set within Princess Leia's spaceship, the Death Star and Han Solo's ship, the Millenium Falcon, were filmed, all of which testify to the skills of production designer John Barry and his team. As in the desert, cheap short-cuts were taken with the building of the sets and the various props, yet in the finished film everything looks substantial and realistic. Effects man John Stears and his assistants also had to produce an incredible number of spectacular explosions, as well as the laser-light swords used by Luke, Kenobi and Darth Vader. These he achieved by coating rods with a highly reflective material that bounces light back with an increased intensity. When the rods were revolved by small motors in the handles they turned into dazzling columns of light. The only problem was that the rods had to keep revolving to maintain this effect, which meant that in the big duel between Kenobi and Darth Vader the two opponents couldn't let their weapons come in contact with each other for fear of halting the rotation – which explains why that sequence isn't as lively as it should have been.

The director of photography on *Star Wars* was Gilbert Taylor, whose previous films included *Dr Strangelove, A Hard Day's Night* and *The Omen*, and though his work appears faultless in the film Lucas wasn't completely happy with it. In an interview with *Rolling Stone* magazine he said: 'By the time I got back to California I wasn't happy with the lighting on the picture. I'm a cameraman myself and I like a slightly more extreme, eccentric style than I got in the movie. It was all right, it was a very difficult movie, there were big sets to light, it was a very big problem. The robots never worked. We faked the whole thing and a lot of it was done editorially.'[56] But in a later interview producer Gary Kurtz said: 'We were unhappy with the interview [in *Rolling Stone*] because it edited out some of our more positive comments. George told them that he wasn't completely happy with the photography – which is probably true. But he went on to say that the end result has turned out fine: and that kind of criticism is a little academic after the fact.'[57] In any event, Kurtz is planning to return to England for the production of *Star Wars 2*, and this time there's the possibility of using British special effects technicians to handle the model and optical work as well. The reason for this may be that John Dykstra, who supervised the model effects in *Star Wars*, will only consider working on the sequel provided he can participate in the profits. This reflects a growing awareness among Hollywood special effects men of *just* how important their work is to the film industry. (British effects man Brian Johnson, who supervised the model effects in *Space 1999*, has been assigned to work on *Star Wars II*.)

Dykstra originally trained under Douglas Trumbull (he assisted Trumbull with the effects in *Silent Running*) and was working at Future General, the Paramount subsidiary set up by Trumbull to research and develop effects techniques, when he was contacted by Kurtz and Lucas and offered the job. Surprisingly, the job was never offered to Trumbull, Dykstra's mentor. 'George didn't want to use Doug,' explained Dykstra, 'because Doug had too big a name. His tendency and preference is to work with people who don't have a big name, for a couple of reasons. One is that he can more easily control them. The other is that he doesn't want to use people who are aware of how much their work is worth.'[58] Dykstra accepted the offer, hired a team of helpers, then took over a California warehouse which was converted into the ultimate special effects studio and named 'The Industrial Light and Magic Corporation'.

Employing as many as 75 people, Dykstra produced 360 different effects shots in eight months, which is quite an achievement given that a single effects shot may have included up to twelve different image components (star backgrounds, planets, various moving spaceships, laser flashes, explosions), all of which had to be photographed separately and then combined onto one piece of film. Unlike Kubrick and his team on *2001* Dykstra was obliged, through lack of time and money, to take short-cuts, the main one being the use of an automatic matting system – the blue-screen process. This invariably produces a blue fringe, or visible 'matte-line', around the models due to the bright blue light from the screen being slightly reflected by the edges of the models, making their outlines look fuzzy in the completed shot. To try and prevent this Dykstra reduced the chance of light being reflected from the models by using only a part of the screen – the immediate area surrounding the model – and blocking off the remainder. For the most part this method worked well and the model outlines in the film are clear and sharp, though in a few shots matte-lines are visible. Dykstra himself was unhappy with some of the necessary short-cuts taken to finish the picture in time. 'Lucas knew what he wanted,' said Dykstra, 'but *I* knew what could and could not be done. Our major problem was being able to do what George wanted. He gave us Second World War dogfight footage cut together as a guide to what he wanted in the battle sequence at the end of the film. But it didn't work very well when it was translated from live action into spaceships in outer space because of problems of perspective and lack of terrestrial horizon. It was hard for Lucas to understand that.'[59]

One of Dykstra's major innovations was to link up his effects camera with a computer system, which meant that the camera could move with the action whereas in the past a camera being used for composite photography had to be kept as motionless as possible to prevent any 'jiggling' between the various image components. This naturally limited the way in which models could be shot (in *2001* all the miniature work was filmed from a fixed camera position). Dykstra's computer system ensured that the camera could repeat exactly the same movements whenever required; for a shot of two spaceships hurtling through space and firing lasers at each other, the camera could separately record each of the various image components – background of stars, the two spaceships, laser flashes, explosions – and ensure that they would all mesh together perfectly in the final composite shot while the whole shot was moved at the same time. This sense of movement added greatly to the realism and excitement of the space battles because it enabled the camera to become part of the action, creating the impression that it was all being filmed from another spaceship rather than from a static point in space.

Dykstra also improved the quality of the model shots by using an old VistaVision camera, which differs from a conventional movie camera in that the film runs through it horizontally, not vertically, and has a larger format frame. Thus more of the film surface catches extra light, and the images of the models were much brighter and sharper than normal.

Over 75 model spaceships were constructed for the film, all of which were extremely complicated, containing miniature lighting systems to provide illumination for the cockpits, engine effects and laser flashes, and some of the models had moving parts such as rotating antennae and articulated wings. Over 300 model kits were cannibalized by Dykstra's team, with the result that bits and pieces from Second World War tanks and planes ended up becoming parts of futuristic space vehicles. For the models that had to be exploded, plastic moulds of the ships filled with foam were used – foam being chosen because it shatters more easily and allows the use of much smaller, slower-burning explosive charges, thus increasing the realism of the miniaturized destruction.

The biggest miniature of all in *Star Wars* was the huge section of the Death Star's surface, where the climactic battle takes place between the rebel fighters and Darth Vader's Imperial interceptors. It consisted of 1,600 square feet of highly detailed architecture, all of which was moulded out of foam. The model of the Death Star used in long shots was four feet in diameter.

The cast of *Star Wars*, like the technical team, was a mixture of American and British artists. Young American actor Mark Hamill made his feature film début as the hero Luke Skywalker; Han Solo was played by Harrison Ford, who appeared in Lucas's previous film *American Graffiti* (he also has a role in Francis Ford Coppola's Vietnam epic *Apocalypse Now*, a project that Lucas was involved in for some time before *Star Wars*);

and Princess Leia Organa was played by Carrie Fisher, daughter of Debbie Reynolds. The British contingent consisted of Peter Cushing as Grand Moff Tarkin; Kenny Baker and Anthony Daniels as the two robots Artoo and Threepio; and Peter Mayhew (a former London hospital porter) as the giant Wookie, Chewbaca. The villainous Lord Darth Vader consisted of two people, one British and one American. Filling his black costume and evil mask was David Prowse, a 6-foot 7-inch-tall strongman who, apart from appearing as Frankenstein's monster in at least two films and performing villainous roles in such films as *Jabberwocky* and *The People That Time Forgot*, also runs a gymnasium in London, while Darth Vader's deep, magnetic voice was provided by black actor James Earl Jones.

The most prestigious British actor in the film was Sir Alec Guinness, who plays Ben Kenobi, last of the Jedi Knights. He was none too enthusiastic about the idea at first: 'The script came through the door and the moment I saw the sci-fi sticker on it I said to myself "Oh crumbs, it's not for me." But then I started to read and I *had* to turn the page . . . it had *vigour* and I finished it at a single sitting. I found the script curious in places and I didn't understand it all but I was held by a certain excitement, a perfectly ordinary, straightforward excitement.

'I hadn't met Lucas previously so I went off and saw his *American Graffiti*, which I found impressive. Soon after that we came together and he struck me as being a very considerable little person – by that I mean he is small in stature. In many ways he is quite untypical of the film industry. When we started work on *Star Wars* it was all so calm, so gentlemanly. No fat cigars, no tough language. I remember someone on the set criticizing Lucas because of his lack of display and announcing that the film was going to be dull. So I took him aside and said: "Mark my words, this film is going to have *distinction*." '[60]

The second big sf block-buster of the late 1970s was *Close Encounters of the Third Kind*, and though in most ways totally different to *Star Wars* it has one basic feature in common: it has more to do with mysticism than with science fiction. Written and directed by Steven Spielberg *Close Encounters* begins in a small, rural town in Indiana where a number of people experience a strange manifestation. It starts in the house of Jillian Guiler (Melinda Dillon) when all her young son's toys come to life. The boy, three-year-old Barry (Cary Guffey), is delighted but his mother's reaction is one of sheer panic, particularly when every electrical gadget in the house starts to run wild. The next person to become involved is electrical-power company worker Roy Neary (Richard Dreyfuss), who sets out in his truck to investigate the sudden power failure only to be caught up in a nightmarish series of phenomena he cannot comprehend – strange lights surround him, the dashboard of his truck goes wild and his equipment in the rear starts to move around as if with a life of its own.

Steven Spielberg sets up a shot for the opening sequence of Close Encounters of the Third Kind.

Then he sees, hovering overhead, the glowing shape of a flying saucer. The night's experiences have a profound effect upon him and from then on he begins to act like a man who has undergone a deep religious experience. He becomes obsessed with UFOs, loses his job as a result and alienates his wife Ronnie (Teri Garr) and his three children when he persists in trying to sculpt the shape of a strange mountain – a vision firmly implanted in his mind since the encounter with the UFO – with whatever material is at hand, be it soap, soil in his garden or even mashed potatoes.

This vision is shared by other residents of the town who have also seen the lights of the UFO. Jillian Guiler is later convinced that her son has been kidnapped by the flying saucers. From then on the film concerns their attempts to discover what the mountain-like shape represents, and this is intercut with another plot concerning a mysterious group of scientific and military experts, headed by a Frenchman called Claude Lacombe (François Truffaut), who are travelling the world trying to decipher and interpret the musical signals that have been recorded emanating from various UFOs. This middle part is the weakest section in the film, Spielberg having been obliged to pad it out with a number of extraneous sequences and sub-plots. The film's last forty minutes are the important ones. Neary, Guiler and the others converge with Lacombe's team at a mountain called the Devil's Tower in Wyoming, which turns out to be the mysterious mountain in the vision. They all wait for the 'encounter', Lacombe and his men having brought along a special electronic console with which they hope to communicate with the aliens. They are not disappointed. The UFOs, in the form of a dazzling display of lights, appear on cue and there follows a barrage of spectacular visuals, accompanied by bursts of electronic music, which culminates in the landing of the vast alien mother ship, a circular object with cathedral-like spires rising from its centre and covered with hundreds of illuminated windows. Then the aliens appear – first a swarm of alien children, glowing and indistinct like humanoid fire flies, followed by the chief alien whom we see in close-up – an ethereal and apparently androgynous figure with a long neck and no hair. As he stands there Lacombe steps forward and smiles. After a pause the alien smiles back.

Like *2001*, *Close Encounters* is a religious film. The aliens in both represent God or gods, but whereas in *2001* they remained beyond human comprehension – cold, impersonal entities playing some kind of cosmic game with mankind for incomprehensible reasons of their own – in *Close Encounters* they reveal themselves as benign, friendly beings who have humanity's best interests at heart. As Pauline Kael observed, the message of the film is: 'God is up there in a crystal-chandelier spaceship, and he likes us.'[61] The main flaw in the film is that it appears to be the result of two entirely different scripts joined together; the mischievous and even sadistic behaviour of the UFOs in the early stages of the film bears no relation to the obviously friendly creatures who are revealed at the end.

Close Encounters' release has coincided with revived interest in UFOs. Reports of sightings are on the increase and even President Carter claims to have seen a flying saucer. NASA has received an official request to investigate possible new methods of approaching the whole question. The growing cult of UFO-ology has been described as a new religion, a reflection of the need of people who can't accept the traditional religions but want to believe that something Out There is interested in them. The anthropologist Ronald Grunloh recently proposed the theory that, like man's oldest religious beliefs, the cult is a modern manifestation of various subjective experiences that have hitherto been interpreted as religious visions. Neatly reversing the theories of Von Daniken and his followers, Grunloh says that people who think they see 'flying saucers' are really seeing the same thing as the Old Testament prophets saw, but whereas the latter tended to visualize lions, chariots and hoofed creatures on fiery clouds, people today visualize bald men in glowing space suits. 'All human beings can have spontaneous visions,' said Grunloh, 'even in groups. If we understood hallucinations better, we might know why the shapes and colours and lights are so often the same.' He believes that these religious visions/UFO sightings increase in number during periods of social upheaval, but that their cause is within ourselves and not in the sky.

Melinda Dillon and Cary Guffey, mother and son, have different reactions to their 'close encounter'.

A UFO comes down to say hello: a profound moment, or simply juvenile wish-fulfilment?

This view is completely supported by sf writer Isaac Asimov, who has publicly denounced *Close Encounters* as a dangerous influence on impressionable minds and contributing to the general move away from rationalism towards mysticism. 'Such people can be stampeded into all kinds of fantasy, folly and warfare,' he warned.

On a purely visual level *Close Encounters* is a superb film, and as with *Duel* and *Jaws* Spielberg demonstrates again how well he can manipulate an audience. His films may not be art but they represent the peak of craftsmanship, perfect machines in which all the parts – story, actors, special effects, editing and music – mesh together in a seamless whole. 'Making movies is an illusion, a technical illusion that people fall for,' he says, 'and my job is to take that technique and hide it so well that never once are you taken out of your chair and reminded where you are.'[62]

The special effects were created by Douglas Trumbull, who supervised the optical effects, and Roy Arbogast, who handled the mechanical effects. Arbogast had previously worked with Spielberg on *Jaws*, and Trumbull had worked on *2001*, *The Andromeda Strain* and his own sf film *Silent Running*. *Close Encounters* presented him with some of the toughest challenges of his career, and the optical effects alone consumed $3,500,000 out of the total budget of $19,000,000. 'I turned down *Star Wars*,' said Trumbull, 'because I felt it was just another space opera – just an extension of the stuff I'd already done in *2001* and *Silent Running* – and I was totally bored with that kind of thing. I liked *Close Encounters* because it was a totally different look with new kinds of effects. The hardest thing about this picture was that we didn't have the advantage of being out in space creating a fantasy. We had to be down on Earth with totally believable illusions. But putting a UFO on the screen is like photographing God – people have a very abstract, mind's-eye view of what they expect to see in a flying saucer. So the general look we went for was one of motion, velocity, luminosity and brilliance. We used very sophisticated fibre optics and light-scanning techniques to modulate, control and colour light on film to create the appearance of shape when in fact no shape existed.'[63]

But Trumbull and his team did build some miniature UFOs as well. Powered by electronic motors that produced up to twelve simultaneous motions they moved on horizontal and vertical tracks in a blacked-out room filled with smoke. 'We made up a sort of erector-set kit – a flying-saucer kit – that was essentially just a flat circular disc with different tops and different bottoms in any combination: cone-shaped, pyramid-shaped, round oblate-shaped, or very shallow disc-shaped. Then we mixed and matched tops and bottoms to make anything we wanted. And these were all rigged with neon lighting systems inside and different kinds of holes and ports and openings. Then we had a system of fibre-optic light sources and scanners built in them which were remotely controllable.

Then there were a few other oddball objects, like wing shapes, which were just big plexiglass boxes with neon on them.'[64]

Trumbull's other tasks included creating vast storm clouds in the sky – which he achieved with liquid white paint in a tank of water – and having a UFO fly straight through a toll-booth, which was achieved with a combination of shots between a full-sized toll-booth and a miniature set complete with a tiny UFO on rails. Another complicated job was to create the illusion that every light in a large town is going out simultaneously and then coming back on again; this was achieved by matting out, by hand, each and every light in the shot.

Trumbull's biggest assignment was to show the landing of the giant mother ship, which was supposed to be a quarter of a mile in diameter. The original idea was simply that a huge black shape would come down through the clouds and block out the light, then open up and emit an intense light from within. But Spielberg decided he wanted the ship to look like an oil refinery at night, a sort of city of light. Sketches were made by Ralph McCory, and Spielberg and Trumbull picked the one they liked the best; then Greg Jein, the film's chief model maker, supervised the construction of the miniature along with Bob Shepherd (effects unit project manager on the film). The finished model was six feet in diameter, weighed almost 400 pounds and was made of plexiglass, steel, plywood, fibreglass, thin aluminium tubes carefully drilled with jeweller's drills, and enormous amounts of plastic model kit parts. It contained a very complicated electrical system because each of the tubes – an average of an inch in diameter – had neon tubes running up and down. It was basically a maze of neon tubes and high-voltage wiring.

For the sequence showing the mother ship opening up a different model was used – an eight-foot diameter dome on which were projected light effects – plus a huge full scale section. The latter was filmed in an enormous hangar (once used for blimps) which became the housing for one of the biggest interior sets ever built. The walls were draped in black velvet and an enormous 100-foot-wide, 38-foot-high screen was used for the front projection of the background sky and horizon. To help create the illusion of a wall of light surrounding the base of the vast ship Trumbull placed 2,000 floodlights and six arc lamps along its edge. The final composite footage of the sequence, incorporating the model, actually consisted of over fifty individual exposures.

Roy Arbogast's mechanical effects are also of an incredibly high standard, as in the sequence where total chaos occurs within the interior of Dreyfuss's truck. To achieve the various effects, like the explosion of objects from the glove box, the whole truck was mounted on gimbals on a huge rig and tilted backward until it was vertical. The sequence shortly afterwards when Dreyfuss gets out of his truck and waves at the lights of a

Sunglasses are obviously required equipment when viewing flying saucers at close range.

The evocative image used in the advertising campaign for Close Encounters of the Third Kind.

car coming along the road – only to see the lights suddenly rise up into the air – was simply done by mounting a number of lights on the boom of a mobile crane. Spielberg himself takes the credit for the film's 'visual effects concepts' on *Close Encounters*. 'I thought it was fair to take a concept credit because all the effects were designed and directed by myself and engineered and supervised by Doug Trumbull. That's the division of labour . . . the same with the other effects – they were my concepts on paper but my problem is that I can't even repair a toaster in my house, so that is where I have to rely on experts like Roy Arbogast.'[65]

The aliens who emerge from the ship were designed by Carlo Rambaldi, the man responsible for the 40-foot mechanical ape that briefly appeared in *King Kong* (1977). The tall alien who smiles at Truffaut took three months to build (the alien children were real children in costumes) and was animated through a combination of mechanical and hydraulic gadgets. The famous smile was achieved via artificial tendons operated by remote control. 'He doesn't have a wide range of expressions,' said Rambaldi, 'because probably very great advances in civilization would gradually bring people to lose much of their emotional nature.'[66]

Trumbull is so proud of his work on *Close Encounters* that he has vowed never again to do special effects for anyone else. Instead he intends to make another film of his own.

After two giants like *Star Wars* and *Close Encounters* the first of the many sf films to follow them, such as *Damnation Alley* and *Capricorn One*, have tended to look like toy ducks bobbing around the wake of two battleships. Both of the latter films, however, would have probably been disappointing even if they'd been released before the Big Two.

Damnation Alley (originally called *Survival Run*) was directed by Jack Smight (whose previous sf film was *The Illustrated Man*) and written by Alan Sharp and Lukas Heller, who based their script on the novel by sf writer Roger Zelazny. The fact that the Hell's Angel protagonist in the novel has become an Air Force officer in the film gives a fair indication of the scriptwriters' approach to the original material. The book's surreal, nightmarish atmosphere has been replaced by one of turgid reality and the film has all the panache of a typical made-for-TV movie, albeit an expensive one.

Capricorn One promises to be genuinely original but ends up the same old thing. Written and directed by Peter Hyams, it begins intriguingly. Three astronauts (James Brolin, Sam Waterston and O. J. Simpson) are removed from a space vehicle perched on top of a huge rocket and taken to a remote desert base, where they are told by the head of NASA (Hal Holbrook) that, due to a malfunction in the vehicle's life-support system, they won't be in the rocket when it takes off; instead, as the success of the mission means so much to NASA in terms of future funding, they have decided to fake the whole thing. The astronauts are blackmailed into letting themselves be filmed in a sound stage complete with Martian scenery and dummy spaceship.

On its remote-controlled return towards Earth the real, but empty, spaceship burns up in the atmosphere when its heat-shield malfunctions. The astronauts realize they are now officially 'dead' and something of an embarrassment to NASA, so, fearing for their lives, they break out of the secret base and head for the desert. At this point the film degenerates into a series of chase sequences across the desert, which take up over half the film's running time. Obviously Peter Hyams had one audacious idea – that of NASA faking a Mars landing – but didn't know what to do with it. So he decided to play safe by turning the film into a simple action-thriller. Amazingly, NASA cooperated with the making of the film, though scientific blunders abound. For instance, after establishing that the TV signals are taking 20 minutes to reach Mars (a miscalculation in itself), there is a later sequence where the wives, at Mission Control, are seen having conversations, via a TV-radio link-up, with their husbands, who are supposed to be on Mars, without any time lapse between questions and answers at all.

After *Damnation Alley* and *Capricorn One* a tidal wave of sf films is in

Fortunately the science fiction cinema still hasn't outgrown its monsters— this over-sized octopus appears in Warlords of Atlantis.

preparation at the time of writing (early 1978) – such as *Starship Invasions*, which is a cross between *Close Encounters* and *Star Wars* and features Christopher Lee as an evil alien in control of a fleet of flying saucers Michael Crichton's *Coma*, based on the novel by Robin Cook about a hospital where patients mysteriously 'die', only to end up in suspended animation while vital organs are removed and sold to the highest bidder; Ronald Neame's *Meteor*, which is about a giant meteor hitting the Earth; Irwin Allen's *Swarm* about a horde of killer bees; George Pal's sequel to *The Time Machine* to be called *Return of the Time Machine*; *The Medusa Touch*, starring Richard Burton as a man with Carrie-like powers who can cause earthquakes and send airliners crashing into skyscrapers; *Warlords of Atlantis*, which is part of the Amicus series that began with *The Land That Time Forgot*; Robert Amram's *The Late, Great Planet Earth* about the end of the world; the two parts of the long-awaited *Superman*; the Dino de Laurentiis production of *Flash Gordon*; Universal's rival production of *Buck Rogers*; *Jaws 2*; *The Terrible Jaw Man* about a scientist who turns into a shark-man; the French space opera *Star Lock*; AIP's *Star Crash*, another space opera; Saul David's *Timescape*; Giorgio Venturini's *Humanoid*; Carl Foreman's *The Weather War*. The list is endless, as is the list of planned remakes of sf film classics: *Things to Come, War of the Worlds, Invasion of the Bodysnatchers, When Worlds Collide, The Thing from Another World.*

The sf film boom is only just beginning.

Epilogue

At the outset of this book I quoted a passage from John Baxter's *Science Fiction in the Cinema* in which he stated that science fiction films have little in common with written science fiction. Eight years later Baxter feels that this is still true: 'It certainly applies to the films I was writing about then. Whether films have changed since then and come closer to science fiction I don't know. I don't really think they have. Special effects are obviously what dominate sf films today but that wasn't true of the films I was writing about. *2001* was the big watershed – it was the ultimate special effects movie and really tried to get the background right. It tried to duplicate the futuristic setting and ever since then sf films have relied heavily on doing the same. I suppose you could say these sf films have come closer to the kind of sf that I read when I was a fan back in the 1950s. *2001* is like a Poul Anderson novel in a way . . . I'm not talking about content, that has to be looked at separately. I don't think sf film-makers these days are very interested in content – they're more concerned with setting and background. They're becoming obsessed with it. When you look at people like Trumbull making *Silent Running* and Lucas with *THX 1138* and *Star Wars*, they're not really concerned with ideology; they're making these big expensive movies tucked away in factories and concentrating solely on getting the background right. Nobody making sf films is really addressing themselves to the issues of the day. . .

'*Logan's Run*, for instance, is almost all background. It tries to work out where the escalators go, where the domes are, what the people do in the evenings, what they eat, what they drink – all the little details that used to be very important to sf fans . . . to me anyway when I read sf. I liked that feeling of knowing exactly how things worked. And these films now seem to have got hung up on all that and I'm not sure why it is. Maybe it's because the movie business lends itself to the evocation of background detail. It's harder to convey things in action and dialogue and it's in those areas that the sf movies tend to fall down. So to my mind all the movies I've seen in the late 1960s and during the 1970s, right across the spectrum from *The Final Programme* to *Star Wars*, share a slightly old-fashioned obsession with detail and a total lack of interest in character.'

However, if one takes 'background' to mean not so much the purely visual background (sets, machinery, etcetera) as the unseen world one should feel exists off-screen, then it is more accurate to say that films like *Rollerball* and *Logan's Run* exist in a kind of limbo. Science fiction writers firmly anchor their stories into well-thought-out social backgrounds, but the makers of many recent sf movies have instead concentrated on the creation of highly-localized settings. Harry Harrison agrees: 'That's why Robert Heinlein's books are so good. You feel when you're reading one that when a detail comes in it's just one of a thousand details he could have included, not something that he's just invented on the spot but part of a whole real world. Only one detail may appear as part of the plot but you're aware of the whole big world behind it. That's what all the best sf has but it rarely gets to the screen.'

During the last decade or so both film-makers and cinema audiences have become a little more knowledgeable about science and therefore sf films have tended to pay greater lip service towards scientific accuracy. Now, however, there are signs that this trend was a short-lived one. Much of the blame lies with *Star Wars*. George Lucas has claimed that his film isn't supposed to be science fiction but fantasy, but unfortunately it masquerades as sf by its use of sf's traditional imagery – spaceships, ray guns, robots, hyper-space, aliens, and so on. The film, though set in a galaxy 'far away and a long time ago', is not entitled to ignore the laws of physics. (If it had been set in another universe Lucas could have invented his own scientific rules with complete justification.) He tries to have it both ways, using science when it pleases him and abandoning it when it doesn't. Some of the scientific absurdities were mentioned in the last chapter, but the cavalier treatment of such a fundamental force as gravity is particularly irksome. Since the Death Star has the dimensions of a small moon it would have a sizable gravitational field, and the gravitational pull would be towards the centre of the station; yet in several sequences people are seen standing parallel to the station's centre of gravity (the equivalent of walking up one's living-room wall). Naturally the Death Star would have no sides as such: there would only be 'up' and 'down'. That old sf standby 'artificial gravity' would have been mentioned by an sf writer in an attempt to paper over the scientific cracks, but Lucas doesn't make even that token gesture.

Since Lucas succeeds in making *Star Wars* so entertaining it's easy to forgive him these scientific lapses, but unfortunately he's setting a dangerous precedent. Less interesting film-makers will no doubt follow suit ignoring the laws of science and before long, perhaps, we'll not only hear sounds in space but see people breathe out there as well. John Baxter maintains that scientific accuracy in sf films isn't very important: 'What I really liked about sf films was the vulgarization of technology. I was never really interested in technology and I don't think any sf reader really is, but it's what the sf films did to technology that interested me. All the arguments by sf fans along the lines of "This is absurd! Rocketships don't work this way!" never mattered to me, any more than it mattered to me that Bette Davis in *The Letter* wasn't an accurate copy of the Malayan planter's wife.' But I see no reason why a science fiction film should not be expected to be scientifically accurate, just as one doesn't expect to see jet planes appearing in the background of a John Ford western. Even films that are anti-science or anti-technology should get their scientific facts right if they are to be effective. Take the film *Holocaust 2000*, for instance; it concerns attempts to prevent the construction of a giant fusion reactor in some unnamed Middle Eastern country, as it seems that the Anti-Christ himself will use the reactor to bring about the end of the world if he can. The film-makers, apart from having no idea as to what a fusion reactor is, absurdly postulate that if the reactor explodes it will set off the reactors in neighbouring countries and thus cause a chain reaction that will destroy the world. An important theme is thus reduced to nonsense, and there does seem a danger that, whereas sf films of the 1950s metamorphosed into the 'monster' cycle, sf films of the 1970s will descend into pure fantasy.

While, in general, sf films of the 1970s cover a wider spectrum of themes, are better made technically and involve the talents of top-name directors and scriptwriters, they do still have one thing in common with 1950s' sf films: very few of them are based on the work of real sf writers. Not only have very few sf novels and stories been adapted into films but the involvement of sf writers in actual scriptwriting has also been extremely rare. One writer who believes that the participation of sf writers can only improve sf movies is John Brunner: 'To be candid, I'm very disappointed in most of the recent sf films. The degree to which the ingenuity of the technical people has increased is not matched by any increase in the sense of the people who hold the purse-strings. I swear to goodness that pictures like *Logan's Run*, for example, would have benefited simply from doubling the fees of the scriptwriters. It's a pretty picture but that's about all you can say about it.

'*Zardoz* particularly annoyed me, mainly because of its pretentiousness but also because of its banality. The storyline might possibly have stood up in a 1940s comic strip. It's very much a writer's reaction to the picture but I have a sort of working rule-of-thumb – anything in which a group of people are described as "*The*-plus adjective", such as "The Abnormals" and "The Deprived", has not been properly thought through. *Zardoz* was full of "*The's*". The other reason is that I think the guy responsible for the film despises science fiction. He comes along and thinks he's created a masterpiece while in fact it's a piece of second-rate hackwork, but he expects to be lauded to the skies and told he's done it much better than a regular sf practitioner could have. This condescending attitude is half the trouble – they say people who like sf are idiots, so we'll make an idiot picture. It's very sad.

'There have been some good sf films made. One thinks of films like *Forbidden Planet* and *The Day the Earth Stood Still*, which is my personal favourite of them all, and it's still impressing people after a relatively long time. An exception to the general drabness of the recent lot was certainly *Rollerball*; I was very favourably impressed by that, much more than I expected to be. I think what possibly made it work was that the makers didn't break what to me is a cardinal rule in sf for the general public – and this applies to TV as well as films: give the public, which is unfamiliar with sf, only one new assumption and then make everything else in your story follow from it according to conventional plotting. This is why, for example, *The Day the Earth Stood Still* was such a tremendous success; a man comes down with a warning from space and everything else flows from that one thing in a perfectly conventional narrative fashion. It's a good, solid, tightly-constructed thriller of the old style. But the more extravagant the set of assumptions you want your audience to follow – and this is where *Logan's Run* breaks down – the less extravagant you must make your story development from those assumptions. A fantasy like *Barbarella*, for example, doesn't necessarily have to abide by these rules, but certainly if you want people to come out of the cinema with the same feelings you get when you close a first-rate sf novel you need to make your story as strong as your assumptions are startling.

'So far I've only written one sf screenplay – for a low-budget Amicus film called *The Terrornauts* (1967) based on a Murray Leinster novel, *The Wailing Asteroid*. That came about because my wife and I are personal friends of Milton Subotsky, the producer. We had no professional involvement until the question of who was going to script this picture came up and I got a phone-call from Milton one day asking me if I'd like to try my hand at it. He knew perfectly well that I would, of course. So I did him the usual two full-length drafts and I must say that I found working with him very pleasant – he was a very reasonable guy. Time and time again he had to tell me: "I'm afraid you can't show this, you'll have to tell it otherwise it will take us over-budget." But it was a perfectly reasonable way of going about things – he would point out the flaws and get me to put them right rather than interfere himself. I wasn't particularly attracted to the book. In fact, quite frankly, I scrapped most of it. It was one of those "experimenter builds spaceship in his backyard" stories that was quite common in the 1930s. I think I made it a little more reasonable and logical within the limitations of what the budget would stretch to. I did get a fan letter from someone in Indiana who'd seen it on TV and who said what a pleasure it was to hear the technical terms used correctly for a change.

'What attracted me to the idea of trying my hand at a film script was that at that time I was not fully established as a writer. I was having to turn out an enormous amount of material in order to make ends meet and the only way I could keep going was to make each project as different as possible from the one before. So the film script provided the kind of variety I was desperately in need of. However, I found that by temperament I'm not a scriptwriter. I don't work very happily in a situation where I am at second remove from the end-product, and afterwards I went back happily to writing straight prose. However I did try to get myself another scriptwriting commission. At odd intervals I'd ask my agent: "Is anybody looking for someone to write an sf picture?", primarily for the same reason as before and partly because I was getting a little disillusioned with the standards of scripting in sf pictures that I'd been seeing recently . . . I was going around for weeks after seeing *Zardoz* saying: "If they'd given me a million and a half dollars and Sean Connery, what a picture I could have made!"

'I'd still be very interested in tackling an sf film project from scratch rather than adapting someone else's work. In fact I had several discussions with a producer about two years ago who was allegedly looking for an sf property, but I don't think he was looking terribly hard because the last time I rang him up (only about six weeks after our initial meeting) it turned out he'd settled for something utterly different – I think he decided to do a historical picture instead. That kind of thing is the bugbear of the movie industry, I'm afraid. An awful lot of people with an awful lot of purchasing power are in exactly the position of the classic editor who, when asked what sort of stories he wanted, replied: "I don't know but I shall when they arrive on my desk."

'I've had hopes that some of my own novels would be bought for the screen but so far, unfortunately, nothing has happened. I have had stuff adapted for television though – two of my stories, 'Some Lapse of Time' and 'The Last Lonely Man', were included in the BBC sf series *Out of the Unknown*. I was extremely fortunate whereas some writers, like Colin Kapp, suffered disasters. They did a version of his story 'Lambda 2' and it was clear after about five minutes that the director didn't have the faintest idea of what was supposed to be going on. And Ray Bradbury's *The Fox in the Forest* was pretty well ruined. I had the guy assigned to script *Some Lapse of Time* round to tea one Sunday and talked *at* him for about two hours, and I thought I'd left him with a clear impression of what the story was all about, but apparently I hadn't. Like all the scriptwriters on the series he'd never done science fiction before. If you were lucky you got a writer like Troy Kennedy Martin and if you weren't lucky . . . well, I won't name the guy *I* got. Five months went by and we moved house, and one day the phone rings and the guy at the other end says: "This is Roger Jenkins" – who I'd never heard of – "I've been trying to reach you at your old address because I've been assigned to direct *Some Lapse of Time*. I have both the story and the script and I've shown them to several people and they all say the story is better than the script. What are we going to do about it?'' So I swallowed hard and said: "Anything I can do I will." It turned out that the scriptwriter had taken ridiculous liberties which had destroyed the story-line. He had simply not bothered with the logic – it was almost as if he'd said to himself: "Oh, this is just science fiction . . . I'll toss it off in an afternoon." In the end Roger Jenkins rewrote the script back to the story at every point he could and did a first-rate job, and as a result *Some Lapse of Time* topped the viewers' rating chart for the first series. But if I hadn't had a conscientious director assigned to the project I would have had a disaster.

'But I am disappointed that none of my novels have made it to the big screen yet because there are at least a handful of my books, *Quicksand* for instance, which I think would come in very nicely as low-budget pictures and be capable of scripting to a very high standard. A lot of people have shown interest in my work. I recall Roger Corman raising and dropping my hopes in the same breath: he said he'd sat down to cost *Stand on Zanzibar* but when he passed $2,000,000 he gave up because he knew nobody was going to give him $2,000,000 to make an sf picture. That, of course, was seven or eight years ago. I've had a number of options picked up on my books but, oddly enough, very rarely on my sf books; one of my thrillers had about three options picked up on it and then dropped again. They never actually put the thing into production so the rights came back to me. So anybody who is reading this who is looking for a corpus of good science fiction from which to choose a theme for a major movie is welcome to ring me up.'

Harry Harrison, after the success of *Soylent Green*, which was based on his novel *Make Room! Make Room!* (see Chapter 9), is another sf writer anxious to see more of his work reach the screen – preferably scripted by himself. 'I'm very interested in becoming a screenwriter,' he said, 'partly for the money, of course, but I would genuinely like to see good science fiction on the screen. I'd like to write one good sf film – or more than one if I could – it's such a rich and full medium and I like working within it. It's absolutely different from doing a novel, and with the visual background I have as a former artist I enjoy doing it. The cinema has always been very important to me – the visual imagery of the cinema should be important to every writer. But it's a whole different world to publishing; to get involved in the film industry you literally have to go and suck the golden teat. You have to go to Hollywood. You have to see everybody, knock on everyone's door and so on, and I find that incredibly boring – I just cannot do it. But that's the only way to break in unless you can manage it from the outside. That's why I was so happy to let them do *Soylent Green* because now when I come up with an idea I can approach them from the top.

'There have been nibbles at some of my other books, particularly *Skyfall* which is a major book as well as being very topical [it concerns a large space station that falls out of orbit] but I have a good agent who doesn't bother me by telling me every time somebody simply asks about it. I was told recently that for every seventy scripts written only one actually gets produced, and even scripts commissioned by companies rarely make it – only about one out of every ten or twelve. And out of every ten films actually made, two or three go on the shelf. Probably for every idea for a film that is conceived, one out of 8,000 actually makes it to the screen. I've done three screenplays in the last twenty years, all of which have been shelved – none reached the shooting stage. One was for Roger Corman. He came to me after he'd done *Deathrace 2000* in 1975, I think. He had this story outline that he'd bought from some young writer and he wanted me to do a screenplay based on it. I thought it was a completely rotten idea and when I came to do the screenplay I tried to throw out the worst stuff, but it turned out that what I'd thrown out was what they had bought the original outline for, so I had to put it back in. It's very hard to describe what it was about; basically a spaceship from Earth is wrecked on an alien planet and the human beings become the slaves of crystal people for generations. And there are renegade humans who live in the swamps and travel about in great wheels. These giant wheels were what sold the outline in the first place but I'm still not sure how they were supposed to work. I even made sketches of them trying to work out how they operated – it was just a rotten idea. I was mainly interested in being involved in a film right from the beginning so I went along with it.

'Roger has a real tight little set-up where he pays Guild standard rates, or just a bit more, for the film writing and gives his director maybe just a thousand dollars for doing the whole film. But the director will be a good one – some guy who wants the chance to direct his first film. Roger will pay him this flat fee but the next time the guy directs a film it will probably be for a major company for about $200,000. So everyone gets something out of it – Roger gets good talent cheap and the guy gets his start as a director. I was quite happy to work with him and he paid me above the Guild minimum – a nice price. Apparently my finished screeplay worked because Roger said he liked it, but he put it on the shelf. In the interim, of course, they've made sf films with multi-million dollar budgets like *Star Wars* and *Close Encounters*, but Roger's success lies in making good films with low budgets.

'I've had screenplays done from my books by some big-name writers but all have gone without a trace. Disney Studios called me one day and said they wanted to do some sf subjects so I gave them a couple of properties. They weren't interested in what I gave them and it took me about a year to find out the sort of thing they wanted. So then I gave them an original idea in the form of a ten- or fifteen-page outline. It was a time travel story and they seemed to like it very much. They gave me a contract so then I did an eighty-page treatment. I worked on it for months but then a screenwriters' strike started and by the time it was over the Disney people had forgotten what my name was, and they also forgot that they liked the idea I'd given them. They just put the treatment on the shelf. They complained that there were too many laughs in the script. Apparently I hadn't managed to work in all the clichés that are necessary for a Disney film. I got paid though, and I got the rights back as well . . .

'At the moment I'm working on a project with Carl Gottlieb, the guy who wrote the screenplay for *Jaws*. It's an sf subject based on one of my novels but I can't say any more about it at this stage. I think it could make a very good movie – I like Carl's screenwriting, he's very, very good. He's working on it with a director at the moment so all I can do now is wait.'

Michael Moorcock, after his depressing experience with *The Final Programme*, is understandably disillusioned with the film industry, particularly the British industry. 'I find being involved with film-making depressing on two counts – on *Final Programme* it was depressing because one was seeing one's own thing ruined, but I also find the industry hacks depressing – the camera crews etcetera. It's no wonder the British film industry is in the state it's in when you've got thirty or so cynical, slightly aggressive idiots on the other side of the camera the whole time. Anything the director might try to do is sometimes actively screwed up by the crew if they're in the mood. Some time back I was involved in a project with Mai Zetterling but she couldn't work in England because the union insisted she couldn't have her own crew. In Sweden she'd been working with a very tight unit, about four people, which is all you really need. There is something absolutely deadly about the technicians in the British film industry and it's a wonder you get any decent films coming out at all.

'I also find meeting film directors depressing. An agency once set up a meeting between me and a director to discuss the making of *Behold the Man*. He was the usual effete type in a leather jacket – they're all called Clive or Lindsay – and I took such an instant dislike to him I actually talked him out of making the movie. I suggested he might as well pinch the story from the same source I did, the New Testament, and he wouldn't have to pay anything for it either. I just don't like directors.

'I really think the professional scriptwriters have a better time working on films than people who have to adapt their own books into film scripts. I remember when Keith Roberts [author of *Pavane, The Furies, The Inner Wheel*] was working on a film a few years ago and all his hair started to fall out. He went to his doctor to find out why and his doctor said: ''Whatever you're working on at the moment – stop!'' Ideally I would like a book of mine taken over by a director like the late Howard Hawks and done in pure Hollywood fashion because at least it would be done professionally, or I'd like to work with someone like Mai Zetterling or Dick Lester. There *are* a number of directors I admire considerably . . .

'In a way I found it refreshing to go and watch an Amicus film like *The Land That Time Forgot* being made because there was no hypocrisy. Nobody was going around saying it's going to be the greatest ever made; instead they treated it like the piece of workmanlike crap they were actually making. I've got a soft spot for Milton Subotsky, who was one of the Amicus producers then, but I'll never forget my first meeting with him years ago at a party. He was introduced to me as this great film producer and he told me they were working on a *real* King Arthur movie, which I thought sounded interesting because he told me it was going to be absolutely authentic in its period detail and everything; but the film that eventually came out covered about 2,000 years of history, largely because of all the library shots they used. They had to keep putting the actors and extras in different costumes to match up with the various library shots.

'The other Amicus producer, Max Rosenburg, sat Jim Cawthorn and me down in his office when we delivered the script for *The Land That Time Forgot* and made it evident that he regarded us as illiterate hacks, and he said what they really wanted to do was make Margaret Drabble movies – which is my personal idea of what really would be crap. It was quite funny, though, to hear from him that's what Amicus is really into – they just do these other films for the money!'

Not surprisingly, Moorcock has strong opinions about sf cinema in general. For instance, he doesn't like *2001 : A Space Odyssey*: 'I thought it was barren of ideas . . . irony is no substitute for imagination. It struck me that poor old Kubrick had innocently got Arthur C. Clarke to do what he thought was going to be a wildly imaginative flight of fancy but Arthur did his usual thing instead. I was on the set twice while they were making it and they'd got technology-heavy: they had all these NASA people around and everything. It's like when you're writing a novel and you start doing the preliminary research – after a while the research becomes the whole thing and you have finally to chuck the whole lot out before you can start writing the fiction. But Kubrick kept everything and got stuck with it . . .

'What I did like about the film were the three-dimensional display systems in the spaceships. If it had all been three-dimensional display systems I would have enjoyed it thoroughly but I didn't like much of the rest of it. I don't like Kubrick as a film-maker. What I've always said about his films is that they would all be very good if they'd had a good director. I didn't like *A Clockwork Orange* or *Barry Lyndon*. The latter is a book I like but Kubrick left out all the fun; all the real irony of the book is missing. By shifting the emphasis and doing his usual "detachment" routine he wrecked the book. I don't think he has much sense of people, though I enjoyed the early film he did, *Paths of Glory*.

'I like *Forbidden Planet*. I liked it when I first saw it and when I saw it again on TV recently I thought it held up very well. The kind of love interest element is horrible but the rest of it is pretty good. The monster, of course, is a bit rotten thanks to the Disney touch – it looks just like a Disney cartoon. And I like both versions of *King Kong* . . . I don't mind the latest version being different from the first one. I thought the tensions were very well maintained in the new one. They learnt a lot from *Jaws* obviously – in fact they pinched a lot from *Jaws*. But just to have everything *moving* the way they did . . . the professionalism of the thing and the special effects were very good, and it was even sadder than the original. I thought they were going to descend into bathos but they didn't – they saved it in time. I still like the original but they both have their own virtues. It's very rare to have a remake that acually amplifies certain elements of the original, and strengthens certain elements as well. Just little things like having the World Trade Center the same, in silhouette, as his mountain home back on the island – you've got to admire that kind of professionalism.

'As for *Zardoz*, I couldn't have believed it was going to be so rotten, and it *was* rotten. Boorman is a director who always has good ideas and subjects but manages to screw them up. I tend to like most sf films, I think, pretty much as I like most westerns. I'm not very critical; it's only when sf films get a bit daft and serious that I get annoyed. Many sf films develop a peculiar, lumpen seriousness that bad directors always think is significant – like when they put in bits about ecology in *Logan's Run*: I was very disappointed in that film. I don't believe that directors should be allowed to think. They shouldn't have so much control over the scripts either. I've decided, after working in films, that the producer is the most important person in the making of a film, which is exactly the way the industry itself thinks too. After the producer the actors are the most important, the director next and the writer comes very low down. But if the producer can actually get a good script and good actors I don't think it matters who directs it. I think half the directors who have good reputations have been very lucky because they've been connected with good scripts.'

Moorcock's views on the big sf movie of 1977 are equally strong: he wrote in the *New Statesman*: 'Star Wars is a ramshackle collage of undigested influences which ran out of the director's control at an early stage. Good directors are reluctant to work on "effects" pictures. *Star Wars* is not so much a story as a naïve compendium of other people's images used haphazardly, without grace or wit. It rips off a sub-culture and gives nothing back to it. It is an empty thing . . . it lacks the humour, the script, the invention, the plot dynamics and the genuine creativity displayed in the best *Dr Who* stories . . . it is the biggest exploitation movie of them all.'[67]

Basically the gulf between sf cinema and written sf, as John Baxter has observed, remains as large as ever. To take the two most obvious examples: both *Star Wars* and *Close Encounters* represent major developments in the field of cinematic effects, but in content they offer nothing new. *Star Wars* may have put traditional science fiction imagery on the screen properly for the first time but its story was almost pure 1930s space opera; and *Close Encounters*, for all its technical brilliance, is a variation on the old aliens-from-outer-space plot, the main innovation being that the aliens come out of their spaceship smiling not blasting.

Practically none of the present concerns of written sf are being reflected in sf cinema. Biology, for instance – in particular the subject of genetic engineering – is a major source of inspiration at the moment for sf writers, yet very few films have exploited this topical scientific development. *Demon Seed* was an exception, and *The Boys from Brazil* ingeniously makes use of the concept of cloning within a thriller context, while similarly the medical thriller *Coma* exploits the darker side of organ transplants. Once again one must conclude this is because so few actual sf writers are involved in the writing of the scripts, and also because so few sf novels and stories are used as the basis for films. At the time of writing the only bright spot is the proposed series of sf films to be produced by Lester Goldsmith of Limelight Films Ltd and based on such well-known sf novels as *The Bicentennial Man* by Isaac Asimov, *The Stainless Steel Rat* by Harry Harrison and *The Forever War* by Joe Haldeman, the screenplays of which will be written by the sf writers themselves. There is also De Palma's planned film version of Alfred Bester's *The Demolished Man* and the various remakes of such films as *The Thing, Invasion of the Bodysnatchers, When Worlds Collide*, etcetera. So, despite the sf film boom, it seems that genuine sf films will remain few and far between. But does this really matter? John Baxter thinks not: 'Film deals in a whole different area of sensibility – a whole different area of mind and emotion; it deals with things that go way down below the intellect, it plays on the deepest fears and desires, it plays on the sensory deprivation of the cinematic experience, whereas written sf primarily appeals to the intellect. I'm not saying you can't make an sf film that is also acceptable to writers and readers but basically they're in different fields and I don't see why they should ever overlap.' It seems that this viewpoint is held – perhaps unwittingly – by the film-makers themselves, and until this outlook changes sf films that are both intellectually satisfying and visually evocative, such as *Forbidden Planet, 2001 : A Space Odyssey, Quatermass and the Pit* and *Dark Star*, will remain the occasional happy accident.

Appendix: SF on Television

1949: CAPTAIN VIDEO
(USA) DuMont. This – the first sf TV series – was primarily aimed at children and ran five nights a week. Originally produced by Larry Menkin and written by Maurice Brockhauser, starring Richard Coogan as Captain Video (in 1950 Al Hodge replaced Coogan in the title role). A juvenile space opera, most of the show was transmitted live but special effects were pre-filmed and somewhat clumsily inserted into the programme. Some well-known sf writers worked on the show over the years, including Jack Vance, Robert Sheckley and Arthur C. Clarke. It lasted until 1953 but was revived in a different format by Hodge in 1955. In 1956 it became *Captain Video's Cartoons*.

1950: BUCK ROGERS
(USA) ABC. Produced by Babette Henry and written by Gene Wyckoff, starring Ken Dibbs and Lou Prentiss. An imitation of the popular *Captain Video*, this series was also aimed at children. Though set in the distant future most of the action took place in Buck's laboratory hidden in a cave behind Niagara Falls. Like *Video* it was transmitted live.

1950: TOM CORBETT, SPACE CADET
(USA) NBC. Produced by Leonard Carlton, originally written by Albert Aley, and starring Frankie Thomas as Tom Corbett, a cadet in the Solar Guides (an interplanetary police force). The show was televised live, as were its special effects (unlike *Video* and *Buck Rogers*). German rocket expert Willy Ley was hired as technical adviser.

1951: SPACE PATROL
(USA) ABC. Produced and written by Mike and Helen Mosier, starring Ed Kemmer as Buzz Corry, the commander-in-chief of the Space Patrol. Like the other children's space opera shows of the time it was transmitted live but had a slightly more lavish budget – $2,500 per week.

1952: OUT OF THIS WORLD
(USA) ABC. Produced by Milton Kaye and narrated by Jackson Beck this series was a mixture of science fiction and lectures on science. The third episode, written by Robbie Robertson, concerned a young couple going to the moon for a vacation; in between the 'dramatized' segments the narrator discussed possible conditions on the moon with scientist Robert R. Cole.

1952: TALES OF TOMORROW

(USA) ABC. Created and produced by George Foley and Dick Gordon this was
one of the earliest sf anthology TV series. Its first two episodes (30 minutes
each) consisted of a dramatization of Verne's *20,000 Leagues* starring Thomas
Mitchell and Leslie Nielsen. Like most TV shows of the time it was limited by
having to transmit live, though filmed inserts were often included.

1953: THE QUATERMASS EXPERIMENT

(UK) BBC. Produced and directed by Rudolph Cartier, written by Nigel Kneale
and starring Reginald Tate as Professor Quatermass. The serial, which
consisted of six episodes, each 40 minutes long, was a clever mixture of sf and
horror aimed at adults (the BBC issued a warning that the programme was
'thought to be unsuitable for children and persons of a nervous disposition').
The story told of an astronaut (Duncan Lamont) who returns to Earth infected
by an alien organism. The serial proved popular and led to two sequels. All of
them were adapted into feature films by Hammer Films (in the USA they were
called *The Creeping Unknown, Enemy from Space* and *Five Million Years to
Earth*). Technically primitive, *The Quatermass Experiment* was transmitted live
via TV cameras which dated back to 1936 and only had one fixed lens each,
thus preventing quick cutting from camera to camera. Special effects
sequences were pre-filmed and inserted into the live transmission.

1953: ROD BROWN OF THE ROCKET RANGERS

(USA) CBS. Starring Cliff Robertson, Bruce Hall and Jack Weston, this was
another juvenile space opera, set in the 22nd century and concerning the
efforts of 'Rocket Rangers' to prevent the spread of 'interplanetary evil'.

1953: ROCKY JONES, SPACE RANGER

(USA) Syndicated. This children's sf show, which starred Richard Crane,
differed from its predecessors in being the first sf TV series made entirely on
film, which allowed for more sophisticated special effects as well as better sets
and location shooting.

1953: SUPERMAN

(USA) ABC and Syndication. The first series was produced by Robert Maxwell
and Bernard Luber but thereafter it was produced by Whitney Ellsworth, who
made it increasingly juvenile. Superman was played by George Reeves, who
first played the role in a low-budget 1951 movie called *Superman and the Mole
Men* produced by Maxwell and Luber. Phyllis Coates played Lois Lane in the
first season but was replaced by Noel Neill in the second one; other actors
included Jack Larson (Jimmy Olsen) and John Hamilton (Perry White). The
series proved popular and lasted until 1957. Like *Rocky Jones* it was shot
entirely on film, with colour added from its third season onwards.

1954: CAPTAIN MIDNIGHT (also known as JET JACKSON)

(USA) Syndicated. Created and produced by George Bilson, and starring

Richard Webb as Midnight (or Jackson, depending on the area in which the series was shown), a super-scientific crimefighter working in a mountain-top laboratory. Sid Melton played his bumbling assistant, Ikky. The series originally began as a radio show in 1940.

1954: 1984
(UK) BBC. Rudolph Cartier and Nigel Kneale, the team responsible for the *Quatermass* serials, produced this TV adaptation of George Orwell's novel. It starred Peter Cushing, Andre Morell and Donald Pleasence and had a major impact on British TV viewers, much of the controversy being caused by a scene involving Cushing and a cage full of rats.

1954: THE LOST PLANET
(UK) BBC. Children's TV serial produced by Kevin Sheldon, written by Angus McVicar, who based it on his book of the same name, and starring Peter Kerr, Jack Stewart and Mary Law.

1955: COMMANDO CODY — SKY MARSHALL OF THE UNIVERSE
(USA) Republic/NBC. Produced by Mel Tucker and Franklyn Adreon and written by Ronald Davidson and Barry Shipman. Judd Holdren starred in this children's series about a super-crimefighter who battles both conventional gangsters and 'The Ruler', an evil genius from outer space.

1955: RETURN OF THE LOST PLANET
(UK) BBC. Sequel to *The Lost Planet* and again produced by Kevin Sheldon and adapted from the novel by Angus McVicar.

1955: QUATERMASS II
(UK) BBC. Second of the Quatermass serials, produced and directed by Rudolph Cartier and written by Nigel Kneale. This time Quatermass was played by John Robinson (Reginald Tate having died) and the story concerned infiltration of the British government by alien entities who have established a secret base in a remote part of the country.

1955: SCIENCE FICTION THEATRE
(USA) NBC. Produced by Ivan Tors, who had previously produced a number of sf feature films, this sf anthology series went out of its way to avoid sensationalism and as a result tended to be boring. Talking about the series in 1956 Tors said 'One of the traps into which such a series may fall is complete dependence on science for interest. This is avoided at the story conference by excluding the scientists at the start . . . after the story is developed it is up to Dr Maxwell Smith, the programme's technical adviser, and the other research people to suggest some scientific fact on which the story can be hung.' The show was hosted by the ultra-dignified Truman Bradley.

1956: THE CREATURE
(UK) BBC. A play produced and written by Rudolph Cartier and Nigel Kneale

about the discovery of an intelligent species of 'abominable snowmen'.

1956 : SPACE SCHOOL
(UK) BBC. Children's serial produced by Kevin Sheldon and written by Gordon Ford, starring John Stuart, Matthew Lane and Julie Webb, about a group of children living in a space station.

1958 : QUATERMASS AND THE PIT
(UK) BBC. The third Quatermass serial, again produced and directed by Rudolph Cartier and written by Nigel Kneale. It starred Andre Morell in the title role and concerned an invasion from Mars five million years in the past which is still exerting a malignant influence over the inhabitants of London. 'In the *Quatermass* serials,' said Nigel Kneale recently, 'I always used what was going on at the time as a basis for the stories . . . in the late 1950s London was being rebuilt after the war and so a number of huge cavities were being dug . . . unexploded bombs were always being found and sometimes old Roman ruins would be exposed. And I thought – what if they found something else far beyond that? What if they uncovered a spaceship? And this led to *Quatermass and the Pit*.'[68]

1959 : MEN INTO SPACE
(USA) CBS. A bland and unexciting series starring William Lundigan and Joyce Taylor which attempted to treat space travel 'seriously'. Much of it was set in outer space or on the moon but budget limitations were reflected in the artificiality of the sets, spaceships and moonscapes.

1959 : MAN AND THE CHALLENGE
(USA) NBC. Another of Ivan Tors' 'semi-factual' productions. George Nader starred as a military medical expert out to test the limits of human endurance and to apply the results in the training of astronauts. Some episodes were interesting (in one, three human guinea-pigs are sealed into space suits and ordered to march across Death Valley, where they are mistaken for invaders from outer space by a group of armed men) but the series soon ran out of plot variations.

1959 : WORLD OF GIANTS
(USA) Syndicated. Produced by William Alland, who had produced so many of Universal's sf/horror movies during the 1950s, the series was built around the giant-size props left over from *The Incredible Shrinking Man*. Marshall Thompson starred as a government secret agent shrunk after a dose of atomic radiation. His full-size partner was played by Arthur Franz.

1959 : THE TWILIGHT ZONE
(USA) CBS. Though basically a fantasy series this features a number of sf episodes. It was created and hosted by Rod Serling, one of the most successful writers for American TV during the 1950s (he won six Emmys and numerous other awards). The show varied in quality but was often very entertaining (the better episodes tended to come from writer Richard Matheson) and was

certainly more thought-provoking and inventive than most TV series at the time. It began as a half-hour series, expanded to an hour in 1963, then returned to a half-hour for its final season in 1964.

1961: A FOR ANDROMEDA

(UK) BBC. A serial produced by Michael Hayes and Norman Jones and written by Fred Hoyle and John Elliot, it starred Peter Halliday, Mary Morris, Esmond Knight and Frank Windsor, and concerned a mysterious radio signal from the Andromeda galaxy which is found to be giving instructions on how to build a super-computer. The computer in turn creates an artificial girl (played by Julie Christie).

1962: THE ANDROMEDA BREAKTHROUGH

(UK) BBC. This sequel to *A for Andromeda* was again written by Fred Hoyle and John Elliot and concerned the discovery of another Andromeda computer, this one being built in South America. Peter Halliday again starred as the scientist attempting to interpret the purpose of the messages from Andromeda, and Susan Hampshire replaced Julie Christie as the artificial girl.

1962: OUT OF THIS WORLD

(UK) ITV. Produced by Leonard White, this sf anthology series was hosted by Boris Karloff and featured adaptations of stories by many well-known sf writers including Isaac Asimov, Philip K. Dick and Clifford Simak.

1962: THE AVENGERS

(UK) ITV. The series began in 1960 under the title *Police Surgeon*, starring Ian Hendry. It was created by Sydney Newman (who later helped create *Dr Who*) and written and produced by Julian Bond, but in 1962 Newman decided to change the format of the show and make it more escapist. The title was altered to *The Avengers* and Patrick MacNee joined the cast as the dandyish John Steed, followed shortly afterwards by Honor Blackman as the leather-clad judo expert Cathy Gale (Ian Hendry had by then left the series). With the arrival of the secret-agent boom, sparked off by the James Bond movies, *The Avengers* became increasingly popular. It peaked in 1965–66 when the production became more lavish and the scripts, under the supervision of Brian Clemens and Albert Fennell, more surreal and sf-orientated. In 1965 Diana Rigg replaced Honor Blackman, and in 1968, the last year of the series, she in turn was replaced by Linda Thorson. (Series revived in 1976.)

1963: DR WHO

(UK) BBC. Created by Sydney Newman and Donald Wilson and originally produced by Verity Lambert, this children's TV serial about a mysterious man, Dr Who, who travels back and forth in time in his time machine the Tardis, accompanied by various people he picks up along the way, is still running on British TV. The series had a modest following when it first started, but the fifth episode, written by Terry Nation, introduced some evil, robot-like creatures called DALEKs (which look like large, mobile salt-shakers); suddenly the show achieved mass popularity, among adults as well as children. Several actors have played the Doctor over the years – William Hartnell, Patrick Troughton, Jon Pertwee, and most recently Tom Baker – and with each change the character has mellowed. Budget restrictions endemic to the BBC usually result in a visible gap between the writer's aspirations and the finished result, but the special effects and costumes are often ingeniously contrived. American audiences might find the show too whimsical.

1963: THE OUTER LIMITS

(USA) ABC. An anthology series created by Leslie Stevens; its first season was produced by Joseph Stefano, who also wrote a number of episodes, and the second season by Ben Brady. Though it leant towards the horror/monster sub-genre of sf it was innovative and unusual in both content and visual style, and – most importantly – it was invariably good fun. Harlan Ellison contributed two episodes; one of them, *Demon With a Glass Hand*, is generally regarded by sf fans as one of the best in the series.

1963: MY FAVOURITE MARTIAN

(USA) CBS. Created and produced by Jack Chertok, this comedy series starred Ray Walston as a Martian who becomes stranded on Earth and is befriended by a young man (Bill Bixby).

1964: MY LIVING DOLL

(USA) CBS. Created by Jack Chertok, this comedy series about a female robot only lasted one season. Produced by Howard Leeds it starred Julie Newmar as the robot left in the care of Bob Cummings while its inventor is out of the country. Cummings decides to train her/it to become the 'perfect woman' but the robot's basic unpredictability places him in embarrassing situations.

1964: VOYAGE TO THE BOTTOM OF THE SEA

(USA) ABC. Created and produced by Irwin Allen and based on his feature film of the same name, this concerned the adventures of Admiral Nelson (Richard Basehart) and the crew of the glass-nosed atomic submarine 'Seaview'. Each week Nelson and crew, which included David Hedison, would try to prevent the sub from being attacked by various giant creatures or being taken over by mad scientists, robots, ghosts, pirates, mummies, lobster men, blobs and sentient seaweed. The series proved popular and lasted until 1968.

1964: THE MAN FROM UNCLE

(USA) NBC. Created by Norman Felton and produced by Sam Rolfe and Anthony Spinner, this series was the first to reflect the James Bond/secret agent craze on American TV. Robert Vaughn starred as Napoleon Solo (the series was to have been called *Mr Solo* but the Bond producers objected), an agent working for UNCLE (United Network Command for Law Enforcement); with the assistance of Ilya Kuryakin (David McCallum), his Russian side-kick, he fights to prevent THRUSH (the Technological Hierarchy for the Removal of Undesirables and the Subjugation of Humanity) from taking over the world.

1965: THE WILD, WILD WEST
(USA) CBS. Produced by Fred Freiberger (first season) and Michael Garrison (second season onwards), this tongue-in-cheek western series was another manifestation of the secret-agent craze. Robert Conrad and Ross Martin starred as Jim West and Artemus Gordon, secret agents operating in the old West during the 1860s. The plots usually involved mad scientists trying to overthrow the government, and anachronistic gadgets were plentiful. Though not as enjoyable as *Uncle* the series lasted until 1967.

1965: OUT OF THE UNKNOWN
(UK) BBC. An anthology series similar in format to *Out of This World* which featured adaptations of stories by many top sf writers including Isaac Asimov, J. G. Ballard, John Brunner, John Wyndham, Clifford Simak, C. M. Kornbluth and Robert Sheckley. It was produced by Alan Bromly; the standard was generally high despite the BBC's customary tight budgets (£4,000 per episode for the first season, rising to £6,000 for the second).

1965: THUNDERBIRDS
(UK) ATV. One of the most successful of the many puppet TV series created and produced by Gerry and Sylvia Anderson. The show was set in the future and concerned a family who run an air, space and undersea rescue service, using a number of spectacular vehicles. The special effects were supervised by Derek Meddings.

1965: LOST IN SPACE
(USA) CBS. The second sf series created and produced by Irwin Allen was aimed at children and starred Guy Williams, June Lockhart, Marta Kristen, Angela Cartwright, Billy Mumy, Mark Goddard and Jonathan Harris as a group who crash-land on a remote planet. Each episode saw the arrival of a new visitor. The story consultant was Anthony Wilson.

1966: IT'S ABOUT TIME
(USA) CBS. A dire comedy series about two astronauts (Frank Alefter and Jack Mullaney) who go back in time to a point when they are befriended by a tribe of gross cave-dwellers (Imogene Coca, Joe E. Ross and Mike Mazurki). The series was created by Sherwood Schwartz (who had previously created *Gilligan's Island*) and the director of the pilot episode was Richard Donner, who has since directed *The Omen* and *Superman*.

1966: TIME TUNNEL
(USA) ABC. Another of Irwin Allen's so-called 'science fiction' series, this starred James Darren and Robert Colbert as human guinea-pigs trapped in a government-run time travel experiment. The time machine's operators are unable to return the two men to the present but can send them forward or backward in time – usually at the beginning and end of each episode. For budget reasons the men tended to visit the past more often than the future, which meant that stock footage could be used.

1966: STAR TREK

(USA) NBC. Created by Gene Roddenberry, this series proved the most popular of all sf shows and is currently being revived. It starred William Shatner, Leonard Nimoy, Deforest Kelley, Nichelle Nichols, George Takei and Jimmy Doohan and was set on a giant spaceship called the 'Enterprise'. The original concept was for a sort of space 'wagon train' – a format that would have provided the writers with endless possibilities for story ideas – but the writers eventually settled for one basic plot, that of the ship being threatened or taken over by various alien entities. By the end of its run there wasn't much difference from *Voyage to the Bottom of the Sea* in terms of plot development. The first two seasons included scripts by a number of sf writers, but the third (and worst) season lacked any well-known sf names (apart from Jerome Bixby). As the series progressed, writer/producer Gene Coon and story consultant Dorothy C. Fontana had an increasing influence on the structure of the show. 'I did three *Star Trek* episodes,' said fantasy/horror writer Robert Bloch, 'and I don't think any of my three scripts were perfectly realized. As the series went on there was more interference and more changes made with the scripts.' Discussing the huge popularity of the series Bloch said: 'It's an interesting phenomenon. The most obvious thing is that the majority of fans are female . . . When *Star Trek* was designed it was presumed that William Shatner, the nominal star and the All-American hero, would emerge as the significant figure in the series but the producers were very surprised when Leonard Nimoy as Mr Spock become the symbol of *Star Trek*. With hindsight it's easy to see why – the late 1960s saw the height of the cult of the cool, and no one was cooler than Mr Spock. He displayed no emotion at all. Girls were attracted to him because *other* females didn't seem to turn him on . . . His coolness was a kind of sexual challenge to them. Of course later on the producers played up this aspect of the character. But *Star Trek* also offered the primary attraction of sf – escape. The world is in rotten shape so let's get out of this world and go take law and order to the lesser breeds of the universe. It also had the appeal of being about a homogeneous family unit with all the races living in perfect harmony aboard the starship . . . it was basic wish-fulfilment.' (*Star Trek* is currently being turned into a lavish feature film with the original cast playing their old roles.)

1967: THE INVADERS

(USA) ABC. Created by Larry Cohen and produced by Alan Armer, this Quinn Martin Production starred Roy Thinnes as a man who discovers that alien invaders have landed in America but is unable to convince anyone in authority of the fact. As the aliens tend to fade away when killed he has difficulty in obtaining evidence of their existence. The aliens also look exactly like human beings, except that their little fingers are rigid (here is a race capable of travelling through space and changing the shape of their bodies but unable to bend their little fingers!). It lasted two seasons, ending in 1968.

1967: THE PRISONER

(UK) ITC. A Kafkaesque and increasingly surreal series created by American actor Patrick McGoohan and produced by David Tomblin. McGoohan played a secret agent who, attempting to resign from the British secret service, is gassed and kidnapped. He wakes to find himself in the Village, a cross between a bland holiday camp and a sanitarium run by a sinister group whose aim is to break his spirit and find out why he resigned. The series proved too far-out for ITC, the company which provided the financial backing, and it came to a premature end after seventeen episodes. Since then it has attracted a cult following and has twice been repeated.

1968: LAND OF THE GIANTS
(USA) ABC. Irwin Allen's sf series exploited the old 'shrunken people' formula. A group of people travelling in a 'strato-cruiser' pass through a space-time warp and crash-land on a planet where everything is hundreds of times larger than normal. The special effects, supervised by L. B. Abbott, were good but the scripts were deadly dull. The regular cast included Gary Conway, Kurt Kastzner, Don Marshall, Heather Young and Don Matheson.

1968: THE YEAR OF THE SEXUAL OLYMPICS
(UK) BBC. A controversial satire by Nigel Kneale about a future world full of voyeurs who spend most of their time watching sex being performed on TV.

1969: UFO
(British) ITC. Gerry and Sylvia Anderson's first non-puppet TV series. Many critics noted that the cast seemed to be trying to imitate puppets, particularly Ed Bishop who played the lead character, Commander Straker. The Commander is in charge of a secret government organization formed to combat a threat of hostile flying saucers.

1969: THE IMMORTAL
(USA) ABC. Based on the novel by sf writer James Gunn, *The Immortal* was originally a TV movie directed by Joseph Sargent (*Colossus: The Forbin Project*). Scripted by Robert Specht it starred Christopher George as a man whose special blood makes him immune to both disease and the ageing process. The movie proved popular and was expanded into a TV series the following year but lasted only thirteen episodes.

1970: HAUSER'S MEMORY
(USA) NBC. TV movie based on the novel by Curt Siodmak, directed by Boris Sagal and scripted by Adrian Spies. It starred David McCallum as a young Jewish-American scientist who is accidentally injected with DNA extracted from the brain of a dead German scientist in an attempt to preserve his unique knowledge; thus two personalities are obliged to share one brain.

1970: THE LOVE WAR
(USA) ABC. TV movie written by Guerdon Trueblood and David Kidd and directed by George McCowan. An alien male called Kyle (Lloyd Bridges) decides to opt out of an interplanetary war and settle on Earth. He becomes involved with an attractive girl called Sandy (Angie Dickinson) whom he

meets on a bus and eventually tells the truth about himself. Sandy, however, turns out to be one of the enemy aliens hunting him.

1970: WINE OF INDIA
(UK) BBC. TV play by Nigel Kneale set in 2050 about an over-populated world where euthanasia is compulsory and the ruling élite keep themselves alive with organ transplants – the organs being acquired from euthanasia victims.

1970: DOOMWATCH
(UK) BBC. Created by Kit Pedler and Gerry Davis and produced by Terence Dudley, this was an anti-science series about a group of scientists who set themselves up as watchdogs over the rest of the scientific community. The cast included Robert Powell (first season only), John Paul and Simon Oates.

1971: CITY BENEATH THE SEA
(USA) NBC. This TV movie was a pilot for a proposed Irwin Allen series which never got off the ground. Outside America it was released as a feature film called *One Hour to Doomsday*. Conceived, produced and directed by Allen from a script by John Meredyth Lucas, it was a confused tangle of sub-plots and scientific absurdities. The cast included Stuart Whitman, Robert Wagner, Joseph Cotton, James Darren and Richard Basehart.

1971: NIGHT GALLERY
(USA) NBC. Created and hosted by Rod Serling, who tried unsuccessfully to repeat his *Twilight Zone* formula. Produced by Jack Laird these fantasies were primarily concerned with the supernatural, though sf stories were occasionally included. The series lasted until 1972 and marked the end of Serling's TV career. He died of a heart attack in 1975.

1972: PURSUIT
(USA) ABC. TV movie directed by Michael Crichton, author of *The Andromeda Strain* and *The Terminal Man*, who later directed *Westworld* and *Coma*. Starring Ben Gazarra, E. G. Marshall, Joseph Wiseman, William Windom and Martin Sheen it featured a mad politician who intends to explode a nerve-gas bomb at a political convention in San Diego. 'I was anxious to direct a movie,' said Crichton, 'but when I realized I wouldn't be allowed to direct a feature right away I finally decided it would have to be a movie for TV. I mean, they can be pretty awful but they still put them on the air. So when one of my books, *Binary*, that I had written under a pseudonym [John Lange] was up for sale to ABC-TV I said: "Okay, you can make it if I can direct it." I wanted to write the screenplay as well but they wouldn't go along with that.'

1972: KILLDOZER
(USA) ABC. Based on the famous sf story of the same name by Theodore Sturgeon about a bulldozer on a remote island possessed by an alien entity, this TV movie was directed by Jerry London and starred Clint Walker, Carl Betz and Neville Brand. Though the script was written by Sturgeon himself the result was disappointing.

1973: GENESIS II
(USA) CBS. A TV movie that was the pilot for a proposed series created by
Gene Roddenberry. Directed by John Llewellyn Moxey and written by
Roddenberry, it was a variation on the old Buck Rogers plot (which in turn
came from Wells's *The Sleeper Wakes*). Alex Cord starred as the 20th-century
man who wakes up in 2133 and becomes involved in an attempt by a group of
humans to overthrow their cruel mutant rulers.

1973: THE STARLOST
(Canada) Syndicated. Short-lived TV series created by Harlan Ellison (who
was so dissatisfied with the production that he had his name removed from the
credits) about a giant spaceship containing several different societies which
have no idea where they are (an idea first used by Robert Heinlein in his book
Universe and later by Brian Aldiss in *Non-Stop*). The cast included Keir Dullea,
Gay Rowin and Robin Ward.

1973: THE SIX MILLION DOLLAR MAN
(USA) ABC. A popular series starring Lee Majors as a former astronaut who,
after a flying accident, has had his badly-injured body rebuilt with artificial
parts, thus becoming half-man and half-machine. Produced by Lionel E. Siegel
and Kenneth Johnson, it was based on a novel called *Cyborg* by Martin Caidin,
an ex-test pilot. Basically an up-dated *Superman* it is very much on a comic-
book level.

1973: MOONBASE 3
(UK) BBC. A serial produced and written by Barry Letts and Terrance Dicks.
Set on the moon in the year 2003 it concerned a group of scientists living in a
domed moonbase. The approach was decidedly non-sensational and 'realistic',
but the result was dull.

1973: THE TOMORROW PEOPLE
(UK) ITV. Children's series created by Roger Price who also – with Ruth
Boswell – produced it. The series incorporated basic childhood fantasies and
concerned a group of mutant children who possess special powers of telepathy
and teleportation.

1974: PLANET OF THE APES
(USA) CBS. Tedious short-lived series based on the movie of the same name,
produced by Stan Hough and starring Roddy McDowall, Ron Harper and
James Naughton.

1974: KOLCHAK: THE NIGHT STALKER
(USA) ABC. Another short-lived series that was a spin-off from a TV movie
called *The Night Stalker* directed by Dan Curtis and written by Richard
Matheson, about a vampire in modern-day Las Vegas. Darren McGavin played
a reporter, Kolchak, who each week uncovers a new supernatural sf menace.
The series was created by Jeff Rice and produced by Paul Playton and Cy

Chermak. Darren McGavin was executive producer.

1974: PLANET EARTH
(USA) ABC. This made-for-TV movie was Gene Roddenberry's second attempt
to launch a new series. Though it used the same basic plot as *Genesis II* John
Saxon replaced Alex Cord as the 20th-century astronaut who finds himself in
the future. The script was by Roddenberry and Juanita Bartlett.

1974: THE QUESTOR TAPES
(USA) NBC. Yet another attempt by Gene Roddenberry to repeat his *Star Trek*
success, this TV movie likewise failed to give birth to a series. Written by
Roddenberry and Gene Coon and directed by Richard A. Colla, it starred
Robert Foxworth as an android called Questor who tries to discover the reason
for his existence.

1974: THE STRANGER WITHIN
(USA) ABC. TV movie directed by Lee Philips and written by Richard
Matheson, who based it on his own short story (written in 1953) called
'Mother By Protest'. It concerns a woman (Barbara Eden) who becomes
inexplicably pregnant and gives birth to a healthy Martian.

1975: STRANGE NEW WORLD
(USA) ABC. This TV movie appears to be part of the *Genesis II* and *Planet
Earth* series, but Gene Roddenberry's name doesn't appear in the credits.
Produced by Robert E. Larson, directed by Robert Butler and written by
Ronald F. Graham, Walter Green and Alvin Ramrus, it again starred John
Saxon as a 20th-century astronaut encountering strange societies in the future.

1975: THE UFO INCIDENT
(USA) NBC. Unusual TV movie that is basically a poor man's version of *Close
Encounters*. Directed by Richard A. Colla and written by S. Lee Pogostin and
Hesper Anderson, it was based on the book *The Interrupted Journey* by John G.
Fuller – a supposedly authentic account of a meeting between a married couple
and aliens from outer space. It starred James Earl Jones and Estelle Parsons.
Ironically, Jones had bought the rights to the book with the intention of
turning it into a feature film but was unable to interest any of the major
companies, so he sold the rights to TV. The following year, *Close Encounters*
got underway, and Jones ended up providing the voice for Darth Vader in *Star
Wars*.

1975: THE NIGHT THAT PANICKED AMERICA
(USA) ABC. A TV movie directed by Joseph Sargent that recreates the events
surrounding Orson Welles's 1938 broadcast of H. G. Wells's *War of the
Worlds*. The movie is convincing when it concentrates on what went on inside
the radio studio but degenerates into cliché when it moves outside to show the
effects of the broadcast on a 'typical cross-section' of people.

1975: SPACE 1999

(UK) ITC. Gerry and Sylvia Anderson unleashed this absurd 'sf' series on American and British audiences in 1975. An explosion of radioactive waste sends the moon hurtling into deep space, taking with it a large lunar base and its inhabitants. Before long they enter other solar systems (the moon appears to be travelling at the speed of light) and encounter alien worlds, just as the characters in *Star Trek* had done. The cast included Martin Landau, Barbara Bain, Barry Morse, Nick Tate and Catherine Schell. The first season was produced by Sylvia Anderson and the second by Fred Freiberger, who had previously produced *The Wild, Wild West* and the third and final season of *Star Trek*. The special effects by Brian Johnson were the most outstanding feature in a series which ended in 1976.

1975: SURVIVORS

(UK) BBC. Serial written and created by Terry Nation and produced by Terence Dudley (who produced *Doomwatch*). It begins with the arrival of a plague that kills 52 million people in Britain in six weeks, leaving about 7,000 people alive. The serial follows the adventures of small groups of survivors who attempt to cope with life in a world without technology, and is in the tradition of that particularly British 'after-the-disaster' genre established by writers like Wells, Wyndham and Ballard. Nation makes it seem rather too cosy, and one has the uneasy feeling that it represents wish-fulfilment on his part rather than a genuine warning.

1975: THE INVISIBLE MAN

(USA) NBC. In the first season of this series, created and produced by Harve Bennett and Steve Bocho and vaguely based on the novel by H. G. Wells, David McCallum starred as the scientist who accidentally becomes invisible while experimenting with a matter transmitter. In the second season he was replaced by Ben Murphy and the title was changed to *The Gemini Man*. Neither changed helped and the series was dropped. (There was a previous *Invisible Man* series made in Britain in 1958, created and produced by Ralph Smart and starring Lisa Daniely and Deborah Walting. The face of the invisible man was never seen but his voice was provided by Tim Turner.)

1976: THE BIONIC WOMAN

(USA) ABC. A spin-off series from *The Six Million Dollar Man* starring Lindsay Wagner as the part-mechanical, super-heroine Jaimie Sommers (as with the bionic man the joins don't show). Like Steve Austin she works as a secret agent for the government, but her series seems more inclined towards sentimentality and 'woman's angle' gimmicks. The producer was Kenneth Johnson.

1977: THE FANTASTIC JOURNEY

(USA) NBC. A boring, short-lived series in which a group of people set out to investigate the Bermuda Triangle and end up on a mysterious island that 'isn't on the map'. They realize that the surrounding landscape consists of segments of time and space from different periods in Earth's history, past and future (an idea first used by Fred Hoyle in his novel *October the First Is Too Late*). This format allowed the characters to encounter a different society each week and the series rapidly became like the worst of *Star Trek*; Dorothy C. Fontana acted as story editor on this show as well.

1977: THE MAN FROM ATLANTIS

(USA) NBC. After the bionic man and the bionic woman came the fish-man. Created and produced by Herb Solow, this series starred Patrick Duffy as the green-eyed, web-fingered stranger with a suggestive style of swimming. Believed to have come from Atlantis he is quickly drafted to work for the Navy and the Foundation for Oceanic Research. The series is so mindless it even makes one nostalgic for *Voyage to the Bottom of the Sea*.

1977: LOGAN'S RUN

(USA). Produced by the creators of *Charlie's Angels*, Ben Roberts and Ivan Goff (both of whom have admitted they know nothing about sf), this series is even worse than the film that inspired it. Starring Gregory Harrison, Heather Menzies, Randy Powell and Donald Moffatt it is set outside the domed city that featured in the movie and concerns Logan's search for the mythical Sanctuary. He is accompanied by Jessica and an android named Rem and during their search they encounter a different group of people each week. Since the show's story editor is the ubiquitous Dorothy C. Fontana the plots are all familiar.

1977: 1990

(UK) BBC. Produced by Prudence Fitzgerald this serial was a weak variation on *1984* and was created by Wilfred Greatorex who, with Edmund Ward, also wrote the scripts. The plot concerns an England ruled by the 'Department of Public Control', an all-powerful bureaucracy which controls all aspects of society; the only people free of its influence are a select élite who possess 'privilege cards'. The story concerns the efforts of a lone journalist (Edward Woodward) to outwit the system.

1977: BLAKE'S SEVEN

(UK) BBC. Written and created by Terry Nation, this inept series represents the BBC's attempt to produce a cross between *Star Trek* and *Star Wars*. Blake (Gareth Thomas) is a rebel who escapes from a totalitarian society on Earth and then, with the help of some companions, sets off to free the galaxy from the tyrant's reign. The concept seems to be the result of a quick skim through a handful of sf novels and the synopsis of *Star Wars*, while the sets, costumes and special effects all reflect the BBC's shortage of finance. The producer was David Maloney.

1978: QUARK

(USA) NBC. Space satire series created and written by Buck Henry. Richard Benjamin stars as Commander Quark, who is in charge of an intergalactic garbage-collecting space vehicle.

References

1. *American Cinematographer,* July 1977.
2. 'Wells, Hitler and the World State' from *Critical Essays* by George Orwell, 1946.
3. *Science Fiction in the Cinema,* John Baxter, Tantivy Press, 1970.
4. *Twenty Years Under the Sea,* J. E. Williamson, Bodley Head, 1935.
5. *Ibid.*
6. *The Bioscope,* 5 June 1916.
7. *Kinematograph Weekly,* 21 June 1923.
8. *King of the Bs,* Charles Flynn and Tod McCarthy, Dutton and Co., 1975.
9. *Twenty Years Under the Sea,* J. E. Williamson.
10. *The Bioscope,* 14 August 1929.
11. *New York Times,* 4 January 1931.
12. *Two Film Stories: Things to Come* and *The Man Who Could Work Miracles.* The Cresset Press, 1940.
13. *Astounding Science Fiction,* July 1950.
14. *Cinema Papers,* March-April 1975.
15. *Cinefantastique,* Vol. 4, No. 4, 1976.
16. *Ibid.*
17. *Photon,* No. 22, 1974.
18. *Cinefantastique,* Vol. 5, No. 4, 1977.
19. *Cinema Papers,* March-April 1975.
20. *Cinefantastique,* Vol. 5, No. 4, 1977.
21. *Ibid.*
22. *Cinema Papers,* March-April 1975.
23. *TV Times,* 24 July 1975.
24. *Cinefantastique,* Vol. 4, No. 1, 1975.
25. *Ibid.*
26. *Cinefantastique,* Vol. 2, No. 3, 1973.
27. *Film Fantasy Scrapbook,* Ray Harryhausen. Tantivy Press, 1975.
28. *Fantascene,* Vol. 1, No. 2, 1976.
29. *Film Fantasy Scrapbook,* Ray Harryhausen.
30. *Photon,* No. 26, 1976.
31. *Stanley Kubrick Directs,* Alexander Walker. Abacus, 1973.
32. *Looking Away: Hollywood and Vietnam,* Julian Smith, 1973.
33. *Film Fantasy Scrapbook,* Ray Harryhausen.
34. *Cinema Papers,* March-April 1975.
35. *Ibid.*
36. *Billion Year Spree,* Brian Aldiss. Weidenfeld and Nicolson, 1973.
37. *Playboy,* 1968.
38. *Psychology Today,* 1968.
39. *Castle of Frankenstein,* 1969.
40. *Cinefantastique,* Vol. 2, No. 2, 1972.

41. *Ibid.*
42. *Films and Filming,* November 1977.
43. *Rolling Stone,* No. 246, 1977.
44. *Sight and Sound,* Spring 1974.
45. *Cinefantastique,* Vol. 3, No. 3, 1974.
46. *Cinefantastique,* Vol. 5, No. 1, 1976.
47. *Sight and Sound,* Autumn 1975.
48. *American Cinematographer,* June 1976.
49. *Cinefantastique,* Vol. 5, No. 2, 1976.
50. *American Cinematographer,* June 1976.
51. *Time,* 30 May 1977.
52. *Rolling Stone,* No. 246, 1977.
53. *Evening Standard,* 29 September 1977.
54. *Rolling Stone,* No. 246, 1977.
55. *Sunday Times,* 14 August 1977.
56. *Rolling Stone,* No. 246, 1977.
57. *Screen International,* 17 December 1977.
58. *Ibid.*
59. *Ibid.*
60. *The Times,* December 1977.
61. *The New Yorker,* 28 November 1977.
62. *Newsweek,* 21 November 1977.
63. *Filmmaker's Newsletter,* Vol. 11, No. 2, 1977.
64. *Newsweek,* 21 November 1977.
65. *Filmmaker's Newsletter,* Vol. 11, No. 2, 1977.
66. *Time,* 7 November 1977.
67. *New Statesman,* 16 December 1977.
68. *Quatermass and the Pit,* National Film Theatre programme notes, November 1977. Interview by Paul Madden.

Acknowledgments

I would like to thank the following people for their assistance in the preparation of this volume: John Baxter, John Brunner, Richard Fleischer, Val Guest, Harry Harrison, Derek Meddings and Michael Moorcock. I would also like to thank the staff of the British Film Institute's reference library and stills archive for their customary invaluable help.

Index

INDEX OF FILM TITLES